ALSO BY WOLFGANG W. E. SAMUEL

German Boy
A Refugee's Story

I Always Wanted to Fly
America's Cold War Airmen

The War of Our Childhood
Memories of World War II

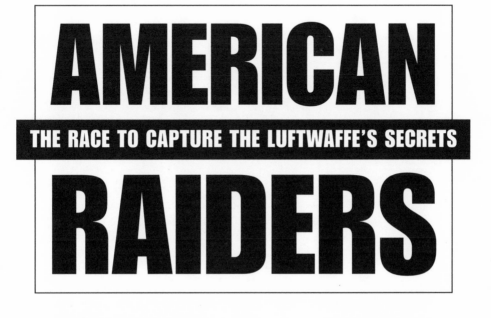

AMERICAN

THE RACE TO CAPTURE THE LUFTWAFFE'S SECRETS

RAIDERS

WOLFGANG W. E. SAMUEL

3/2006

UNIVERSITY PRESS OF MISSISSIPPI / JACKSON

*Publication of this book was made possible
through the support of Dudley J. Hughes.*

www.upress.state.ms.us

The University Press of Mississippi is a member of the
Association of American University Presses.

Manufactured in the United States of America

12 11 10 09 08 07 06 05 04   4 3 2 1

∞

Library of Congress Cataloging-in-Publication Data

Samuel, Wolfgang W. E.
    American raiders : the race to capture the Luftwaffe's secrets / Wolfgang W. E. Samuel.
        p. cm.
Includes bibliographical references and index.
    ISBN 1-57806-649-2 (cloth : alk. paper)
    1. Aeronautics, Military—Research—United States—History—20th century. 2. Technology
transfer—Germany—History—20th century. 3. Technology transfer—United States—History—
20th century. 4. World War, 1939–1945—Science. 5. World War, 1939–1945—Technology. I. Title.
UG643.S36 2004
940.54′8673—dc22   2003023251

British Library Cataloging-in-Publication Data available

To my wife, Joan, and in memory
of my friend Stephen E. Ambrose

CONTENTS

PREFACE AND ACKNOWLEDGMENTS

American Raiders provides a glimpse of the complex story of the *disarmament* of the Luftwaffe after its defeat in the spring of 1945 and the *exploitation* of its aeronautical secrets. Disarmament and exploitation were two distinctly separate acts executed by unique organizational entities created for those specific purposes. The umbrella plan under which the disarmament of the Luftwaffe was implemented was Operation Eclipse. Eclipse took over where Overlord left off, Overlord having been the plan which provided for the invasion of Europe up to the defeat of the enemy, while Eclipse covered the disarmament and permanent military neutralization of Nazi Germany. For American airmen tasked to exploit the aeronautical secrets of the Third Reich, Operation Lusty provided the authority, direction, and concept of operation. These two groups, the disarmers and the exploiters, worked hand in glove, one feeding the other, and by doing so ensured each other's success. Although the process as it unfolded was anything but orderly, they succeeded in their respective tasks beyond anyone's expectations.

This army of dismemberment and discovery came from varied sources within the European theater of operations, the ETO. Combat crew replacement squadrons, no longer needed as the war neared its end and bomber losses diminished, were turned into disarmament squadrons. Specially trained Air Technical Intelligence teams were formed and directed to find and recover the secrets of the Third Reich. A small group of volunteer P-47 combat pilots rounded out this diverse group of men charged with disarming and exploiting the once feared and mighty Luftwaffe. Although they had held up their hands and volunteered, they had no idea that they were signing up to fly enemy jets and receive their training from German pilots. The war had been bitterly fought, but it left behind a surprisingly small residue of personal animosity among its American and German combatants, who suddenly found themselves working and flying together for a common cause.

American Raiders is the story of Operation Lusty, of the disarmament of the German air force, and of how its secret and advanced weaponry, developed too late to play a significant role in saving the crumbling Third Reich, became the basis for America's technological rejuvenation. The Nazis could never have imagined that the weaponry they built in such secrecy to defeat the western Allies would loom large in the ultimate defeat of the Soviet Union—only fifty-some years later. Of all the captured hardware, the Me-262 jet fighter and the Arado 234 jet bomber fascinated most and elicited the greatest attention. On the one hand, their capture symbolized the magnitude of the American military victory over a sophisticated enemy; on the other, these very airplanes pointed to America's own technological deficiencies and backwardness. As Americans went about the task of collecting German hardware, drawings, blueprints, and documentation, some quickly understood that hardware was only a small part of what needed to be brought home. What was much more important was to tap the minds of the innovative scientists who had come up with these ideas in the first place. The *Wissenschaftler* were the real prizes of war. This shift in focus, on the ideas of men rather than on yesterday's hardware, quickly became a struggle between those wanting retribution and others who wanted to get on with the business of securing America's future. The eventual transfer of the German scientists to the United States and their integration into American society became known as Project Overcast and Project Paperclip. That the two projects did not die on the vine is a credit to the farsightedness and perseverance of men like Arnold, Spaatz, Cannon, Knerr, McDonald, Putt, Watson, and many other dedicated American warriors. It was their persistence in overcoming bureaucratic inertia, misguided patriotism, and outright hostility which in the end provided this country with the means to emerge from the Cold War victorious. Because of them there was no repeat of the World War II technology debacle when the MiG-15 challenged American air power in Korea in 1951, and American strategic bomber and intercontinental ballistic missile superiority assured that the Cold War would be resolved in its favor. How it all came about is the story of *American Raiders*—the story of the last battle of World War II in Europe, which was not for military victory but for the technology of the Third Reich and America's future military security.

I want to express my thanks, gratitude, and appreciation to the many men and women who helped and assisted in this undertaking and who consented to being interviewed for *American Raiders*. In the process I had the pleasant experience of making new friendships and sharing in the lifetime experiences of men who helped shape the history of our nation for over fifty years. I have a personal preference for portraying history through the eyes of its participants, and therefore, wherever possible, I use their words to describe events. History is, after all, the story of ordinary men and women who do extraordinary things when called upon; why not let them tell their stories in their own words? I edited interviews for brevity and clarity of expression. The interview with General Putt was in its original form, and, as I did with interviews which I conducted personally, I edited it for readability. With Lieutenant Charles Johnson's permission, I extracted his story from his unpublished manuscript, "Memoirs of a Navigator, WWII."

The following people not only agreed to be interviewed but also freely provided rare pictures and documentation in support of

American Raiders: Ruth Watson, the wife of the late Major General Watson; Roy Brown, a former P-47 and Me-262 pilot; Frederick McIntosh, also a P-47 pilot and flyer of many German airplanes; Colonels Lloyd Wenzel, Kenneth Chilstrom, Robert Anspach, John Sutton, and Mr. Dennis Freiburger, the son of the late Master Sergeant Freiburger; Carl Daughters; and Robert Drew, who on June 6, 1944, landed on Omaha Beach. My sincere thanks to all of them for helping me capture a piece of American history. I extend my appreciation and thanks to Douglas N. Lantry, research historian at the United States Air Force Museum at Wright-Patterson Air Force Base, Dayton, Ohio, for generously providing copies of flying logs and other pertinent material on the life of Major General Harold E. Watson; to Dr. Roger Miller of the Air Force Office of History, AF/HO, at Bolling Air Force Base, Washington, D.C., for his support and the insights he provided on command relationships, aircraft identification, and practices of flying units; and to Yvonne Kinkaid, also from the Air Force Office of History, without whose assistance my research efforts would have been much prolonged. Yvonne readily provided the hands-on help I needed for delving into enormously large files to look for the few buried nuggets about an air force few remembered, the 1st Tactical Air Force (Provisional), and an operation few recalled, Operation Lusty. Last, but not least, my thanks go to Axel Kornfuehrer, who agreed to be my technical reviewer on Luftwaffe aircraft.

I thank my always supportive wife, Joan, for her hard-nosed editorial assistance, and my late friend Stephen E. Ambrose, the historian and writer, who like no other historian of our time brought to life on the pages of his books the experiences of America's fighting men in World War II. Finally, my thanks go to the director of the University Press of Mississippi, Seetha Srinivasan, and its editor-in-chief, Craig W. Gill, for their continued support. This is the fourth book of mine that Seetha and Craig have shepherded through the publication process at University Press of Mississippi, which is staffed by exceedingly competent, helpful, and friendly people. I thank them all for having me as one of their authors. It was a pleasure writing this book, and it is my sincere hope that the experience for readers will be equally enjoyable.

—WOLFGANG W. E. SAMUEL

Colonel, U.S. Air Force (Ret.)
Fairfax Station, Virginia

ABBREVIATIONS

AAF	Army Air Forces
AC/AS	Assistant Chief of Air Staff
AC/S	Assistant Chief of Staff
ADS	Air Disarmament Squadron
AGF	Army Ground Forces
AMC	Air Materiel Command
AMG	American Military Government
ASF	Army Service Forces
ATI	Air Technical Intelligence
ATSC	Air Technical Service Command
AWOL	Absent without Leave
Bf	Bayrische Flugzeugwerke (builder of the Bf 109 and Bf 110) renamed Messerschmitt A.G. in 1938. All subsequent aircraft designs received the Me instead of the Bf prefix.
BMW	Bayrische Motorenwerke
BOQ	Bachelor Officers' Quarters
CCTS	Combat Crew Training Squadron
CG	Center of Gravity
CIOS	Combined Intelligence Objectives Subcommittee
CO	Commanding Officer

Comint	Communications intelligence
CPMB	Captured Personnel and Materiel Branch
DFC	Distinguished Flying Cross
DP	Displaced Person
EGT	Exhaust Gas Temperature
Elint	Electronic intelligence
EM	Enlisted Men
ETO	European Theater of Operations
FE	Foreign Equipment Number
FG	Fighter Group
FIAT	Field Information Agency Technical
Flak	Fliegerabwehrkanone (antiaircraft gun, World War II)
FS	Fighter Squadron
GAF	German Air Force
GCI	Ground Controlled Intercept
HQ	Headquarters
ICBM	Intercontinental Ballistic Missile
i.G.	im Generalstab (General Staff Officer)
JCS	Joint Chiefs of Staff
JIOA	Joint Intelligence Objectives Agency
LFA	Luftfahrtforschungsanstalt
MIS	Military Intelligence Service
MIT	Massachusetts Institute of Technology
MP	Military Police
NACA	National Advisory Committee for Aeronautics
NAS	Naval Air Station
NYA	National Youth Administration
OKL	Oberkommando der Luftwaffe
PGM	Precision Guided Munition
Photint	Photographic intelligence
POW	Prisoner of War
PW	Prisoner of War

RAE	Royal Aircraft Establishment (Farnborough)
RAF	Royal Air Force
RATO/JATO	Rocket Assisted Take-off/Jet Assist Take-off
RLM	Reichsluftfahrtministerium
ROTC	Reserve Officer Training Corps
SRW	Strategic Reconnaissance Wing
RTU	Replacement Training Unit
SHAEF	Supreme Headquarters Allied Expeditionary Force
Sigint	Signals intelligence
TDY	Temporary Duty
TFW	Tactical Fighter Wing
UK	United Kingdom
USAFE	United States Air Forces in Europe
USFET	United States Forces European Theater
USSTAF	United States Strategic Air Forces in Europe
VFR	Visual Flight Rules
WD	War Department
WDGS	War Department General Staff
ZI	Zone of Interior

THE WAY THINGS
WERE—1945

A West Pointer who first saw aerial combat in World War I, Lieutenant General Carl A. "Tooey" Spaatz commanded the largest fleet of combat airplanes ever assembled to wage war. The United States Strategic Air Forces in Europe, USSTAF, with its eleven thousand first-line combat aircraft, had, by 1945, for all practical purposes destroyed the Luftwaffe and with that Germany's ability to wage war effectively. In late April, with the strategic bombing campaign terminated and within days of Germany's unconditional surrender, General Spaatz kicked off the final military operation against the Third Reich—Operation Lusty. To ensure Lusty's success, Spaatz gave it a priority equivalent to a combat operation. Although American arms were clearly poised to win the greatest military victory ever, this moment of triumph paradoxically revealed America's technological backwardness when measured against the technology of a conquered Germany.

Many senior military officers, including the Commanding General of the Army Air Forces, General of the Army Henry Harley "Hap" Arnold, knew that the Germans were far ahead of the United States in numerous fields of military technology. The imminent, and to all appearances overwhelming, victory over Hitler's Germany was therefore less impressive than it appeared—there was just too much luck involved. Luck is not something senior military officers like to rely on. Colonel Harold E. Watson, a Wright Field engineer and test pilot and an up-and-coming young officer handpicked by General Spaatz as a key Operation Lusty participant, pointedly put it this way: "If Germany flew the first jet-propelled plane before the German army marched against Poland . . . why hadn't we learned those secrets before?"[1] A good question. Yet this was not the time for recrimination, but rather an opportunity to set things right. The obvious thing to do was to face facts and take the enemy's superior technology and run— one purpose of Operation Lusty. "The Germans were ahead of us, in some instances from two to fifteen years . . . in the fields of rockets and guided missiles, jet engines, jet-propelled aircraft, synthetic fuels and supersonics," said Colonel Donald L. Putt, another Wright Field aero-nautical engineer and test pilot. "If we are not too proud to make use of this German-born information, much benefit can be derived from it and we can advance from where Germany left off."[2] This was Yankee pragmatism at its best, but unfortunately it was not a point of view shared by many. The decision by General Spaatz not only to disarm the Luftwaffe but also to exploit its technological treasures to the fullest was farsighted and timely. Few comprehended at the time the urgency behind Operation Lusty and that others were about to engage in a sim-ilar technology exploitation process, most notably an ally and possible future adversary, the Russians.

As American and British armies advanced ever farther into Germany and Air Technical Intelligence teams and disarmament squadrons gained access to German facilities, the true scope of German scientific progress became increasingly visible and in many respects awe inspir-ing. There were, of course, the German jet and rocket planes already encountered in combat, of which only anemic counterparts were found in the United States and England. Wind tunnels of incredibly large dimensions were discovered with simulation characteristics American scientists could only dream of. When American aeronautical experts gained insight into German wind-tunnel test results it suddenly became clear that the much-heralded sound barrier had already been conquered by futuristic-looking, swept-wing aircraft models tested in the German tunnels. They discovered precision-guided air-to-ground missiles, such as the Fritz X and the Henschel 293, using radio, wire, and even TV guidance, the latter pooh-poohed as "Buck Rogers" technology by one of America's leading and most respected scientists, Dr. Vannevar Bush of the Massachusetts Institute of Technology and chairman of the Office of Scientific Research and Development. A plethora of surface-to-air, surface-to-surface, and air-to-air missile designs was discovered in varied stages of development, including the V-2 ballistic missile—a truly unique, one-of-a-kind development. Fortunately, German scientists, who in time would populate American laboratories and test centers, would continue to evolve the V-2 into a two-stage vehicle with intercontinental reach, which in yet another form took Americans to the moon. The Nike surface-to-air missile, an offshoot of the V-2 missile program, would in years to come defend not only the American heartland but also the Germany of its World War II origin. When all there was to be discovered was discovered, the total tally of German missiles under development in the Third Reich came to 138.[3]

United States Strategic Air Forces disarmament squadrons and Air Technical Intelligence teams worked hand in glove to accomplish the critical and gargantuan task of discovering Germany's technological secrets, secrets which began to astound Allied military commanders as early as the summer of 1944. As Patton's and Dever's armies moved ever farther east, the disarmament squadrons and ATI teams extended their areas of operation into American-occupied sections of Czechoslovakia and portions of the future Soviet zone of occupation. Similar U.S. Army Ground Forces and U.S. Navy technical exploitation teams, as well as a multitude of other teams representing various joint, combined, and unilateral British and American interests, went about the business of discovery and disarmament. A curious word was chosen to describe this scramble for Nazi technology: exploitation. It was the Exploitation Division of the Directorate of Intelligence at Headquarters USSTAF which ran this comprehensive, multinational and multidepartmental effort for the Army Air Forces. Exploitation was the word used to describe the discovery and eventual shipment to the United States of scientific documentation, advanced weaponry, test equipment, entire research laboratories, and later even the transfer of Germany's engineers and scientists. Although historians frequently report this undertaking as preplanned and orderly, close scrutiny reveals it was anything but that.

Instead, War Department intelligence teams, Army Air Forces disarmament squadrons, Navy Department teams, State Department teams, and scientific teams of learned men from various other government agencies, Military Government of Germany teams, scoundrels, black marketeers, and sellers of secrets fell over one another in the technology scramble, racing to find for their own constituencies or their own accounts whatever "secrets" and discoveries they could lay their hands on. They came with lists—black lists, blue lists, brown lists, grey lists, A and B lists—from which they attempted to determine what technology to pick up and what to leave lie, what to retain and what to destroy, whom to take and whom to leave behind. All too frequently the disarmament and exploitation team members were ill prepared to differentiate between the golden nuggets of technology and fool's gold, so they took it all. Assembly points overflowed with the detritus of war. Active competition arose between Brit and Yank, between Army ground forces, Army Air Forces, and Navy teams, between West and East, all trying to deprive one another of the prized technological loot and the all-important German scientists. Spring and summer of 1945 in Germany might best be described as an Alice in Wonderland setting; a Macy's bargain basement atmosphere prevailed in a land without law and with little order, a land wherein the quick and daring went away with the most prized possessions.

Those closest to the action perceived that the wartime alliance between the western Allies and the Soviets had serious limitations. With Hitler's armies destroyed, neither had much need for the other. The lines for future East-West confrontation were being drawn quite clearly in German soil in those sunny April, May, and June days of 1945. As the Nazi empire expired, the most astute among the exploiters could see on the military and political horizons a trace of fog auguring future confrontation, maybe even war. One of those perceptive men was Colonel Donald Leander Putt. In late April 1945 Putt was leading a USSTAF technical exploitation team at the Luftfahrtforschungsanstalt (LFA) Hermann Göring at Völkenrode, on the western outskirts of Braunschweig. Putt quickly became uninterested in collecting hardware—although that was his charter and he did a good job at it—instead deciding to focus on matters he considered much more important. Hardware, as Putt saw things, was representative of yesterday's ideas—like the B-17 and the B-24 which by April 1945 were no longer viable weapons of war. Putt wanted the ideas of the future, the thoughts in men's minds which he felt would in no small measure define tomorrow's America. He wanted to bring to the United States the *Wissenschaftler,* the German scientists, the men and the women who designed and developed the futuristic military weaponry and equipment he was so assiduously collecting.

Putt determined to go after the intellectual capital of the former Third Reich, the scientists who had designed the jet and rocket planes and other advanced weapons never brought to bear against the Allies simply because the Nazis ran out of time. More than any of his peers, Putt clearly grasped the importance of the German scientist to the technological future of the United States and wanted as many of them as possible, and as soon as possible, brought to Wright Field, the research, development, and test center for the Army Air Forces. There, he thought, the scientists should resume work, making up the technological deficit America had allowed itself to accumulate in the prewar years. Why else was he here at the LFA picking up the Nazis' scientific scraps, if not in recognition of the fact that something had gone terribly awry and needed to be put right? The only question in Putt's mind was how he was going to pull off his plan of getting the German scientists back to the United States. He had some stripped-down B-17s and B-24s at his disposal which had been relegated to transport duties at war's end. Using his small fleet of war-weary bombers, he was ready to fly some of the German scientists directly to the United States. He even set his plan in motion. It had been done often enough in the waning days of the war. The U.S. Navy spirited Professor Wagner and his Hs 293 air-to-ground missile team to a remote estate on Long Island. Why couldn't he do the same? Unfortunately, by the time Putt was ready to put his idea into practice, war in Europe had ended. Conditions changed. Someone raised a question or two, and Putt's plan fell apart. Although his initial attempt at bringing German scientists to the United States failed, he persisted relentlessly, and in time his efforts were crowned with success.

While Putt was doing his thing at the LFA, a group of war-weary American P-47 combat pilots and German jet test pilots and mechanics came together at the bomb-scarred airfield of Lager Lechfeld near Augsburg to rescue Germany's most visible technological treasures—its revolutionary jet fighters and bombers—which late in the war had begun to upset the order of things in the skies over Europe. Revolutionary, because the German jets could undoubtedly have altered the course of war, if not its outcome. As it was, they were harbingers of a new era of flight. This disparate group of airmen working together as a binational team of victors and vanquished under the auspices of Operation Lusty was led by a flamboyant colonel named Harold E. Watson, better known to his friends as Hal, a form of address he much preferred to Colonel, or, later in life, General. Not that Watson didn't appreciate his military rank and achievements—quite the contrary—but Hal fit his informal, unpretentious style of leadership much better than the formal title of Colonel or General. All who knew him saw Watson as a hands-on man, inspiring deep loyalties among the many who worked directly with him. Hal liked to move freely among enlisted men and officers at a time when the U.S. Army somewhat resembled a caste system rather than the cooperative enterprise it is today. Watson was less formed and shaped by the Army and its rituals than by his engineering background and love for flying and its liberating sense of freedom. He led with a smile, insisting on being the first to expose himself to the risks of flight in a new, untested aircraft. A German Messerschmitt test pilot wrote about Watson in his 1945 journal, "Even the Colonel himself is not afraid of his status and gives a helping hand when needed. Can you imagine an *Oberst* of the German Air Force giving his crew a hand? Unthinkable."[4]

Putt and Watson knew one another from their early days at Wright Field, and both were to be major players in Operation Lusty. Both were test pilots and engineers; both earned master's degrees in aeronautical engineering from prestigious American universities; and both were assigned to USSTAF headquarters at St.-Germain, France, in early 1945. Watson's specific task was to bring home the German jets as quickly as possible. Over lunch one day in late 1944, General Spaatz tasked Watson to find those jets wherever they were and bring them home as quickly as possible. Recalled Watson of this meeting, "He stressed his keen interest in German V-weapons, the Me-262, the Arado-234, the Me-163, and other unusual aircraft."[5] Spaatz had good reasons for ordering Watson to get the German jets, reasons Watson wasn't fully aware of at the time. But by spring of 1945 Watson understood the big picture and learned of the urgency behind the general's request—the Germans had provided much, if not all, of their advanced technology to their Japanese ally. The war in the Pacific was

The business end of a German Me-262A jet fighter at Lager Lechfeld, Germany, May 1945. Colonel Mark Bradley, a friend of Watson's, poses for the camera. (RW)

still raging, and, while its end was in sight, that end was viewed as potentially very bloody for both sides. Getting the German jets home for quick analysis and testing had everything to do with being ready for the Japanese should they suddenly field some German-inspired surprises of their own. The first question senior American military leaders wanted to have an answer to was: what specific technologies did the Germans provide to the Japanese? That knowledge would be critical to the timely development of appropriate countermeasures.

The Japanese connection was the initial impetus behind Operation Lusty and Watson's incentive to find and move the German jets to the United States as quickly as possible. These same aircraft could, of course, also provide a technological leap forward for a lagging, even stalled, jet development effort at home—reason number two for Watson's hurry-up-and-get-it-done mission. Although the United States had developed its own jet fighters by 1944, the YP-59 Airacomet and the P-80 Shooting Star, the programs developed too many snags and provided no operational capabilities. By summer of 1945 there were no American jet fighters sitting on ramps ready to go to war.[6] As for pilots, whether American, British, or German, they were awed by the very sight of the sleek Me-262 fighter jet and its lesser-known companion, the Arado 234 Blitz reconnaissance bomber. The Me-262 was a creation of great functional beauty making most airmen want to fly one, no matter which side they fought on. Wrote Watson years later, "When I first saw the Me-262 I was spellbound. Just sitting there on the ground it looked as though it was doing almost Mach 1," the speed of sound.[7]

Scientific development in Nazi Germany can point to remarkable achievements, yet its usage was as unfocused as its underlying Nazi ideology—neither providing for the longevity of the Thousand Year Reich. History shows that scarce resources were committed to projects promising little return for investmen, and when there were scientific developments which coincided with pressing needs of the moment, such as the Me-262 jet fighter, their implementation was delayed and modified until the advantage melted away and was lost. Nazi Germany expended vast amounts of its limited resources on research; in retrospect this proved irrelevant to its overall war effort and actually inspired much of the end-of-war technology collection frenzy by the western Allies and the Soviets. The German V-2(A4) ballistic missile is a clear example of unique scientific achievement, yet the missile was redundant to what was needed to stem the Allied bomber offensive or to inflict comparable damage. "There were six main centers for aeronautical research in Germany," Colonel Putt recalled in a speech in 1946. "How much did they cost the German public? One center alone, Peenemünde, where the Germans developed the V-2 rocket, cost more than $100 million for just the physical construction of this one center. . . . For the buildings and grounds of another center the Germans paid $50,000,000. Still another cost roughly $12,000,000. At war's end new construction was still being carried out at many of these establishments."[8] Without the focus enjoyed by

American and British scientific efforts, German science had little impact on either the course or the outcome of the war. Ironically, its legacy was to leave behind for the victors a plethora of futuristic and far-reaching technological innovation, such as the Me-262 jet fighter and the Arado 234 jet bomber, for exploitation and use in a future confrontation.

THE GERMAN JETS

The Luftwaffe entered war in 1939 equipped with first-line fighter air-craft as good as any flying anywhere else in the world. Hitler, however, subscribed to a short war scenario in which each attack against a newly chosen enemy would be overwhelming and brief. In such a scenario there seemed to be little reason to pursue technological innovation—no need for jet fighters, proximity fuzes, or radar. The groundbreaking advances in aviation and related technologies by Germany's engineers and scientists were largely ignored by its political leadership during the heady days of victory in the early forties. Critical research was suspended, engineers drafted, and the focus remained on producing more of the old, rather than expending limited resources on new, unproven science. But wars seldom are as brief as men would have them; nor is a war's course ever clearly discernible.

Colonel Raymond E. Toliver, in his book *Fighter General: The Life of Adolf Galland*, made the point of missed opportunities quite clearly. "Four months prior to the Bader incident [Bader was a colorful and legless British fighter pilot shot down over the Pas de Calais in August 1941], an aircraft took off from the Heinkel factory that demonstrated Germany's vast technical lead in fighter development. The He 280 was a sleek twin-jet with tricycle landing gear, capable of over 500 miles per hour even on primitive turbojets. Intended armament was initially three 20 mm cannons. . . . The He-280 flew as a pure twin-jet aircraft more than 15 months before the Me-262. The Germans thus had within their grasp, during the RAF's first nonstop offensive, the weapon needed to abort the ruin that would later descend on them from the daylight skies."[1] Politicking by no less a figure than Dr. Willy Messerschmitt himself, the designer of the competing Me-262 jet fighter, helped to scuttle the He 280 jet project. The smart course of action for the Luftwaffe would have been to pursue both the He 280 and the Me-262 projects with the aim of augmenting and eventually replacing its conventionally powered fighter inventory. That scenario never materialized. History abounds with examples of the value of new technology not being recognized when it first surfaces, and the German jets were no exception. The He 280 design was in some ways even more innovative than the competing Me-262, featuring a tricycle landing gear, when the Me-262 was still relying on a tail wheel, directing its jet blast into the runway. The He 280 featured an ejection seat; the Me-262 never did. On the downside, the He 280 retained the constraints imposed by a straight wing and a twin-fin tail, yet it would have been a formidable opponent to any conventionally powered Allied aircraft of the time, especially the lumbering bombers of the U.S. 8th Air Force and RAF's Bomber Command, bombers that led to Germany's ruin.

The Me-262 jet was one of the most visible elements of late-war German aeronautical prowess. As a result the Me-262 served as a marker of Nazi Germany's technological lead over the Allies. Flying at speeds of up to 560 miles per hour at 20,000 feet, the Me-262 could operate with near impunity against anything the Allies were able to put up. And the Arado 234 jet reconnaissance bomber, using the same engines as the Me-262, could fly with equal ease over England without fearing American or British fighters on its wide-ranging forays.[2] Fortunately for the western Allies, the introduction of these advanced jets by a technologically obtuse Nazi leadership was too little and too late. If not for that, the American and British combined bomber offensive, using aircraft of vintage design, could have faced unsustainable losses. Even the landing on the Normandy coast would likely have been thrown into question had this new German technology been introduced early enough and in sufficient numbers. The German jets clearly had the potential to alter the course of war if not its outcome. Lieutenant General Putt noted in 1974, "If he [Hitler] had let them use that [Me-262] as a fighter when it first came out, we would have been in bad shape."[3]

No one really knows how the course of history might have changed if its ingredients had been varied at critical moments in time. We can only speculate. One thing, though, is not subject to speculation—by 1940, American aeronautical research and development had been far surpassed by German and British engineers and scientists. America's aviation industry seemed stuck on conventionally powered aircraft, while others were looking at an entirely different approach to aircraft propulsion. On the British side, Frank Whittle, made a Knight Commander of the Order of the British Empire in 1948 for his development of a turbo jet engine, found even less support for his ideas at the Air Ministry than did his German counterpart, Hans von Ohain, at the Reichsluftfahrtministerium (RLM). Not until the outbreak of war in late 1939 did the British Air Ministry show more than passing interest in Whittle's jet engine design. The first flight tests commenced on May 15, 1941, and the W2B engine which would power the Gloster Meteor twin jet fighter was put into production by Rolls-Royce in 1943. The Gloster Meteor never saw actual combat but was instrumental in shooting down a number of German V-1 cruise missiles over England in 1944. Drawings of the W2B engine were provided to General Electric as early as 1941, eventually providing GE a substantial lead in jet engine technology over its competitors, most of which appeared totally uninterested in such unproven gimmickery. The RLM wasn't much more supportive of Hans von Ohain's jet engine design, but in spite of substantial political and material obstacles, the German jets came into being sooner than comparable British jets.

The fact that the Me-262 flew at all in any numbers is a credit to people other than the Nazi leadership. Its large-scale introduction as a fighter was delayed and compromised by repeated internal Nazi political machinations and not by faulty design or technological limitations. Hitler, never one to stay out of anything, forced its conversion to a fighter-bomber, and by so doing delayed the effective introduction of the Me-262 as an interceptor by as much as a year. Albert Speer, Hitler's armaments minister, wrote, "On March 22, [1945,] Hitler invited me to one of his armaments conferences. . . . Although armaments production had long since come to an end, they occupied themselves with projects as though the whole of 1945 were still at their disposal. . . . He wished to have our jet fighter-bomber, the Me-262, rearmed as quickly as possible as a fighter plane. In ordering this last action, he was tacitly conceding the error he had made a year and a half before, when he had persistently refused the advice of all the experts" and ordered the conversion of jet fighters to bombers.[4] Although Hitler gets much of the blame for delaying the introduction of the Me-262, there is no evidence that Göring and his air staff pushed the revolutionary technology ahead of conventional aircraft programs. To the contrary, Speer and his armaments ministry prided themselves on how many Bf 109s and FW 190s, as well as useless medium bombers for which there was no fuel, were produced in 1944. Other than a few far-sighted men, such as the German fighter ace Adolf Galland, there was no one vocal in the Reich to champion the new jets. Men like Speer, in influential positions, did not appear to fully understand the jet's potential any more than Hitler did.

The Me-262 had two major limitations. First was its short engine life, dictated by a lack of critical materials required to harden the high temperature enduring turbine blades of the Junkers Jumo 004 engines. The second limitation was that frequently the pilots who flew the

Me-262B night fighter, with an external antenna array and two belly-mounted fuel tanks, at Schleswig, Germany, June 1945. (RB)

Me-262 were inexperienced. There were other problems, such as the unreliable synthetic tires, caused not by the design of the aircraft but by a lack of natural resources. "When the war ended," wrote Dr. Walter J. Lee in August 1945 in a Synthetic Rubber Survey conducted under the auspices of Operation Lusty, "their factories were still trying to make a useable airplane tire out of nylon fabric. From captured planes, they had analyzed our equipment and found our nylon tires were much stronger than their rayon tires." Quality problems were also associated with the manufacture of parts and their assembly by unskilled labor. Aircraft coming off the assembly lines had a dented, unfinished look; smoothness of skin was achieved with a putty-like substance applied to dents and seams and taped over when dry, much the way we go about fixing a rust spot on a favorite automobile. Yet, the rough-skinned Me-262 fighter still outperformed smooth-skinned, highly polished American and British jets built under ideal conditions and in a controlled factory environment with highly skilled and reliable personnel.

Each of the Me-262's engines provided just under two thousand pounds of thrust, not enough for its fourteen-thousand-pound gross weight. But then every jet fighter until the mid-seventies was under-powered, including the famed F-86, until the emergence of the F-15 with its two enormously powerful turbofan engines, the F100-PW-229, each providing twenty-nine thousand pounds of thrust. Long runways and RATO/JATO supplementary power packs were solutions for getting the early jets into the air. RATO was a device first used with the Arado 234 jet bomber. A Jumo 004E improved engine was in test at war's end with a static thrust of nearly three thousand pounds.

As for the men who piloted the new German jets, there was no quick fix for suddenly producing pilots equal in flying skills to American or British airmen. A one-time bomber pilot suddenly thrown into a jet fighter and given an hour's actual training in the aircraft wasn't going to turn into an instant Adolf Galland. Even Galland had problems adjusting to the rapid closure rate of the Me-262 upon a slow-moving bomber—over 150 miles an hour faster than what he experienced flying the Bf 109 or FW 190. Frequently pilots failed to fire their guns at all as they passed through a bomber formation—everything happened too fast for them to react properly. The Luftwaffe ran out of resources, out of real estate, and out of time to develop a coherent training program for its new jet pilots, much less come up with effective tactics against Allied fighters and bombers by the time the aircraft became available in increasing numbers in late 1944. Young German pilots were lucky to get one brief flight in the new jet before launching on their first operational mission. The resultant accident rate for the Me-262 was high. Captain Eric Brown notes, "While obviously proud of the Me-262, the German pilots were equally obviously somewhat apprehensive of it and especially of the two-seat night fighting version. . . . Firstly, the turbojets were unreliable and had, we were told, an overhaul life of a mere 10 hours. . . . Secondly, the single-engine safety speed on take-off was daunting; an engine failure before 180 miles per hour had been attained produced dire results. In fact, accident fatalities on Me-262s had been appalling."[5]

Chuck Yeager's encounters with Me-262 fighters illuminate both the aircraft's advantages and its vulnerabilities. He wrote:

> Blow jobs, the bomber crews called them, but no one was eager to be on the receiving end of the twin-engine German jet fighters that screamed down on our formations to quickly hit and run. The jets had a 150 mph speed advantage over the Mustang, but their pilots tried to avoid dogfights, concentrating instead on hammering the bombers. So, rarely did we encounter any jets. The word on them was that they were wing-heavy; the Mustang, with its laminar flow wing, could easily turn and dive with them, but in a level chase there was no contest; the Me-262 easily sped beyond gun range. . . . German jet pilots . . . just teased around, let a Mustang get close, then cobbed the throttle and thumbed their nose. If one of our pilots got off a shot, it was a quick burst at long range. So, I could hardly believe my good luck when I looked down into broken clouds from 8,000 feet and saw three jets cruising about 3,000 feet below. I was leading a flight of four Mustangs, just north of Essen, Germany, and I dove after them. I fired a few bursts before losing them in the cloud deck. My gun camera recorded that I put a few bullets into two jets. Chasing those guys, I was a fat man running uphill to catch a trolley. I was doing 450, but they zoomed out of sight. I climbed back to 8,000 feet to search for my flight. . . . I saw a large airdrome [Achmer] with a six-thousand-foot runway and a lone jet approaching the field from the south at 500 feet. I dove at him. His landing gear was down and he was lining up the runway, coming in at no more than 200 mph, when I dropped on his ass at 500 mph. . . . I came in full-throttle at 500 feet and fired above and behind the jet from four hundred yards. My hits slapped into his wings and I pulled up 300 feet off the ground with flak crackling all around me. Climbing straight up, I looked back and saw that jet crash-landing short of the runway, shearing off a wing, in a cloud of dust and smoke.[6]

Notwithstanding some occasional successes against the German jets, like Yeager's, the Me-262 represented an unresolved problem to escorting fighters. Since there was no possibility of catching the new fighter in level flight, certain tactics were suggested to minimize the jet's advantage during attacks, such as maintaining several thousand feet of altitude above the bombers, which, it was hoped, would give American pilots the chance to catch up to the jet in a dive. Turning directly into an attack, another tactic for the escorts, provided a split-second chance to inflict damage before the jet reached the bombers. A lucky hit on a vital part even at maximum range might slow the Messerschmitt sufficiently for the escorts to catch and destroy it. While these measures offered at least a chance of success, no entirely satisfactory solution to the problem of the Me-262 was ever reached during the war.[7]

Fred McIntosh, a P-47 pilot who flew out of England with the 56th Fighter Group, Zemke's famed Wolf Pack, recalled his first encounter in 1944 with an Me-262 on a bomber escort mission over Holland. "Before I knew what was happening, that P-51 was in flames and the German jet was gracefully swooping through our formation of several hundred fighters. If he wanted to get you, you were dead meat. There was nothing you could do about it." McIntosh reveals how his group commander, Colonel David C. Schilling, the eighth-highest-scoring American ace in World War II, with twenty-two and one-half victories, wanted nothing more than to fly one of those German jets. "I can taste it," Schilling said to me, he wanted to fly it that badly."[8]

Wright Field test pilots wanted to get their hands on one of those jets as well to put it through its paces. On March 31, Hans Fay, a Messerschmitt factory test pilot, decided that for him the war was over. Fay had taken off in a newly assembled Me-262A day fighter from a field at Hessenthal, several miles east of Darmstadt, for a brief functional test flight. Part of the magic of the Me-262 was that its component parts were not designed to close tolerances, allowing assembly of aircraft subsections in remote areas of Germany by unskilled laborers. Subsections then were transported to a final assembly point, such as Hessenthal, for integration. Here the airframe was assembled, fitted with the cockpit module and avionics and the two Jumo 004 power plants. It was necessary then to give the newly assembled aircraft a one-time operational flight check before turning it over to a combat unit. That's what Hans Fay was tasked to do on the last day of March in 1945. Instead, Fay headed his brand-new jet fighter northwest, toward Rhein-Main airport, on the fringes of Frankfurt, a field he was thoroughly familiar with and which was only a few minutes' flying time from Hessenthal. Fay never raised his landing gear, a universally understood gesture of surrender, and, staying at treetop level, made his way to Rhein-Main without incident. An Air Technical Intelligence team quickly disassembled the unexpected war prize, moved it by land to Rouen, and on the eighth of May the Me-262 was on its way to Wright Field, on what a report by the USSTAF Intelligence Directorate referred to as a "fast boat."[9] After reassembly at Wright Field, the Me-262 was test-flown for the first time on August 29, 1945. After a total of twelve flights of nearly eleven hours, the aircraft suffered an engine fire on August 20, 1946. Its pilot, Lieutenant Colonel Walter J. McAuley, abandoned the aircraft with difficulty. McAuley's experience of exiting the flaming jet was harrowing, and he relived it many times in his nightmares. The incident underlined the need for an ejection seat in jet aircraft. Test flying in the forties was dangerous business, and death or close encounters with it occurred frequently. Liz McAuley, Walter's wife, wrote, "Half our friends went down with their planes."[10]

McAuley thought the Me-262 "performed slightly better than the F-80 but was a dog as far as handling characteristics, and a maintenance man's nightmare." McAuley's finding was contrary to the experience of Hal Watson and his men at Lager Lechfeld, where in the course of their exploitation efforts they recovered a number of Me-262 jets for return to the United States. Another Wright Field test pilot, Gustav Lundquist, felt that the "engines did not hold up well when operating near the red-line limits and I had to make a couple single engine landings."[11] After the war Chuck Yeager chose to become a Wright Field test pilot. It was General Arnold's policy to allow his fighter aces to choose any assignment they wanted, and Yeager wanted to try his hand at test flying. Yeager was one of several aces flying under Major Kenneth O. Chilstrom, the chief of the Wright Field Fighter Operations Section. Chilstrom had

The suspended nose section of this Me-262 at Lechfeld shows how easily the aircraft could be disassembled. Engines and major subassemblies could be removed in twenty to thirty minutes. (RB)

Yeager fly the Me-262. Yeager commented, "I was busy doing air shows and flight test work; being the most junior test pilot in the shop, I was lucky to be asked to make coffee, but I did manage to get a few interesting jobs. One of them was comparison testing between the *Shooting Star* and a captured German Me-262 jet fighter. . . . I was fascinated to discover that the 262 and *Shooting Star* performed identically—the same range, top speed, acceleration, and rate of climb."[12]

The final report published by Wright Field on the Me-262 concluded that it suffered from poor brakes, something common to all German aircraft and certainly no reflection on the Me-262, and that engine changes were a frequent requirement. The latter finding, of course, attested only to the early stage of jet engine development and the German inability to obtain critical raw materials such as chromium, nickel, and molybdenum. As for the 262's handling characteristics, the Wright Field test pilots rated them as poor. The probable cause was aileron and elevator servotabs which had for some reason been disconnected. This may have occurred during disassembly for shipment, with the servotabs never being reconnected during reassembly. "The overall conclusion was that T2-711"—the number assigned to the aircraft by Technical Intelligence at Wright Field—"was superior to the average Lockheed P-80A in acceleration and speed, and comparable in climb perform-ance, despite a weight penalty of 2,000 lbs. A maximum True Air Speed of 568 mph was measured at a pressure altitude of 20,200 feet."[13]

Any way one chose to look at the Me-262 jet fighter, it was a remark-able airplane. Bob Strobell, a P-47 pilot and one of Watson's Whizzers, said about the Me-262/P-80 comparison tests, "The final test report stated that the comparison tests were pretty close. No enormous advantage of one over the other. I don't really believe that. I think the Me-262 was superior to the P-80 across the board. I flew the 262, and that's what I believe." Other Whizzer pilots who flew the German jet, like Bob Strobell, felt that the Me-262 was a superior airplane, the very best of its day.

Finally, it is important to note that the Me-262 was an interceptor and not a fighter able to engage in classic dogfight maneuvers. It had a terrible turning radius, and in a dogfight even the Arado 234 jet bomber could outturn it. Some academic commentators, impressed by the high speeds attained by jet aircraft, thought that the days of the dog-fight were over. Dr. Vannevar Bush, the head of the Office of Scientific Research and Development during World War II, wrote in 1949 that "dogfighting in the air, as a determining feature of really modern war, is probably now a thing of the past." Jet engines "made speeds in the air so high and turning radii consequently so large that dogfights became almost impossible. To conduct a dogfight, one has to be able to keep the enemy in sight for more than fleeting seconds."[14] Knife fighting, as we refer to it today, is still with us.

The Me-262 excelled at fast hit-and-run tactics to blow slow-moving B-17 and B-24 bombers out of the sky. Its low-velocity 30 mm guns were rather unimpressive, but they were designed to inflict maximum damage on a B-17 or B-24 bomber. Its rocket armament was, however, what made the 262 a truly lethal aircraft, allowing it to deliver destruction without having to enter within range of the victim's guns. Besides its unique power plants, the aircraft incorporated a number of other new features, including a built-in starter motor hidden in each engine's nose cone, an eighteen-degree wing sweep delaying the onset of compressibility and resultant drag, and wings incorporating automatic leading edge slats to provide stability at low airspeeds. For a pilot a first look at a new airplane often settles the relationship; it's a gut feeling each pilot develops over time and learns to trust. Some planes look like dogs, and they fly like dogs, trying to kill the pilot at every turn. Others look like they were made to reach for the sky and touch the face of God. The Me-262 was built to reach for the sky.

The other German jet to become operational in late 1944, less well known yet no less important, was the Arado 234 bomber and reconnaissance aircraft. Although at war's end there were numerous Arado 234 versions on the drawing boards of its designer and manufacturer, the Arado Flugzeugwerke, the one version which saw considerable combat as both a bomber and a reconnaissance aircraft was the Ar 234B, a twin-jet aircraft with its engines slung under its wings, as on the Me-262. The four-engine C-model included bomber, reconnaissance, and night fighter configurations. Only a limited number of C-models were built; none ever flew in combat. The lack of Jumo 004 turbines and the high priority given to the Me-262 fighter program forced Arado engineers to consider the less-powerful Bayrische Motorenwerke BMW 003 turbine. They hung four of the BMW 003 jets on the two hardpoints under the wings of the C-models as an interim measure to be rectified when more Jumo 004 engines became available. Before that could happen, time ran out for the Thousand Year Reich.

The Arado was a straight-wing bomber, in contrast to the Me-262, with its eighteen-degree wing sweep. Although conventional

A captured Arado 234B bomber at Schleswig airfield, Germany, in the British zone of occupation. (RB)

in appearance, the Ar 234 was exceedingly innovative. Among those innovations was a new approach to aircraft braking. German engineers had made significant advances in parachute design. Instead of conventional types of chutes, familiar to everyone since the waning days of World War I, ribbon chutes were developed which could be employed to deliver large loads from low-flying transport aircraft, and others were to be used for aircraft emergency braking. The Arado 234 was the first aircraft in the world to use an advanced design ribbon brake chute to shorten its landing roll. Later this new chute was to find application in America's first swept-wing jet bomber, the B-47. Not only was the German-developed ribbon chute used as a brake chute in the B-47, but a second chute of similar design was installed as an approach chute to stabilize the B-47's final moments of flight prior to landing.

Wrote Captain Eric Brown, "When I saw my first Arado at the Danish airfield of Grove . . . I was immediately impressed by its aesthetically attractive contours. . . . This airplane looked right and in my experience this was always a good omen with regard to flying qualities. With its slender shoulder-mounted wing, slim underslung engine nacelles and smooth fuselage profile, it exemplified careful aerodynamic design."

Brown, like Watson, was enthralled with this new German jet bomber and flew it in subsequent weeks more than any other German aircraft. "I found the *Blitz* a delightful airplane to fly," swooned Brown, and a "top speed of 475 mph was what made the *Blitz* so appropriate a name for the Arado 234B."[15] The single-seat Arado provided the pilot with a superlative view, had a steerable nose gear, a pressurized cockpit, and two fixed, aftfiring 20 mm cannons, although few of the operational Arados had cannons installed. With a range of sixteen hundred to eighteen hundred miles at an altitude of thirty thousand feet, the Arado could easily reach the British Isles. Nearly all German bombers were designed for dive-bombing, which found its extreme application in the four-engine Heinkel 177. The Arado got away from this limiting approach of bomb delivery by providing its pilot with a computerized bombsight the Germans considered superior even to the Norden bombsight, which they had gained access to soon after its introduction in 8th Air Force bombers and rejected as inferior to their own developments.[16]

The Arado pilot had the option to deliver his bombs in a shallow dive aided by a periscope tied into a computer. This was the principal mode of bomb delivery. The second mode was a straight and level high-altitude approach to the target. On August 26, 1944, Kampfgeschwader 76, KG 76, the only combat wing to be fully equipped with the Arado 234B, received its first aircraft equipped with the new and, for German bomber pilots, revolutionary bombsight. It was a hands-off type operation where the pilot put the aircraft on autopilot, fixed the crosshairs of the bombsight on the target, and bomb release was automatically initiated at a computer-calculated release point. This device was rudimentary by today's standards and had no way to calculate various factors affecting the trajectory of a bomb, but in 1945 this was a highly advanced approach to bomb delivery. Most Arado pilots rejected this option, being used to the dive-bombing techniques they had learned flying the Ju 87 Stuka and the Ju 88 medium bomber. The level bombing approach also required a clear sky and had its limitations in the cloud-heavy European environment. When conditions were right the high-altitude delivery method took the bomber largely out of AAA range and denied enemy fighters the opportunity to successfully intercept the Arado with its superior airspeed.

Radar-controlled American AAA guns, some using proximity fuzed shells, made dive-bombing a hazardous undertaking by late 1944, yet most of the KG 76 pilots chose the shallow dive-bombing technique over the high-altitude attack option. Arado engineers found the reluctance of their best pilots to use the new equipment disheartening. Colonel Storp, the commander of KG 76 in 1944 "was a convinced dive bomber man and the whole technical effort of the alternative method was wasted," lamented the bombsight's designer in 1944. All photo reconnaissance missions had to be flown straight and level, of course, and flying at thirty-three thousand feet, even if detected, provided little chance for American or British fighters to catch the high-speed intruder. Had the Arado been introduced prior to the June 6 Normandy landings, it could have provided much-needed information to the Germans and revealed Patton's sham army tying down German forces at the Pas de Calais. Its subsequent flights over the east coast of the United Kingdom, although spectacular, came at a time when the information could no longer be acted upon.

By October 1944, KG 76 had fifty-seven Arados operational, yet its pilots were still learning to understand the aircraft. Most transitioned straight from their previous assignments in Ju 88s, or the dated Ju 87 Stuka dive-bomber into the Arado 234B. In time KG 76 acquired a two-seat Me-262B-1 trainer and provided some entry-level jet training for its pilots. But many just received classroom instruction and then took off into a totally new experience of flight. As in the Me-262 program, Arado training claimed its victims. On landing, for instance, pilots tried to make a three-point landing, being unfamiliar with the new tricycle gear arrangement on the Arado. Collapsing nose gears finally convinced them that they should approach in a nose-high attitude, touching down on the main gear and then slowly letting the nose gear settle down.

The sound barrier, so familiar to every aviation buff since Chuck Yeager broke it in October 1947, was a totally unknown phenomenon to the flyers of KG 76, who manned a new jet which in a dive could quickly find itself entering a zone of high compressibility where drag suddenly increased exponentially and lift faltered. Many a Bf 109 or Mosquito pilot, diving to escape a pursuing foe, had paid the price as his aircraft disintegrated in a downward dive while entering the region of high drag and low lift when approaching Mach 1. Pressure and consequently drag built up on the edge of a straight wing as it approached Mach 1, quickly destabilizing the aircraft and frequently causing structural failure. Germany's engineers, operating the most advanced wind tunnels in the world at Peenemünde, later moved to Kochel, knew all about the effects of high-speed flight on an aircraft at speeds just below, at, and beyond Mach 1, but evidently none of these learned men thought of or had the opportunity to pass this information on to the combat flyers of KG 76. Sergeant Ludwig "Rieffel was practicing a gliding attack when he experienced a reversal of the controls approaching Mach 1. He bailed out successfully but the shock of the parachute opening at that speed ripped three of its six sections from top to bottom. A freshly ploughed field prevented him from being seriously injured. This happened later to Oberleutnant Heinke. . . . He was unable to escape from the aircraft which crashed into the ground in a vertical dive on March 7, 1945."[17] The German flyers still had much to learn about their new ship.

When American flyers encountered a German jet their experiences very much depended on the type of aircraft they were flying. If it was a fighter, the pilot could defend himself by either using escape maneuvers or ganging up on the German jet and attempting to overwhelm it with superior numbers. For the bomber crew an encounter with an Me-262 jet was a mostly terrifying experience, their plane being little more than the proverbial sitting duck.

JET ENCOUNTERS

Although over a thousand Me-262 jet fighters were built by the Germans, fewer than half were ever delivered to combat units, and fewer still were committed to actual combat. Although American airmen heard of these German jets, actual encounters were infrequent considering the thousands of American aircraft that roamed across German skies on a daily basis. Yet when they occurred, they were very different experiences for fighter pilots and bomber crews.

Captain Frederic B. McIntosh, a gung-ho fighter pilot if there ever was one, flew P-47s. Like many other Americans, his heritage was German. "My stepfather's name was Heinrich Warnholz," Fred reminisced. "I was born on June 8, 1918. I don't remember when my mother married Heinrich. I was still very young. She changed her name; I kept mine. People and things in my life were pretty much German. Eleanor Vollmer, my twenty-some-year-old high school German teacher, was from Berlin. I picked up her accent. Years later in 1945 when I was retrieving captured Luftwaffe aircraft, Germans frequently asked me if I was a Berliner. After high school I went to work for the Pacific Gas & Electric Company in Oakland. I graduated on Friday and on Monday night I was digging ditches for the gas company for fifteen cents an hour. I worked nights and went to school during the day. In college I took Navy ROTC with the idea of becoming a naval aviator. When I applied for flight training the Navy recruiter told me that a junior certificate just wouldn't do. I had to have a college degree to get into naval aviation. I went across the street to the Army recruiter, who didn't care what my educational pedigree was, and signed up with the Army Air Corps, class 43C.

"I reported to Santa Ana in southern California, no more than a wheat field then and a bunch of tents. Next came Thunderbird II, again a new airfield near Phoenix with few amenities. But there at least we didn't have to sleep in tents. After graduation in March 1943 I went to Williams Field near Tempe, Arizona, where I spent a year as an instructor pilot in the P-38 Lightning. Whoever set the date for the invasion of the Continent must have foreseen the need for replacement pilots. Four hundred of us from training command were picked to 'volunteer.' When we arrived in Florida we were introduced to the P-47. Hell, you could just look at that airplane and tell it wouldn't fly. We all signed up for P-38s. We got about four hours' flying time in the P-47 and then were sent to New York and put on a seventy-two-ship convoy, mostly tankers, heading for Europe. Sitting on the tankers were fighter planes. We didn't see any P-38s, but we saw lots of P-47s and P-51s. When we got to England, we second lieutenants were met by several 'bird colonels,' commanders of P-38 fighter outfits. Some of us thought this kind of odd and we trotted over to the intelligence section to take a look at some mission summaries for different types of combat aircraft. What fell out of it for me was that for every P-47 lost, they lost two P-51s, in round numbers, that is. And for every P-51 they lost two P-38s. You didn't have to be a blackjack player to figure out the way Jimmy Doolittle [who commanded the 8th Air Force] was running the air war, the first airplane to stay out of was the P-38, the second the P-51. I didn't know what they were doing with the P-47, but I decided that airplane was for me after all.[1]

"I arrived at the 56th Fighter Group at Boxted, near Colchester, on June 5, 1944. I was assigned to the 62nd squadron. They had been in

England almost a year and a half by that time. The 56th Group was the most successful fighter group in the 8th Air Force. It had more aces than any other outfit - Gaby Gabreski, Hub Zemke, Dave Schilling, Walker Mahurin, Fred Christensen, Gerald and Bob Johnson, Joe Powers, Paul Conger, Leroy Schreiber, Jimmy Stewart—not the actor and bomber pilot—and many more. Zemke was our group commander through the invasion. Schilling was Zemke's deputy and my squadron commander. Schilling and I took a shine to one another. I flew twenty-five missions on his wing. Zemke then went to a down-and-out P-38 outfit to shape it up, the 479th Fighter Group at Wattisham, part of our Wing, the 65th. They were scheduled to receive P-51s. Zemke transitioned into the P-51 and ended up bailing out over France when his aircraft iced up and spun into the ground. Zemke escaped by the skin of his teeth and ended up as a guest of the Germans at Stalag Luft I, near Barth, Pomerania. Schilling took over the 56th when Zemke left. Both Zemke and Schilling were full colonels in their twenties.

"On the first of November 1944 we were escorting over three hundred B-24 bombers of the 2nd Air Division. There were nearly as many fighters escorting the bombers as there were bombers. The sky was filled with airplanes. We were on our way home, over Holland, when suddenly an Me-262 jet jumped a bunch of P-51s flying high cover. The German jet went after a straggler, and blew him out of the sky before I knew what was happening. Then the Me-262 peeled off and came down through our formation." The 56th Fighter Group history states, "The jet was at 38,000 feet and at first only its heavy brown intermittent contrail was visible. It was approaching the bombers, which were withdrawing from the target area on a course of 320 degrees. As the group turned into the jet, it went into a shallow dive of about thirty degrees and came on the tail of a P-51 above and to the rear of the bombers. The P-51 burst into flames. The Me-262 continued its dive over the bomber formation." From then on all the P-51s and the P-47s were "in a mad scramble to destroy the Hun. It made a diving turn to the left in

The stubby-winged P-47 fighter, dubbed the Jug, was a rugged airplane, handling much of the close air support in the ETO. This one, named Pick, *was flown by Lieutenant Roy Brown of the 86th Fighter Group, 1st TAF (Provisional). (RB)*

a south-westerly direction. At about 10,000 feet it made a climbing turn of 180 degrees right and headed full throttle toward the Zuider Zee in a northerly direction just above the cloud layer. At that time, if the enemy pilot had gone into the cloud undercast, he undoubtedly could have evaded our fighters. Evidently he felt that he could outrun our fighters because he kept above the clouds. As he made his last turn to the right, both P-47s and P-51s cut him off, getting strikes on the left side of the fuselage and the left wing." The Me-262 jet made a climbing turn to the left, in front of one of the flights of the 56th Fighter Group, and Lieutenant Groce fired. "It was then that the right jet burst into flames. The *blow-job* went into a spin, and the pilot bailed out."[2]

McIntosh recalled that "Schilling went after the German pilot and killed him in his chute. When we got back he got everybody in the debriefing room and said, 'OK, I know some of you probably think I'm an SOB because I killed a man in a chute. Did you ever think of all the mistakes that guy made?' And he enumerated them. 'And what would happen if he got back? Some of us, including you, are not going to outlast the war. It's just that simple. So think what you want, that's why I did it. Any questions, gentlemen?' Of course nobody said a word. But he was right. As Schilling went through the man's mistakes—his last mistake was to open his chute too high, giving Schilling an opportunity to kill him." The act of shooting a jet pilot in his chute was not all that unusual, although it was distasteful to many airmen. Colonel Raymond E. Toliver described Galland's actions to save his own life when his Me-262 was damaged on April 26, 1945, days before war's end. "His stricken Me-262 was still flying, and he did not want to risk parachuting and landing as a corpse. Jet pilots were regarded as valuable targets by the Allied commanders, although most Allied fighter pilots disagreed with the principle of shooting at para-chuting enemies."[3] Chuck Yeager wrote, "Early in my tour, I heard that one of the guys had seen a 109 strafe an American bomber crew in their chutes. I thought it was bad practice in every way. Both sides at least gave lip service to a gentleman's agreement not to do it. And if I had to jump for it again, I could hope the agreement was being honored that day."[4]

"The British had developed a jet of their own," Fred McIntosh continued. "After our encounter with the German jet on November 1, we occasionally practiced against the British jet, teapot, the Brits called it. We tried to devise maneuvers and tactics for the P-47 against jet fight-ers. Even though the British airplane was not as good as the Me-262, it became obvious to us that if the German pilot knew what he was doing, you were dead meat. I learned to love the P-47; it was a tough little airplane. I once flew one through the trees and made it home. Gaby Gabreski tried the same thing with a P-51 and ended up in Stalag Luft I along with his buddy Hub Zemke. When Stalag Luft I was liber-ated toward the end of April 1945, they brought all the POWs from Barth to Camp Lucky Strike, near Le Havre. On May 4, I got word that Zemke and Gabreski were at Camp Lucky Strike and I flew over in a Martin B-26 Widow Maker and flew them back to Boxted."

While the fighter boys had a fair chance of coping with an attacking Me-262 jet by either taking evasive action or ganging up on the enemy plane and overwhelming it with their sheer numbers, the bombers had no such options. They flew straight and level in their ponderous formations designed to maximize their defensive fire power against conventional fighters. They stood little chance of surviving a deter-mined attack by a swift-moving German jet—especially if it was armed with the new fin-stabilized RLM 4 air-to-air rockets. Lieutenant Charles P. Johnson learned this lesson firsthand on March 20, 1945, during a bombing raid against the already bomb-scarred seaport of Hamburg.

Charlie Johnson hailed from Mount Rainier, Maryland, and was drafted on April 28, 1943, along with a slew of his high school buddies. While being processed by a gruff Army sergeant he asked about flight training, and to his surprise the sergeant obligingly got him the applica-tion forms which would send him on his way to the Army Air Forces. "That's a good idea, young fella," the sergeant said, smiling, when he handed Charlie the forms. "That's a really good idea. I do hope it works out for you, kid"—and there was that smile again. Greensboro, North Carolina; Spartanburg, South Carolina; Nashville, Tennessee; Montgomery, Alabama; Fort Myers, Florida; Valdosta, Georgia; San Marcos, Texas; and Lincoln, Nebraska, were the many way stations Charlie passed through before he found himself at an overseas replace-ment center at Dyersburg, Tennessee. In Dyersburg Charlie became part of a newly formed B-17 crew. "The pilot was both competent and tough, a real no-nonsense-looking kind of guy," Charlie recalled. "He hailed from St. Louis, Missouri, and was a second-generation German. Francis Taub didn't talk a lot, but when he did, people listened. We called him Taub. John Cooper, the copilot, had a soft Memphis drawl and was a very competent pilot as well. Warren Chrisman was our flight engineer and top gunner; Mike Dugan served as armorer and waist gunner; Jim Hollowell, a little guy, was the ball turret gunner;

Chester Maluchnik served as radio operator; Elmer McWilliams was the waist gunner; and Jim Spencer served as tail gunner.

"On January 2, 1945, we set off for the war in Europe in a brand-new B-17G. Our route took us over the snow-covered plains states, across Pennsylvania, New York, and into New England, where we landed at Manchester Army Airfield, New Hampshire. It wasn't until January 6 that we received departure clearance for Goose Bay, Labrador. We landed at Goose Bay in the evening darkness with the surface temperature twenty degrees below zero and a forty-mile-per-hour wind. Mike Dugan got frostbite while he tried to cover the engines with canvas. He lost part of one ear. Not until January 17 did the weather ease and we were cleared for a night departure. We took off for Reykjavík, Iceland, where we landed after fourteen anxious hours in the air. The next afternoon we departed for Prestwick, Scotland, and arrived that same evening safely and without incident. Our final assignment was to the 303rd Bomb Group at Molesworth, England. On February 14 I flew my first combat mission against Dresden. We were flying within sight of a B-24 formation which had a different target than ours. The B-24s came under heavy attack by flak. In a matter of only a few minutes, nearly half of the B-24s had fallen out of their formation—some severely damaged, struggling to regain contact with the main body. Others spun away into the mist or exploded in a bright flash. Parachutes appeared on the horizon, but not enough to account for all the flight crews whose planes had been hit and were going down. No training film had prepared me for such an awful sight. This frightening scene put me in a cold sweat. I was shaking. I felt I was getting a preview of what would happen to us over Dresden. Fortunately the opposition over Dresden was light. Only one plane in our formation was seriously damaged.

"On my second mission against an oil refinery on February 16 my plane sustained major damage. Two engines had to be shut down, the props feathered to prevent them from running away and shearing off into the crew compartment. Then a third engine quit on us—we were flying with only one good engine over Germany, losing altitude rapidly. Our immediate problem was to get through our own formation without a midair collision. Once Taub and Cooper had accomplished that feat, they managed to get a second engine running again. Then Taub and Cooper nursed our ailing craft back home, steadily losing altitude as we went, but we got home without having to ditch or a German fighter picking us off. Our escort was nowhere in sight. On February 22 we became part of a two-thousand-plane raid against the rail system of the Third Reich. Bombers and fighters from the 8th, 15th, and 9th Air Forces and the 1st Tactical Air Force participated in this mass raid, code-named Operation Rail Smash. Our assigned target was the marshaling yard at Uelzen. Although we flew only at twelve thousand feet, our bombing was mediocre. The next day we attacked Bad Kitzingen, then Ulm, and on the twenty-sixth of February the big B—Berlin. By March 20 I had flown seventeen of my required thirty-five combat missions. This day we were assigned another brand-new B-17G, like the one we had flown over to England. I remember the crew chief as he was closing the hatch yelling up at us, 'Bring her back in one piece.' I studied my maps as we made our way across France, there wasn't much for me to do. Our position was on the extreme right flank of our squadron of twelve. We were the high group at twenty-six thousand feet. Neither I nor Taub had been told where or what our target was, that information was passed to us before we crossed into Germany. After crossing the Rhine River we set course for Hamburg. From the initial point of our bomb run onward, Taub and I saw several German planes pacing us, just out of range of our guns. Obviously they were passing our altitude to controllers on the ground. As we neared Hamburg the flak grew in intensity. I watched for the lead plane to drop its bombs, and when it did, Mike Dugan, the waist gunner who also served as bomb toggler, dropped our bombs. Our group initiated a sharp turn, heading for the North Sea and home. About halfway through our turn all hell broke loose. I felt a tremendous jolt shaking the entire plane. My first thought was that we had had a midair collision. As I turned my head to the right I glimpsed a Messerschmitt Me-262 jet fighter streaking past my window—a plane I had heard about but never seen before. I switched my radio from the group channel to intercom just in time to hear Spencer reporting extensive damage to the tail section. Taub then came on the intercom and warned that he had trouble controlling the aircraft and that we should prepare for bailout. I hollered at Taub, 'Don't you do that. We are still over Hamburg. If we bail out now we will be captured by the people we just bombed. Our chances of remaining alive will be slim to zero! Stay on a northerly heading and try to make Sweden, or at least Denmark.' 'I'll try,' Taub replied. The aircraft was shaking badly. I started to plot an alternate course when I felt two explosions. I looked out and saw two engines burning fiercely. The wings were shredded. Taub yelled, 'Bail out, bail out.' This was the end of my war, maybe the end of my life. I tightened the straps of my parachute. At the escape hatch Chrisman was struggling; he could only open it a crack. He started to squeeze out, feet first, and got stuck. I stepped on the hatch handle and pushed him out. Then I squeezed out the hatch, plunging away from the plane, which exploded in a fiery flash. The nose section separated from the fuselage at the escape hatch from which I had just exited. Mike Dugan, still in the plunging nose section, climbed out as the nose dove toward the ground, and parachuted to safety. Cooper and Taub never had a chance. I think about them every day, every day of my life. If I hadn't tried to talk Taub into going on, maybe . . .

"After a painful landing I evaded capture for a couple of days, eventually ending up at Stalag Luft I near the former resort town of Barth on the Baltic Sea, a sprawling, ugly camp, holding nine thousand British and American airmen. Colonel Hubert 'Hub' Zemke was the senior Allied camp officer, and Lieutenant Colonel Francis 'Gaby' Gabresky was the senior officer of my compound. During the last days of April, artillery fire could be heard coming from the east. For several days the sounds of battle increased in intensity and volume. On the first of May the rumor mill had it that the guards, who were all old men, *Volkssturm* home guards, were preparing to abandon the camp before the Russians arrived. The following morning some of us climbed out the windows of our barracks. When there was no response from the guard towers we knew that the guards had left. Prisoners from throughout the compound followed our example. Doors were ripped off their hinges, fires were lit, the gates of the interior fences were broken down, and within a short time all the camp inmates were outside shouting, laughing, crying, and hugging one another.

"On May 8, VE Day, 8th Air Force B-17s landed at the nearby Barth airfield and flew us to a military airfield in France. From there trucks drove us to a railway station where we boarded a train to Camp Lucky

Charlie Johnson's crew. L to R front: Francis Taub, pilot; John Cooper, copilot; Charles Johnson, navigator. L to R back: Warren Chrisman, flight engineer/gunner; Michael Dugan, bomb toggler/gunner; James Hollowell, gunner; Chester Maluchnik, radio; Elmer McWilliams, gunner; James Spencer, gunner. (CJ)

Strike. While we waited for the train we noticed a tank car on a siding. A sign on its side said it contained *vin*. One of our guys spoke French and asked the stationmaster if he would allow us to tap the tank car. Without hesitation the Frenchman proclaimed, 'As allies and liberators of France you are entitled to have as much wine as you want.' He broke the seal and opened the valve and we filed by the tank car, filling our canteens with red wine. The wine was not very good, but who cared. This was the happiest and drunkest bunch of passengers a train had ever carried. The French conductors joined in the merriment, and in the end they were as drunk as the rest of us. Camp Lucky Strike, a huge tent city, became our temporary home until transportation was arranged for our return to America. In my mind I retain that picture of an Me-262 fighter flashing past my window. I think of Taub and Cooper. The war just goes on for me. It never ends."[5]

4

THE DEFIANT FEW

The fighter pilots of the Luftwaffe held their own against the western Allies for years, nearly always outnumbered and flying aircraft of increasingly vintage design. The Messerschmitt Bf 109 first flew in 1935, the Focke-Wulf 190 in 1939. By 1944, Allied air superiority had become intimidating to even the most hardened Luftwaffe veterans. Allied air forces swept before them anything the Luftwaffe managed to put up. The *Jagdflieger* couldn't remember anymore when they had had enough fuel, spare parts, or well-trained replacements to make up for the steady attrition that sapped the morale of all but the most steely nerved. By the summer of 1944 the *Jagdflieger* were at the end of their ropes; fatalism took over when morale faltered. Then, suddenly, a jet fighter entered their inventory that was superior to anything the Allies could muster. For a brief defiant moment their spirits soared, if only to show the enemy that they still knew how to fly and fight if given first-rate equipment. For one last time the *Jagdflieger* rallied around their admired leader Adolf Galland. They were, Galland told them, the first and the last.

The Me-262 jet fighter downed over the Zuider Zee on November 1, 1944, by a P-47 pilot of the 56th Fighter Group, belonged to a fledgling German jet squadron led by Major Walter Nowotny. Nowotny, a seasoned fighter pilot with 258 aerial victories to his credit, was killed one week later on November 8, by pursuing P-51 fighters while trying to land his damaged jet at his home base of Achmer near Osnabrück. Nowotny was twenty-three years old when he died. Most fighter pilots, whether German, American, or British, were very young. Upon Nowotny's death Jagdgeschwader 7, JG 7, Fighter Wing 7, was formed from the remnants of Nowotny's group of Me-262 flyers.

The Me-262 which shot down Charlie Johnson's B-17 over Hamburg on the afternoon of March 20, 1945, with a salvo of twenty-four 50 mm RLM 4 rockets belonged to JG 7. The 1st Air Division lost three B-17s to the German jets that March day over Hamburg, an insignificant number for a force of over three hundred bombers. But men like General Spaatz, the experienced and farsighted commander of the United States Strategic Air Forces in Europe, saw the Me-262 and its futuristic rocket armament for what it truly represented—not the last gasp of a nearly defeated tyrant, but the tools of wars yet to come.

The aggressive Jagdgeschwader 7 pilots were led briefly by Colonel Johannes Steinhoff, who had 176 aerial victories to his credit. In later years Steinhoff would rise to three-star rank as chief of staff of the reconstituted Luftwaffe of the Federal Republic of Germany. By the time of Charlie Johnson's shoot-down, however, Colonel Steinhoff had joined the rebellious Adolf Galland, who was forming Jagdverband 44, JV 44, from one of the squadrons of JG 7 operating out of Brandenburg-Briest airfield, north of Berlin. General Galland, the youthful one-time leader of Germany's fighter forces, had the audacity to challenge Reichsmarschall Hermann Göring, whom most thought a pompous and incompetent leader. Angered by Galland's actions, Göring relieved Galland of command, charged him with mutiny, and attempted to put him before a *Kriegsgericht,* a military court, and have him shot. Göring, thwarted in his efforts by no less than the Führer himself, reluctantly let Galland off the hook and permitted him to form his own squadron of experts, JV 44.

When word went out that Galland was forming his own squadron of Me-262 jets, many of Germany's best pilots dropped whatever they were doing and flew, drove, rode bicycles, or walked into Brandenburg-Briest to have the honor of flying with Adolf Galland. "From the Russian Front came Major Gerd Barkhorn, credited with 300 victories," wrote Colonel Toliver. "Major Krupinski, the fabled "Count Punski" with 197 victories, was coaxed out of the hospital, as were Erich Hohagen and "Bubi" Schnell. Günter Lützow [103 victories] returned from exile in Italy, where he had been banished by Göring as one of Galland's co-conspirators." Galland himself requested the transfer of Hauptmann Erich Hartmann, the most successful of all Luftwaffe fighter pilots, with 352 victories. Hartmann came and checked out in the Me-262, but he wanted desperately to be with his own men in JG 52 who were fighting their war on the Ostfront. Hartmann's decision to return to his unit led to ten years of imprisonment in the Soviet Union upon his capture by the Russians. "These aces and their illustrious squadron commander had almost 900 victories between them. When the numerous captains, lieutenants, and sergeants who were aces were included, the squadron became the only one in the world whose personnel had downed over 1,000 aircraft! . . . In the history of aerial warfare, there had never been such an elite fighter squadron."[1]

Although outnumbered and outgunned, for a few dangerous weeks the pilots of JV 44 flaunted their jets in the faces of Allied airmen. "With an average serviceability of six aircraft, JV 44 destroyed some forty-five to fifty American and British planes in the short time it operated."[2] While claims were difficult to verify in the hectic aerial battles of the last months of war, reviewed and revised postwar records seem to indicate that JV 44's greatest victory against the hated bombers of the 8th Air Force came on April 7, 1945. "In the span of a few minutes, the long stream of bombers lost between twenty and thirty aircraft. The Me-262 pilots claimed that twenty-five had been downed by their rockets."[3] The official history of the Army Air Forces in World War II records that 1,200 heavy bombers of the 8th Air Force were attacked on April 7 by 150 German fighters, including over 50 jets, admitting to a loss of 15 heavy bombers.[4] The rocket-equipped Me-262 appeared to be the German answer to the American bomber boxes with their withering defensive firepower. Armed with rockets, the fighters no longer had to fly within range of the bombers' guns. This capability and great advantage for the *Jagdflieger* came, however, at one minute to twelve o'clock. The show was nearly over.

JV 44 operated predominantly from Lager Lechfeld and Munich-Riem airfields, ending the war in Salzburg and Innsbruck, Austria. JG 7 operated from bases near Berlin and from Parchim in the north of Germany, frequently changing operating locations as dictated by the ever-constricting geography of the Reich. From the ranks of JG 7 emerged the highest-scoring jet ace of World War II, Oberleutnant Rudolf "Rudi" Rademacher, with twenty-three confirmed victories in the Me-262. Heinz "Pritzl" Bär, a Luftwaffe legend with two hundred twenty confirmed victories going back to 1939, was the leading scorer for JV 44, with sixteen victories. And Leutnant Klaus Neumann, at age twenty-one the youngest JV 44 ace, added five victories in the Me-262 to the thirty-two he had gained in the previous two years flying the Bf 109. But the cost to the jet flyers came high.

The Me-262 required nearly six thousand feet of hard surface runway for takeoff, and air bases with runways of that type and length, such as Lager Lechfeld in the south and Achmer in the north, were easily identified by Allied fighters. A favorite American tactic was to wait for the German jets to return and catch them as they tried to land. On landing and takeoff, even the most experienced Luftwaffe flyers were totally vulnerable. Lieutenant Urban L. "Ben" Drew was a P-51 pilot with the 361st Fighter Group, the Yellowjackets, based at Little Walden, England. On October 7, 1944, Ben Drew was leading the 375th squadron, escorting bombers returning from a raid against an oil refinery at Brüx, Czechoslovakia. Passing Achmer airfield, Drew looked down and noticed two enemy aircraft taxiing into position for takeoff. Accompanied by two wing men, Drew rolled over from fifteen thousand feet in a nearly vertical dive and began firing at the second Me-262 "when he was about 1,000 feet off the ground. I was indicating 450 MPH and the jet aircraft could not have been going over 200 MPH. . . . They didn't see me and I pulled in behind the number two man and the first burst hit his starboard fuel tank where the wing fares into the fuselage, and he exploded—I mean complete explosion, there was nothing left." Still indicating four hundred miles per hour, Drew was able to close with the leader and open fire at a range of four hundred yards. "If he'd cobbed it, if he'd have thrown the throttle wide open, if it wasn't already there, I think he'd have gotten away. But he started a tight climbing turn to the left. I pulled up and my bullets started hitting. . . . Then he was losing speed which enabled me to pull in tighter and my bullets walked up to the cockpit and I saw the canopy blow off but I never saw him go over the side." The plane rolled over, hitting the ground at about a sixty-degree angle. Although Drew did not witness the German pilot's escape, he survived the low-level bailout. Drew had shot down two of Nowotny's jets.[5]

Several other small units were equipped with the fighter-bomber version of the Me-262, principally KG 52, Kampfgeschwader 52, at Brandenburg-Briest. The KG 52 jets carried two 250-kilogram bombs. As the war came to a close in early May 1945, the remaining Me-262s– night fighters, day fighters, and fighter-bombers alike–scattered to bases wherever they could find a last sanctuary. For JG 7 pilots it was Prague-Ruzyne and Gbell, Eger, Saaz, among others, and Lager Lechfeld near Augsburg. As for JV 44, Adolf Galland attempted to surrender the squadron as an operational unit to the XII Tactical Air Command of the 1st Tactical Air Force.

On the morning of April 26, 1945, Galland and five other jets took off from Munich-Riem; spotting a formation of 1st TAF B-26 Marauders near Neuburg, they attacked the American bombers. Galland's aircraft was armed with twenty-four air-to-air rockets. As he closed on an unsuspecting Marauder, he failed to throw the second safety switch to arm the rockets, and when he pushed the firing button nothing happened. The B-26 loomed large, and Galland instinctively fired his four 30 mm nose guns. The B-26 exploded in a bright flash. Galland hammered a second B-26 in passing. Unsure of his victim's fate, he turned to look back and became a victim himself. Lieutenant Jim Finnegan of the 50th Fighter Group, flying escort in his P-47 Thunderbolt, gained on Galland and fired a desperate burst from his eight .50 caliber guns. Galland's jet was hit by Finnegan's stream of bullets, fragments lodging in Galland's right knee. Galland nursed his jet back to Munich-Riem, and as he touched down he came under attack by strafing Mustangs. He miraculously survived, ending up in a hospital bed in a private home near Tegernsee from which he attempted to negotiate the surrender of JV 44. Arrangements for JV 44's surrender were negotiated by the deputy commander of the XII TAC, Colonel Dorr E. Newton, and Galland's representatives, Major Herget and Hauptmann Kessler.[6] According to the agreement worked out between Newton and Herget, the Me-262s were to fly from Salzburg and Innsbruck along predetermined routes and altitudes to airfields occupied by the 50th and 86th Fighter Groups. The 86th was located at Gross Gerau, near Darmstadt. The 526th Fighter Squadron history of the 86th Fighter Group notes, "The big event of the day was Command assigning the Group a special mission. Thirty-six planes from the Group were to go to the Munich area, pick up some enemy fighters and escort them back to the field, where the enemy planes would land. Some arrangements had been made with the enemy but bad weather prevented the show from taking place."[7] With the weather-induced failure of JV 44's surrender, most of its planes were destroyed by their German crews.

The few Me-262 night fighters the Luftwaffe fielded put up as spirited a fight as the more numerous day fighters. NJG 11, Nachtjagdgeschwader 11, Nightfighter Wing 11, operated from Schleswig and Fassberg airfields. Their Me-262B-1/2 jets were two-seater night-fighter versions of the Me-262B-1 trainer equipped with the FuG 218 Neptun search and tail warning radar using the cumbersome nose-mounted stag antler antenna array. Oberleutnant Kurt Welter, flying with NJG 11, demonstrated what a skilled pilot could achieve by night with a superior airplane such as the Me-262 with six nose-mounted 30 mm and 20 mm guns. On the night of March 30, 1945, Welter and his radar-intercept officer downed four Mosquitos. The Mosquito was a British two-seat, twin-engine, high-speed fighter and reconnaissance aircraft, largely of plywood construction and accustomed to roaming Germany's night skies unmolested much of the time. Welter was undoubtedly one of the most able German night fighter pilots, with a total of sixty-three victories, twenty of which he achieved in the Me-262, an all-time jet record. Of Welter's sixty-three victories, thirty-five of his victims were Mosquitos. Feldwebel Karl-Heinz Becker, although a latecomer to NJG 11, in the remaining weeks of 1945 demonstrated that he was equally comfortable in the Me-262. He and his radar intercept officer downed six Mosquitos in two weeks, two within three minutes of each other on the night of March 23, 1945.[8] As either a night or day fighter the Me-262 posted an impressive combat record in its brief operational history under decidedly adverse circumstances.

There were fewer of the Arado 234 jet bombers built than Me-262 jet fighters, and only one combat wing became fully operational, KG 76. When encountered by Allied fighters the Arado jet was frequently mistaken for an Me-262. On February 22, 1945, late in the afternoon, fourteen KG 76 Arados attacked targets in the vicinity of Aachen using their usual bomb delivery method, the shallow dive. The attacking aircraft were intercepted by P-47 Thunderbolts of the 366th Fighter Group. The after action Report of Operations for Mission No. 2 of the 366th Group reported that "15 to 20 Me-262s were encountered northeast of Aachen at 14,000 ft going West. Enemy a/c glide bombed behind our lines when jumped by our ships. 1 was destroyed 10 miles northeast of Aachen . . . shot down by 1st Lt David B. Fox.[9] Lieutenant Fox had not shot down an Me-262, but an Arado 234. Hauptmann Josef Regler, the pilot of the damaged Arado jet, belly-landed near the village of Selgersdorf, northeast of Aachen. The aircraft came down between the American and German lines, and Regler made a hasty exit to escape capture. The following day the American advance progressed beyond the location of the hapless Arado, and an American ATI team salvaged the nearly intact jet and shipped it over land to RAE Farnborough. This was the first intact Arado 234 jet captured by the Allies, and a much sought after trophy.

In March, KG 76 was tasked to destroy the Ludendorff railroad bridge spanning the Rhine River at Remagen. The bridge was captured on March 7, 1945, by Able Company of the 27th Armored Infantry Battalion, led by German-born Second Lieutenant Karl H. Timmermann. Timmermann, who was decorated with the Distinguished Service Cross for his courage, leadership, and initiative, was the first American across the bridge, and his battalion held the bridge until reinforcements arrived. The Remagen bridge proved to be the gateway into the heart of the Third Reich, and Hitler ordered its destruction at all cost. Floating mines, frogmen, and counterattacks failed to destroy the bridge or dislodge its American defenders.[10] "It was not until twenty-four hours after it was taken," noted the 56th Fighter Group history, "that the enemy made his first air attack on the bridge. . . . On March 10 the attacks were becoming so frequent that Eighth Air Force fighter groups were requested to patrol the area to destroy enemy dive bombers."[11]

Lieutenant Colonel Robert Kowalewski, holder of a Battle of Britain Knights Cross and new commander of KG 76, led the first Arado 234 attack against the Remagen bridge on March 9, losing one of his aircraft to antiaircraft fire. The Arados continued their attacks on March 11 and 12. The weather was largely uncooperative, low cloud decks forcing the attackers to altitudes where they preferred not to operate. The weather cleared on the fourteenth, and KG 76 launched a major attack, losing four of its aircraft without damaging either the railroad

With the exception of the Remagen bridge, all other Rhine River bridges were blown up by the Wehrmacht. This bridge across the Main River near Mainz was bypassed with pontoon bridges laid by Army engineers. (JH)

bridge or the pontoon bridge constructed by Lieutenant Colonel David E. Pergrin's 291st Combat Engineer Battalion downriver from the Ludendorff railroad bridge. The Ludendorff bridge eventually collapsed on its own accord.

KG 76 moved its aircraft from airfield to airfield as British, American, and Canadian troops penetrated farther and farther into the Ruhr Valley and then proceeded northward toward the German-Danish peninsula. Some airfields KG 76 was forced to use had runways not long enough to accommodate a fully fueled and loaded jet on takeoff. The Arados began to use rocket assisted takeoff, RATO, a procedure that was later adopted by the U.S. Air Force and used in the fifties and sixties on fighters and bombers, and was known as jet assisted takeoff, JATO. Flying from Achmer the *Geschwader* eventually moved to bases in Schleswig-Holstein, then to Grove airfield in Denmark; finally on

May 5, 1945, upon the surrender of German forces in Denmark, nine Arado 234Bs of KG 76 made a final defiant dash from Grove to Sola airport at Stavangar, Norway. KG 76 flew its last combat mission from Grove on May 3. On May 8, at 2301 hours, Admiral Dönitz unconditionally surrendered all remaining German forces. British forces didn't arrive at Sola airfield until May 10.

When the sound of guns faded into history, only a few Arados remained intact. Of the nearly two hundred 234Bs built, most were destroyed by Allied bombs and bullets, claimed by accidents, or destroyed by their German crews upon surrender. The nine aircraft ferried to Sola, however, survived intact, as did seven Arados at Grove airfield and one at Schleswig, for a total of seventeen.

The Russians found only one flyable Arado 234B in their zone of occupation, but several of the four-engine C-model test aircraft were found intact at Alt Lonnewitz airfield, the Arado test center. Soviet postwar jet bomber design quickly adopted the insights gained from the capture of the Arado 234. Major General Harold E. Watson noted in 1981 that "the Russian IL-28 [Beagle] jet bomber looks like a copy of the Arado 234." And so it did; and so it was.[12]

COLONEL
HAROLD E. WATSON

While war raged in Europe, Colonel Harold E. Watson served his country on the home front. Hal became less and less enchanted with his position and applied to his bosses several times for a European assignment. On June 6, 1944, he was still at the Wright-Aero Factory in Cincinnati, an aircraft engine assembly plant, assuring a steady flow of engines to aircraft assembly plants throughout the country. Watson tried to tell himself that his job was just as important as flying a B-17 bomber over Germany, but he didn't really believe it. Most of his flying school classmates were in combat assignments and getting shot at in either the ETO or the Pacific. There he was, watching it all from afar, just like any other civilian. Watson was frustrated. He promised himself to keep on trying—one day someone would have to listen to him and let him go before it was too late. It would be embarrassing, he thought, to end the war with a slick chest, without even a lowly campaign ribbon.

Watson was born in November 1911 to Charles E. Watson, the Farmington, Connecticut, stationmaster for the New York Central Railroad, and Louise Kaeufer Watson. Charles was of Scottish descent, and Louise's ancestors had emigrated from Alsace-Lorraine sometime in the mid-1800s. Friends frequently asked Hal, "What are you?"

meaning, is your ancestry German, French, English, or what? Hal's answer never varied. "I'm a Connecticut Yankee," he would say, smiling broadly. Yankee or not, he had the charm of a southern gentleman. Yankee pragmatism and a southerner's charm were defining characteristics of Hal Watson's character, as was an underlying belief that to move forward in life required a certain willingness to take risks—calculable risks, but risks nevertheless.

Hal was the boy in the middle. His brother Allan was two years older, and Donald was two years younger. Hal had only good memories of growing up in Farmington. He loved the four seasons—the colors of autumn and the deep snows of winter. He liked roaming through the nearby woods with his brothers after school, or just lying on his back on a sunny day looking up at the clouds and the sky and wondering what lay beyond. Watching birds flying above as he scrutinized the endless depth of blue, Hal decided one day he would learn to fly. When and where and how he didn't know, but he would learn to fly.

On occasion Hal's father arranged for him to ride in the cab of a locomotive as far as the next station. He recalled with pleasure the searing heat from the firebox and the hooting of the train whenever they approached a road crossing. Now and then the engineer would allow Hal to pull the handle to make it go hoot, hoot. Exciting stuff. The railroad got into Hal's blood, becoming part of the sights, sounds, and smells that define life. In later years, after retirement in West Palm Beach, Florida, the sound of a train passing in the night would wake him from the deepest sleep. Hal would listen intently to the sounds made by the passing railroad cars, the roar of the straining engines and the whistle of the train. He would listen until the sounds faded into the black of night. When all that remained behind was dark silence, then Hal Watson would drift off to sleep again. That the sounds and smells of childhood never faded for Hal in their intensity indicated a deep sentimental streak carefully hidden and revealed only to his closest friends.

In later life Hal added sailboats to the short list of things he liked more than any other—except for girls, of course. Girls were in a class all by themselves, and they seemed to love him as much as he loved them. Ruth Watson, Hal's second wife, recalled that among his treasured memories was Miss Porter's Finishing School, just down the road from where Hal lived as a young boy. At Miss Porter's Hal learned about girls from the girls. "I was practically raised by Miss Porter's ladies," Hal confided many years later to Ruth as he was steering their sailboat into a Caribbean rain squall. "Miss Porter's was the school where the really rich girls went," Hal told Ruth. "Some arrived in their own railroad cars at the start of the school year, accompanied by personal servants. My father arranged for the cars to be parked on a siding and I would watch the comings and goings of those beautiful young ladies. I made their acquaintanceship when they first arrived, and bid them farewell when the school year ended." Ruth recalled the big smile that crossed Hal's face whenever he spoke of Miss Porter and her girls. But then Ruth mused wistfully, "Hal was a cute youngster, and as he grew older it is understandable that the girls loved to go out with him. I did, that's for sure. And I didn't meet him until many years later."[1] Next to Hal's picture in the Rensselaer Polytechnic Institute's yearbook for 1933 is written, "The big blond hero from the South who makes the female hearts palpitate. . . . Where there are women there is Hal Watson. There have been women killers before, but not so mighty as he."

Although brothers Al, Hal, and Don were close, Hal was unique in the things he sought out, what he chose to focus on. He liked mechanical things, figuring out what made them work and how they could be made to work better. Al and Don preferred to watch things work. Hal liked doing numbers. Al and Don were inclined toward the arts. His brothers went to Yale. Hal went to Rensselaer Polytechnic Institute in Troy, New York, to study engineering. When he arrived at Rensselaer in 1929 Hal had five dollars in his pocket. His father cautioned him when he handed him the money to "spend it carefully." The stock market crash that October made Hal's financial situation even more precarious.

Hal pocketed his puny endowment and marched straight into the president's office at Rensselaer. He was seen almost immediately, and announced to the startled president that he wanted to be an engineer and that he had no money. "I passed the entrance exams," Hal pleaded, "but I am going to have to work my way through school. All I have right now is five dollars. Please take a chance on me." That engaging smile, which made Hal so attractive to Miss Porter's girls, never left his face while he was pleading for his future with the president of Rensselaer. His smile worked its magic on a college president just as it had with Miss Porter's girls. The president said to Watson, "If you are that willing to do what you must to graduate, I am willing to take a chance on you." Hal found an older lady near the campus who, in exchange for his taking care of her house and grounds, allowed him to room for free. He worked in the university's dining room and at the soda fountain of Peter's Drug Store. He worked his three jobs and others to get through school.

In 1932 Hal decided it was time to make his dream come true and learn to fly. He had been going to the Troy airport watching the planes take off and land. When Gates' Flying Circus, a well-known group of barnstormers, came to town, Hal's mind was made up. The only question was how to talk one of those stunt flyers into teaching him to fly the way they did. Simon Peter Bittner, better known as Si, was one of the flying circus's most daring performers, and Hal decided to stake out Bittner. Bittner saw the youngster staring at him, watching his every move, each afternoon before he took off to do his stunts. After he landed, there was the kid again, staring at him. On the fourth afternoon of their two-week engagement at Troy, Bittner decided he had had enough. After landing his biplane he taxied up to the kid and shut down the engine. Then, looking down from the cockpit, he shouted, "What the hell do you want from me, kid? What are you staring at me for? You are getting on my nerves. If you want to go for a ride, get in. It's only five bucks. You can swing five bucks, can't you?"

For a brief moment Hal didn't know how to respond. But the moment of hesitation passed quickly. "Sir," Hal said, pronouncing the word precisely and respectfully, "I have no money, but I really want to learn to fly. I don't just want to take a ride in your airplane. I want to learn to fly the way you fly. Isn't there something I can do to earn my way? I can't come up with five dollars. I don't have any money." Si rubbed his forehead with his left hand and pulled his aviator's cap off his head. He ran his right hand through his hair several times, scratched his head, and then said, "What are you studying in college, boy? I assume you are a college kid? You look like one anyway."

"Ahhh. I'm nearly finished," Hal replied. "Electrical engineering."

"OK, kid. I make you a deal. I need to learn more mathematics. You teach me what I need to know with the numbers, and I teach you how to fly. Does that sound like a deal to you?" They shook hands. Watson had himself a deal. But there was one thing Hal didn't know about his teacher: Si not only flew in a crazy way, but, like many flyers of that day, he *was* a little crazy, in an adventurous, risk-taking way. Every morning for a week Si and Hal flew circles around the Troy airport. One morning Si shouted from the backseat of their plane, "Watson, you are ready to solo. See ya in the coffee shop." And with that, Si Bittner, his parachute strapped to his butt, bailed out of the airplane. Hal thought Bittner was joking. He turned around to look for Si—the backseat was empty. Hal remembered the sweat breaking out of every pore of his body. Within the span of ten seconds he felt as if he were sitting in a warm bath. The panic passed quickly. He calmed down. He noticed the engine was running smoothly just as it had when Bittner was still on board. He took his hands and feet off the controls—and the plane kept on flying straight and level. Hal felt a sudden sense of elation. No, he felt more than elation; it was utter euphoria. He was the pilot of the airplane. He was flying it all by himself, and he would land it just like

Bittner had taught him to land, with one wheel slightly down, catching the wind in the wires. Hal let out a loud yell of joy and circled the airport a couple of times. Then he flew the downwind leg, turned into the wind and lined up with the grass strip they had been practicing on, and brought her in. It wasn't a pretty landing, but he walked away from it, and the plane was still in one piece. "Any landing you can walk away from," Bittner had said to him, "is a good landing." This was a good landing. With long, hurried strides Hal cantered toward the coffee shop. No longer able to contain his excitement, he broke into a run. He couldn't wait to tell Bittner he had actually landed the plane. He was a pilot. Hal threw open the coffee shop door. There sat Bittner sipping a mug of coffee. Before Hal could get a word out, Bittner said, "What took you so long, boy?" and a smile crossed his weather-beaten face.

Nineteen thirty-three was a watershed year for young Watson. He graduated from Rensselaer with a degree in electrical engineering, second in his class. In September, Pratt & Whitney Aircraft Company opened a research and production facility in East Hartford. Hal was driving a truck for a gas company to make ends meet, unable to find a job as an engineer. One day as he drove past Pratt & Whitney Aircraft he stopped his truck on a whim and went in to see Mr. Parkins, the chief engineer. Parkins was impressed by the impetuous young man and hired him on the spot as an engineer in the experimental and research department. There Hal studied production and assembly methods and assisted in the design and test of new aircraft engines. The joy of finally finding a job where he could apply his college learning was dampened by the untimely death of his father, who at age forty-five succumbed to the effects of a burst appendix. Hal was the boy who was there for his mother when she needed someone to lean on. Hal remained that pillar of support for Louise Watson until her death in 1972.

Hal worked at Pratt & Whitney for three years. He convinced himself that to be successful in this business of building and selling aircraft engines he had to understand his customers' needs. Pratt & Whitney sold its engines to the Army Air Corps, so it seemed the natural thing to become a military pilot. His boss thought it was a good idea and told Hal that his job would be waiting for him when he returned. In 1935 Hal applied for aviation cadet training, initially failing the physical examination because of a deviated septum which he had acquired during a one-bout boxing career at his alma mater. "I got into the ring," Hal told Ruth, "and the next thing I knew I was counting the beams on the ceiling. My opponent laid me out with one punch and broke my nose in the process."

After getting his septum fixed he passed his physical and entered the aviation cadet program on February 17, 1936. He departed Hartford, Connecticut, the following day for Randolph Field near San Antonio, Texas. On February 24 an enthusiastic Hal Watson sent a postcard from San Antonio to his mother at 771 Farmington Avenue in West Hartford, Connecticut. "Dear Mom," Hal wrote. "Well, I'm here at last—staying at hotel with three other fellows going to same place. Met them on train from St. Louis. Temperature today is 78 degrees. How do you like that? Hal." At Randolph Field Hal's flight commander was Lieutenant Curtis E. LeMay, who in time would rise to four-star rank and command America's strategic air forces during the Cold War. When Hal reported to LeMay he said to him, "Now look, I am not in here for the long haul. I serve out my time, but I have a job waiting for me at Pratt & Whitney."

"It won't do you any good, Watson," LeMay replied caustically.

"What do you mean, it won't do me any good? I serve my time. I ought to be able to get out when my time is up."

"Do you know what's going on in Europe right now?" LeMay asked. "If you get out, we'll have to call you right back."

One of Hal's fellow cadets was Hubert "Hub" Zemke. In the war yet to come, Zemke would become an ace, leading the 56th Fighter Group, the Wolf Pack, against the Luftwaffe. Philip Cochran, another of Hal's fellow cadets, would organize the 1st Air Commando Group in 1943 and lead it into Burma against the Japanese. For his exceptional leadership and courage, General Arnold, the Commanding General of the Army Air Forces, awarded Cochran the Distinguished Service Cross—the second highest decoration for valor after the Medal of Honor. Cochran became so popular in the public's eye that he served Milton Caniff as a model for the character Major Flip Corkin of the *Terry and the Pirates* cartoon strip. Caniff again chose Cochran for General Philerie in the popular *Steve Canyon* strip.[2] Many of Hal's classmates, as well as Hal himself, would rise to fame and general officer rank in the war that would define their generation.

While Watson was at Randolph Field a movie scout noticed him and offered to give him a screen test. "Come out to Hollywood and be in pictures," the fellow said to him. "You are a handsome man, and we need people like you. You can become very famous, believe me, and make a lot of money too!" Hal did the screen test, and met Claudet Colbert, Spencer Tracy, and Joan Crawford. "Joan came on to me," he confided to Ruth, "but I was too young and too dumb to know what to do." Over drinks, Spencer Tracy told Hal, "If you get into this business, acting in films is a job. Anybody who thinks it's more than that is wrong—be on time, know your lines, and hit your mark. It's hard work and you have to watch your back every moment." Hal thought about the offer only briefly. "I knew how to fly," he told Ruth. "I didn't know a thing about pictures." He said good-bye to Hollywood and went back to Randolph Field to finish out his contract.

Pilot training was demanding, and Hal's flight commander, Lieutenant LeMay, didn't put up with much nonsense. On March 24, after eight hours of dual-control time with an instructor pilot, Hal soloed in a PT-3. In February 1937, all thirty-five cadets of his pilot training class went on a final graduation flight, passing through towns in Alabama, Louisiana, Georgia, and Texas. The trip was a payoff to the cadets for the many months of hard work—a sort of graduation present. "It was a fun trip," Hal reported, "without the usual hassle from

A Consolidated PT-3 open cockpit aircraft at Kelly Field, Texas, 1937. America's Air Corps was not much to look at. (RW)

the instructors." The Air Corps bureaucracy justified such trips as providing students with training in navigation, formation flying, and aircraft maintenance at strange fields. Others saw the trips as a means of recruiting future officers and airmen for a still-struggling Army Air Corps.

On February 17, 1937, Harold E. Watson, along with thirty-four classmates, received his pilot wings in formal graduation ceremonies at the Kelly Field post theater, exactly one year after he entered the aviation cadet program. With graduation from flying training normally came a promotion to second lieutenant. Unfortunately in February 1937 the Army Air Corps was out of money to pay for additional lieutenants, and the new graduates had to remain in cadet status for pay purposes for another four months until the beginning of the new fiscal year, July 1. Cadet pay was seventy-five dollars a month. After subtracting charges for room, food, and uniforms, each cadet had about ten dollars of spending money remaining. On June 22, 1937, Watson finally was appointed a second lieutenant in the Army Air Corps reserve. This meant he was a soldier with a time contract, one who would be sent home to

Graduation picture of Watson's pilot training class before a P-12 fighter. Hal Watson, standing, second from right, second row from top; Hub Zemke, standing, second row from bottom, third from left; Phil Cochran, sitting, bottom row, third from right. (RW)

an inactive reserve unit after completion of his initial tour of active duty. Getting flying time in a reserve unit would be difficult. But less than two years after graduating from pilot training, Hal was informed of his selection into the regular Army, effective October 1, 1938. When he learned of this he immediately sent his beloved mother, Louise, a telegram to share with her the good news. "YOUR SON NOW LEFT TENANT REGULAR ARMY DON'T GET DRUNK LOVE = HAL." Throughout his long active-duty career, upon promotion to the next higher rank Hal Watson would share with his mother these moments of joy by sending her a telegram.

Watson's first assignment out of flying training was as engineering officer for the 96th Bombardment Squadron of the 2nd Bombardment Group at Langley Field, Virginia. In 1937 the 96th was the first bombardment unit to be equipped with the new B-17 Flying Fortress. The 96th quickly moved out to explore the full range of capabilities of the huge four-engine leviathan. The B-17 represented a gigantic step forward for the Air Corps from the twin-engine Keystone biplane bombers. While stationed at Langley Field, Watson took advantage of flying other aircraft, such as the open cockpit P-6, a biplane flown by the 36th Pursuit Squadron.

At Langley Field, Hal worked for Lieutenant Colonel Carl "Tooey" Spaatz, a fighter pilot in World War I, who made a reputation for himself fighting for the recognition of air power in a hidebound Army. Spaatz was a West Pointer and a personal friend of Hap Arnold's, and in 1929 he served as one of the pilots who flew the Fokker trimotor Question Mark to demonstrate the potential of air-to-air refueling. Lieutenant Hal Watson and Colonel Spaatz (spelled Spatz at birth, meaning sparrow in German, later changed to Spaatz) became off-duty friends. Until Spaatz was reassigned to Washington in late 1938, Hal, along with other junior officers at Langley, enjoyed the off-duty hospitality of Ruth and Carl Spaatz. Ruth was affectionately called "Mama Ruth" by the young lieutenants. Those were good years for the young men who would soon have to shoulder the burdens of war and build an air force from scratch.

In 1939 Hal received orders to report to the Power Plant Laboratory of the Materiel Division at Wright Field, near Dayton, Ohio. There he was to do the kind of work he did at Pratt & Whitney and would have the opportunity to fly many different kinds of airplanes. Wright Field was where the Army Air Corps did its flight testing. Hal quickly became friendly with a clerk who scheduled flight tests on newly arrived airplanes delivered by civilian contractors. This way he got the opportunity to fly many different types, mostly fighters. "Everything was pretty informal in those days," Hal related to Ruth. "As a pilot you were expected to be able to fly anything and everything with a propeller at the front." Hal recalled being sent to the West Coast in March of 1942 to pick up a P-38E Lightning fighter for testing at Wright Field. The P-38 was aircraft designer Clarence L. "Kelly" Johnson's first creation.

At the Lockheed plant at Long Beach, Hal asked who was going to check him out in the airplane. He had never even set eyes on a P-38 until he arrived at Lockheed. People looked at him skeptically and told him to go home if he didn't know how to fly the plane. Hal asked a sergeant for help in getting into the aircraft; then he figured out how to take off and fly it. He landed in Tucson and El Paso to refuel. As he approached Dallas, one of the P-38's engines quit. He made a single-engine landing in this twin-boom aircraft, a type in which he had less than ten hours' total flying time. His landing was uneventful, meaning that it wasn't pretty but he didn't crash. He changed the fouled spark plugs in both engines and took off for Memphis, where he remained overnight. He flew on to Wright Field the following day. Watson was not only a superb pilot; when it came to aircraft engines he knew them like the back of his hand and felt that he could fix any problem.

There were not very many officers assigned to Wright Field and they were mostly low in rank. The country didn't spend much money on military salaries in the 1930s, and the opportunities for advancement were limited. In April 1940 the Materiel Division with all of its laboratories had only one colonel and nine lieutenant colonels assigned, and all the rest were lower-ranking majors, captains, or lieutenants. At Wright Field, Hal met two other junior officers he would be working with in years to come—Second Lieutenant Bernard "Bernie" Schriever, a German immigrant, future four-star general, and father-to-be of the American ICBM program, and Captain Donald L. Putt, another future general who with Watson would be involved in the acquisition and exploitation of foreign technology in the war that was looming ever larger on the horizon. A small officer corps meant that nearly everyone knew everyone else. Said Ken Chilstrom, a former Wright Field test pilot, "These people all grew up together. It was a very small group. As time went by and the air force grew they all got promoted, and they promoted the people they grew up with."

*Watson's first flight assignment was in the new B-17B Flying Fortress bomber,
shown in this 1937 picture flying in echelon formation over Langley Field, Virginia.
Langley was the bomber base for the Army Air Corps. (RW)*

Hal's speciality in pilot training had been bombardment, the reason for his assignment to Langley Field in 1937. The fighters were at
Selfridge Field, Michigan. So Hal was surprised in September 1940
when he was selected to go to the University of Michigan to obtain a
master's degree in aeronautical engineering. At this time he was also
promoted to first lieutenant. Hal loved his year at Ann Arbor. He was
paid to go to school and on Saturdays he watched Tom Harmon play
football. "That was the life," Hal reminisced many years later. "It doesn't
get any better than that." While at Michigan, Hal got married to
a woman he had first met while stationed at Langley Field, Louise
Applewhite Brown. Louise (his mother had the same first name), was
the daughter of a Newport News dentist. Hal was attracted to the
unconventional in life; he nearly always took the path less traveled if
given a choice, and it was no different with his women. A brief

announcement in the New York *Herald Tribune* revealed that "Harold Ernest Watson, 28, an Air Corps officer, formerly of Farmington, now of 345 East 57th Street, New York, and Mrs. Louise A. Brown, 31, a divorcee, of 18 East 64th Street, New York, procured a license to marry here Tuesday in the Municipal Building. . . . Her marriage to Alexander C. Brown was terminated by a Virginia Divorce granted on August 1 last." The divorce was granted in Reno, Nevada; otherwise the announcement was correct, although unnecessarily explicit in revealing the age of Watson's new bride and her former marital status.

Of course, Watson was at Michigan to obtain an education–not to enjoy the pleasures of life. His master's thesis was as unconventional as his marriage in a time when both divorce and older women were unmentionables. In his thesis Watson proved to the satisfaction of his academic committee "why man would never be able to fly faster than the speed of sound." The learned professors nodded their heads when Hal made his presentation in 1941, and he was awarded his master's degree in aeronautical engineering. Ruth Watson recalled that in later years Hal had a good time telling that story at assorted social events. "I was no fool," Hal would tell his listeners. "I proved my theory that man would never break the sound barrier to the complete satisfaction of my academic committee." Hal Watson never took himself too seriously and knew how to joke and laugh at his own expense—people liked him for that.

After graduation Watson returned to Wright Field. He continued working in the Power Plant Laboratory. As an engine specialist he worked with manufacturers to resolve engine problems that developed in the field and affected aircraft production. Aircraft production in the United States ramped up steeply in 1941 and engines were a critical choke point. In 1940 the United States produced a total of 3,807 military aircraft of all types. That number rose to 19,433 in 1941, and in 1944 the United States turned out 96,318 aircraft, more than all the other belligerents put together.[3] Clearly Watson's engineering skills were needed at home. It made much more sense to use his skills in keeping the production lines moving than it did to stuff him into a bomber and send him off to perish over Schweinfurt or Berlin. Yet, Watson was a competitive man. He closely followed the exploits of his flying-school classmates. Their rapid promotions made him wonder if he was going to be left behind doing his job on the home front.

In February 1942 Hal was promoted to captain. His older brother, Allan, had also joined the Air Corps and was assigned to Wright Field as well, and his younger brother, Donald, served at Fort Belvoir, Virginia, with the Army Corps of Engineers. All three brothers served their country in its epic struggle against the Axis powers. A month later, in March, Hal was promoted to major. Wright Field was undergoing substantial expansion, and reorganization became a way of life. A technical data laboratory was formed in the Materiel Division to evaluate enemy equipment, and in May 1942 the first captured German fighter, a Bf 109E, one of Germany's first-line combat aircraft, arrived for testing and evaluation. In January 1943 Watson was promoted to lieutenant colonel. Hal followed the war news in both the Pacific and the European theaters of war, but particularly the war in Europe. Hal's one-time commander at Langley, Carl Spaatz, formerly a lieutenant colonel, was now a lieutenant general, and commanded the 8th Air Force in England and the 15th Air Force in Italy. General Spaatz had established the headquarters for the United States Strategic Air Forces at Bushey Park, a leafy London suburb. His headquarters occupied a number of wooden, one-story barracks built on the grounds of an estate adjacent to Eisenhower's headquarters. The place for an air commander was at the side of his ground commander, and that's where Spaatz always put himself. Spaatz also had administrative control over the 9th Air Force, which had been moved to England to support the planned invasion of the Continent. Administrative control meant that Spaatz wrote the 9th Air Force commander's efficiency report. In other words, General Spaatz was the top airman in Europe and ran the air war. Watson knew that. The question for Watson was, how could he get to General Spaatz to wangle an assignment to Europe? He needed help to get relieved from his assignment at the Wright-Aero Factory in Cincinnati, a position which was classified as "wartime critical."

In March 1944 the Deputy Commanding General for Administration at Headquarters USSTAF, Major General Hugh Knerr, established the Air Technical Intelligence section within the Directorate of Technical Services, which was commanded by Colonel H. G. Bunker. Most of the people assigned to the directorate came from Wright Field. It seemed like a good idea to both Knerr and Bunker to be ready to exploit captured German equipment once the invasion of Normandy, planned for late spring of 1944, got under way. Air Technical Intelligence collection teams were formed, modeled after, and initially trained by the British, who had much experience in that business. Although ATI implied an intelligence function, the teams actually focused on the technical aspects of their finds, which then would be relayed back to Wright Field for use by the laboratories, rather than providing any useful intelligence to USSTAF and its component air forces.

In early 1944 American combat intelligence support for the Army Air Forces in Europe was still largely an oxymoron. The United States had some of the best code breakers in the world and daring special operations operatives, but providing intelligence information for use by its military forces was still a work in progress. The established practice of the 8th Air Force was to rely on the British for such support until an equivalent American capability was brought into being. Before the arrival of General Spaatz, little had been done to make that happen. Why duplicate things the British were doing so well? The problem was that when the war moved to the Continent, the British support structure remained behind. When Spaatz first arrived in England and established USSTAF headquarters in January 1944, he brought along Brigadier General George C. McDonald as his director of intelligence. Spaatz and McDonald had served together in North Africa, and Spaatz had great confidence in McDonald's ability to fix things. Spaatz was appalled at what he found when he arrived in England. No one could give him an accurate count of Luftwaffe fighter opposition. The numbers were all over the place. Recalled General Spaatz at a meeting of intelligence officers of American air forces in Europe in January 1945, "When I first came to England . . . there were all sorts of vague guesses as to how strong the GAF was. Estimates ranged from 15,000 to 50,000 first line planes."[4] McDonald eventually remedied that situation, but change came slowly. Until such time when McDonald could place Knerr's ATI teams under his command, where he thought they rightfully belonged, the teams continued to receive their direction from the laboratories at Wright Field. Watson, still assigned to the Power Plant Laboratory, was well informed of what was happening across the Atlantic, and he put out feelers to Bunker and Knerr, angling for an assignment. He would make a great ATI team leader, he gave them to understand, with his aeronautical engineering background, practical experience in aircraft engine problem solving, and experience as a pilot who had flown the latest jet, the YP-59. Nothing happened. Watson soon learned why.

The greater part of the first half of 1944 in the European theater of operations had been one of preparation for the invasion of the Continent. The June 6 landings on the rugged coast of Normandy was as much a surprise to Watson as it was to men and women in the street. The ensuing battles were brutal, but American and British tactical air power quickly gained the upper hand, smashing trapped German armored columns decisively at Argentan. On August 15 the U.S. 7th Army landed in the south of France, linking up with Patton's 3rd Army on September 15. The retreat of the defeated Wehrmacht continued at a precipitous pace. Perhaps the war would end by Christmas. Watson worried that the war would end before he could get over there. On August 25, Paris was liberated. Brussels and the port of Antwerp were freed from German occupation on September 3 and 4 respectively. Allied headquarters began their relocation from London to the mainland in early August. General McDonald put together a mobile intelligence support cell housed in trailers to allow General Spaatz to accompany any forward movement of the supreme commander's headquarters. The mobile unit could be moved quickly from one location to another, moving first to advance headquarters at Granville on the French coast south of Cherbourg; in August, with the capture of Paris, the main USSTAF headquarters shifted from London to St.-Germain. The mobile unit was parked next to General Spaatz's residence at St.-Germain. Later it would move to Reims when Eisenhower moved his headquarters there.[5] Volatility was the order of the day from June 1944 onward. Then someone at USSTAF headquarters took a close look at future personnel requirements—and Watson's name popped up.

German countermeasures to Allied successes in France showed all the marks of desperation. On June 13 the Germans launched their first V-1 cruise missiles against London, and on June 26 the first encounter with a German Me-262 jet was reported by an American bomber crew. On July 28 a new German rocket plane, the Me-163B Komet, made its appearance flying an intercept against aircraft of the 385th Bomb Group over Merseburg. The first V-2 ballistic missile exploded in London on September 8. The German jets and rocket planes had General Spaatz's full attention because of their potential impact on his bomber operations. The V-weapons represented no threat to the general's operations and future plans. He could afford to ignore them. The V-1 attacks against London were quickly countered by the massive deployment of antiaircraft batteries along the coast of England, including American 90 mm guns, guided by the newly fielded SCR-584 gun-laying radar, firing proximity fuzed shells. The proximity fuze was a closely guarded American secret and was employed only with the concurrence of the Combined Chiefs of Staff under conditions and circumstances where it was felt the fuze would not fall into German hands. If the Germans developed an effective proximity fuze for their antiaircraft guns, in conjunction with the timely introduction of large numbers of Me-262 jet fighters, the combination would have the potential of stopping the Allied air campaign in its tracks. The VT fuze, as the proximity fuze was called, remained a closely controlled item until late in the war, when it was used again by artillery in the Battle of the Bulge and by antiaircraft guns in the defense of the Remagen railroad bridge. On those occasions when the proximity fuze was employed, its effectiveness proved devastating. During the last large-scale V-1 attack against London in September 1944, the VT proximity fuze was employed for the first time. Of 104 V-1s "detected by early warning radar, only 4 reached London. Some 16 failed to reach the coast, 14 fell to the R.A.F., 2 crashed thanks to barrage balloons, and antiaircraft accounted for 68."⁶ The V-1 threat diminished substantially when the fixed launch sites in France and Belgium were overrun by British forces. Sporadic V-1 launches after September 1944 were made from converted Heinkel 111 bombers flying off the coast of Holland.

Against the V-2 ballistic missile there was no effective defense, although there were relatively few launched and their impact areas

A captured V-1 missile at a Wright Field display in 1947. (RW)

were widely dispersed. A total of 9,782 V-1s were successfully launched from sites in France and Holland against the United Kingdom, while only 1,403 V-2s were launched and these killed or seriously wounded fewer than forty thousand people. Their overall impact on the war's direction or outcome was negligible. One estimate put the total cost to the Germans of the V-1 and V-2 programs at around three billion dollars, an immense investment for a resource-limited country like Nazi Germany.[7]

In September 1944 Watson learned he had been selected for promotion to full colonel. The date when he would exchange his silver oak leaves for a pair of eagles had yet to be announced and depended on where he stood in line with other selectees. It was a happy occasion, duly celebrated at the officers' club, and as always shared with his mother, Louise, with the customary telegram. But even before his promotion to colonel became effective he received orders assigning him to Headquarters United States Strategic Air Forces (Rear) in London, England, with subsequent assignment to be determined. HQ USSTAF (Rear) in London functioned as an interface with the British, who at that point in the war were still the major suppliers of intelligence information for the 8th and 9th Air Forces. Watson hopped a ride across the Atlantic on a C-54 transport and moved in with a friend, Lieutenant Colonel Ed Walker, who had found a small flat near the Air Ministry. Watson recalled, "I asked Ed about V-1 attacks on London. . . . Ed had a recording of a V-1 and over dry gin martinis he played it for me. I listened to the putt-putt sound of the V-1. The recording ended, but the sound continued. Synchronized with his recording of a V-1 was an actual V-1 flying overhead. Shortly the V-1 engine cut off and the missile exploded about five blocks away—creating considerable damage and jiggling the hell out of me and my martini. The very next night around seven o'clock, while we were having another cool martini, there was a fantastic explosion, and that was a V-2, the world's first ballistic missile."

A V-2 ballistic missile, part of a Wright Field enemy equipment display, 1947. (RW)

The V-1 and V-2 episodes were an appropriate initiation for Watson into the European war zone, his first exposure to the sounds of war. In addition to an ETO indoctrination, Watson told of spending "hours and hours with British intelligence getting boned up on everything they knew about German science and technology, where they were headed and what new things might appear on the scene. Having flown the Bell YP-59 in early 1944, the first American noncombat jet, and having been briefed on the noncombat Lockheed YP-80, I was interested in anything the British knew about German development in jet aircraft."[8]

His indoctrination complete, Watson grabbed a flight on a "little known airline" run by a former P-47 fighter pilot, First Lieutenant Robert "Bob" Strobell, who worked for Headquarters USSTAF, flying its staff back and forth between the main headquarters at St.-Germain and the rear headquarters at Bushy Park. Strobell's little airline consisted of an odd assortment of aging liaison and transport aircraft no one else had any use for. Strobell flew Watson across the English Channel, across Omaha Beach, then northeast toward Paris. He knew just by looking at Watson that this was a new guy, so he stayed low to give Watson a chance to see the war-ravaged land below. Lieutenant Strobell didn't talk to Watson during the flight, nor did Watson make an effort at polite conversation. One was the pilot, the other a passenger; one was a lieutenant, the other a colonel-selectee. As soon as Watson stepped off the plane at Villacoublay airfield near Paris he forgot about Strobell, grabbed his bags, and headed straight for base operations to get a staff car to take him to picturesque St.-Germain.

6

THE 1st TACTICAL AIR FORCE (PROVISIONAL)

Within days of his arrival at St.-Germain, Hal Watson was issued a blue Eisenhower pass. The pass gave its bearer the authority to go anywhere and request assistance from any U.S. or British military command in the execution of his duties. Bearing General Eisenhower's signature element, the pass stated in English, French, and German that "Harold E. Watson, the bearer of this card, will not be interfered with in the performance of his duty by the military police or any other military organization: By Command of General Eisenhower." It was an extraordinary door opener, and Watson was to use it to his advantage on more than one occasion. The pass stated that its bearer was authorized to examine and remove any captured aircraft or item of enemy air and radar equipment, whether found in the field or in factories, workshops, or dumps, and was permitted to travel anywhere in Allied forces' zones throughout the theater. Military commands were to provide its bearer with gas, oil, rations, accommodations, or anything else required. Watson had all the authority he needed to get whatever enemy equipment he chose to go after.

Once assigned a desk in the Technical Services Directorate at Headquarters USSTAF, Watson began familiarizing himself with collection requirements levied by the Wright Field laboratories, many of whose scientists he knew personally. High on the Wright Field "A List" of wants were the German jet and rocket-powered aircraft. Also listed were advanced versions of the Focke-Wulf 190 fighter. Watson learned that the French had two captured German fighters at Villacoublay, the former French experimental flight test center outside Paris, and he decided that it wouldn't hurt to take advantage of that opportunity and get familiar with German aircraft as well as establish some French contacts which might come in handy in the future. Additionally, he needed to get his monthly flying time to qualify for flight pay, so by flying the German planes he could satisfy the flight time requirement and also familiarize himself with German aircraft. "At Villacoublay," Watson wrote, "I met several French Air Force people and French underground members of the Maquis. From them I learned much about German aircraft and equipment. Here I became acquainted with the Bf 109 and the FW 190 fighters. These two aircraft were the backbone of the fighter arm of the Luftwaffe. The French were very liberal about my use of their two German aircraft. Flying these airplanes, and studying their systems, was an opportunity for me to get acquainted with the German color code markings for oil, fuel and hydraulic systems as well as with the cockpit layout."[1]

On October 1, 1944, Watson exchanged his silver oak leaves for the eagles of a full colonel. There is no report as to whether the occasion warranted the customary celebration, but one can presume that it did. Hal Watson was neither a teetotaler nor averse to having a good time. Several days later Watson was invited to lunch with General Spaatz, an unexpected honor, but something he had hoped for. The men knew each other from way back at Langley Field when the B-17 was a novelty and General Spaatz was still a lieutenant colonel. Brigadier General George C. McDonald, the USSTAF director of intelligence, as well as General Spaatz's two deputies, Major General Knerr, administration, and Major General Anderson, operations, were

DATE : 26 April 1945   PASS No. 3694
PERMIT TO ENTER ZONE OF

Issued to Col. Harold E. Watson, ISO Card No. 153
DÉLIVRÉ A   IDENTITE

Organization   USSTAF
SERVICE

Permit to visit   6th Army Group Area
DONNANT ACCES A

Purpose of visit   Investigate Air Targets.
MOTIF

This pass expires   26 May 1945.
VALABLE JUSQU'AU

Issued by
ETABLI PAR

DATE   April 1945   PASS No. 1402

SIXTH ARMY GROUP

Issued to   Col. Harold E. Watson
DÉLIVRÉ A

Organization   USSTAF
SERVICE

Permit to visit   6th Army Group Area
DONNANT ACCES A

For the following purpose only   Investigate Air targets
UNIQUEMENT POUR

This pass expires   26 May 1945.
VALABLE JUSQU'AU

SUPREME HEADQUARTERS
ALLIED EXPEDITIONARY FORCE

29 September 1944   **2089**
Date of issue   Card No.

This Card of Identity Certifies That

Name HAROLD E. WATSON

Rank Lt.Col., AC,   Military Identity Card No. or
Serial No. O-21537

THE BEARER OF THIS CARD WILL NOT BE INTERFERED
WITH IN THE PERFORMANCE OF HIS DUTY BY
THE MILITARY POLICE OR ANY OTHER MILITARY
ORGANIZATION.

BY COMMAND OF GENERAL EISENHOWER

Eisenhower and 6th Army passes issued to Colonel Watson. Passes were in English, French, and German. (RW) also invited. Knerr was Watson's immediate boss, instead of McDonald, because the Directorate of Technical Services, where Watson hung his hat, ran the Air Technical Intelligence teams which scoured the liberated areas of western Europe for German aircraft and equipment. Watson didn't know at the time that McDonald was waging a relentless campaign to consolidate intelligence functions scattered throughout the headquarters within his directorate. It wasn't anything personal with McDonald, but was just the right thing to do as far as he was concerned, and he never missed an opportunity to raise the issue with General Spaatz. "Over lunch General Spaatz stressed his keen interest in German V-Weapons, the Me-262, the Arado-234, the Me-163, and other unusual aircraft that could possibly give the Air Corps some problems," Watson later wrote. Watson clearly understood that the general wanted a number of those aircraft in flying condition sent back to Wright Field for evaluation at the earliest opportunity.

Watson's nearly idyllic life in Paris was short lived. Soon after the meeting with General Spaatz, he found himself in General Knerr's office to learn that he had been assigned as director of maintenance to the newly established 1st Tactical Air Force (Provisional). The assignment was a surprise, but Watson saluted smartly, packed his bags, and departed for his new duty station in Vittel, France, where the 1st TAF had established its headquarters. General Knerr gave Watson to understand that his new assignment in no way affected the task he had been assigned by General Spaatz, but right then his talents were needed elsewhere. With his background of building, testing, and managing the production of aircraft engines, Watson made the perfect director of maintenance for what turned out to be a hodgepodge of American and French fighter and medium bomber groups, many in need of good maintenance advice.

The 1st Tactical Air Force (Provisional), 1st TAF in Army Air Forces parlance, was formally activated by Headquarters USSTAF on October 20, 1944, under General Order number 81. There was already a 1st Air

Force in existence in the United States, so "tactical" had to be added to the name to differentiate this temporary organization from its permanent namesake. "Provisional" meant that the 1st TAF was a creation of General Spaatz and that Washington wasn't going to come up with additional manpower spaces. Knerr's personnel directorate at Headquarters USSTAF combed through its files and pulled the names of every officer and enlisted man not assigned to a combat element or combat support organization; anyone in transit, personnel overages to existing positions, and anyone else in a float status became a potential candidate for assignment to the 1st TAF. During this intensive search for personnel to staff the 1st TAF headquarters, Watson's name popped out, as well as the name of 1st Lieutenant Robert C. Strobell—neither being assigned to an authorized position. The 1st TAF had no T.O., table of organization, of its own. In the arcane language of the military, a T.O. was the giver of organizational life, providing for the essential supplies, manpower, and equipment necessary to establish and support an organization. The 1st TAF had to rely on the T.O.s brought along by its assigned units to flesh itself out, and headquarters staffing therefore came out of the hides of the combat groups. It was going to be a challenge for its first commander, Major General Ralph Royce, to stand such an improvised organization on its feet.

The American flying squadrons assigned to the 1st Tactical Air Force were P-47 Thunderbolt groups which had become surplus to needs in the Mediterranean theater of operations or were transferred from the 9th Air Force to flesh out the 1st TAF. The XII Tactical Air Command, XII TAC, was the principal American fighter organization assigned to the 1st TAF and consisted of the 27th, 50th, 86th, 324th, and 358th Fighter Groups. General Spaatz believed that every numbered air force should have its own reconnaissance capability, so the 1st TAF was augmented by the 69th Tactical Reconnaissance Group flying F-5 (P-38) and F-6 (P-51) aircraft. The 17th and 320th Bomb Groups of the 42nd Bombardment Wing, equipped with new B-26 twin-engine medium bombers, were also allocated to the 1st TAF, as well as the IX Troop Carrier Command, giving the 1st TAF its own airlift capability. The 1st French Tactical Air Force completed the 1st TAF's assigned combat elements.

The French flew a mishmash of P-39, P-47, older vintage Spitfire fighters, and the short-wing Martin B-26 Marauder bomber, referred to by its American pilots as the Widow Maker or Flying Vagrant (in GI humor "vagrant" meant that the airplane had no visible means of support). The short-wing B-26 had very high wing loading; in practical terms that meant it had a very small wing area to support its weight. According to Colonel Donald Putt, who was the Wright Field project manager for both B-25 and B-26 development and acquisition, it "probably was pushing the state of the art as we knew it in those days. . . . It never was really a very satisfactory airplane." Not only that, but "it was kind of a tricky airplane which you had to fly every minute or, boy, it would get you." In Putt's words, the B-26 "was *a real dog*. However, the people that flew those things thought the world of it." That was a characteristic of all pilots, Putt maintained. "Whatever piece of equipment they were flying that brought them home, particularly from combat missions, they feel pretty good about." But Putt stuck to his opinion about the airplane, reaffirming that the Martin B-26 "was a dog."[2] Watson would have to work the kinks out of those "dogs." The usual support aircraft were assigned to two liaison squadrons to provide transportation for the staff of the 1st TAF and to perform miscellaneous support functions, such as hauling spare parts from one airfield to another.

One unspoken reason for the establishment of the 1st TAF was to integrate the French air force into overall combat operations and give them experience for future independent action. The French, although spirited combatants, were at times thought to be a difficult ally to deal with. Their planes were scattered all over the Mediterranean and the south of France, too far removed to be effectively employed in support of their own 1st French Army. The 1st French Army operated as part of

A 1st TAF Martin B-26 Marauder down for the last time in Luxembourg, March 1, 1945. Not even Watson with all his skills could resurrect this airplane. (JH)

General Devers's 6th Army Group, which the 1st TAF was tasked to support. The French air component needed to be pulled together into a cohesive combat organization, and the 1st TAF was the vehicle to do that. The French also needed better equipment. They were flying cast-off, worn-out aircraft such as P-39s rejected by the British and long ago phased out by the American Mediterranean Air Forces. And of course they flew the earliest models of the B-26 Marauder, which had been phased out much earlier by the 9th Air Force. As a result it was no surprise to find that the French sortie rates were dismally low when compared to rates of American fighter and bomber squadrons.

Vittel, a fading resort town once known in France for its mineral springs, surprised every new American arrival with its abundance of females. Located thirty miles southwest of Strasbourg, the Germans had used the resort as an internment camp for women. At first only American and English women were held at Vittel, but later women of many nationalities were interned in Vittel's resort hotels in what the official history of the 1st TAF Service Command refers to as a "veritable city of women." The thirty-six hotels of Vittel were crowded with women from a host of nations and from every walk of life. Apparently they did not fare too badly under German rule. The women elected Mrs. Robinson, an American, as their president to represent them in their dealings with Captain Georg Hilpisch, the German commandant, who had been an American POW in World War I, and again found himself a captive of the Americans. An abundance of Red Cross packages was received at Vittel for the internees, and the Germans were apparently scrupulously honest in their handling. When the Americans entered Vittel, they found several hundred Red Cross packages which the women had not even troubled to open. Because most of the hotels were enclosed with barbed wire, wooden catwalks were built above the enclosures to allow the internees easy access to the other hotels. So extensive were these wooden thoroughfares that it was possible to travel around the entire central portion of Vittel without once descending to the pavement. "Sanitary conditions in Vittel were, to put it mildly, distinctly on the unhygienic side. In fairness to the Germans, the onus for this situation should fall on the lack of personal pride on the part of the interned women rather than on the attitude or official actions of the Nazi authorities."[3]

The 1st TAF advance element arrived in Vittel on October 23, 1944, and chose the Hotel des Thermes for its headquarters. Another five hotels were cleared of their female occupants to provide office space and quarters for the 1st TAF staff. The reason for choosing Vittel was obvious. The town was the location of General Devers's 6th Army Group headquarters, and the 1st TAF existed to provide Devers with tactical air support. Watson was assigned to the 1st TAF Service Command, which provided engineering and logistics support for the fighting elements. Not only was the Service Command colocated with the 1st TAF in the Hotel des Thermes, but many of the officers performed dual operational and logistics functions. There simply weren't enough people to properly staff the 1st TAF headquarters under the austere setup of a "provisional" organization without its own table of organization. Watson had his hands full from the minute he arrived.

The first order of business for Watson was to get the French out of his hair. To that end, the French squadrons had to be moved up near Vittel. "There were B-26 Groups in Corsica and French units dispersed on many, tiny and well-nigh undiscoverable airfields in southern France," states the 1st TAF Service Command's history. "The French units of the new Air Force had just received their P-47s. They had been flying P-39s and they knew little about the servicing and maintenance of their new ships. In addition, they had no Technical Orders and no servicing facilities. . . . These units had to be moved to fields within a reasonable radius of the newly established Headquarters. . . . They were moved, and moved with a surprising minimum of mishaps." Watson wanted the French to be on their own so he could concentrate on providing support to the American flying units. The easy way out would have been to assign American mechanics. But mechanics were in short supply. Watson recommended to Brigadier General Langmead, the commander of the 1st TAF Service Command, that the French be allowed to learn to do things for themselves. Langmead and Watson agreed to put a number of American maintenance men on temporary duty with the French units to teach their airmen proper servicing and maintenance procedures, an approach which ensured that once the war ended and the French were on their own, they would have a functioning support organization. In addition, Watson located a French-speaking American officer among his men, Lieutenant Colonel Paul Rockwell, who had served in the French Foreign Legion. Watson placed Rockwell on the 1st TAF French Advisory Section formed to resolve numerous issues which arose between the French and the Americans. Soon things began to run smoothly, and Watson could concentrate on supporting American fighter and bomber groups of the 1st TAF.

A 1st TAF team surveyed existing airfields near Vittel, and the American squadrons began to arrive from their former locations in the

Mediterranean theater of operations and from other locations in France. The 50th and 358th Fighter Groups bedded down with their P-47s at Ochey airfield near Toul. The 324th and 371st Fighter Groups operated out of Tavaux airport, on the outskirts of Dole; the 86th bedded down at Tantonville; and the 27th Fighter Group moved to St.-Dizier airfield. The recce folks flew their P-38s and P-51s out of Azelot, near Nancy, while the B-26 bombers of the 17th and 320th Bomb Groups bedded down at Longvic airport near Dijon. Bron airfield near Lyon became the home of the 31st and 34th Bomb Groups. Over the following months, fighter and bomber groups continued to shift forward as the front lines moved east, finally ending up in 1945 on airfields in Germany.

Winter came early in 1944 and soon turned bitterly cold. Freezing rain, sleet, and snow was the order of things. All the airfields had been formerly used by the Luftwaffe and had been "completely ruined by concentrated bombings. Hangar space was almost an unknown phenomenon. Such luxuries as Kill Frost and wing covers were completely unknown. In spite of the freezing weather, it was necessary for mechanics to work on planes in the open air. Ruts in the mud, which covered the fields, and ice which formed on the runways caused innumerable accidents. Operating conditions were difficult in the extreme," laments the Command's history. At all the fields, improvised shelters were built out of whatever material was available to keep mechanics and planes out of the elements. Next, landing-gear failures threatened to ground a large part of the P-47 fleet. Finding a solution became Watson's highest priority. Most of the former Luftwaffe airfields were nothing more than level meadows, rutted from constant use and hard on the airplanes. Building their own test equipment, the maintenance men discovered that gear failures were caused by cracked axles. Further, many of the planes still flying had cracked axles and were heading for accidents. "The securing of new axles was a difficult and lengthy task," records the 1st TAF history, and "therefore steps were taken to make it possible for the damaged axles to be repaired here."[4] GI ingenuity won the day for Watson; some pretty unorthodox approaches were used to keep the P-47s flying and their axles in one piece. Had Watson's people waited for new axles to reach them through normal supply channels, a large part of the P-47 fleet undoubtedly would have been out of action. That, obviously, was not an acceptable alternative. In spite of the difficult winter, B-26 and P-47 in-commission and sortie rates rose steadily and by early 1945 equaled those of American fighter and medium bomber squadrons in the 9th Air Force. The 1st TAF, including its French units, went from a dismal 66 percent of aircraft in commission in December 1944 to a high of 84 percent by March of 1945, when Watson was reassigned from Vittel to USSTAF headquarters in Paris. Watson was, after all, an experienced engine designer who could analyze many of the problems faced by his maintenance crews on the spot to give expert advice. Watson was out there with his men in the rain, snow, and mud, solving problems by day and night; the men liked and respected that kind of an officer and responded accordingly.

The fact that Watson was able to instill in his men his own positive approach to problem solving was key to his success. He encouraged them to use their initiative and come up with their own solutions to problems, rather than going by the book. Today this might seem like something too obvious to mention, but in the world of 1945 it was quite a remarkable achievement, since Army Air Forces rules frowned on fraternization between officers and men. A sort of medieval caste system existed, in which pilots rarely dealt with anyone but other pilots and had very little contact with fellow officers who were nonflyers. Pilots talked to pilots, officers talked to officers, sergeants spoke to sergeants, and the lower ranks were at the proverbial bottom of the hill. Gravity assured that everything flowed downhill, landing on the enlisted men's backs. Watson found a way to move freely among all the groups—pilots, enlisted men, sergeants, and the nonflying officers, even though he had never flown a combat mission himself.

A 1st TAF P-47 Jug fighter bellied in at Azelot airport, A95, Nancy, France,
bending its props. It was a frequent problem Watson had to deal with as 1st TAF
director of maintenance. (JH)

He was a Wright Field test pilot, an extraordinary engineer, and not a
man who stood on rank and its perquisites—and those qualifications
made him acceptable. His personality carried him the rest of the way.

One action that made Watson popular with his maintenance men
was bringing in civilian technical representatives, "techreps," to help
them troubleshoot difficult mechanical problems. John Love, John
Danish, Phelps Mace, and Marion Ford arrived from the Glenn L.
Martin Company to support the B-26 Marauders; William Sheehan,
Foster White, and John Howard came from Pratt & Whitney Aircraft
Corporation to provide hands-on technical support for the P-47
Thunderbolts, as did Edward Driscoll and Charles Holowchak from
Republic Aviation Corporation. Blake Bailey from North American
and John Marin from Packard Motor Company supported the P-51s
of the 1st TAF.[5] Watson pulled off a difficult organizational and air-
craft maintenance task and upon his departure from Vittel in March
1945 was recognized for his stellar achievement with the award of the
Bronze Star Medal specifically for keeping the 1st TAF airplanes flying
through a difficult winter.[6]

Lieutenant Bob Strobell, like Watson, had shown up as an "overage" when General Knerr's personnel people looked for bodies to staff the 1st TAF headquarters. He suffered the same fate as Watson and had to relinquish his cushy job running his little airline for the USSTAF headquarters staffs in Paris and London. Before Strobell headed for Vittel, Watson reviewed his records, after watching him coming in for a landing one October night at Villacoublay. Watson was getting his flying time at Villacoublay on one of the French-owned German fighters when an aircraft suddenly appeared, buzzing the field and apparently wanting to land. The only problem was that at this late hour the airfield was pitch black with no lights anywhere to guide the pilot to the runway. Watson, along with others, stepped outside Operations to see what the hell was going on. A quick-thinking sergeant drove a jeep out and pointed its headlights down the dark runway, providing enough light for Strobell to come on down. The following morning Watson went over to Operations to meet Strobell, but when he arrived he found a bunch of guys congratulating Strobell on his daring night landing. Watson left without talking to him, intending to check Strobell out at a later time. The lieutenant looked like a pilot who had his head screwed on right, someone he might need in the future.

Strobell arrived at Vittel about the time Watson did. Their desks were on the same floor of the Hotel des Thermes. There was no real contact between the two until one day when Watson came to see Strobell. "It was puzzling," Strobell recalled. "Colonel Watson came to my office and said, 'We are going to pick up a B-17. I need a copilot and you are going with me.' I said, fine, but you have to understand that I have never flown a B-17 before. Also, I don't really care about big birds. Watson kind of laughed and said, 'That's all right, Lieutenant, you just do what I tell you.' So we hopped into a B-26 and flew to this 1st Tactical Air Force fighter base where the commander was screaming his head off because this great big B-17 bomber was sitting on his ramp and doing all sorts of awful things to his operations. The colonel, red in the face, shouted at Watson and me to get that big-ass bird out of there. So Watson, I can still see him vividly before my eyes, walked up to the crew chief and said, 'Will this thing fly?' The chief replied without batting an eye, 'Yeah, it's ready to go.' We did a ground check, and that's when I discovered the reason why the B-17 was on the base. It was battle damaged. It had very large holes in it. This was a sad-looking airplane. We got in and Watson took the left seat, I the right. Watson cranked her up and we took off. In flight the B-17 sounded like a wind tunnel. There was no hydraulic fluid in it. I couldn't get the gear up. I couldn't get the flaps up. I couldn't close the bomb bay doors. This thing was down and dirty and messy—and Watson was flying it at five hundred feet off the ground into Nancy, a depot for dead or nearly dead birds. When I got out of that airplane I said to him, Colonel, sir, I don't like big birds. And I sure as hell don't like this airplane. Any airplane that can flap its wings like this one does, I don't want to have anything to do with. Watson got a kick out of what I said and laughed loudly. Then he said to me, 'How about flying an Me-262 jet, would that suit you better?' I didn't know what he was talking about."[7]

7

ORGANIZING TO DISARM THE LUFTWAFFE

"During the summer of 1944, with the invasion of Europe well under way and the end of war in Europe a reasonable possibility, considerable attention was being given to plans for the post-hostilities period," states the History of the Directorate of Intelligence for the United States Strategic Air Forces.[1] While planning and organizing isn't a terribly exciting aspect of military operations, it is fundamental to success. Nazi Germany did little of either. When success on the battlefield came, it was frequently as great a surprise to the victors as it was to the vanquished. For those with such a cavalier approach to waging war, failure was an inevitable outcome. Without adequate attention to the mundane tasks of planning and organizing for the future, the Nazis squandered their limited resources, and options diminished, until finally only unconditional surrender remained. By late summer of 1944 Germany had largely run out of both options and resources to influence in its favor the war it had begun in 1939.

In contrast to Germany, Great Britain and the United States were ill prepared when war began, but one of the first things the western

Alliance partners did was initiate a coherent planning process. They agreed on a set of priorities to effectively mitigate the constraints imposed by a lack of infinite resources. The defeat of Germany was given first priority; Japanese aggression was to be contained in the interim, then defeated. Detailed plans evolved on how to conduct a combined strategic bomber campaign against Germany, how to defeat the U-boat threat in the Atlantic, and how, when, and where to land on the European mainland to overwhelm the Nazi war machine. Plans followed plans. By the time of the landings on the beaches of Normandy, planning and organizing for success was a routine and well-practiced part of every Allied military operation. The disarmament of Nazi Germany upon surrender or collapse required detailed planning, like any military campaign, to ensure that resources were ready to tackle the enormous task when the time came.

The code name for the invasion of the European mainland was Operation Overlord. Overlord not only provided for the initial landings but also for operations beyond the beachhead until the presumed successful conclusion of the conflict. Operation Eclipse then took over and provided guidance and direction "from the moment of a GERMAN surrender until control in GERMANY is taken over from the Supreme Commander by the Tripartite Military Government [U.S., British, and Soviet] or by separate UNITED STATES and BRITISH Commanders."[2] Every major Allied command developed a supporting plan to the SHAEF master Eclipse plan. Eclipse planning was held close to the vest in accordance with SHAEF security directives which ordered that "The surrender terms will not be distributed to or discussed with subordinate formations or units." The directive cautioned that "The plan may be discussed verbally with commanders of lower units. Talks can be given within units in general terms of our intention to occupy the whole of Germany, to disband the German Armed Forces, to establish Military Government and eradicate Nazism."[3] The effect of this security directive was that few junior officers and nearly none of the enlisted men who eventually had to do the disarming of the German air force, the GAF, were made aware of any aspects of Operation Eclipse. They wondered and speculated and groused about their state of ignorance, and in good old GI fashion eventually wrote it all off to "the Army way"—do as you are told, don't ask why.

Eclipse outlined in detail British and United States disarmament responsibilities and objectives, which included: (1) disarmament and control of German forces, including paramilitary and police units to prevent renewal of hostilities; (2) enforcement of the terms of surrender or in the event of no surrender the suppression of organized resistance; (3) establishment of law and order; (4) initiation of steps to complete the control and disarmament of German forces; and (5) redeployment of Allied forces in their respective national zones in Germany. "This operation will be executed in two main phases," the plan directed. In the primary phase Allied forces were to "secure important strategic areas deep inside GERMANY and to extend the Allied Air threat." In the secondary phase, these phases were expected to overlap; detailed instructions were provided for disarmament tasks to be accomplished by the 6th, Devers's, and 12th, Bradley's, Army Groups and the supporting 9th Air Force and 1st TAF.[4] Eclipse was the umbrella plan under which newly formed air disarmament wings and squadrons of the 9th Air Force and the 1st Tactical Air Force assumed the ultimate responsibility for disarming every Luftwaffe unit and facility in Devers's and Bradley's areas of responsibility, including areas which would eventually revert to the Russians. To accomplish this gigantic undertaking, planning commenced as early as October 1944. It quickly became clear that thousands of men would be needed to accomplish the task. General Arnold made it quite clear in a letter to General Spaatz that he was not going to come up with additional personnel for this purpose. In a September 19, 1944, letter, however, Arnold concurred with an earlier suggestion from Spaatz "that upon cessation of hostilities all U.S. Air Forces in Europe should be placed under the control of one U.S. Headquarters" and in the same letter Arnold designated the commanding general of the USSTAF "until that time as the senior representative of the U.S. Army Air Forces on all post-hostilities matters in Europe including the Mediterranean theater."[5]

Initially Spaatz agreed with his staff's suggestion to pass the disarmament responsibility to the Combat Crew Replacement Center of the 8th Air Force Composite Command headquartered in London. It was in fact a sound suggestion. The workload of combat crew training squadrons in the United Kingdom had diminished significantly as bomber losses declined. These squadrons, relates the history of the 9th Air Force Service Command, were "probably more familiar with the GAF than any other group of allied personnel, since the training job required knowledge of GAF methods and equipment."[6] The decision was made to take the 1st, 2nd, 3rd, and 4th Combat Crew Replacement and Training Squadrons as well as a number of other 8th Air Force units and turn them into disarmament squadrons.

On October 8, 1944, the combat crew training squadrons slated for conversion to disarmament functions were transferred from the 8th Air Force and attached to Headquarters USSTAF, where an office known as the Air Disarmament Command (Provisional) had been established. The word "provisional," as in the case of the 1st Tactical Air Force, indicated the stark fact that Washington wasn't providing manpower for the new command arrangement, and General Spaatz had to come up with the resources from within his own organization. Its existence was short lived, General Spaatz not being especially fond of additional intermediate command arrangements with their inevitable manpower requirements. On paper the creation of the Air Disarmament Command looked like a good idea. In practice it didn't work out. The 9th Air Force agreed to assume the disarmament responsibility under the Eclipse plan, and with that the need for a disarmament command vanished.[7] The 9th Air Force and the 1st TAF then took control of the already forming disarmament squadrons. Detailed instructions of how the two air forces

were to go about their disarmament tasks were provided by Headquarters USSTAF in a lengthy, top-secret directive on January 16, 1945.[8]

The 9th Air Force and 1st Tactical Air Force quickly passed their
newly acquired disarmament function to their respective service commands, which were in the business of providing maintenance and
logistics support for the flying groups. It was the 9th Air Force Service
Command and 1st Tactical Air Force Service Command which actually
took control of the disarmament squadrons, directing their formation,
training, and subsequent employment. What finally emerged was a disarmament division under both the 9th and the 1st Tactical Air Force
Service Commands. Each division consisted of a disarmament wing
with five squadrons. The 1st Air Disarmament Wing (Provisional) of the
9th Air Force had the 20th, 21st, 28th, 29th, and 30th Air Disarmament
Squadrons assigned to it. The 2nd Air Disarmament Wing (Provisional)
of the 1st TAF controlled the 52nd, 53rd, 54th, 55th, and 56th Air Disarmament Squadrons. The 1st Air Disarmament Wing was assigned to
exploit the area occupied by the U.S. 12th Army Group, Bradley's
command, which was composed of the 1st, 3rd, and 9th Armies commanded by Generals Hodges, Patton, and Simpson, respectively. The
2nd Air Disarmament Wing was assigned to support the 6th Army
Group, Devers's command, consisting of the U.S. 7th Army and the
French 1st Army commanded by Generals Patch and de Lattre de
Tassigny.

For the men of the disarmament squadrons, "disarmament" was
defined as separating the GAF from its arms, aircraft, and equipment.
The term "German air force" referred to all military and paramilitary
personnel assigned to the Luftwaffe, including such units as the Nazi
Flying Corps, but not German air force units operating as a part of the
German ground forces, such as the Hermann Göring Panzer Division.
Specific instructions were issued down to the squad level on how to
disarm an airfield, an aircraft, ground weapons, rockets, and motor
vehicles. There were detailed instructions on how to dispose of captured

equipment, where and how to ship it, and whom to notify if items required by Air Technical Intelligence teams were located. The relationship between ATI collection teams and the disarmament squadrons became a very close and essential one right from the beginning. ATI exploitation teams also relied on the logistical support provided by disarmament squadrons, such as housing (tents), food (C and K rations for the most part), transportation (jeeps with trailers and weapons carriers), and the storing and packaging of confiscated materials.

Training for the newly designated disarmament squadrons began immediately, if only to keep the men busy and out of trouble—a problem faced by every army since the days when the Roman legions ruled this part of the world. The training program was based largely on intelligence reports received from the Office of Strategic Services and from whatever information the cooperative British were willing to part with. Use was made of a limited amount of captured German equipment and of more or less accurate replicas of German arms and aircraft. Identification courses on German aircraft and uniforms were given, as were courses in German history and language, augmented by instruction in the psychology of the German people. Survey teams were organized within each squadron. The surveyors were to be the first to enter an enemy installation, inventory and report its contents, and on the basis of these reports additional men could then be sent to complete the disarmament task. To aid team members in the identification of enemy equipment a technical intelligence catalogue was developed which included available pictures and descriptions of items wanted by the Wright Field engineers. The latter task—to identify advanced German technology—was not a disarmament function and required technical expertise which very few of the young soldiers possessed. Although various crutches were provided to assist the disarmament people in their difficult task of identifying new German technology, the plan never worked out very well and led to collection centers being innundated with ordinary "junk."

The Air Technical Intelligence teams which after December 1944 worked directly for the USSTAF intelligence directorate operated from a Category A Collection List provided by Wright Field engineers and scientists. This was a complex "want list" of German technology arranged in order of priority. The disarmament squadrons, however, were issued Red, Blue, and Brown collection lists, which were simplified compared to the more complex Category A Collection List. The Red List was the rough equivalent of the Wright Field Category A Collection List, and the disarmament units used it as their Bible. The Blue List addressed items which were required immediately by Allied forces for their own operational use, such as telephone equipment, aircraft spare parts, and engines. The appropriately named Brown List (brown being the Nazi color) included items which didn't fit into the Red and Blue categories and were designated for use by the German civilian population. Brown List material was surplus "junk" to its American collectors.

In 1945 as the disarmament squadrons surged through France and into Germany on the treads of advancing Allied tanks, their productivity became prolific. The History of the Air Disarmament Division of the 9th Air Force Service Command laments, "It is hardly possible to realize the difficulties involved in the packing of the thousand and one items that were sent to the 45th Air Depot Group [at Kassel]. Along with the really valuable equipment were sent tons of material that was worthless as far as technical intelligence was concerned." This situation was, of course, unavoidable due to a lack of basic technical knowledge by the enlisted men and the rapid expansion of the disarmament squadrons at a time of constant personnel turnover, which accelerated in the weeks following VE Day. The disarmament squadrons were, after all, made up of young, untrained personnel, only vaguely familiar with German advances in technology. Experts in signal, radar, photo, weather, and other fields of technical intelligence were not available in sufficient numbers to advise ATI field teams, much less disarmament squadrons, on the many problems of identification that presented themselves.

Aerial view of Wright Field and Building 89, the large warehouse which held Lieutenant Strobell's "stuff." The Wright Field flight line, a typical prewar triangle layout, can be seen in the background. (WS)

As the hodgepodge of items—radios, flying clothing, aero-medical equipment, radar sets, flak pieces, searchlights, meteorological equipment, and all the rest—poured in, the warehouses were piled deeper and higher. Finally, the 9th Air Force was forced to order a collection moratorium for the "field units to become familiar with disarmament procedures and to relieve the congestion at the warehouses."[9]

Lieutenant Bob Strobell was reassigned to Wright Field in September 1945 and recalled what happened to much of the "stuff," as he referred to it, sent back to Wright Field from collection points in Germany. "After I got out of the Me-262 program I was ordered to Building 89 at Wright Field, working under Colonel Watson, taking care of all the equipment gathered up in Europe and along the Pacific rim. I had a warehouse full of enemy aircraft and a lot of the experimental stuff— glide bombs, V-1s, V-2s, right down the line. I had a warehouse full of tons and tons of 'stuff' of thousands of pieces and parts. The idea was to inventory everything, which we did, and hold it for further testing and evaluation. In the couple of years I was there I don't recall anyone ever calling for one piece to be tested or evaluated. In my opinion, a lot of that stuff was on the fringe of being of no further value when it was collected and shipped to Wright Field. We had guided bombs, but our people were thinking in terms of atomic bombs, not precision guided bombs with their small conventional payloads. So all that stuff just sat there getting older by the day. When I left Wright-Patterson Air Force Base [Wright Field had been consolidated with adjacent Patterson Field by 1947 after the Air Force gained its independence from the Army], people referred to building 89 as the Museum Division of Technical Intelligence. That, I believe, was the genesis of the present Air Force museum at Wright-Patterson AFB."

8

OPERATION LUSTY

In addition to planning for disarmament of the Luftwaffe, there was an obvious need to develop a companion plan for the exploitation of Germany's advanced technology. Disarmament was simply a security measure, while finding the Nazi technological treasure had huge implications for the nation's future and was therefore accorded the highest priority. A first and important step along those lines was the establishment of the Combined Intelligence Objectives Sub-Committee (CIOS) on August 21, 1944, by the Combined Chiefs of Staff in Washington. The committee consisted of representatives from British and United States diplomatic, naval, air, and scientific intelligence organizations, and was charged with the responsibility to exploit intelligence of political or military significance, other than normal operational intelligence.[1] In plain language, CIOS represented an organized and gentlemanly approach to the sharing of Germany's advanced scientific developments among the victors. CIOS would in due course field binational exploitation teams and try to ensure that the spoils of war would be shared and shared alike. The word exploitation was the operative term to describe the acquisition of Germany's highly sought after technology, including the scientists responsible for the design and development of jet aircraft and ballistic missiles. CIOS technical intelligence collection teams, as well as their U.S. national counterparts, the USSTAF ATI teams, exploited targets—a curious word choice, yet quite accurately describing ATI and CIOS team functions.

As enemy installations in the occupied territories were overrun, one function of CIOS was to process all requests for intelligence information emanating from British or American civil or military authorities. CIOS was to prioritize requests for information, prepare intelligence folders, and assign expert personnel to investigate targets. The information gained by such CIOS investigative teams would then be shared with both British and American organizations—meaning that reports would be disseminated through the customary intelligence channels. In its efforts to develop target folders and prioritize targets, CIOS took over what was referred to as the Black List, developed by its predecessor organization the Combined Intelligence Priorities Committee. The Black List was useful in that it provided focus for CIOS collection teams in terms of what to collect and what to ignore as they rummaged through a particular enemy installation. The list consisted of thirty-one target types such as (1) radar, (3) bombs and fuzes, (6) directed missiles, (25) aircraft, (26) aircraft engines, and so on, up to 31. Each target type was then broken down into finite elements of specific equipments desired for collection.[2] The CIOS Black List was similar to the Wright Field A List.

The British members of CIOS were also looking toward the economic revitalization of Great Britain. At their suggestion a Grey List was created to address targets of economic value, including industrial methods, techniques, and know-how, while the Black List focused on end products of immediate military importance. Both lists, Black and Grey, were eventually merged into one, which reflected the collegially derived exploitation requirements of the United States and the United Kingdom. The bureaucratic structure of this multinational organization was, of course, large and multilayered, its processes slow, and its response to field requirements predictably ponderous and at times inadequate. The CIOS field teams were derisively referred to by their ATI colleagues as CHAOS teams, a play on the acronym CIOS. By February 1945 even the staunchest bureaucrats in London and Washington had to admit that something must be done. They came up with a revised field team concept called CAFT—the Consolidated Advanced Field Team. Reorganization was and is a time-honored method for getting out of an all-too-obvious mess, and this mess was no exception.

Under the CAFT approach teams of experts were stationed in the forward area directly at the headquarters of each Army group—the 6th Army Group commanded by General Jacob L. Devers in the south, the 12th Army Group commanded by General Omar N. Bradley in the center, and the 21st Army Group commanded by Field Marshall Sir Bernard L. Montgomery in the north. The team disposition was to make CIOS more responsive to actual developments in the field. The USSTAF provided the leadership for teams at the 6th and 12th Army Groups, while the British led the team at the 21st Army Group. The two American-led teams consisted of five officers each, functioning as assessors. The CAFT teams were organized in London at Headquarters USSTAF (rear), which was commanded by Lieutenant Colonel John H. O'Mara, and proceeded in March of 1945 into the field "armed with complete dossiers on all known targets in their respective areas. Their duties were to determine the value of the targets inspected" and when additional specialists were deemed necessary they could call for help through SHAEF headquarters at Versailles, which would then contact the CIOS secretariat in London to send out a CIOS team.[3] It was a bureaucratic approach, devised not totally by accident. The slower response by CIOS teams, of course, allowed national intelligence collection teams, both American and British, quick and easy access to important targets before the arrival of jointly staffed CIOS teams. The cumbersome CIOS technical intelligence collection effort was spawned by alliance relationships which often denied the teams the operational flexibility needed to be truly effective. General McDonald, USSTAF's intelligence chief, fully understood that—after all, men from his directorate were directly involved, some leading a number of the CIOS teams. However, until late December 1944 McDonald had little or no control over the USSTAF technical intelligence collection effort and its ATI teams. The ATI collection teams in the field didn't belong to him.

From the very beginning in 1942 the Army Air Forces in England relied on the British for their operational intelligence. What there was in terms of a U.S. intelligence component was largely derived from the Wright Field aircraft design, development, and test community. Not surprisingly, when technical intelligence teams were formed and employed they worked for Major General Hugh Knerr, the USSTAF Deputy for Administration. Knerr was a Wright Field product, and his responsibilities included all of the special and administrative staffs at headquarters USSTAF in his role as Deputy Commanding General Administration. Additionally he was the Commanding General Air Service Command. The only functions Knerr didn't control were those under the Deputy Commanding General for Operations, Major General F. L. Anderson. The Directorate of Intelligence headed by Brigadier General George C. McDonald fell under Anderson. Although USSTAF had a requirement levied on it by General Arnold to collect technical intelligence as far back as September 1944, with McDonald not owning the necessary collection assets, the ATI teams, he was effectively stymied and it frustrated him to no end. Knerr, who "owned" the ATI collection teams, felt their duties "were inspection and determination of new industrial devices of value to Wright Field. Any intelligence by-products of such inspection and determination were of secondary importance."[4] Sadly, that statement summarized the situation for McDonald until December 1944. McDonald made it quite clear to General Spaatz that this situation was unsatisfactory and a reorganization at USSTAF headquarters was not only in order, but overdue. McDonald wanted everything that smacked of intelligence at USSTAF put under his control. Better yet, he advocated the creation of an intelligence command. "This war has taught us," McDonald said, "the need for adequate and timely intelligence. This can only be achieved by having sufficient trained personnel, equipment and other facilities to achieve this end." As for technical intelligence, he emphasized, it is "one of the most important of all forms of enemy understanding. The wars of tomorrow will be fought with tomorrow's weapons, and the Air Forces must know the weapons that can be used against them." According to McDonald, an Air Technical Intelligence Command would, and could, allow him to cut the umbilical cord to British intelligence, provide self-sufficiency in this critical area, and preclude future technological surprise.

On November 4, 1944, General Spaatz finally sat down with his divided staff and listened to McDonald's proposals. He shot down the intelligence command idea as soon as McDonald brought it up. He agreed, however, to centralize all intelligence functions within USSTAF under McDonald. Spaatz listened to the objections of his staff, some of whom were vehemently opposed to the concept of centralization. Then Spaatz declared that technical intelligence was a clear-cut responsibility of the director of intelligence and not of the Air Technical Section. "There will not be two agencies of this headquarters roaming around Europe under separate instructions, looking at the same piece of equipment," Spaatz admonished his staff. "Technical intelligence is an intelligence function. This operation will have to be tied in such a way that there is no duplication of agencies going around and treading on each other's toes all over the face of Europe." Spaatz ended the meeting by saying, "See what you can work out."[5]

It took a month, until December 8, 1944, for Colonel Bunker, the Director of the Technical Services Directorate at USSTAF headquarters, to inform his officers and men that "By direction of General Spaatz, the Director of Intelligence will be responsible for all intelligence functions" and "will take over the Field Teams and C.I.O.S. affairs formerly dealt with" by the Technical Services Directorate. Bunker cautioned his officers and men to cooperate and make the new organization work to continue "the flow of information on enemy equipment." That same day General Knerr wrote General Anderson that in accordance with General Spaatz's decision the director of intelligence would as of that date have full responsibility for technical intelligence. On December 8 the Technical Services Directorate transferred from Knerr's domain to McDonald's, as did counterintelligence, the CIC, and other security functions within the headquarters which until then had reported to Knerr.[6] With that far-reaching realignment within USSTAF headquarters, McDonald finally had the resources to implement General Arnold's directive—the collection of technical intelligence, with emphasis on the intelligence aspect of the operation rather than its technical attributes.

When briefed by McDonald in Washington on the centralization of intelligence functions at USSTAF, General Arnold agreed and gave his blessings. It was a precedent-setting reorganization which would lead to greater independence from British sources for the USSTAF and provide an organizational model for the future. In a subsequent letter to General Spaatz, Arnold wrote that he looked "with favor upon the intelligence program which has been submitted to me to discharge your commitments in this respect, and favor its implementation as soon as possible and practicable." In addition to providing his support to efforts to centralize intelligence functions at USSTAF, Arnold again reminded Spaatz that "I shall look to you as my senior representative on all post-hostilities matters."[7] That tasking led McDonald to establish an office of posthostilities planning, which immediately set to work writing the plan for the exploitation of German aircraft and missile technology—code-named Operation Lusty.

Although the headquarters reorganization was an essential prerequisite for the effective implementation of Operation Lusty as a concept, it had little effect on the way the ATI teams operated in the field. Air Technical Intelligence collection teams normally consisted of two officers and a sergeant jeep driver and were pretty much self-contained;

they roamed around the liberated countryside at will, inspecting newly captured airfields, military equipment dumps, factories, and crashed and captured enemy planes. The teams were encouraged to use their initiative and had a great amount of latitude and flexibility in terms of where they could go and what they could look at. Like Watson, they carried special passes, issued by the Army group commanders, allowing them to go anywhere, anytime, within their areas of responsibility. The collection teams were structured to take advantage of sudden opportunities, in contrast to the more hidebound CIOS teams, which worked according to a static plan that at times could not keep up with the demands of a fluid battlefield situation.

To prepare for their challenging assignment, ATI team members underwent a headquarters-prescribed training program which included much useful information and skill training, as well as a fair amount of bureaucratic eyewash. High on the list of training objectives prescribed by Colonel Bunker, the USSTAF Director of Technical Services, was "complete cooperation with British Intelligence Staff and field units." That subject was sure to inspire any freshly minted ATI officer. Then they were to learn "the power and prerogatives of Technical Intelligence Inspectors," which translated into what it was one couldn't do. Finally, the eager students got down to something practical—learning about measures to protect captured equipment, methods of removal, packing, and shipment. A high-interest curriculum item was the recognition of booby traps. Every ATI team member stayed awake and paid attention to this particular lesson, as well as the one on how to recognize mined areas (if cows are grazing happily in the meadows, the area isn't mined). Gas mask training, first aid, use of rubber dinghy for river crossings, tent building, and how to "enjoy" C and K rations followed. The bureaucrats had one last go at the ATI students before sending them out in the field, and team members were immersed in lectures on geography, airdrome locations, how to communicate in the field, and what to report to higher headquarters as a FLASH report. Finally, the director prescribed an ample measure of "physical hardening" for the men during their training—a widely adhered-to Army practice to help keep young men's minds on their assigned tasks.[8]

On D-day plus one, June 7, 1944, the first ATI team landed on the Normandy beachhead, and as the armies advanced inland, additional teams were added. Only two months later they could point to their first big success. "On August 10, 1944, two officers of the Air Technical Intelligence Section received the surrender of approximately five hundred and fifty (550) German troops garrisoned at adjacent radar sites near Perros-Guirec, Brittany, which had been by-passed by our ground forces," noted an Air Technical Service Command Europe report. "During these early operations in Brittany, numerous radar sites of all known types were examined, consisting of Benito, Coastwatcher, Electra, Freya, Hoarding, Windjammer, as well as both small and giant Würzburg units.[9] A large Signals warehouse was entered, which contained not only many varieties of radio equipment, but cryptographic devices and probable small flying missiles of a new type. Numerous articles of captured enemy equipment were secured and forwarded to the Air Technical Service Command, Wright Field, Ohio, for further study. One outstanding example was the first intact V-1 which was couriered to Wright Field by an officer of the Air Technical Intelligence Section (USSTAF) and shown to interested personnel in Washington. It was from this article that the JB-2 program was initiated in the United States." The American copy of the V-1, the JB-2, was soon rolling off production lines at Republic Aircraft and the Ford Motor Company for use against the Japanese.[10]

In December 1944 an ATI team searching the small town of Stolberg, east of Aachen, the first large German city occupied by American forces, discovered jet engine components in a small factory. The important find was immediately sent back to the rear and flown to Wright Field. "We shipped this evidence back to the U.S.," Colonel Watson recalled in a speech on April 10, 1946, "because at this time the

G.E. people were having a devil of a time with buckets [the combustion chamber for the jet engine that was to power the P-80 jet], and this information helped in the development of a new [engine] bucket." The first complete jet engine Wright Field engineers laid their hands on was from an Arado 234 reconnaissance jet shot down by a P-47 Thunderbolt from the 324th Fighter Group of the 1st TAF, on April 4, 1945. The German plane crashed in an open field near Colmar, on the French side of the Rhine River.[11]

ATI field teams were the principal collectors of technical intelligence for the Army Air Forces and received full support in whatever they needed from their new boss at USSTAF headquarters. In fact, as Colonel Bradley, the new chief of McDonald's Technical Intelligence Division, proudly explained to him in an April 16, 1945, memo, "The Air Technical Intelligence (ATI) personnel are independent of SHAEF by their own directive and are the only people doing technical intelligence work in the field who are under your direct control. They are directly working for the interests of the USAAF and no other Air personnel whatsoever other than the ATI teams of A.I.2(g) [British] enjoy the same degree of freedom. . . . ATI being unhampered in their movements are only limited by their numbers to getting in on all targets as soon as same are uncovered. C.I.O.S. personnel invariably have to wait three or more days before being allowed to proceed to a target, as it is necessary for them to secure clearances from the Armies and various other controlling sections. Technical intelligence obtained by the ATI teams is reported directly to this Directorate. . . . By mutual agreement ATI teams are now cooperating with Disarmament units of the Ninth Air Force, thereby greatly expediting the return of material to Wright Field."[12] Things were definitely looking up since the December reorganization, and McDonald, with the assistance of the 9th AF and 1st TAF disarmament squadrons, was effectively inserting his teams into every captured German Luftwaffe research establishment, factory, and military facility they came across.

There were, of course, concerns that the various disarmament and technical intelligence collection teams would get in each other's way, or in the way of Army combat units. After all, the war wasn't over yet. In addition to McDonald's ATI teams and the binational CIOS teams, there were State Department and Navy Department teams which crisscrossed Germany looking for unique targets. The Naval Technical Mission ran its own operation for the Navy Department, focusing on air-to-surface missiles, wind tunnels, and submarine technology. A specially constituted and top secret ALSOS team had the mission to capture Germany's leading atomic scientists, such as Nobel Prize—winning nuclear physicist Werner Heisenberg. ALSOS was run by Army Colonel Boris Pash, who worked for General Groves. General Leslie Groves, the chief administrator of the Manhattan Project, averred that "Heisenberg was one of the world's leading physicists, and, at the time of the German break-up, he was worth more to us than ten divisions of Germans. Had he fallen into the Russian hands, he would have proven invaluable to them."[13] There were teams from the Army Ordnance Department and engineers in army uniform who were looking for mundane technical industrial intelligence under the auspices of the Technical Industrial Intelligence Committee (TIIC). There were British teams, French teams, and clandestine teams composed of anyone with enough clout to elbow his way into the evolving technology collection frenzy. Competition among the various groups was unavoidable. One may wonder how such a multiplicity of teams scrounging for enemy technology in the same area could possibly be an orderly undertaking. It wasn't. Recalled Colonel Watson, "I can say that the whole scheme of things was completely disorganized."[14]

In spite of A Lists, Red, Blue, Brown, Black, and Grey Lists, in spite of all the confusion and chaos, the collection job was done more or less effectively. At a later date Watson raised one other issue, the question of why all this was necessary in the first place. "Germany flew the first jet propelled airplane before the German army marched against

Poland," said Watson. "Revolutionary developments in aeronautical engineering had been in progress in Germany for a long time before we fired our first shot against the Nazis. . . . Yet, a long time after that shot—after we had managed, with considerable difficulty, to gain the upper hand over our enemies—there we were out in no-man's-land, scrambling around for the secrets of Nazi air power, while Nazi bullets whistled in our ears. Why were we out there then? Why hadn't we learned those secrets before that late date?"[15] Watson, with his European ATI experience, would in time have the opportunity to fix the problem, creating a permanent and effective technical intelligence collection and analysis organization.

On April 22, 1945, the Exploitation Divison replaced the former Technical Intelligence Division at Headquarters USSTAF under the direction of Colonel Huntingdon D. Sheldon. The division soon grew sizable, with its own staff sections including personnel, administration, intelligence, operations, and supply. One additional collection list the new division quickly added to its many tasks was the Air Staff Post Hostilities Requirements List. This was not a collection list of hardware, as all the other lists were; rather, it proposed study topics, to be initiated by the Exploitation Division, which would make use of captured German senior officers. An example of the quality and detail of such studies was one entitled "German Air Defenses." It analyzed in detail the flak defenses of key German cities such as Bremen, Bremerhaven, Hamburg, Hannover, Münster, Nürnberg, and Augsburg. Officers writing the study interrogated General von Axthelm, the chief of GAF flak units, and his staff, as well as members of flak units at the division and brigade levels. The study included a detailed examination of Grove airfield in Denmark, where a complete fighter defense installation was captured intact with plotting center and key personnel.[16]

General Spaatz, who received his fourth star in March 1945, personally kicked off Operation Lusty on April 25 with a message to his commanders: "Each Air Force of this command is hereby notified of initiation of . . . Operation Lusty, which has equal priority with operations." The first priority of Operation Lusty was defined as the thorough and detailed exploitation of German technical intelligence in support of the prosecution of the war against Japan. Its second objective was the collection of equipment and documentation for longer-term research. "You are therefore directed to render all possible assistance to insure successful accomplishment of this mission," Spaatz cautioned his commanders, "and are expected to provide communications support, vehicle maintenance, billeting, messing and transportation as required."[17] Just in case some of his commanders still didn't understand how much importance he attached to Operation Lusty, Spaatz reminded them that the "prompt exploitation of this intelligence will expedite the termination of this war, be of material assistance in the prosecution of the war against Japan and aid in the future development of Army Air Forces Technical material." Then he directed them to make available for Operation Lusty "all military and civilian technical personnel not engaged in critical operational duties of immediate importance in this theater . . . for the purpose of exploiting technical intelligence objectives. . . . Personnel desired are those who have technical training or experience in connection with the research and development of aircraft, aircraft engines, jet propulsion, instruments and equipment, radar, bomb sights or any other subjects in connection with the overall development of aerial warfare. Personnel who have had technical training experience at Wright Field or with agencies of aeronautical research, development, etc., are particularly desired."[18]

McDonald's Exploitation Division's first priority was to learn what technology the Germans had transferred to the Japanese. To everyone's surprise, that riddle was quickly solved.

SOLVING THE JAPANESE RIDDLE

The implementation of Operation Eclipse, which provided for the occupation of the whole of Germany, the dissolution and disarmament of the German armed forces, and the establishment of a military government, wrapped up the war in Europe as far as the western Allies were concerned. Eclipse was the final operation of a long war that had changed the world in ways yet to be fully understood. Beyond Eclipse loomed an indefinite period of occupation for Germany and a future which at this point in time was as much an enigma to the victors as it was to the vanquished. Operation Lusty, an acronym for Luftwaffe science and technology, was that portion of Operation Eclipse assigned exclusively to General Spaatz and his staff at St.-Germain—the exploitation of Luftwaffe technology. On April 16 Spaatz ended the strategic bombing offensive against Germany. There were no more targets of a strategic nature to bomb. He committed the 8th and 15th strategic air forces to tactical missions for the duration of the war.[1] On April 29 the German forces in Italy surrendered. The general's focus and that of his Exploitation Division became Operation Lusty and the disarmament of the Luftwaffe.

The first priority of Operation Lusty was to determine which of their advanced scientific developments the Germans had provided to their Japanese ally and what possible use the Japanese might have made of that German technology. Finding and capturing Hermann Göring and his air staff would be a giant step toward answering those critical questions. Help came unexpectedly with the interception of German radio traffic on May 1, 1945, between a location in Austria and Admiral Dönitz's headquarters in Flensburg, near the Danish border. Dönitz had assumed command of the German armed forces upon Hitler's suicide on April 30, and the greater part of Göring's staff, the Oberkommando der Luftwaffe, had assembled in the picturesque lakeside village of Thumersbach on the Zellersee, a few miles south of Berchtesgaden. "At a medieval inn . . . the German General Air Staff patiently awaited the outcome of surrender negotiations taking place in the North," reflects the USAFE history of Operation Lusty. "They had arrived by car and plane during the past weeks, when the fall of Berlin was imminent, and had kept in contact by radio with Admiral Dönitz at Flensburg. Through the interception of one of these messages, their location, which had previously been unknown, was discovered. Within twenty-four hours Lt. Col. O'Brien and his small party, representing the Exploitation Division of the Directorate of Intelligence, USSTAF, had arrived, located the party and conducted the first of a series of discussions with General Koller, who was then in command. All documents and records that had been brought by the High Command were immediately turned over, and the first unearthing of buried records and documents, in and around Berchtesgaden, as well as the initial interrogation of the staff officers present, took place."[2] SHAEF quickly got involved in the act, sending a large team of English and American officers, previously selected for this purpose and standing by in London, to conduct the interrogation of the German air staff.

The entire staff of the OKL was not at Thumersbach, of course. A small remnant of about sixty officers remained in Flensburg with

Admiral Dönitz and surrendered on May 8, or went into hiding. As a result, a number of German air staff members remained unaccounted for, but the greater part of the Oberkommando der Luftwaffe was in captivity by May 8, at either Berchtesgaden or Flensburg. These included the Reichsmarschall and head of the Luftwaffe himself, Hermann Göring; Lieutenant General Koller, chief of staff of the air staff; Brigadier General Schulz, chief of the Luftwaffe operations staff; Brigadier General von Rohden, chief of the Luftwaffe history office; Lieutenant General Wolfgang Martini, chief of Luftwaffe intelligence; Major General von Griegern, chief logistician; Brigadier General Hitschold, ground attack operations; Major General von Massow, Luftwaffe training; Lieutenant General Dr. Schröder, chief Luftwaffe medical services; Brigadier General Morzig, chief of air transport services; Brigadier General Narsewisch, chief of reconnaissance operations; Major General Nordmann, commanding general of day fighters; Major General Dahlmann, flying safety; and many other general officers, including the Reichs Minister of Armaments and War Production, Albert Speer. Speer was detained at Flensburg. General der Jagdflieger Adolf Galland, the famed former chief of Germany's fighter forces, was captured on May 5 at a villa near Tegernsee where he lay recuperating from wounds received on his last combat mission on April 26. Galland was transferred to Berchtesgaden along with the rest of Göring's staff for interrogation. In addition to the general officers, a large number of lesser ranks was captured at Thumersbach.[3]

The entire OKL group was quickly moved from Thumersbach to Strub, a village adjacent to Berchtesgaden. In Strub, the Germans were quartered in a spacious girls' school, a facility built for the *Bund Deutscher Mädel*, the Hitler Youth counterpart for German teenage girls fourteen years of age and older. At Strub the preliminary interrogation began. A casual remark by a lower-level engineer undergoing routine interrogation revealed that he had recently been offered a position in Japan. That revelation was of high interest and was quickly followed by intensive questioning. The engineer revealed that in the middle of April ten submarines loaded with Luftwaffe equipment had sailed from Kiel for Japan. Headquarters SHAEF was quickly notified and a major search was initiated along possible routes the U-boats may have taken on their way to Japan. By "the end of June, six of these ten submarines had been captured intact, some a relatively short distance away from their ports of departure, others perilously close to Japan."

Another OKL officer revealed the location of a large cache of documentation hidden in a concealed air raid shelter. On close examination the cache of documents provided many of the answers the interrogators were looking for—the answers to the Japanese riddle. Apparently the Germans had supplied "Japan all types of equipment for aerial warfare, including models of the Me-262 and Me-163, quantities of V-1 equipment, high explosives, incendiary bombs, bomb sights, radar apparatus of all descriptions, including models of the Würzburg and Freya, radio and signals installations, telephone, teleprinters . . . and all types of aircraft parts. Another [document] contained the precise location of every plant in Japan presently engaged in the manufacture of the latest aerial plane designs, every research institution connected with the Japanese Air Force, and many vital targets hitherto unknown and unsuspected by Army Air Force Intelligence officers. These volumes were flown at once to Washington, D.C., and shortly thereafter bombers of the 20th Air Force were doing precision bombing of the secret targets whose existence had been disclosed in the documents captured at Berchtesgaden."[4]

Not only did the Germans provide the Japanese with AAA guns and their latest radars, but "the Germans made complete disclosures of flak tactics and techniques of fire control to the Japanese."[5] *Telefunken* had an active training program in Germany under its chief of research and development, Dr. Brandt, who "trained 2,200 Japanese in radar and infra-red technique."[6] ATI team discoveries and the capture of the German air staff in large part answered the questions regarding

German-Japanese wartime cooperation and its implications for the ongoing war in the Pacific. The answers had come more quickly than anyone had expected.

As the interrogations of the OKL members progressed, it became clear that it had been German policy for many years to share with the Japanese all information on German weapons systems. Noted an Exploitation Division report of July 17, 1945, "It was the policy of the Germans to give to the Japanese all information regarding weapons and implements of war. The extent to which this general policy was carried out varied with the individuals who were carrying it out." Hitler, in a letter dated August 7, 1942, had expressed his own strong feelings on the subject, ordering that "basically there is no objection of any kind against fulfilling the Japanese requirements." Subsequent interrogation of German officials confirmed this policy. Said Albert Speer, the armaments minister, "On the German side there had been a general order to give them access to all information they wanted. Göring said: Hitler ordered that the blueprints for the Me-262 be handed over to the Japanese despite my objections, because the last thing is not given even to an ally." Interrogation of Dr. Adolf Busemann, Director of the Institute of Aerodynamics at Völkenrode, revealed that "A Japanese group visited Völkenrode and were to be shown the wind tunnels, but LFA had been instructed to hold back data on work in progress." In February 1943 this generous policy of releasing all and everything to the Japanese was apparently changed by the Oberkommando der Wehrmacht. The OKW sent a letter to concerned staff agencies stating that "Hitler had decided that the Japanese were to receive only the apparatus which they themselves could manufacture and use operationally in their theater of war. Apparatus and documents with respect to new developments were not to be released."[7]

Despite the vacillations of individuals as to how to carry out Hitler's policies, it appeared that the Japanese received vast quantities of equipment and design information. The Junkers company shipped diesel and gasoline engines and drawings. Henschel Flugzeugwerke in Berlin shipped plans for new aircraft construction methods. Elektrochemische Werke provided data on rocket fuels. In December 1942, Rhein Metal Borsig shipped fifty-seven MG 15 aircraft machine guns, one hundred nineteen MG 17 aircraft machine guns, five 20 mm machine guns in aircraft mountings with twenty-five thousand rounds of ammunition, and eighteen 20 mm antiaircraft guns with one hundred fifty thousand rounds of ammunition. In 1943 Rhein Metal Borsig shipped additional machine guns, antiaircraft guns, and ammunition, as well as bombs ranging from four-pound incendiary bombs to four-thousand-pound general purpose bombs. The Technical Air Armaments Section of the Luftwaffe provided the Japanese with drawings of the Me-262 jet fighter and the Arado 234 jet reconnaissance bomber, as well as actual turbines, gyros, automatic pilots, oxygen apparatus, and Walter rockets. The list of aircraft deliveries to Japan between 1937 and 1943 was extensive, including the Ju 87, Ju 88, and Do 217 bombers and the Bf 109, FW 190, and Me-210 fighters, as well as numerous support, training, and liaison aircraft. Reciprocating engines of all types, bombs of all sizes, fuzes, antiaircraft guns from 20 mm to 105 mm, and fifty-three Würzburg radar sets, various other equipment, drawings, and operator manuals were shipped to Japan over the years.

Japanese personnel frequently visited German military installations and factories. General Galland recalled that "at Rechlin we demonstrated in the presence of the Japanese the Me-262, Ar 234, and Do 335."[8] That aircraft demonstration took place on June 12 and 13, 1944, with Generalfeldmarschall Milch, Minister Speer, and General der Jagdflieger Galland in attendance. Hitler apparently also made a gift of two submarines of the latest type to the Japanese emperor in the spring of 1944. Dr. Herbert Wagner, an engineer with Henschel Flugzeug Werke, recalled that "In 1943 and 1944 the military people demonstrated the HS 293 and HS 294 [air-to-surface antiship missiles] to the Japanese

An Me-163B Komet at Freeman Field, one of ten shipped to the United States in the hold of HMS Reaper. *(DF)*

at Garz Usedom Airdrome," and there appeared to have been negotiations regarding the purchase of patent rights for the HS 293 and 294. Professor Lutz, an aircraft engineer and instructor at the Technische Hochschule in Braunschweig, revealed that additional technical information was provided to the Japanese only "eight weeks ago," which would have placed the delivery at about April 27 or 28 of 1945.[9]

The traffic between Japan and Germany was not one-way. The Japanese provided the Germans with critical raw materials in compensation for their arms shipments, or paid in gold. How were the deliveries effected? Over the years shipments were made by rail across the Soviet Union (before Stalin and Hitler became mortal enemies), then by surface ship, later through "neutral" countries such as Spain and Portugal, and by German and Japanese submarines. In June 1944 the huge Japanese submarine I-52 was en route from Japan to German-occupied France with a cargo of 290 tons of rubber, tin, tungsten, and gold in exchange for German technology. "The Japanese submarine rendezvoused with a German support submarine in the mid-Atlantic to take on fuel and technicians who, ironically, were going to install anti-aircraft radar on the Japanese vessel for the dangerous sail to the Bay of Biscay." Unknown to the Japanese, the United States had broken their naval code. "Each night when the Japanese submarine surfaced to recharge its batteries, its coded messages, which included its location, were being monitored." The escort carrier USS *Bogue* was tasked to find and destroy the Japanese submarine. "On the night of June 24, 1944, an Avenger got a blip on its radar and dropped flares." The submarine dived, but sonobuoys dropped from antisubmarine warfare aircraft soon relocated the 357-foot target and commenced attack. "The first aircraft dropped depth charges and then a Mark 24 *mine*. The Mark 24 was a code name for the then top secret acoustic torpedo that was being used for the very first time in the war.... Another Avenger, piloted by Lt. William Gordon, arrived on the scene, its sonobuoys picking up the sounds of the damaged submarine's cavitating propeller noises. Another acoustic torpedo was dropped; finding and critically crippling the Japanese submarine as it tried to get away." Over one hundred Japanese sailors and technicians died on that starlit night, taking all that critically needed tungsten, tin, rubber, and gold with them to the bottom of the South Atlantic.[10] Submarine traffic of this nature between Japan and Germany continued right up to April 1945.

The German U-234 could carry an estimated 250 tons of cargo and sufficient fuel and provisions for a trip of several months' duration. The U-234 departed Kristiansand, Norway, on April 15, 1945, for Japan. On board the submarine were "74 tons of lead, 26 tons of mercury, 12 tons of steel, 7 tons of optical glass, 43 tons of aircraft plans, instruments, arms, and medical supplies, 5 tons of 20 mm and 37 mm ammo, 6 tons of equipment for the U-boat bases, 1 ton of mail, films, and courier post, 1,232 pounds of uranium-oxide ore," and one disassembled Me-262 jet fighter. In addition the submarine carried a number of passengers, including Messerschmitt engineers August Bringewald and Franz Ruff. In *Hitler's U-Boat War: The Hunted, 1942–1945*, Clay

Blair writes, "When Germany capitulated, Fehler [the U-boat's captain] was in mid-Atlantic and he chose to surrender to the Americans, so he surfaced and headed westward. After disposing of his *Tunis* radar detector, *Kurier* transmitter, and all *Enigma* and other secret papers, Fehler met the American destroyer *Sutton* [on May 14]. Rather than be captured, the two Japanese officers [on board the submarine] committed suicide, each swallowing a dozen Luminal sleeping pills. Fehler secretly buried the bodies in weighted seabags. *Sutton* took control of the boat and escorted U-234 into Portsmouth to berth with U-805, U-873, and U-1228." The uranium ore aboard the U-234 would have yielded about 7.7 pounds of U-235, "about one-fifth of what was needed to make an atomic bomb." Subsequently this ore "disappeared," probably finding its way to the Manhattan Project's diffusion plant at Oak Ridge, Tennessee. When the Germans capitulated on May 8, 1945, there were four additional German supply U-boats in Japan, which were then taken over by the Japanese navy.[11]

In October 1945, Karl Baur, a Messerschmitt Me-262 test pilot, was at NAS Patuxent River, Virginia, assisting the U.S. Navy with its recently acquired Arado 234 and Me-262 jets. There Baur unexpectedly ran into two former Messerschmitt colleagues from Lager Lechfeld, who in April 1945 had set out on their way to Japan on the ill-starred U-234. August Bringewald, a close associate of Willy Messerschmitt's, and Franz Ruff had been interned at Portsmouth, New Hampshire, after the U-234's surrender to the destroyer USS *Sutton*. Shortly, along with the rest of the submarine's crew, they were transferred for interrogation to Fort Hunt, Virginia, and subsequently sent to "Pax River" to cool their heels. In the isolation ward of the Navy hospital where Baur had been assigned a room for the duration of his stay at Patuxent River, he met his two bored and dispirited colleagues.[12]

A young American fighter pilot, Lieutenant John L. "Larry" Sutton, was one of that select group of American and English airmen who had been biding their time in London hotels, waiting for a call that would send them on their way to interrogate Göring's air staff. "I was born in 1917 in Zanesville, Ohio, of English, Irish, and German descent," Larry revealed. "I spoke a little German, of course. My mother's maiden name was Derwächter. Her ancestors came to Zanesville in 1752 from Freckenfeld, near Karlsruhe. Most of my boyhood I spent in Memphis, Tennessee. I graduated from Notre Dame and stayed around to obtain a master's degree in political science. I believe I must have been the only fighter pilot in England with a master's degree, because few of us even had any college. I was a little late getting into the military for World War II. The Navy turned me down twice for physical defects which I did not have. I finally decided to try the Air Corps. I remember the moment when I sat in my first fighter, a P-40 Warhawk. It was one of the highlights of my life. I eventually ended up flying a combat tour in P-51s with the 339th Fighter Group of the 8th Air Force, out of RAF Fowlmere.

"I was a twenty-six-year-old second lieutenant. My group commander was a twenty-seven-year-old full colonel. On a good day the 8th Air Force launched as many as seven hundred fighters out of England. The sky was filled with airplanes—it was an awesome sight to behold. Most of my combat missions were uneventful, flying bomber escort or strafing targets of opportunity. By December 1944 I had flown the required number of combat hours, but I didn't want to go home yet. I found a job with the rear element of Headquarters USSTAF in London. I was assigned to a CIOS team which had been established for the purpose of interrogating the Luftwaffe air staff, the Oberkommando der Luftwaffe, OKL for short, once they were captured. We Americans knew very little about the Luftwaffe air staff, but the British knew a great deal and readily shared with us all they knew. I spent several months at RAF headquarters in London learning all about the OKL before going over to Germany.

"On May 17, 1945, only days after the surrender was signed at Reims, I landed at Munich-Riem airport with several other CIOS team members on our way to Berchtesgaden. My team chief was Wing Commander R. J. Cullingham. In Munich we stopped at the headquarters of Luftgau 7, which was a regional Luftwaffe headquarters and air defense command and control center. It had the responsibility for the air defense of the southern part of Germany. Luftgau 7 had a unique hard-wire communications system which ran around the city of Munich as well as a remote radar ground-control intercept capability which was fed real-time data from regional radar sites through a system of coaxial cables. It was a very advanced and automated air defense command and control center with unique features which we studied, copied, and expanded on in later years. When we arrived in Berchtesgaden, most of my outfit was already busy interrogating the German air staff. The POW compound consisted of a number of nice buildings in a walled-in enclosure where the Germans had established their offices as well as personal quarters. We lived in Berchtesgaden in the Berchtesgadener Hof, the Post Hotel, and various other hotels taken over by the U.S. Army. Every morning the interrogation teams would drive over to Strub from their hotels to continue with their investigations. The Germans continued to function as a staff, although they no longer had a mission or subordinate units. Every day they published a *Tagesbefehl*, orders of the day, and distributed copies to each staff office. The *Tagesbefehl* was signed by the U.S. Army colonel in command of the compound.

"Most members of our CIOS interrogation team were intelligence officers; the British as well as many of the American officers were bilingual. The British interrogators had done this sort of thing for a number of years. Initially we didn't know what to do with the Germans. There was some talk of trying them as war criminals, but that didn't hold up, so we had them doing studies on the campaigns they had undertaken. For example, we asked them to give us a report on how they organized the attack on Crete. There were about two hundred officers in the camp. They located those with knowledge of the Crete campaign and put together a working group. We had kept about twenty German secretaries behind for that purpose. So they had typists, who could also take dictation and prepare the report. Senior generals in any army don't type very well. I did wonder after a while why they were so eager to cooperate with us. Of course there were the terms of surrender—unconditional. Also, just after the end of hostilities, things were in a mess in Germany. Nor were they heroes in their own country. And then of course—very important in a hungry country— was the fact that we were feeding them.

"Three German generals who had been captured earlier were sent back to us from England. I met them, along with a U.S. Army group headed by a lieutenant. The Army group wanted to process the generals before accepting them into the camp. As part of the in-processing they told the three to take off all insignia with a swastika on it. When one of the generals prepared to hand over his pilot wings to the Army lieutenant, I intervened. I believe I am the only pilot here, I said to the lieutenant. I was a junior captain then. And if you don't mind I will take the general's wings. The German handed his wings to me and then said in faultless American English, 'I want you to know that I am the fourteenth pilot in the Luftwaffe.' I said, 'Where did you learn to speak like that?' 'Brooks Field,' he replied. This was Generalleutnant Gerd von Massow, General der Fliegerausbildung, the chief of their air training command. Ten years later I went down to Starnberg on the Starnberger See, where the general lived in retirement, and offered to return his wings to him. He declined and asked me to keep them.

"We did have a few famous flyers among the OKL staff. One was, of course, Generalleutnant Adolf Galland, the one-time chief of Germany's fighter force. We also had Oberst Gordon Gollob, a nice Scottish name, who was a big ace with over 160 victories. Galland made some noises that Gollob had screwed him out of his job and wanted to get even. Gollob replaced Galland temporarily as General der Jagdflieger when Galland was fired by Göring and reduced to command a squadron of Me-262 jets, JV 44. I talked to Galland and he gave his word that he would not cause any trouble while he was in the camp. After that, things quieted down. There came the day when the British wanted some of our German generals sent back to England for interrogation, among them Generals Galland and Koller, the chief of staff. I was present when General Koller read the last *Tagesbefehl*—a simple good-bye message. The group of German officers standing at attention outdoors between the buildings murmured "auf Wiedersehen." That was the end of the Luftwaffe general staff.

"It was during this Berchtesgaden period that I went to Nürnberg-Roth to fly a P-51 to get my monthly flying hours to qualify for my flight pay. It was a nice sunny day, so I decided to buzz the Berchtesgaden camp. That done, I was just boring holes into the sky, when I noticed an American transport, a Gooney Bird, flying near Salzburg. I buzzed the slow-moving transport a couple of times just to rattle the pilot's cage. Only later did I learn that General Arnold was on board that plane. [Fortunately for Captain Sutton, General Arnold loved his fighter pilots, and nothing ever came of the incident.] After landing back at Nürnberg-Roth, the crew chief who tended to my borrowed P-51 asked me if I wanted an aircraft of my own. He had been flying a German trainer, a Bücker Bü 181, and his commander had told him in no uncertain terms to destroy the aircraft. Instead, the sergeant had hidden the Bücker in a wheat field and removed all of its instruments, planning to take the instruments back home with him. But, as he said, the engine still ran well, and did I want the aircraft? I took it. He ran up the Bücker's engine and taxied it out onto the grass for me and I took off. I didn't need a compass for the return flight to Berchtesgaden. The autobahn was a reliable guide and led me straight to Salzburg airport, where I put down and parked the airplane. The sergeant had removed the German crosses and swastika and applied American markings on the fuselage, tail, and wings.

"At Berchtesgaden I thought it might be a good idea to consult with a German pilot who had flown an aircraft of this type. I put out the word and soon a young major reported to my office who said he had flown the Bü 181 in pilot training. Major Werner Reppening, who had been captured at Thumersbach along with the rest of the OKL staff, agreed to accompany me to Salzburg, just a few miles east of Berchtesgaden, and look over the aircraft. Reppening, Flight 'Leftenant' Clark, a Spitfire pilot who was a member of our CIOS interrogation team, and I drove over to Salzburg airport. Major Reppening walked around the Bücker, patted it, and muttered something about it being '*in Ordnung*.' I wasn't quite ready to take a ride with him, so I asked my English friend, Would you want to fly around the field with the major? 'Oh, I don't mind,' Clark replied in his very British accent. So Reppening and Clark got in—the Bücker had side-by-side seating— and they took off and flew around Salzburg for a while. As I watched them drawing lazy circles above the city I wondered if Reppening was the first German pilot to fly in Germany after the war. I ran into Reppening twenty years later in Paris when I was the U.S. military representative to SHAPE, the military headquarters of NATO. Reppening, as a brigadier general in the new Luftwaffe, had become my opposite number. I was then a colonel in the U.S. Air Force.

"I participated in some of the interrogations at Berchtesgaden, but mostly I went out searching for and retrieving OKL files which had been hidden in nearby caves, castle ruins, and air raid shelters. In late July the Combined Chiefs of Staff in Washington approved our move to England, and we brought in a large number of C-47 transports and flew all prisoners out. In England we put them up on a country estate that had been used by the English as an interrogation center for German aircrews during the war, Latimer House. I flew to England alone in my Bücker 181, crossing the English Channel at the narrowest point and landing at a famous Battle of Britain field outside London, Biggin Hill. No one seemed to care about this German aircraft being on the field. I flew the Bücker a couple more times and then gave it to one of our people."[13]

Adolf Galland, along with several other high-interest prisoners of the OKL staff, was flown to England as early as May 14 to begin detailed interrogation. Galland ended up in Camp 7 at Latimer, the Joint Services Interrogation Center, along with all the other members of the OKL staff. In *Fighter General*, Colonel Raymond F. Toliver writes, "Since Allied interest in jet fighters remained high, Galland was first interrogated about the Me-262, as were other pilot POWs who had flown the jet. A special report on the Me-262 was compiled at Latimer. Famous American aces like Colonel David Schilling and Colonel John C. Meyer [a future commander of the Strategic Air Command] came to interview Galland and other Me-262 pilots."[14] There at Camp 7, Galland, a thirty-three-year-old flyer who received his first battle experience in Spain and who obtained a reputation among Allied officers as perhaps the most brilliant general in the German air force, prepared a historical narrative of fighter tactics employed for all campaigns, beginning with the Spanish civil war and ending with the last concerted attacks against Allied fighters and bombers in 1945. Galland's report formed the basis of his book *The First and the Last*, initially published in Germany in 1953.

Additional studies were tasked and written by the captured members of the OKL. General von Rohden, the German air staff historian, and his staff prepared a report on the history of German theories on the application of air power. General Marzik and his staff assistants wrote up the German airborne campaigns planned and executed, including the planned airborne landing of Malta, which was never undertaken. Additionally, to satisfy Air Force Post-Hostilities Requirements tasking, over the following year the captured German officers prepared papers and studies on every imaginable subject in which they had expertise and were involved. Topics ranged from aviation medicine to flying safety, from troop carrier operations to night fighter operations, from air defense to propaganda in the Luftwaffe. The final list of studies comprised forty-five volumes which, in great detail, laid out the "military mistakes made by German Air Force generals, the clash of strong personalities that was so detrimental to their cause and purpose, the magnificent military plans created but never executed, tactics employed, principles of air power devised and used, adopted methods of communications, supply and training . . . all lucidly and scholarly presented."[15]

The capture and intense interrogation of Göring's staff yielded an immense amount of useful information and provided important leads pointing at other sources of German-Japanese collaboration. On May 18, a German civilian Japanese language interpreter, Heinz Weber, was flown to Headquarters Army Air Forces in Washington, D.C., accompanied by numerous files which shed light on Japanese-German collaboration. On June 23, 1945, Weber was followed by Oberleutnant Schumann, who accompanied a planeload of documents and hardware destined for the Captured Personnel and Materiel Branch, CPMB, in Washington. The documents flown to Washington National Airport were considered primary source material "for determining the extent of information furnished by Germany to Japan." It was an immensely large cache which included detailed drawings, tool and parts lists, and detailed photographs of the TA 152H advanced fighter aircraft, the BMW 003 jet turbine, and the Jumo 004 jet engine. Correspondence dealt with deliveries of radars, munitions, searchlight lenses, guns, and numerous other military and technical paraphernalia, including Japanese wish lists. As soon as the documents were located, and without any intervening translation or evaluation by either the Exploitation Divison at USSTAF or SHAEF, the documents were packed and shipped to Headquarters Army Air Forces in Washington on the first plane available.[16]

The pressing questions related to German-Japanese collaboration and their continuing implications for the United States in the ongoing war in the Pacific were answered quickly and acted upon promptly. With that high priority task largely accomplished, the time was right to focus on Operation Lusty's second objective—the exploitation of Germany's advanced aviation and missile technology for the benefit of America's lagging aviation industry.

10

A MOTHER LODE OF AVIATION TECHNOLOGY

The Air Technical Intelligence teams and the disarmament squadrons received their direction as to where to look for critical materials from detailed target folders prepared by the targeting sections of the 8th and 9th Air Forces. The folders were derived from target dossiers initially prepared for bombing purposes. With minor additions and changes, the target folders were adapted to provide all the information an ATI team would need to locate a particular GAF installation or research facility. Without such specific guidance, the teams undoubtedly would have been running around blind. By March 1, 1945, fifteen hundred targets were identified for inspection and appropriate folders prepared for areas already occupied or soon to be occupied by American forces. With the capture of the Remagen bridge on March 7, and the subsequent northward movement of American and British armies into territory that was soon to become the Russian zone of occupation, along with Patton's move into Czechoslovakia and Austria, there was suddenly a requirement to develop additional target folders to take advantage of the unexpected opportunity.

The areas which would subsequently fall under Russian control yielded a bonanza of material. Much of it probably would not have been uncovered in the brief time available without the help of the meticulously prepared folders. Still, much was left behind for the Russians when the time came to evacuate the area.[1] Wrote Norman M. Naimark in *The Russians in Germany*, "CIOS teams removed equipment in staggering quantities from the region. From Nordhausen alone, 1,000 technicians and the parts for 100 V-2 missiles were evacuated to the West." Yet, when the Soviets occupied these same areas they found entire armaments factories still operable, such as the BMW jet engine factories and the Junkers aircraft plants.[2]

The collection of large quantities of captured equipment required an adequate support structure for its assembly, packaging, and subsequent shipment to its ultimate destinations. To that end McDonald's people in the Exploitation Division at Headquarters USSTAF had by May 1, 1945, settled on three Air Technical Intelligence collection points—ATICPs, in military jargon. The first ATICP selected was Merseburg airfield, one mile west of the town near the Leuna synthetic oil refinery complex, heavily bombed during the war. Merseburg was in what would soon become part of the Russian zone of occupation and, according to Allied agreement, had to be vacated by not later than July 10. In turn, the Russians were to hand over the American sector of Berlin to American forces in early July. Nürnberg-Roth airfield, about ten miles south of Nürnberg, became the second ATICP. An airfield seven miles east of Stuttgart became a third collection point. When on June 2, 1945, Merseburg was abandoned by ATI teams, Munich-Riem airport was designated an ATICP in its place.[3]

The ATI teams were assigned to the three ATICPs in almost equal numbers. Each ATICP command post was radio equipped for twenty-four-hour communication with USSTAF headquarters, and it disposed of a number of mobile jeep-mounted radio sets to allow the field teams to stay in touch with their respective command posts. The radios allowed a high degree of tasking flexibility as the teams fanned out in their jeeps from the three collection points to inspect GAF facilities and arms factories. Based on daily inventory reports submitted by the three ATICPs, the Exploitation Division ordered the movement of German aircraft to a depot at Hanau, while engines and other equipment went to Kassel. At each depot, collected material was prepared and packaged for shipment to destinations in the United States and the United Kingdom. The 9th Air Force and 1st Tactical Air Force Service Commands provided the necessary airlift, which included several stripped-down B-17 and B-24 bombers serving as long-range transports between the ETO and the Zone of Interior, or ZI, as the United States was then referred to. Heavier items were moved by ship from ports in France. Documentation was shipped to the Joint Documentation Center in London for translation, indexing, and subsequent distribution. Tons of this paper was to show up at Wright Field by late 1945 for evaluation and translation.[4] The entire disarmament and intelligence collection task proved to be in its own way as demanding of resources as any battle fought to bring the Nazis to their knees.

While John Sutton and his team were interrogating the one-time Luftwaffe leaders in Berchtesgaden, and the ATI teams were scrambling around war-scarred Germany looking for loot, access to German technology became a hot priority item for the American defense industry. Companies involved in the development of jet-powered aviation, such as Bell, Lockheed, and General Electric, clamored for direct access to plants, equipment, and scientists. Generals Spaatz and McDonald had worked for some time with the Pentagon to obtain approval for the participation of American engineers and scientists in Operation Lusty. Major General James P. Hodges, the Assistant Chief of Air Staff for Intelligence, personally worked the problem in the Pentagon, and by late April and early May engineers and scientists arrived in the ETO by the planeload. Scientists came by the hundreds to augment ATI teams and interrogate German scientists, to study engineering plans and technical documentation, to conduct equipment tests, and to visit factories and laboratories. A group headed by Dr. Theodore von Karman, an aerodynamicist from the California Institute of Technology and director of the Army Air Forces Scientific Advisory Group, arrived in the United Kingdom in April. Dr. von Karman was accompanied by some of America's leading scientists in guided missile technology, radar, television, aircraft design, rocket motors, and jet propulsion, including Dr. Hugh L. Dryden from the Bureau of Standards, Dr. L. A. DuBridge, director of the radiation laboratory at the Massachusetts Institute of Technology, Dr. Vladimir K. Zworykin of the RCA research laboratory, Dr. Hsue S. Tsien and Dr. Fritz Zwicky from the California Institute of Technology, and Dr. Frank L. Wattendorf from the Wright Field laboratories.[5]

Dr. von Karman and his group were not idle curiosity seekers, but were on a mission of extreme national importance, seeking to define the future composition and look of the Army Air Forces. General of the Army H. H. "Hap" Arnold had long ago recognized the technological deficit of his own air force and in late 1944 formed the AAF Scientific Advisory Group. Arnold secured the services of Dr. Theodore von Karman, renowned scientist and consultant in aeronautics, who agreed to organize and direct the group. Dr. von Karman then gathered about him a group of scientists from every field of research to analyze developments in the basic sciences and evaluate the effects of their application to air power. Soon after the formation of the advisory group, on November 7, 1944, General Arnold sent Dr. von Karman a memorandum asking him to "investigate all the possibilities and desirabilities for postwar and future war's development" and "give me a report or guide for recommended future AAF research and development programs." Among the axioms General Arnold chose to bring to Dr. von Karman's attention to frame his study efforts were: "(1) our prewar research and development has often been inferior to our enemies;

(2) offensive, not defensive, weapons win wars; (3) our country will not support a large standing army; and (4) it is a fundamental principle of American democracy that personnel casualties are distasteful. We will continue to fight mechanical rather than manpower wars." In addition, General Arnold encouraged von Karman to "look at all and everything, leave no option unaddressed." He asked, "Is it not now possible to determine if another totally different weapon will replace the airplane? Are manless remote-controlled radar or television assisted precision military rockets or multiple purpose seekers a possibility?"[6] These were the guidelines von Karman and his group were to consider. It was this specific tasking by General Arnold which had brought von Karman's group to Germany.

In addition to von Karman's high-level team of scientists, engineers and technicians arrived from every segment of America's defense industry. They came from the Boeing Aircraft Company, Bell Aircraft, Lockheed, Douglas, Bendix Aviation, Jack & Heintz, Sperry Research, Ladish Drop Forge, Cincinnati Milling Machine, American Aviation, Aerojet Engine, Curtiss-Wright, and General Electric. Still others arrived from General Motors, United Aircraft, Standard Oil of Indiana, and Minneapolis Honeywell. In April and May 1945 Air Technical Intelligence teams spread out from their collection points at Merseburg, Nürnberg-Roth, and Stuttgart and were frequently accompanied by American civilian engineers and scientists. These civilians quickly became a vital part of the search and evaluation process, providing sorely needed technical expertise.[7] They arrived in Germany with suitcases and trunks stuffed with suits, ties, fine leather shoes, fedoras, and the hundred and one other items evidently deemed essential by Americans for life in Europe. General McDonald was forced to issue practical guidelines for life in postwar Germany. In a memo aimed at new arrivals, among them many prominent and high-ranking professionals, it was politely pointed out that those assigned in connection with "exploitation of German aircraft and research establishments have, in many cases, burdened themselves with unnecessary clothing. In general, both officers and civilians need only have what dress uniforms and personal linen they should need for normal post life. Much of their duty will be in the field." Further, "Laundry facilities are very limited and a minimum of ten days and normally 2 weeks is required for laundry. Laundry soap is issued in the PX and it is often necessary for officers to wash their own personal linen and socks." The memo went on to say, "Field duty usually involves riding in jeeps as mud is often encountered. Wool OD slacks, battle jacket and combat boots can be purchased here in the theater [ETO]. Cleaning facilities are scarce."[8] This must have sounded like a combat assignment for those who had up to then followed the war from behind the safety of a desk. They adjusted.

Bell Aircraft was immensely interested in German technology for its own development projects. Its chief test pilot, Jack Woolams, was one of the first to arrive on the scene. Bell's YP-59A jet fighter had made its first flight in October 1942. The Me-262 first flew in July 1942. It seemed at the time that the two development programs were on a nearly equal footing and jet combat aircraft should enter their respective national inventories at about the same time. While the Me-262 proved to be a superb design, appearing for the first time in combat in mid-1944, the YP-59 turned out to be a flawed design from the start, deemed by its Wright Field test pilots as not much better than what the best piston engine aircraft could deliver in terms of speed and maneuverability, maybe even not as good. Nathan Rosengarten, a Wright Field flight test engineer, summed up the YP-59 by saying, "It could hardly be considered a combat airplane—at best it was a good safe airplane, a training vehicle for indoctrinating pilots into the Jet Age."[9]

By early 1943 General Arnold found himself over the proverbial barrel. His new YP-59 jet was useless for combat. Arnold had good reason to be concerned. The possible impact of the German jet on his bomber operations in Europe, if employed smartly and in sufficient numbers, could be disastrous. He had nothing to put up against the Me-262. The obsolete B-17 and B-24 bombers, surviving in European skies only by resorting to cumbersome formations and massive fighter cover, were totally defenseless against a jet fighter armed with air-to-air rockets. General Arnold turned to "Kelly" Johnson at Lockheed Aircraft, the designer of the P-38 fighter. A contract was signed for the YP-80 in June 1943. By November, the first YP-80 was on its way to Muroc Field, later renamed Edwards Air Force Base, in California. Things appeared to be looking up. Unfortunately, this was as good as it was going to get for the P-80 program for some time.

In the end, what saved Arnold's bombers was not the YP-59 nor the P-80 Shooting Star. The Me-262 threat simply never materialized, and by the time Operation Lusty was moving through Hitler's technological pantry in May 1945, the YP-80 was still struggling. Trouble began early with the P-80 project. In October 1944 Lockheed's chief test pilot died in a crash of an XP-80—the experimental version. Uninhibited by this ominous development the Army Air Forces in late 1944 shipped four YP-80s to Europe under the command of General George Price, supposedly to demonstrate to American flyers that "we too have a jet"—"if the Germans can do it, we can do it better" sort of thing. Lieutenant Colonel J. H. Carter, Chief of the Fighter Production Branch at Wright Field, came along to brief General Spaatz and his staff on that wonderful P-80 jet. His briefing, like all too many contractor briefings, was filled with hyperbole and promise, but there was little substance to back it up.

In his briefing on January 19, 1945, at USSTAF headquarters in St.-Germain, Colonel Carter swooned confidently to General Spaatz, "This is the P-80 [showing a slide of the airplane]. Its wing span is 37 feet; its length, 35 feet. Going from the nose aft, there is a landing light in the nose which can be tilted down for landing or takeoff. It carries 6.50s in the nose, with 300 rounds of ammunition for each gun. Access to the gun compartment is through—as the British would call it—a bonnet. The airplane is equipped with tricycle landing gear. The cockpit canopy is of the full-vision bubble type, with a pressurized chamber. It is equipped with a K-14 computing gun sight. The visibility from the cockpit is excellent; it has a 9 degree visibility over the nose. The engine is an air duct I-40 General Electric type thermal engine, with a duct on each side [Carter was talking about the Whittle engine built under license by GE]. The airplane carries 400 gallons of fuel. There is one main fuel tank behind the pilot with a capacity of 260 gallons, and three in each wing. The bombs or wing tanks are carried on the ends of the wings by shackles with a special fairing around them. The engine is just behind the main fuel tank. . . . This airplane is the most maneuverable I personally have flown. The first P-80 flew about a year ago. It was powered with a different engine. The results so far in 250 hours of test have been very successful. All the pilots who have flown it are extremely enthusiastic about it. One characteristic of the airplane that must be remembered is that the fuel consumption at sea level is twice that at altitude. When speaking of range, altitude must always be taken into consideration. The best altitude for economic fuel consumption is 35,000 feet. . . . So far the engine life is limited to 50 hours, with careful 25 hour inspections. However, at the speed it can go, the P-80 covers a lot of miles in 50 hours."[10]

On the same day Carter briefed General Spaatz on the virtues of the P-80, his intelligence people provided the general with their estimate of German capabilities for 1945. A principal conclusion of the report was that "The highest priorities in the Reich are devoted to a program of producing jet aircraft. The purpose of this program is to regain aerial superiority first over Germany and then over Europe, the armies and the sea approaches to the Continent. The superiority of an air force composed of jet aircraft, in sufficient numbers, is indubitable. It is estimated that at the present rates of production and training, if the program is unchecked, the Germans could possibly have roughly

1,000 jets operational by mid-summer," and, in the absence of appropriate countermeasures, this "could conceivably make further strategic bombardment of Germany too expensive to continue."[11] McDonald's assessment of the situation would prove to be quite accurate.

If General Spaatz actually believed Colonel Carter's overly optimistic P-80 presentation, he had cause to worry when one of the four YP-80 demonstrators sent to Europe crashed on January 31, 1945, killing its Wright Field test pilot, Major Fred Borsodi. Another aircraft was diverted to Rolls-Royce for installation of the RB-41 gas turbine power plant, an uprated Whittle engine. This aircraft too was to crash on a test flight on November 14, 1945. The remaining two YP-80s continued to perform moral boosting demonstration flights for the 15th Air Force in Italy. In spite of continuing development problems, General Arnold went ahead with a production order for a thousand P-80s. Optimism and production orders however do not make an airplane fly. The P-80's troubles were far from over. The first production P-80 was delivered in February 1945. Although "VE Day in May 1945 ended the Me-262 and Me-163 threat to Allied Forces in Europe and reduced the critical urgency condition," wrote Major General Warner E. Newby, a former Wright Field test pilot, "the U.S. still needed to achieve comparability or preferably superiority in jet technology. . . . In July 1945 a production test P-80A crashed on takeoff killing the pilot. Early in August 1945 a YP-80A exploded and crashed killing the pilot." On August 6, 1945, a black-letter day indeed for the P-80 program, Major Richard I. Bong crashed in a P-80 on takeoff from Muroc Field, Burbank, California, and was killed. Major Bong was a Medal of Honor winner and America's greatest World War II flying ace, with forty victories. "The loss of a national hero," wrote Newby, "triggered strong media, then public and political reaction. Concerns over the hazard of flying jet aircraft reached a crisis stage when the opposition began to allege that jet technology was just too risky to fly if test pilots and our top Ace could not safely handle the aircraft."

Lessons learned from German wind tunnel test data and captured turbine technology were hastily applied to end the P-80's bad luck streak. Additionally, General Arnold, in a message to the commanding general of the Air Technical Service Command at Wright Field, Major General Hugh Knerr, who had just returned from his assignment at Headquarters USSTAF in Paris, outlined for Knerr the importance of "the P-80A jet technology program," Newby recalled, and "the crisis that had emerged as a result of the recent accidents and especially the loss of Bong. He was now faced with serious political threats to cut back, cancel or withdraw funding for the jet programs." Arnold's message in so many words directed Knerr to fix the P-80's problems. And Arnold added prescriptively that "all P-80A aircraft flying be suspended, five new P-80A aircraft be carefully checked and updated with all possible improvements by the contractor and then expeditiously flown 50 hours each." The message closed with the profound directive, underlined: "There will not be an accident. I repeat there will not be an accident."[12] Knerr understood loud and clear what his marching orders were. There were no further accidents.

Although the F-80 was phased out of the active air force inventory soon after the Korean War, several generations of American military pilots cut their teeth on its trainer version, the T-33. Still, it took a long time to get there—several years beyond 1944 when the Me-262 first began to terrorize the skies over Europe and threaten to take away the air superiority so essential to the success of European combat operations. Bluntly put, the F-80 was a failure as a fighter aircraft. The United States fell behind in a critical technology where many thought it was a leader both in manufacturing prowess and technological innovation. Major General Knerr summarized the situation in a letter written in the summer of 1945 just before departing St.-Germain for Wright Field. Wrote Knerr to Spaatz, "Occupation of German scientific and industrial establishments has revealed the fact that we have been alarmingly backward in many fields of research."[13] One of the

A trainer version of the P/F-80, the T-33, at the March Air Reserve Base museum, Riverside, California. This version of the F-80 was a very different airplane from the initial X/YP-80. (WS)

many fields of research the United States was dangerously backward in was jet propulsion.

In April, May, and June 1945, information gathered from German design centers and manufacturing facilities provided a much-needed boost to the stalled YP-80 program. The Bayrische Motorenwerke plant in Munich was an exceptional source of information. ATI team members, Wright Field engineers, and civilian scientists interrogated BMW personnel from the Munich plant, as well as the company's personnel from its plant in Spandau, near Berlin, who had been evacuated to Munich. Then they actually tested BMW 003 jet engines in the only high-altitude test chamber in existence anywhere in the world to establish general performance characteristics. States the Exploitation Division report, "A series of performance tests have been conducted in the high-altitude engine test beds of the BMW plant at MUNICH. This test bed equipment appears to be one of the most, if not the most, elaborate in the world, being capable of supplying refrigerated low-pressure air both for engine cooling and combustion, and simulating atmospheric conditions at approximately 40,000 feet." The findings were promptly provided to American and British companies engaged in jet engine design and development. The Wright Field engineers were thrilled with the high-altitude test chamber at the BMW plant. Soon they discovered two test chambers of even greater capacity which were immediately identified by Exploitation Division personnel for shipment to the United States. The work at BMW was carried out with the assistance of its German engineers and technicians, including the designer and builder of the high-altitude wind tunnel. The team recommended these German experts should be "sent to the United States with the equipment to assist in its erection and calibration."[14] The test chambers were dismantled and shipped, and the turbine's designer, Dr. von Ohain, a young and brilliant engineer, soon was on his way to the United States—but not without first facing down some thorny issues.

At Garmisch-Partenkirchen, an ATI team located Dr. Schmidt, one of the outstanding authorities in the field of jet turbine research. Dr. Schmidt had conducted research on the injection of oxygen into aircraft engines at high altitudes to obtain increased power, and he developed and tested new theories on fuel combustion in engines. Dr. Schmidt was immediately held for further interrogation by American engineers. A secret cache of jet engine data and drawings was found at Hallein, in Austria, and BMW jet engine manufacturing plants at Stassfurt, Bamberg, Eisenach, and Abterrode were gone over in minute detail and their key engineers interrogated. Then additional plans and specifications were uncovered of a high-thrust experimental jet tied to a conventional propeller drive, a turboprop, "as a means of reducing excessive fuel consumption rates at low altitudes." The search for Germany's jet turbine secrets was unrelenting, thorough, and successful.[15]

On June 17, 1945, a team of specialists from the Exploitation Division, including four officers and seven enlisted men, took charge of the Aerodynamische Versuchsanstalt (AVA) and the Kaiser Wilhelm Institut (KWI) at Göttingen. Although colocated, each was an independent research center. AVA had a strong reputation in aerodynamic research, including studies on wind tunnel design, engine ducts, subsonic compressibility effects, swept-back wings, suction and blowing of air to increase lift, laminar flow, wing flutter, icing, and research on axial flow compressors. The AVA research teams did nearly everything essential to enter the jet age. At the KWI, fundamental research in fluid motion was conducted and a variety of special effects tunnels were in use to test practical, as well as theoretical, applications. The U.S. ATI team found research "with respect to transition from subsonic to supersonic flow, cavitation, laminar boundary layers, turbulence, heat transfer, lubrication" and more. Soon the German professors at the two institutes were preparing reports under the guidance of a USSTAF ATI team. ALSOS and CIOS teams swarmed through the two institutes as well. Competition for Germany's jet secrets was a fact of life, a real-life aspect of exploitation work.[16]

Reports of strange-looking aircraft seen flying near Salzburg reached McDonald at his headquarters in St.-Germain, and he sent an ATI team to investigate. Lieutenant Colonel O'Brien, the team leader, found a jet-propelled helicopter, the Dh 243, as it was referred to by McDonald's people in their report, the only one of its kind in the world. Its designer, Dr. Friedrich von Doblhoff, and his staff had labored for the past ten years on Doblhoff's creation and guarded it "as one would a precious jewel. The helicopter was examined and a preliminary superficial interrogation of the staff was sufficient to reveal its tremendous importance. It was carefully loaded in a large truck and taken to Munich. From there it was trucked to Cherbourg together with the confiscated notes, drawings and meticulous records of experiments conducted by" Dr. Doblhoff, for eventual shipment to the United States.[17]

Jet-related design and manufacturing data was not the only item of interest to McDonald's teams. Plenty of leading-edge development was discovered in numerous other fields that proved to be of great value and interest. At the Robert Bosch factory in Stuttgart, an ATI

Flettner 282 single-seat helicopter at a 1947 Wright Field exhibit of enemy aircraft and missiles. The FE (foreign equipment) numbers were assigned to captured enemy equipment by Technical Intelligence at Wright Field. (WS)

team found a working fuel injector mechanism. "Although American industry has long known the theory and operation of fuel injection, it has never been able to manufacture a product that was completely operationally satisfactory," wrote an enthusiastic investigator. "As the GERMANS seem to have overcome many of the difficulties with which we have been faced, the BOSCH manufacturing methods have been carefully exploited." There was also the two-stage supercharger developed by Daimler-Benz, "which achieved a supercharger efficiency far greater than ours," and its hydraulic coupling drive permitted "a far more accurate control over supercharger impeller speed than we have attained. Two engines incorporating the two-stage supercharger have been located," and were shipped to Wright Field.[18]

Documents found at a research center at Halle, in the future Soviet zone of occupation, provided "complete instructions in the handling of plastic welding, a process which had been employed by the German aircraft industry for joining of plastics by flame gas welding and enabled the sections joined together to possess the same strength at juncture as the original material."[19] Much of Germany's technological research facilities and factories had been relocated into underground structures hewn into lime and sandstone formations of the German *Mittelgebirge.* The large tunnel systems caught McDonald's attention and caused him to worry about the future. In August 1945, after the atomic bomb drops on Japan, McDonald wrote Lieutenant General Cannon, the current USAFE commander, about the large number of underground structures found by his investigators.[20] He informed Cannon that he personally had inspected a number of them. One of the underground factories he visited was at Nordhausen, south of the Harz mountains, in the Soviet zone of occupation. Nordhausen was a huge V-2 missile assembly plant captured on April 11, yielding over one hundred V-2 rockets. These underground installations varied in size, according to McDonald, from approximately five to twenty-six kilometers in lineal measurement, anywhere from four to twenty meters wide, and five to fifteen meters high. The floor space varied from 25,000 to 130,000 square meters. He did not think they were preferable to above-ground structures, but they were impervious to bombardment from the air with available bombs. General McDonald then recommended to General Cannon that his letter be forwarded to Headquarters Army Air Forces in Washington, where they should select "targets of above mentioned types [meaning the tunnels] for secret experiment of rocket propelled atomic bomb."[21] Fortunately nothing ever came of McDonald's absurd atomic bomb test idea.

At a research laboratory at Köthen, complete information on the Freya, Würzburg Riese, and Jagdschloss radars was discovered. The Jagdschloss was the latest German early warning radar, and the Würzburg and Freya were used for ground control intercept of enemy aircraft. An acoustically controlled guided missile research program, together with its operating personnel, was found at Bad Kissingen. The experimental system consisted of four electrical circuits activated by sound with the intended purpose of guiding a rocket-propelled missile into the space occupied by a heavy bombardment formation, constantly correcting the missile's course by means of incoming sound waves from the aircraft engines. "The group of scientists working upon this development are being retained at the laboratory to develop the program for our possible use," it was reported. Even more surface-to-air missile research was in progress by the Germans aimed at ending the dominance of America's heavy bomber formations over Germany. "A rocket propelled guided missile upon which a great deal of faith was apparently pinned was the 'GREAT ENZIAN.' This unit carried a 500 kilogram explosive head and could operate to 53,000 feet altitude at speeds approaching Mach numbers of 0.9. Sixty had been produced for test purposes, forty flown, and a very high production schedule projected when the organization fell into Allied hands and the remaining twenty were destroyed before capture. Dr. Würsten, the designer, is now in our hands and he has given us the following information on this unit: Take-off is assisted by four powder type assist take-off units which operate for the first five seconds only, producing a thrust of 3,200 pounds each which, when added to the 4,400 pound thrust of the main rocket, gives a total thrust of over four times the total weight of this missile. The assist take-off units drop off when the powder has been consumed and the main rocket motor runs on for forty-five seconds gradually decreasing its thrust, as the missile becomes lighter, to roughly one-half its initial value. When the missile is guided within 500 feet of the airplane target, it is automatically exploded by a radar device destroying the bomber. The unit, when traveling at a Mach number of .9 is not very maneuverable; minimum turning radius being about 1,650 feet. This permits evasive tactics to be successful. Speeds of thirty to forty per cent greater than those of the target aircraft are best. The range of this unit is fifteen miles when the trajectory is arranged to achieve the maximum. It can be fired safely at an angle down to 30 [degrees] above horizontal. Launching is accomplished from modified 88 [millimeter anti-aircraft] gun mounts with twenty-three feet guide rails attached."

An equally deadly surface-to-air missile development was an outgrowth of the V-2 ballistic missile project, the Wasserfall. Wasserfall was a brainchild of Dr. Wernher von Braun and his mentor, General Dornberger. In contrast to the Enzian, which was still subsonic, Wasserfall was supersonic, tested in the supersonic Peenemünde wind tunnel [evacuated to Kochel in 1943] and controlled by two radars, one aimed constantly at the target, while the other guided the missile. Wasserfall was designed to be launched against high-flying bomber formations as well as individual aircraft. Thirty-five of the Wasserfall missiles were test-flown before the V-2 and the Wasserfall teams moved to Bavaria in early 1945 and testing was terminated. Other similar missile developments discovered by ATI teams were the Rheintochter and the Schmetterling. The Schmetterling, or Hs 117, "has been found and is being examined," reported an ATI team. In fact the Schmetterling was remarkable for its light weight of less than a thousand pounds, and it could be fired from a stand at various angles.

For the Great Enzian and other German surface-to-air missile developments to be effective, a proximity fuze was needed. To no one's surprise, one of McDonald's teams reported, "A proximity fuze development for artillery shells has been recovered. It has been ascertained that the fuze operates on electro-static principles and, accordingly, will be a very difficult fuze against which to employ countermeasures. . . . German research had under development no less than fifteen different projects involving proximity fuzes. Although it is evident strict supervision from a central agency should have controlled the related projects, it is now apparent no such control existed and that activities were poorly coordinated. A number of the projects originated in 1930, were halted in 1940, and revived in 1943 when the danger from air bombardment became more acute. Not a single proximity fuze has seen service, and only two could have been placed in mass production within two years."[22]

The mother lode of advanced German technology appeared endless. Teams reported finding air-to-surface antiship missiles such as the SD 1400X, also known as the Fritz X, and the Hs 293, both of which had been used against the Allies and were of high interest to the U.S. Navy. The wire-guided air-to-air rocket X-4 was almost ready for action as

An SD 1400 Fritz X air-to-ground guided missile designed for use against armored naval combatants. Two Fritz X missiles sank the defecting Italian battleship Roma *on September 9, 1943. (RW)*

the war ended, and also a smaller antitank version, the X-7, all developed by Dr. Max Krämer as an outgrowth of his experience with the Fritz X. "Several complete V-1s have already been evacuated," wrote the Exploitation Division in a status report, "and a piloted V-1 is being shipped on project 'Seahorse'. . . . Seven complete A4 rockets (V-2s) have been evacuated to the Zone of the Interior." Less spectacular finds, yet important to future American aircraft development, included a de-icing research station, together with its director, Dr. Eder. "Among the items of interest are an electrical propeller de-icing method previously unknown to us. Documents describing this, and the heat exhaust methods used in the GAF, have been secured and are being evacuated. . . . The Benger plant at Stuttgart was exploited with respect to a ribbon type parachute used for dropping mines. . . . The BMW plant at Munich yielded unilever controls, drawings and propeller governors of a highly simplified and accurate design."[23]

Documents on varied subjects were discovered by the ton, such as the records of the German patent office, which were stored fifteen hundred feet underground in an abandoned potash mine. The records of Albert Speer's production ministry, which dealt with the development of the V-1, V-2, and Germany's jets, were immediately shipped to the Document Evaluation Center in London. No matter how carefully the Nazis attempted to hide facilities, equipment, or documentation, they were soon uncovered, sent onward to Kassel or Hanau for packing, and then shipped to the United States or London.

Documents were found in such great quantities that they required a special handling process. In June 1945 the Air Documents Research Center was established in London. There the thousands of tons of German documents from the British and American occupation zones in Germany and Austria were assembled. Over a period of only three months, 111,000 tons of documents were flown from Germany to the center in London. Army and Navy enlisted men fluent in German separated the documents into technical and nontechnical categories. The nontechnical documentation was then distributed to agencies interested in the subject matter; the technical documents received detailed screening and were catalogued and microfilmed. Technical libraries were established for such prominent manufacturing and research firms as Messerschmitt, BMW, and Daimler-Benz. Prominent American scientists and aeronautical engineers from universities throughout the United States assisted in the process. All of the material was made available for use by government agencies, research centers, universities, and private industry.

As extensive as the quantity of captured equipment and documentation proved to be, a yet more important source of information and scientific theories were the German scientists and engineers involved in the research and development programs of the Third Reich. Stated a report, "During the early phase of Operation Lusty, ATI teams and skilled American aeronautical engineers and scientists investigating intelligence targets carried out such detailed and extensive interrogations that a wealth of technical information of extreme importance was extricated from brilliant minds once directed to our own destruction." Typical of such interrogations was one conducted by engineers and researchers from Curtiss-Wright and General Electric who inspected the BMW jet engine production facilities and interrogated their personnel. The final reports covered the jet propulsion program at BMW, their nonreciprocating power plant programs under development, and the metallurgical aspects of gas turbine development, and described in detail the BMW 003 power plant. Interrogations of such prominent scientists as Professor Willy Messerschmitt, Dr. Alexander Lippisch, who researched supersonic wing design, Dr. Franz Tank, chief designer for Focke-Wulf, and the Peenemünde V-2 ballistic missile design team headed by Dr. Wernher von Braun proved extremely time consuming. The Germans were therefore put in indefinite detention for future interrogation—possibly in the United States.[24] "Eminent scientific personnel are available for interrogation," reported the Exploitation Division in July 1945, "concerning GAF activities in all the fields of scientific and industrial research. A list of some of the outstanding individuals in this category" was prepared, as well as a "further list of German scientists recently removed for interrogation from areas evacuated by U.S. troops," to keep them out of the hands of the Russians.[25]

To exploit the knowledge and experience of these men of science required more than quick hit-and-run interrogation. A way had to be found to bring the Germans to the United States, where a thorough debriefing, as the interrogation process was euphemistically known, could be conducted by Americans of equal stature in the proper setting and without distractions. Both General Knerr and Colonel Putt were to take on that difficult and thankless task of bringing German scientists, enemy aliens, to the United States. Theirs was to be a rocky road.

THE SECRETS OF VÖLKENRODE AND KOCHEL

When Colonel Donald Putt reported for duty at Headquarters USSTAF in January 1945 he was appointed director of technical services. He expected to go to work for General Knerr, his mentor, but, on his arrival at St.-Germain, Putt learned the headquarters had reorganized and technical services had been moved over to intelligence under General McDonald. Putt recalled that "my outfit turned into more of a technical intelligence operation than it did technical services." As fate would have it, he wouldn't be there long enough to put down roots. In April, "the ground armies traveling east uncovered this secret research and development facility outside Brunswick in a place called Völkenrode. I got instructions to go there and take over the place."[1]

Donald Leander Putt was born on May 14, 1905, in Sugar Creek, Ohio. In a 1974 interview General Putt reminisced, "As early as grade school I was interested in mechanical things. By the time I got to high school, I was sure I wanted to be an electrical engineer." Donald was especially interested in what was then referred to as "wireless," and built his own rig to intercept the Arlington time signal and other radio transmissions. Putt obtained a commercial radio operator's license by the time he was eighteen and graduated from high school. "I stayed out of school and spent the following winter in Cleveland working at the Ford assembly plant until spring came and the ice went out of the Great Lakes, when I got a job as a wireless operator on one of the lake freighters hauling iron ore, coal, wheat, and grain." But Donald had his eyes on bigger things and took the time to take the entrance exam for the Carnegie Institute of Technology in Pittsburgh, "and that fall enrolled there with the idea of becoming an electrical engineer." In the spring of his senior year "one of the chaps in one of my classes brought to the class a little yellow-covered pamphlet that was entitled *Flying Cadets of the Army Air Corps*. He passed the pamphlet to me in class and said, 'Gee, this sounds interesting.' So I stuck the pamphlet in the back of my textbook. That evening at the fraternity house I read the pamphlet and it sounded intriguing. You know, go to Texas at Uncle Sam's expense and learn to fly around like an eagle." Putt decided to apply, to "see what happens." He learned that there was a large percentage of washouts: first when people took the physical exam to get in, and later, when at least 50 percent washed out of flight training. He took his physical examination and was surprised to learn he passed. He received orders to report to San Antonio, Texas, July 1, 1928. Putt still thought of it as a lark and figured he wouldn't last through flight training. So he went ahead and interviewed for a job. "I accepted a job with General Electric for their training course but asked to report on the first of October. I figured that would give me enough time to get washed out of flying school. Well, when the first of October came, I had to write G.E. and tell them I was sorry I couldn't report because I was in the Army. I suppose because I was so relaxed about it all, I sailed right on through flying school." Putt accepted a reserve commission and signed on for one year of active duty, thinking that "at the end of the year, why, I'll get out and make an honest living. My regular commission came through in October 1929. I was ordered to Selfridge

Field, Michigan, flying with the 36th Pursuit Squadron until February 1933 when I was reassigned to the Flight Test Branch at Wright Field.[2]

Donald Putt nearly lost his life at Wright Field. It was Halloween day, 1935, and he was part of a flight test crew to put the X-299 through its paces, the earliest model of what would become the B-17 bomber of World War II fame. "The first X-model had bubble windows on its sides, the principal exterior difference between the X-299 and follow-on production aircraft," Putt recalled. "This was the largest airplane built to that time. This was also before checklists, the things you do before you take off. That morning I flew as copilot with my boss, Pete Hill, chief of flight test. The test called for us to conduct a series of climbs to different altitudes to established optimum climb speeds. We got behind schedule and were in a hurry, and that's always bad. Boeing's chief test pilot, Les Tower, came along. He was standing between us, just a little bit aft of the pilot and copilot's seat, probably hanging onto the back of our chairs. A flight test observer was also along, sitting in the navigator's position, and a crew chief mechanic. We taxied out to take off, and we sat there for a little bit and ran the engines up, moved the controls, and then gave it the gun. As the airplane picked up speed the nose kept coming up. Hill pushed forward on the stick to keep the nose down, nothing happened. The nose kept coming up and up. When we got to an alarmingly steep angle I got on the controls too, attempting to help Hill shove them forward; I was of no help. And so, with full power, right over the center of the field, we went up until we were vertical, and then we did a wing-over. That is, we stalled and came back down in a dive. We had almost leveled off when we hit the ground full speed ahead. So we came down a little bit left wing low. I think having hit wing low is the thing that saved those that made it, because that absorbed some of the shock, and it wasn't a direct impact. But it split open the wing, and we had a full tank of gas, and the plane immediately caught fire. Pete Hill was killed when his head was thrown forward into the control column; I was knocked out and

A YB-17 at Langley Field, Virginia, 1939. Very similar to the X-299 flown by Don Putt. The Y prefix, in the YB-17, indicated the source of funding. (RW)

suffered a severe scalp laceration, bleeding profusely. Regaining consciousness I escaped through where the windshield normally would be onto the nose of the ship, and dropped off onto the ground. The Boeing test pilot, Les Tower, was severely burned and died nine days later.

"Well, one of the other chaps that got there real quick was standing beside me right after I got out. I said to him, Has somebody checked to see whether or not the controls were locked? And that's exactly what happened. We took off with locked controls. All airplanes we had up to that time had external control locks. You slipped in a wedged piece of wood with red streamers to lock the aileron. The same way with the tail and the rudder. In the case of the X-299 Boeing decided to use internal locks. A plunger was activated by a small button—a two-inch movement was the difference between the controls locked and the controls unlocked. To unlock them, you just stepped on that thing, and it pulled all the pins that were inside the control surfaces. Always before I had thought to unlock the controls, but that morning I hadn't and neither had Hill. The main controls were fixed in such a position as to give us a nose high attitude on liftoff. Obviously the investigating board found it was pilot error. As a result of the accident there was a great hue and cry that an airplane of this size was just too much for the human being to handle, and the whole program almost got scuttled. It took a lot of effort to continue the program. We were under the War Department then, and there was an awful lot of pressure to cut it out."[3]

In September 1937 Putt entered the California Institute of Technology, earning his master's of science in aeronautical engineering. He returned to Wright Field in 1938 and was assigned to the Aircraft Projects Branch of the Materiel Division, where he continued to work in aircraft evaluation from the engineering perspective rather than doing any actual flying. He remained in engineering at Wright Field throughout the prewar years and most of the war years, as did Watson. While Watson worked on improving the performance of aircraft engines, Putt's focus was the general improvement of combat aircraft to give the men at the front lines the best possible flying equipment. "Most of the effort was really on model improvement, on upgrading the performance, and just solving some of the mumps and measles that kept occurring," Putt recalled.[4] He worked on the B-25 and the B-26 programs, and just before reporting to Europe, in December 1944, Putt was involved in a jet bomber design and selection project. When he departed Wright Field for Headquarters USSTAF (rear) in London he thought he was finished with that project.

On April 13, 1945, the Luftfahrtforschungsanstalt (LFA) Hermann Göring, the Hermann Göring Aeronautical Research Center, fell into American hands. By April 22 an ATI team from the USSTAF Exploitation Division led by Colonel Donald Putt arrived at Völkenrode to take control. Völkenrode, on the western outskirts of the city of

Braunschweig, hid in its dense forests seventy-six buildings ranging from munitions storage facilities to a structure that housed an eight-meter wind tunnel. Buildings were so carefully camouflaged that the few structures visible from the air appeared to be nothing more than innocent-looking farmsteads, endowed with the traditional stork's nest on the roof and surrounded by gardens, planted and harvested as any farm garden would have been. Colonel Putt recalled that, frequently when American planes landed on the three-thousand-foot sod strip at Völkenrode, "Pilots and passengers would inquire as to the location of the large research center they had heard so much about. They were greatly surprised when they learned that it was in the woods just off the edge of the field and that they had been flying over it but had not observed all of the man-made construction. The extent to which the Germans went to ensure concealment is evidenced by the fact that the design of some of the buildings, and particularly the large wind tunnels, had been influenced by the height of the trees which grew in the forest. In one instance the height of the wind tunnel slightly exceeded that of the tree height. In this case a large concrete platform had been built over the building on which several feet of earth had been placed and sod and trees planted, which blended well with the natural forest.[5]

"I moved in a housekeeping detail from one of the operational units and opened up a mess and quarters and things like that, and ran it like a little base." Putt had maps prepared, buildings named, and signs put up so people could find their way around. Heating, lighting, telephone, telegraph, and radio facilities were made operational or installed. The 9th Airdrome Squadron of the XXIX Tactical Air Command, 9th Air Force, was given the housekeeping duties for Völkenrode. Within days Putt had things running his way, and he could concentrate on what he had come for—the exploitation of the LFA and its scientists.

The LFA consisted of six independent institutes, equipped with "large quantities of the finest and most superb instruments and test equipment," Putt reported back to the Exploitation Division at St.-Germain.

Even the names of the institutes relayed the importance of what they were doing: the Aerodynamics Institute, the Gasdynamics Institute (Supersonic), the Statics Institute, the Engines Institute, the Special Engine Institute, and the Weapons Institute.

Professor Blank was administratively responsible for all six institutes, but each institute dealt directly with outside agencies on technical matters. This led to a curious situation whereby scientists in the varied institutes had no knowledge of what was going on in any other institute outside of their own, and as a result had no way of learning about progress made in their respective fields by others either within or outside the LFA.[6] Putt rounded up the German scientists who had gone into hiding. They "scattered all over the place, and buried documents and laboratory equipment in the forests, and we had to dig that stuff up," Putt observed. "One scientist had taken some things home and buried whatever it was on his property. With a little bit of persuasion, we got him to take us to his home. He took us out through the back door to a little toolshed at the back of a glassed-in hothouse where he grew his flowers and vegetables. The toolshed had a brick floor and he starts digging up the bricks, and digs a deep hole and comes out with some sealed tin cans that had formula for rocket fuel and things like that in it. There was a lot of laboratory equipment in addition to experimental items, like propulsion units and wind tunnel models. In fact, it was as a result of what we found there that the B-47 had swept-back wings. It appeared that it would be desirable to get some of this stuff back to Wright Field as quickly as possible."[7]

"During the period from 22 April to 10 June 1945, approximately seventy-five American and British scientific and technical personnel visited for varying periods of time," reported the Exploitation Division. "As a result of these investigations, 119 reports were written on the facilities, the research conducted there, and on the interrogation of many of the German scientists previously employed in the various institutes." Nearly five thousand scientific documents were retrieved from hiding places as far away as thirty miles from Völkenrode. Colonel Putt established a library and had the documents catalogued and photographed for later distribution to whoever was interested in the material and cleared to look at it. There were many who were interested, not the least of which was America's aviation industry. It was obvious to Don Putt that Völkenrode was unique. It was home to seven wind tunnels of varying sizes and speeds, allowing the study of the effects of swept-back wings on aircraft. A July 1945 status report from the Exploitation Division observed on the sweepback of wings, "The results of this research and development should be immediately applied to all jet propelled aircraft now under design as it is possible to increase the high speed from 50 to 75 m.p.h. before the detrimental effects of compressibility become serious." At the time many scientists still believed there was a sound barrier which could not be penetrated by manned aircraft. Hal Watson had written his master's thesis on that subject. But Dr. Busemann of the LFA had already devised successful wind tunnel techniques allowing him to study behavior of swept-wing aircraft models in the critical transitional region between Mach .8 and Mach 1.2. "Application of the same theory," the report continued, "to the design of propellers was being studied in order to increase their efficiency at high rotational and forward speeds." As an aeronautical engineer Putt immediately recognized that these findings were explosive stuff, probably the very thing needed for the jet bomber design evaluation he had been involved in before coming to Europe.

Other research projects undertaken at Völkenrode, and of immediate interest to the Army Air Forces, included the development of interference techniques and equipment which made the airflow around wings, streamlined bodies, or turbine blades under test conditions in a wind tunnel both visible and photographable. When photographs were taken, quantitative measurements could be made. "The German scientist in charge of this development had been working on it for the past ten years, whereas similar development in the United States had just barely started," the report noted. Dr. Theodor W. Zobel, Putt recalled, "had worked out a means of making airflow visible by the use of interferometry, which is actually using mirrors and optics" to make interference patterns visible. "He could make visible the airflow over a body in the wind tunnel. . . . One of the large pieces of equipment that we dismantled in the hours of darkness and hauled away from Völkenrode was this equipment, along with him and three or four of his assistants. That equipment was sent to Wright Field and was later put into operation there."[8]

Using Zobel's equipment and techniques, the Weapons Institute at the LFA had constructed a thirteen-hundred-foot underground tunnel "equipped with a series of stations at which projectiles being fired in the tunnel trip light and camera equipment, thus taking photographs of themselves in flight. This firing tunnel was capable of being evacuated to an altitude equivalent of approximately 98,000 feet," and could accommodate an 88 mm antiaircraft artillery projectile and depict the airflow around the projectile as it sped through the tunnel. "Another tunnel, 325 feet long, was provided for studying ballistics of projectiles when subjected to the effects of a crosswind . . . up to 350 to 400 miles per hour."[9] Professor Dr. Adolf Busemann had done "wind tunnel tests of compressor sections, little air foils," as early as 1934. "They were running what they called cascades where they put three or four of the compressor blades in the wind tunnel and measured the forces exerted on them."[10]

Another high-interest study dealt with "the use of ceramic materials in the manufacture of turbine and stationary turning blades. Although the Germans were forced to this development because of lack of high alloy steels, this work may lead to turbine designs which will permit operations at high gas inlet temperatures, thus improving the operating efficiency of turbo-jet engines," noted the Exploitation Division study. Other reports dealt with water cooling for turbine blades; rockets for use in flight-testing aircraft models at supersonic, transsonic, and subsonic speeds; nitrous oxide injection for aircraft engines to increase the horsepower available for limited periods of operation; the induction of multiple shock formations by artificial means so that they might be properly controlled; and research on rocket fuels and propellants "believed to be far more extensive than anything that has been undertaken in the United States."[11]

Don Putt decided that Dr. Theodore von Karman, General Arnold's scientific advisor and head of the Scientific Advisory Group, had to see this place before the British took over. Putt had first met Dr. von Karman in 1938 when he was studying for his master's degree at Cal Tech. They maintained a professional and personal relationship over the years until Dr. von Karman's death in 1963. In April 1945 Putt tracked him down at another location in Germany, and Dr. von Karman was all too glad to oblige. "Of course, von Karman was from Germany to start with," Putt noted. "Well, he was Hungarian, but he spent a number of years at the University of Aachen and had lots of German friends. So he had known Busemann before the war. In fact, he knew quite a number of the German scientists at this particular establishment.

"My one big job just before I went overseas in December 1944," Putt recalled, "was the running of the competition that had the B-45, B-46, B-47, and B-48 in it. All of them were straight-wing aircraft, very conventional looking except for hanging some engines on the wings that had no propellers on them. They were perhaps more streamlined and refined aerodynamically than prior aircraft, but basically they were pretty conventional designs. Boeing had presented a couple of configurations varying the placement of the engines, but it was still a straight wing." At Völkenrode, Putt's ATI team found wind tunnel models with swept-back wings, and he brought that discovery to the attention of Dr. von Karman. Dr. Busemann had been running those wind tunnel tests and Putt arranged a meeting between Busemann and von Karman. Also present at the meeting was the chief designer of the Boeing Aircraft Company, George Schairer. During the meeting von Karman asked Busemann, "Why the swept-wings?" Busemann explained in simple layman's terms that "by sweeping the wings you fooled the air into thinking that it was not going as fast as it really was, or not so fast as the airplane itself was moving through the atmosphere, and therefore, you delayed the onset of compressibility drag. When you get close to the speed of sound, drag just takes off and goes up like that [moving his hand up vertically], but by sweeping the wing back and fooling the molecules of air, they don't think they're going as fast, and you delay that great rise in the drag curve." Von Karman then asked Busemann, "How did you get this idea?" Busemann said, "Karman, don't you remember, at the Volta Congress in Rome in 1934 you gave a paper that gave me a suggestion for doing just that." "I remember," von Karman replied, slapping his forehead. "Oh, yes." Busemann and von Karman continued to talk, George Schairer listening. Immediately after the meeting, according to Putt, "Schairer wired Boeing and told them to hold up on the design that was to be the B-47 until he got home. When he got home they sat down and started all over again." As a result of the Busemann-von Karman meeting arranged by Colonel Donald Putt, and the fortuitous presence of George Schairer, the B-47 had swept-back wings, among many other innovative features. "We did build a few B-45s," Putt recalled, "which was a North American jet, and a lot of B-47s."[12] The B-47 bomber took the U.S. Air Force into the jet age, and it became the design baseline for the 707 airliner, which led to the KC-135 jet tanker and to subsequent Boeing Company commercial aircraft designs. The B-47 put Boeing on the road to becoming one of the world's premier military and commercial aircraft companies.[13]

Von Karman was impressed with what Putt had found at Völkenrode and wrote to General Arnold that "probably 75 to 90 per cent of the technical aeronautical information in Germany was available at this establishment and that information on research and development which had not previously been investigated in the United States would require approximately two years to accomplish in the United States

An RB-47E of the 91st Strategic Reconnaissance Wing, Lockbourne AFB, Ohio, refueling from a KC-97 tanker, 1954. (HA)

with the facilities available there." Von Karman further noted that "the information on jet engine developments available at this establishment would expedite the United States development by approximately six to nine months." This was important information for an Army Air Forces chief who was struggling with the introduction of America's first jet fighter, the P-80.[14]

But there were things not yet past the drafting board which were "probably more important than those immediately available in the form of models and production items." This presented a dilemma, because to take advantage of the ideas stored in the minds of creative scientists required that they be transported to Wright Field for practical work assignments.[15] The Exploitation Division boldly announced that "The following key scientists of this establishment [Völkenrode], each being considered preeminent in his field, are being returned to the United States for further interrogation and exploitation by American scientists of comparable status: Professor Adolf Busemann, Dr. Theodor Zobel, Engineer Bock, Engineer Rister [both assistants to Dr. Zobel],

Dr. Guderley, Dr. Braun, Dr. Schmidt, Dr. Wolfgang Nöggerath, Dr. Edse, Dr. Schugt, and Professor Rossman."[16] The Exploitation Division's unilateral decision unfortunately found little resonance in Washington, and the German *Wissenschaftler* were in for a long and uncertain wait.

Völkenrode was a scientific gold mine and it was in the British zone of occupation. Putt decided to "midnight-requisition" as much of the equipment as he possibly could before the British took over. "I had a little airline of my own, one B-24 and one B-17. The trick was to get whatever test equipment and documentation out of the place without the British noticing. As soon as everybody was in bed and the lights were out, we'd spring into action. There was an airfield just across town, and with trucks we'd haul this stuff over there, and quickly load it on my B-17 or B-24. By the time people woke up the next morning, they were at Lakenheath or in Ireland refueling to get to Wright Field. So I had these two airplanes shuttling back and forth. This went on for some time until the British caught on. At the Potsdam Conference [July 17 to August 2] the British threw this up to General Arnold. Of course, I'm sure he must have pleaded ignorance."

In early June 1945 General Knerr showed up at Völkenrode and informed Putt that " 'I've got orders to go back to Wright Field and take command. I'd like to have you back there. In addition, I think we'd better get you out of here.' Knerr knew what I was doing; there was no question about it. In fact, he had approved it. Very shortly after that I departed for Wright Field." In October "I was at the Northrop Company," Putt explained. "I arrived in the morning, and Jack Northrop said to me, 'Gee, General Arnold is coming in this morning also.' I said, Well, that will be interesting. I didn't know about the Potsdam incident at the time. We were already out on the factory floor looking at something, when General Arnold arrived. Jack Northrop introduced me and said, 'You know Colonel Putt?' General Arnold said, 'Oh, yes, I know him all right,' and then he told them about Potsdam." The British had complained bitterly to him about Colonel Donald Putt appropriating all of their "stuff" and flying it out of Völkenrode in the dark of night.[17]

Unknown to Putt at Völkenrode was that another wind tunnel of even greater dimensions than those at the LFA had been located by a CIOS/CAFT team at Kochel. Kochel, a picturesque Bavarian town at the north end of the Kochelsee, just a skip and a jump northeast of Garmisch-Partenkirchen, was host to the Aerodynamische-Ballistische-Versuchsanstalt Kochelsee, which in 1945 accommodated the extraordinary Peenemünde wind tunnel. The station and the tunnel were discovered by a CAFT team on May 15. Colonel James J. Stone, the USSTAF Exploitation Divison liaison officer at Headquarters XII TAC in Darmstadt, learned of the find within minutes of its discovery. Grasping the importance of the situation, Stone immediately tasked XII TAC to dispatch a team of officers and men to Kochel to guard the all-important wind tunnel. The XII TAC had a team of 130 officers and men at nearby Holzkirchen, only a few kilometers east of Kochel, and immediately complied with Stone's request.[18]

The wind tunnel had been built between 1937 and 1939 at the RLM test facility at Peenemünde and was subsequently moved to Kochel after British and American air raids against Peenemünde in late summer 1943. The tunnel was used to test ram jet experiments and the Me-163 rocket plane, the A4/V-2 ballistic missile, and the Wasserfall surface-to-air missile. The tunnel was superior to any other tunnel in Germany, including those at the LFA in Völkenrode and others found at the University of Aachen research center and at the Kaiser Wilhelm Institut at Göttingen. American scientists were quickly dispatched to Kochel to examine the tunnel. They reported that "Not only does this wind tunnel have the largest testing sections of any known supersonic wind tunnel, and the greatest airflow [the maximum being 4.4 times the speed of sound], but plans have already been completed whereby large increases in air speed can be obtained by using compressors with tremendous suction capacities. These compressors are already at Kochel and would provide not only phenomenal air flow speeds but would also increase the duration of testing time from the present possible 35 seconds to a possible continuous operation. The measuring apparatus used in this installation is also without equal in Germany." The report continued, "Another important part of this installation is the air drying apparatus. Because dry air is essential for supersonic testing, research in the supersonic test section of the wind tunnel at the Hermann Göring Institute at Völkenrode was limited by the lack of such apparatus."

The importance of the Peenemünde tunnel for research on long-range rockets, jet-powered swept-wing aircraft, and transsonic and supersonic experimentation was immediately grasped, and steps were taken to begin the process of dismantling the tunnel and shipping it to the United States. The uniqueness of the tunnel produced an active level of "competition between the U.S. Navy, U.S. Ordnance, and USSTAF teams" for its ultimate location in the United States. "From the point of view of Army Air Forces, it is considered of exceptional importance for research in connection with jet fighter and fighter bomber priority projects" argued the air staff in Washington.[19] The U.S. Navy felt it had equally important test requirements.

A United States Navy Technical Mission in Europe report of June 1945 was ecstatic about the value of the Kochel wind tunnel. Wrote Professor Zwicky, "The Peenemünde supersonic wind tunnel has been in operation for over five years and the scientists and operators involved have gained invaluable experience in operating the tunnel and the great number of measuring instruments. The specific work done covers . . . fin stabilized rockets [and] resulted in the successful completion of the V-2(A4) rocket. Stable and controllable flight paths with velocities up to 5000 feet/sec were thus achieved for the first time. . . . The work on the 'Wasserfall' resulted in the first wing-borne, jet propelled and fin stabilized missile to fly in a stable and controllable manner through the whole range of subsonic, transsonic and supersonic speeds up to Mach numbers 2.5–3.0. . . . The work on the interrelations between an exhaust jet and the aerodynamic characteristics of a rocket propelled missile opens up new and important vistas on the possibility of materially lowering the intrinsic aerodynamic drag of bodies flying at supersonic speeds." Dr. Fritz Zwicky was a professor at the California Institute of Technology and a member of Dr. von Karman's SAG. Zwicky conjectured that the basic information for the launching, stabilization, and control of heavy rockets over ranges of several hundred miles was now available, and supersonic, wing-borne, and jet-propelled controllable missiles of the Wasserfall type promised to be of utmost importance. Dr. Zwicky estimated "that about three years may be gained in the development of the missiles mentioned if the Peenemünde supersonic wind tunnel were evacuated along with key German personnel. If the tunnel is moved to the United States, provisions should be made to have projects of the Bureau of Aeronautics, the Bureau of Ordnance, and the Army Air Forces handled by the supersonic tunnel in question. This tunnel, with the working sections, is now capable of running semi-continuously at Mach numbers below 3.9 with each section in intermittent operation. However, if two additional compressors (in storage at the Kochel railway station) are installed, the tunnel can be run continuously at Mach numbers greater than 3.9."[20] Zwicky's recommendation to make the tunnel available to multiple users helped defuse the contentious situation that had arisen between the U.S. Navy and the Army Air Forces over control of the tunnel. It was subsequently agreed that the tunnel would be installed at the Naval Ordnance Facility at White Oak, Maryland, where everyone would get a chance to use it.

Something that had already become an issue at Völkenrode again became one at Kochel—the fact that removal of the hardware alone would not yield satisfactory results. To get the most out of this extraordinary wind tunnel in the shortest possible time would require that the scientists who designed and operated the tunnel accompany it to the United States. As in the case of the scientists at Völkenrode, the Exploitation Division, this time supported by the Navy Technical Mission, initiated action to move twenty of the German specialists to the United States, including Dr. Rudolph Hermann, the director of the wind tunnel, to assist in reassembly and tunnel operation. The problem was that there was no existing program for bringing large numbers of German scientists, enemy aliens, to the United States so soon after war's end. The need for such a program was obvious to military officers and American scientists deeply involved in the exploitation process, but not necessarily to others in distant Washington, D.C.

Individual Germans, such as Oberleutnant Schumann, were brought to the United States on a case-by-case basis. Schumann was flown on June 23, 1945, to Washington National Airport to assist in the evaluation of documentation on weaponry furnished by Germany to Japan. Schumann's evacuation to the United States was an act in support of the war effort against Japan, and in that way quite different from the situation faced by the Völkenrode and Kochel scientists. Heinz Weber, the Japanese language interpreter, had also been moved to the United States on May 18, 1945, to assist in a similar task.[21] Traveling on the same plane with Heinz Weber was Professor Herbert Wagner, chief missile design engineer for the Henschel Company, and two of his assistants. Wagner designed the Hs 293 air-to-ground antiship missile, a rocket-assisted glide bomb, which had been used successfully against Allied shipping in the Mediterranean and the Bay of Biscay. The Navy put up Wagner and his team on the 160-acre Gould estate at Sands Point, Long Island, to assist in the development of an American version of the Hs 293 for use against the Japanese.[22] Again, it was a move in direct support of the war against Japan. Other than POWs, no large groups of Germans had ever been moved to the United States for a lengthy stay to work on America's most advanced and secret technical projects.

Once the requirement for bringing German scientists to the United States was justified in Washington by the War and Navy Departments, Project Overcast emerged as a compromise solution to allow the entrance of enemy aliens for a period not to exceed two years. Project Overcast became a vehicle for bringing to the United States not only the Völkenrode scientists and Kochel wind tunnel experts but also large numbers of German scientists held under indefinite detention at various locations in Germany to keep them out of the grasp of the Russians, including Dr. von Braun's large V-2 rocket design team.

On his way home to the United States to assume a new position under General Knerr at Wright Field, Colonel Putt was unaware of the important role he was to play in Project Overcast.

12

THE FEUDIN' 54TH

While the Air Technical Intelligence and CIOS/CAFT teams garnered most of the glory in their search and discovery of Nazi technological treasure, they would not have succeeded without the support provided by the disarmament squadrons. The disarmament squadrons provided everything the ATI teams didn't have or couldn't do for themselves— trucks, jeeps, food, tents, skilled and unskilled labor, any number of items and services required for large and small projects. Both teams and squadrons worked hand in glove to strip Nazi Germany of its technological treasure.

The 54th Air Disarmament Squadron, one of ten such squadrons formed under the umbrella of the 9th Air Force Service Command Disarmament Division, came into being in December 1944. Other squadrons had been forming since October, when the conversion of aircrew replacement training squadrons into disarmament squadrons was first authorized by General Spaatz. The men of the newly designated 54th ADS struggled with their new identity, having no clear idea what the term disarmament implied. The men felt unprepared for a task they didn't understand and had not been trained for. They wanted to continue training aircrew replacements, not knowing that those days were gone, never to return. Their new assignment, however, recognized and drew on their varied technical skills as well as their language abilities, present in most American combat units. They were all young men in their teens or early twenties, whose backgrounds were as varied as the nation they came from. Their names spoke volumes as to their heritage—Freiburger, Berkowitz, Cummings, Kadansky, Maxwell, Smith, Brown, Jones, Fiedler, Hanclosky, Higgins, Ninneman, Harasmisz, Preston. Some had a high school education; most didn't. Some spoke German, Polish, Hungarian, or another European language; some spoke more than one language, useful skills, as it would turn out, for their new and still ill-defined tasks. They were innovative and creative; they groused at the arbitrariness of Army life; they would in time lament the nonfraternization policies imposed by old men who didn't seem to understand the needs of the young.

The men of the 54th ADS all knew, though, why they had come to England. One of the first things nearly every one of them had done upon his initial assignment to a double-decker bunk stuffed into a crowded Quonset hut was to hang a calendar above his bed and begin marking off the days. Going home became the goal. (Actually, hanging a calendar may have been the second thing the new arrivals did. The first probably was to put up a picture of a bathing-suit-clad Esther Williams, a 1940s pinup girl.) Although they were airmen, they were in the Army Air Forces and wore brown uniforms like any "dogface" in an infantry platoon. When they eventually deployed from England to France, they wore helmets, carried M1A1 carbines or M1 rifles, .45 caliber pistols for the officers, along with their A bags slung over their shoulders. When seen from a distance, they looked just like any other group of dogfaces.

In December 1944 the 54th ADS historian, an additional duty levied on the most junior lieutenant in the squadron, was 1st Lieutenant Robert L. Smith. Smith did a commendable job of recording the human side of war. "The squadron received a new birth beginning with this month," Lieutenant Smith noted. "Till that memorable day we were the 3rd Replacement and Training Squadron, but now all our personnel in addition to the old designation are placed on duty with the 54th Air Disarmament Squadron (Provisional). This double identity causes difficulty to many of us in understanding exactly what we are, but our hands are tied until the 'Provisional' is removed from our name and we legally come into existence." The lieutenant's lament was all too understandable—the troops on the line often were never told about the little details which shaped the routines of their military existence. Lieutenant Smith also had no idea that the 54th would never again function as a replacement and training squadron, and that the PROVISIONAL appended to their new unit designator was a fact of life which provided for their squadron's demise upon completion of their newly assigned task—the disarmament of the Luftwaffe.

Personnel turnover in the 54th, as in nearly every other combat unit, whether fighter, bomber, or ground support, was constant and at times heavy. "The job of adjusting our personalities to each other" and learning new duties was "a great one," explained Smith. At the same time the unit was experiencing an influx of new people and the departure of old friends, they shifted to a new location, Army Air Forces Station number 162, APO 639, at Chipping Ongar. Everything was a secret, even the name of their station and its associated APO number. There was an upside to the move. "Now we have only a short walk to the Officer's Mess," exalted Smith. He noted with tongue-in-cheek humor that "The movement itself wasn't carried out in an orderly manner. This is usual for the Army. The trouble seemed to lie in that the unit commanders involved didn't take proper charge of their men being transferred. As a result a few were 'lost' and others took the liberty of going AWOL for a few days. Nothing serious though."

On the fifth of December, the 54th held its first formation at the new location and formed four new platoons. The first platoon was assigned to Master Sergeant Eugene E. Freiburger. Freiburger was initially assigned to a B-26 Marauder Combat Crew Training

Squadron in Northern Ireland and later transferred to the B-17 CCTS, which had now become the 54th ADS. On the twenty-first of December, unit training was implemented for all four platoons as defined by Headquarters, 2nd Air Disarmament Wing, the wing to which they were assigned along with four other squadrons—the 52nd, 53rd, 55th, and 56th. Keeping the men occupied and tired was the order of the day for the officers and the sergeants. The four platoon sergeants, the squadron commander, Captain Ernest L. Hubbard, and his operations officer, Captain Zenneth D. Ward, decided that Thursdays would be unit training days when the men would practice infantry drills. On every Saturday morning they had a parade, just the way it was done in a peacetime garrison. Nothing in their daily activities had the smell of war about it; it was garrison life at its worst. The squadron's first sergeant, Master Sergeant Brown, when looking at his bunch of spitting and scratching GIs, conferred upon them their new name—Feudin' 54th.

"The meaning of feudin' is that we have clashes amongst ourselves due to men coming from various units on the station rather than feudin' with the other squadrons," Sergeant Brown explained. By Christmas the Feudin' 54th finally worked itself into a holiday spirit. "On Christmas day morale reached a new high," Lieutenant Smith reported, "when we entertained about three hundred kids from the towns of Romford, Ongar, Chelmsford and Brentwood. Some of the youngsters were bombed out of their homes recently and sure deserved a good break for the Holidays. They seemed to have enjoyed their Christmas turkey dinner with ice cream, and the entertainment and presents that followed." A collection was taken up to bring together nine-year old Jimmy Osborne, "a blind pianist who played very often in the Aero Club, with the famous blind pianist, Alec Templeton. All the other squadrons on the station also contributed to help him get a good musical education as he is very talented." December 1944 came to a close with a focus on what was really important to everyone, regardless of rank—going home. "The rotation plan for sending wor-thy applicants back to the States was welcomed and the First Sergeant was given the GI rush to get those applications in." To remind every-one that they were still in the Army, Lieutenant Smith concluded the squadron history for December 1944 with this somber notation: "We passed the parade with flying colors but bigger and better ones are in store for us in the coming year."[1]

January passed wet and cold, miserable as only an English January could be. In February Lieutenant Smith reported rampant rumors of an impending move to the "far shore. This, as a consequence meant a great deal of work for Air Corps Supply personnel and a lot of the equipment was being flown to France." The men continued with their Thursday training activities and Saturday parades. Basketball was added as a new activity to keep a restless bunch of GIs busy. In the ensuing tournament, the 54th team, led by Master Sergeant Freiburger, emerged victorious over everyone except the other two air disarmament squadrons on station. "A most disappointing outcome," Lieutenant Smith lamented. The "stirring" news came that their APO number had been changed from 639 to 149. There was one event the men truly put their hearts into—the GI carnival. The carnival was held for the purpose of "obtaining supplemental funds for Jimmy Osborne, the nine year old blind pianist." Lieutenant Smith reported gleefully that "Many of the fellows enjoyed it immensely even though they did walk away from the Aero Club 'pound less.' "

There were official clothing inspections and warnings to get rid of extra clothing or anything else that didn't fit into an A bag. Then "Captain Hubbard filled our training days with lectures on infantry maneuvers. This was all new to most of us, never-the-less just what we needed as we did not yet definitely know what we might run into on the continent." Each man in the outfit fired his weapon on the rifle range "getting the 'feel' for it." And then there was an endless string of training films on personal health and hygiene, water purification, and numerous other subjects. The highlight of the film festival was without doubt the movie which provided in boring detail the army's official explanation of why and how to properly use a pro-kit. On that stirring note the month of February ended for the 54th ADS.[2] On March 13, 1945, the Feudin' 54th was trucked to the port of Southampton for movement to the Continent. It was five o'clock in the morning when the groggy troops dismounted from their trucks, lined up, and marched three miles to an empty warehouse where they were ordered to wait for further instructions. They ate C and K rations for breakfast, and a mobile Red Cross unit served hot coffee and doughnuts. "Some of the fellows secured food from the sailors," reported Lieutenant Smith. "One of them came across with two large containers of flap-jacks."

Late in the morning of the thirteenth the order came down to board the French Liberty ship *Antenor*. "All men of our Squadron were assigned to duties on the ship during the trip and within a short time all were at their posts. We set sail in the early afternoon of the 13th of March. . . . At 1245 hours on the following day, an announcement came over the ship's tannoy that we were to prepare to disembark by landing craft. . . . Shortly after 1400 hours, our squadron filed down the gangway onto an LST [landing ship tank], carrying our full equipment and A bags." Once loaded, the LST set off for Le Havre, several miles east of the *Antenor*'s anchorage. They landed on the beach just like the GIs of June 6, 1944, disgorging from their crowded craft carrying carbines, ammunition pouches, and A bags—with the important difference that no one was shooting at them. "We carried our A bags for a mile and a half into the battered city of Le Havre where troop trucks were lined up to transport us to transient Camp X, a distance of about forty five miles" from Rouen. The tired and weary men reached Camp X at ten-thirty that night, where they moved into tents, took advantage of the hot chow, and then hit the sack. "Our stay at Camp X was alright and we enjoyed sunny weather which was quite different from our past months and years in the United Kingdom. Our days were routine there and we were given liberty time in the evenings until 2300 hours."

Camp X was to be their home for five days, after which the men again loaded onto trucks and in a convoy of considerable length, joined by the men of the 52nd ADS, were driven back to the railroad station in Rouen. "At Rouen we boarded freight cars and drew C rations for a two day journey to Luneville. We slept as best we could in the box cars and had breakfast of C-rations when awakened. We remained in the marshaling yard until early afternoon." The train arrived in Nancy at 0100 hours in the early morning hours of March 21. In Nancy "we were side tracked until the afternoon. We were able to secure water to wash up and also get a bit of exercise. Some of the boys wandered too far to get drinks from a bar and Captain Ward restricted them to the inside of the box car." Not until late that afternoon did a new locomotive show up. Upon arrival in Luneville they disembarked, stiff, dirty, and tired of having been in the same uniform for days. Once more they mounted waiting trucks for a brief and bumpy journey to their final destination—A96, Ochey airfield, near Toul.

Ochey turned out to be another tent city. "The fellows started fixing up their tents with all the modern conveniences the wilderness afforded. About the most difficult feat as far as personal cleanliness went was the way you'd have to take a bath in your helmet. This type of bath was very appropriately nicknamed by some in words just a little too harsh for usage here. Plans were eventually drawn up and equipment procured for the building of a shower house, but alas, word of it must have gotten out because it was no sooner started that we again received word to move."[3] Smith's report continued, "Everything was packed quite hurriedly the night of April 3, and on April 4, at 0845 hours" the squadron departed for Darmstadt, arriving at a former German airfield late that afternoon. Immediately upon arrival, details

Camp X was like any other Army camp in the forward area—tents filled with cots and blankets. It beat a foxhole every time. (JH)

were appointed to clean out their living quarters, "a barracks once occupied by Jerries." Though the Germans had apparently left in a hurry, "most of the utilities and facilities on the field were damaged. The amateur plumbers and electricians had a field day improvising," reported Captain Ward, the 54th ADS operations officer. In the following days the men settled in "even to the extent of Sgt. McClure repairing the water system and firing up the boilers to give us hot showers."

Captain Ward recalled that "The first disarmament job was to recover an intact Me-262 aircraft located at Giebelstadt Airfield. As soon as the plane was dismantled a C-46 flew in and took the result of our labors to Bovingdon, England. . . . The main activities of the squadron while at Darmstadt were at Auerbach and Neckarelz. The former was an underground factory for the manufacture of gyroscopes for automatic pilots, the latter was the largest underground engine factory in Germany. This factory produced Daimler-Benz aircraft engines. As the disarmament procedures had not crystallized, all the squadron was able to do was to inventory these factories and to check for Red and Blue List material." By the nineteenth of April the men of the 54th had achieved a high level of comfort in their new surroundings at Darmstadt, but they were again ordered to relocate, this time to Mosbach. Mosbach was a little town about eighty-five miles southeast of Darmstadt, just on the east side of the Neckar River, which flowed in a big bend from north to west, past Heidelberg into the Rhine River at Mannheim. The move was made the following day with the use of squadron trucks which shuttled back and forth between Darmstadt and Mosbach. Target folders were passed out to inspect and disarm diverse targets ranging from a GAF radar installation at Eppingen to an experimental wind tunnel at Rothenburg, from jet engines at Acholshausen to a furniture factory near Bamberg which had been converted into a salvage and testing plant. There was a supply warehouse near Wertheim, and an aircraft brake and wheel factory at Brombach. A squadron of twelve Bf 109s was discovered near Nassig, and the airfield at Schwabisch Hall "was almost completely demolished by the terrific aerial bombardment of the Allied Air Forces," reported the inspection team assigned to that location. In a railroad tunnel near Wertheim they found stored aircraft wings. "The main effort was spent on unraveling the Me-109 complex at Wertheim. The Mannheim Me-109 plant had been bombed, so the remaining machine tools had been dispersed around Wertheim. Here it was a matter of locating machine shops in breweries, barns, etc. Work was also done on the airfield at Schwabisch Hall, a German salvage yard at Odenheim, and several railroad tunnels converted into machine shops. As at Darmstadt, our activities were restricted to inventory and collecting of items of technical intelligence interest."[4]

At Mosbach the 54th ADS was housed in a requisitioned apartment house and two adjoining private homes. "The place had more or less become home to us," wrote Smith, so when orders were received to move to Augsburg, the men were "not too elated." However, "orders were orders."⁵ They loaded up early on the morning of May 4, using their own trucks, and after "a very scenic journey," according to the historian, they arrived at their new base of operation—Lager Lechfeld. Smith's commander, Captain Hubbard, saw the trip a little differently, writing, "This move was made difficult by the number of other army vehicles on the road following the final drive into the redoubt area [the Alps]. Traffic was further snarled by the masses of Displaced Persons on the move."⁶

The other nine disarmament squadrons of the 1st and 2nd Air Disarmament Wings moved into Germany alongside the 54th ADS. The squadrons' experiences and problems were largely similar.

The 20th Air Disarmament Squadron was assigned to the 1st Air Disarmament Wing, and was tasked to move east into German territory that would in time revert to the Russians. "From the city of Frankfurt we moved to this quiet city of Mühlhausen in Thuringia," the 20th ADS historian, First Lieutenant Charles J. Klingman, recorded. "This community for some reason was left untouched by bombing; in fact, in traveling around the vicinity only one house has been noticed destroyed by bombs. We found the Germans here going to great lengths to be friendly with our troops. They all seemed relieved that the war was over for them and the occupation troops were Americans. Our allies, the Russians, were held in mortal fear by most of the people. The local AMG officials told many of our officers that residents were in, every day, inquiring if the American troops were to remain.

"One of the interesting visitors we had was Bill Jack of 'Jack and Heintz,' a large manufacturing concern in the States. He was interested in locating where the famous German 'Patin Automatic Pilots' were made and it was our intelligence officer, 1st Lt. David H. Jenkins III, who was able to supply him with this information. The automatic pilot was made here near Mühlhausen in an underground factory. Four complete automatic pilots were taken by Mr. Jack back to the United States."

An aerial view of Lager Lechfeld reveals extensive bomb damage. The large hangar in the center was where the 54th ADS set up shop to refurbish Watson's Me-262s. (RB)

High on the list of complaints for officers and enlisted men alike was the nonfraternization policy. Noted Lieutenant Klingman, "The present policy of fraternization is rather difficult for men who having been stationed so long in France and England find it hard to avoid pretty girls. The locality here is governed by Major General Oliver, Commanding General, Fifth Armored Division. It is his policy to allow association with Displaced Persons; however, this is impossible for us as our group has required a strict policy of avoiding all civilians in accordance with Ninth Air Force instructions and enforced by our own unit." Nonfraternization was more or less enforced by American commanders as war approached its end, causing those men serving under overly zealous officers to be resentful and to look for ways to circumvent the policy. American ingenuity was not to be denied, and the policy soon collapsed through massive noncompliance.

The July 1945 history for the 20th ADS noted that "Our residence in Mühlhausen ... was to be terminated in early July. The Russian Zone of Occupation included Mühlhausen and both the American Forces and a large number of civilians were leaving prior to the scheduled arrival of the Russians on 4 July 1945. The advance party of 18 Russian Officers arrived on 3 July 1945, and immediately demonstrated their well-known unlimited capacity for Cognac and other more volatile liquids. They were a jolly crew and we had a brief 'good will' party on our last day in Mühlhausen. The move to Fulda was accomplished in the approved manner ... and the bulk of the squadron arrived at Fulda on 4 July." The squadron was billeted in a bomb-damaged area of a large post. Living conditions, initially at least, were reported to be unsatisfactory, especially regarding washing and toilet facilities. But then the solution to the problems presented itself. "Now that we were in enemy territory there was no need to 'stand short' in the comforts of home. The enemy could and would provide these. New washing, showering and kitchen facilities were built with civilian labor." It was not only the facilities problem that was quickly resolved but also the nonfraternization dilemma. Fulda had displaced persons, and the men quickly took advantage of that opportunity. Russian and Polish girls were hired to work in the mess hall and to maintain the quarters. "The chatter of female voices sounded good even though we couldn't understand them," recorded Lieutenant Klingman. Doc Huntsberger set up his office and continued to give his periodic venereal disease lectures. The long-promised liberal-leave policy was implemented at last, and "officers and men visited Ireland, Scotland, England, Paris, Brussels and the Riviera. The leave center at Creil, 23 miles north of Paris, was officially opened and the officers and men were able to see a little bit more of Montmartre, Place Pigalle, and the Eiffel Tower."[7]

The 21st Air Disarmament Squadron, also a part of the 1st Air Disarmament Wing, moved on April 20 from its base in Boulange,

France, to Rhein-Main airfield. The squadron immediately initiated disarmament operations in the assigned target areas. Typical targets were abandoned airfields and dispersed factories manufacturing the necessities of war up to the day they were overrun by American troops. Lieutenant Harry Eissner led his team onto an abandoned German airfield on May 1, and reported that "It was in fair condition with no GAF personnel and 26 aircraft of various types." On May 3, Lieutenant Johnson inspected an airfield and repair depot at Stodten. "There were 2,500 various types of aircraft engines, 16 hangars and buildings full of aircraft parts, 40 88 mm AA guns and many AAA parts. This field is being guarded by AAF personnel," Johnson reported after moving on to another target at Lauringen, where he discovered warehouses filled with aircraft parts and "an Me-109 assembly plant." On May 15 Lieutenant McNamara led a team onto an airfield near Oschersleben. There he discovered a large quantity of gasoline which he turned over to American Military Government representatives. In addition McNamara's team found "thirty-four FW 190 fighters, and all the necessary parts for the assembly of an additional fifty FW 190 aircraft. There was some damage to all aircraft on the field," he reported, "done by pillaging U.S. troops." The 21st ADS, like its sister squadrons, found nonfraternization a burden. "Due to General Eisenhower's Non-Fraternization rule there were no social activities as all people in this area outside of the U.S. Army are either enemy civilians or displaced persons. There were of course," the historian reported candidly, "the usual Army poker and crap games, soft-ball and volley-ball."[8] Getting around nonfraternization policies varied from ADS squadron to ADS squadron, depending on how adept each squadron's commander was at interpreting the restrictive and often conflicting policies and orders issued by various commanders. Everyone quickly learned to abide by the least restrictive orders.

The history of the 52nd Air Disarmament Squadron reflects the close cooperation between air disarmament squadrons and ATI teams.

On May 1, 1945, the squadron departed from Karlsruhe for its new duty station at Nellingen airfield. "On our arrival there," wrote the squadron historian, First Lieutenant Charles L. Pemix, "we found that the field had been plowed up and that there were furrows running all over the landing strip. This strip was immediately repaired and made suitable for landing of C-47's and other transient aircraft." The barracks at Nellingen were in fair condition "but were cluttered with trash which the enlisted men soon cleaned out. All the men agreed that it was a nice place, and in a few days after our arrival the field had taken on a perspective of an American air base." The 52nd ADS was assigned to the 2nd Air Disarmament Wing as were the 54th, 55th, and 56th ADS. The 52nd set up a depot at Nellingen where USSTAF Air Technical Intelligence teams collected items of interest and had them sorted and packed for subsequent shipment to the United Kingdom or the Zone of Interior. The 52nd formed support teams which accompanied ATI teams into the field. "On the 18th of May 1945, we departed Nellingen airfield for Kirchheim, Germany, by motor convoy and on arrival there, proceeded to set up and continue operations for and with Air Technical Intelligence. We were housed in a large hotel which was a former resident hotel. The conditions which existed at this new station were ideal and everyone liked this assignment. Clubs were opened both for the officers and enlisted men. A swimming pool was . . . filled and swimming parties were started every evening, weather permitting." Their idyllic existence soon came to an end as the squadron was again transferred to a new location.[9]

The 56th Air Disarmament Squadron, like all the other squadrons, was constantly on the move. Between May 9 and May 31 the squadron moved from Ellwangen to Munich-Riem airfield, then to Göppingen and again back to Ellwangen. "May was a beautiful month with little rain and plenty of sunshine," rejoiced an unidentified historian. "Most officers and enlisted men took advantage of the tropical sunshine and many acquired suntans which would meet with wide-eyed approval by their wives or sweethearts. Sun bathing, swimming, and other outdoor sports helped tremendously toward keeping everyone in good physical condition." Although there appeared to have been plenty of time to take in some rays, the men did their jobs as the tasking arrived from the Exploitation Division through the 9th Air Force Service Command. "The total number of targets visited during the month was 67. Most unusual of these targets was the Holzkirchen Flugplatz, where one of our teams stumbled upon a Nazi lair which had previously surrendered formally to General Barcus of the 12th [XII] TAC [part of the 1st Tactical Air Force]. It consisted of 71 officers and 360 enlisted men plus an additional 8 alleged WACS of the ill-fated Luftwaffe. Members of this squadron were assigned the task of guarding these prisoners until further disposition could be made."[10] A very different target was the discovery of "a dummy airfield made entirely of wood with wooden airplanes dispersed about the field. It is rumored that the British 'bombed' this place with wooden bombs."[11]

"On 7 May, at 1441 hours," the 55th Air Disarmament Squadron historian recorded, "news of the end of the hostilities in Europe and the complete unconditional surrender of the German forces on land, in the air and on the sea was received in the squadron; not with any calamity, but rather with an almost unbelievable calmness. This news, which we had been waiting to hear for such a long time, came so sudden that it had an odd effect on everyone; an effect which might be considered as leaving everyone stunned. Of course there was a little celebration, but for the most part everyone accepted the news as if it were just the end of another campaign, which in reality it was, for there still remains another battle to end; the one which is raging on the other side of the world, among the treacherous islands of the South Pacific." The historian lamented, "The end of the war in Europe brought with it the problem of keeping everyone occupied in such a way that thoughts of home would not prey upon their minds to too great an extent. . . . During May, five enlisted men were granted furloughs to the United Kingdom. Such furloughs came as a welcome surprise, in as much as the non-fraternization regulations became quite an imposition on all personnel of the squadron and any chance to mingle again with the citizens of an allied country was quickly grasped." The 55th history concluded, "The end of May arrived; a month which saw the end of the Nazi rule in Germany; a month which we had been looking forward to with great anticipation."[12]

As for the Feudin' 54th, on May 4 they occupied the main headquarters building of the Messerschmitt Aircraft Company at Lager Lechfeld. "After a good deal of work on our part, with the assistance of Krauts obtained from the American Military Government, we had things fairly organized, including showers," reflected Lieutenant Smith. Without leaving their assigned squadron area, the men found an abundance of work to do on the Messerschmitt factory premises. "Documents were located in the building, covering all phases of activity of the Me [Messerschmitt] Corporation. Contracts with Japan, experimental data on the Me-163 and Me-262 aircraft, plans for new underground factories and complete data on the Enzian Flak Rocket were uncovered. These documents were screened by the squadron interpreters" and subsequently turned over to CIOS and ATI teams.[13]

At Lager Lechfeld, a few miles south of Augsburg, the 54th counted fifty Me-262 jet fighters, many of them damaged beyond repair by rampaging GIs as they swept through the airfield in late April.[14] Recalled Sergeant Freiburger, "Lechfeld was a sight to behold. There were approximately thirty-five jets the infantry had shot full of holes, hit with their tanks or bulldozed off to the side—really tore them up." Freiburger became even more chagrined over this level of destruction when he learned that he and his team of men had been selected to recover up to fifteen of these unique jets for a colonel by the name of

One of more than fifty Me-262 jets scattered about Lager Lechfeld. This one, with its 30 mm cannon shells littering the foreground, would never fly again. (DF)

Watson. Among the many German aircraft the 54th ADS found at Lechfeld were several Heinkel 219 Uhu night fighters and Focke-Wulf 190 day fighters, as well as a number of Heinkel 177 Greif four-engine bombers. German aircraft continued to fly into Lechfeld to surrender. A late model Ju-88G-6 night fighter with *Hirschgeweih* antennae protruding from its nose arrived in broad daylight on May 7. The aircraft came from NJG 100, which operated against the Russians in the east. The German aircrew, flying in from Saaz, Czechoslovakia, had painted out the *Balkenkreuz* on the aircraft's fuselage with a four-pointed star looking much like the current NATO star. Its crew had no desire to surrender to the Russians, and instead chose to surrender to the Americans, from whom they expected more lenient treatment.[15] At Lager Lechfeld, among the wreckage of a once-proud Luftwaffe, Colonel Watson's interests converged with those of the 54th Air Disarmament Squadron.

WATSON PICKS HIS TEAM

Colonel Watson had been busily planning for the recovery of the German jets since his reassignment in late March from the 1st Tactical Air Force Service Command at Vittel back to Headquarters USSTAF in St.-Germain. Watson was attached to McDonald's Intelligence Directorate, making his home in the Exploitation Division when it was formed in late April. Watson had about as free a hand to do as he saw fit as any man could want. No one required him to give an accounting of his day-to-day activities, nor did anyone specifically ask how he was going to go about finding and delivering the German jets he had been tasked to obtain. In later years, long after his retirement from the Air Force, Hal Watson would reflect on this period of his life and say, "Those were my wild years."

Since its formation, the Exploitation Divison had grown by leaps and bounds as the disarmament function began to assume increasing importance and combat support requirements diminished to zero. Under Operation Lusty the division broadly defined its mission as the exploitation of the German aircraft research and industrial establishment to derive all possible technical intelligence to further the prosecution of the war against Japan. The Exploitation Division viewed its second priority, which soon became its first and primary objective, as increasing the overall efficiency of American aircraft equipment and the support of ongoing research and development efforts. "The success of this operation will be measured by the quality and amount of intelligence which is expeditiously delivered to the U.S."—that was the standard the division established for itself. No one should forget in the execution of their duties, Colonel Sheldon unfailingly reminded anyone who had anything to do with Operation Lusty, that American interests always come first.

Quality and quantity were defined by the Wright Field Category A list of desired enemy equipment. Priority I items were defined as those which promised to further "our war effort to shorten the Pacific War; priority II and III items are of longer term interest affecting our national security. Desired priority I subjects include: Jet propulsion, electronics, medicine, select items of equipment, rockets and controlled missiles. Most highly desired intelligence items are the top secret and secret developments not now known which are the priority I. Intelligence items include documents as well as equipment." In other words, anything that looked intriguing or interesting was fair game for shipment to Wright Field.

Some haggling went on between SHAEF-controlled CIOS/CAFT teams and USSTAF's ATI teams about who controlled what territory and had authority to do this or that. CIOS, the combined United States/United Kingdom exploitation operation, rightfully saw Operation Lusty as a national competitor for the technological riches wanted by both the United States and the United Kingdom. After all, USSTAF's ATI teams represented purely American interests. No decision emerged from the SHAEF bureaucracy to inhibit American efforts to exploit whatever facilities were captured by American arms, and Operation Lusty proceeded full speed ahead. On April 25, Watson obtained a fully crewed C-47 from one of the air transport squadrons of the 1st Tactical Air Force and surveyed the forward area. When he returned to St.-Germain on April 28, he briefed General McDonald and the intelligence staff on his findings and explained in general terms how he intended to implement his portion of Operation Lusty. To Watson it was obvious that the Me-262 recovery operation should be run from Lechfeld, the airfield adjacent to the Messerschmitt headquarters and production complex. Aerial reconnaissance had detected numerous jets scattered about the field, but equally important was the fact that Lechfeld and the nearby city of Augsburg were the places where many of the German test pilots and jet assembly workers lived. These Germans were an important part of Watson's plan. The Arado jet bombers, on the other hand, were up north in the British zone. Watson would have to see what he could work out with the British once they took control of the German airfields. For the collection of conventionally powered aircraft Watson recommended the use of Merseburg, already identified as one of three collection points, along with Nürnberg-Roth and Stuttgart.[1]

Operation Lusty seemed to have been tailored for Watson the man, aeronautical engineer, and test pilot, rather than just the military officer that he was. His unique technical skills as an aircraft power plant engineer and test pilot were of vital importance, but so were his sense of bravado, his willingness to take risks and, not least, his engaging personality. To succeed at his task and get what he wanted and needed, Watson would have to motivate, lead, cajole, befriend, bully, bribe, and, if necessary, cheat and steal from French, English, American, and German airmen, victors and vanquished alike. He would do whatever it took. Watson went into Operation Lusty the way he learned to fly— feet first, never looking back. What made Watson's "boat float" was the thrill of discovery, and Operation Lusty had lots of that.

By April 24, 1945, the 1st Tactical Air Force had relocated its headquarters from Vittel to Heidelberg, and the 1st TAF Service Command took up quarters in Schwetzingen, just to the west of Heidelberg.

Watson knew that the 1st TAF's days were numbered, and that its attached P-47 fighter groups would soon be redeployed or disbanded. Hundreds of fighter pilots and maintenance men would be out of a job—something that most of them were looking forward to. All he needed was to persuade a few competent "volunteers" to delay their return to the ZI by a month or two. Watson tasked the personnel section of the Exploitation Division to find him ten experienced pilots and twice that many top-notch maintenance men from the P-47 squadrons of the 1st TAF. He stipulated that the pilots should have about a thousand hours' flying time and preferably instructor pilot experience. Flying a new jet would be a challenge, he knew that, but instructor pilot experience should lessen the chances of someone smacking himself in the face with Mother Earth.

In addition to pilots, Watson needed a couple of guys to run the Lechfeld and Merseburg operations—Lechfeld for the jets, Merseburg for the "windmills," as some pilots referred to the propeller-driven aircraft. He knew he would be moving about frequently and couldn't be tied down at either location. One lesson Watson learned and never forgot was that delegation, pushing work downward, was the key to freedom and success. It didn't take him long to figure out whom he wanted at Lechfeld—Bob Strobell. He liked the way Bob had handled himself on their flight in that beat-up B-17 from St.-Dizier to Nancy. He had also seen him make a crazy night landing near Paris on a totally blacked-out airfield. Watson knew Strobell hadn't gotten rattled on either occasion, an attribute Watson valued in himself and in other pilots. Strobell also had run an assorted pool of support aircraft for USSTAF headquarters out of an airfield near London, and later from fields near Paris. For a young lieutenant, Strobell readily assumed responsibility when it came his way, and he discharged his duties competently. Watson's mind was made up.

For the Merseburg operation, Watson decided to take over an existing ATI team already in place. That team was nominally headed by

Colonel David Schilling, the fighter ace and one-time commander of the 56th Fighter Group. As the strategic bombing campaign was halted by General Spaatz on April 16, Schilling saw his opportunity to fly an Me-262 jet.[2] Unfortunately, the 8th Air Force was slated to move to the Pacific, and shortly after Schilling arrived at Merseburg he was recalled and assigned to the Intelligence Directorate at 8th Air Force headquarters to help plan the movement of the 8th. Schilling's dream of flying a German jet remained a dream. His small ATI team at Merseburg, however, stayed behind and included two hand-picked men from his old outfit, the 56th Fighter Group—Captain Edwin D. Maxfield, a nonrated engineering officer, and Sergeant Edmund R. Namowicz, an outstanding mechanic fluent in both German and Polish. When Watson learned that Captain McIntosh, who once flew as Schilling's wing man, was on his way to join the Merseburg team, he decided that McIntosh was the pilot he wanted to head up that operation.

Watson still needed to fill one other important position to complete his team, a position which required the skills of a logistician and politician. It would have to be someone who could take care of all the paperwork, make the necessary support arrangements to assemble the fleet of German airplanes, and move them to a port and ship them back to the ZI. He didn't intend to have his precious aircraft disassembled, boxed, and shipped home on Liberty ships as captured aircraft had been shipped in the past. He knew they were almost never put back together right. Instead, he thought in terms of an aircraft carrier, which meant that the planes would have to be properly prepared to protect them from the ravages of the salty ocean air. Aircraft preparation for an open-deck carrier voyage involved encasing each aircraft in a layer of pliofilm and silica gel to keep the sea air from turning them into junk. The job required someone he could work with, and who could work with the Army, Navy, the French, and the British as well. Watson's choice was Lieutenant Colonel Malcolm D. Seashore, whom he knew from his days at the 1st TAF in Vittel. Seashore served as the executive officer to the commander of the 1st TAF Service Command and did an impressive job. He had helped Watson on many occasions solve tricky personnel, supply, and maintenance problems, was thoroughly familiar with the USSTAF and SHAEF organizational structure, and most of all knew the right people to get the job done. When asked, Seashore quickly accepted Watson's offer to be his "man Friday." Seashore, like Watson, had been reassigned from the 1st TAF headquarters to the Exploitation Division in St.-Germain, and was available.

Upon learning that the 54th Air Disarmament Squadron would be the one to move into Lechfeld, Watson tasked them to assist in the recovery of Me-262s at Lechfeld and from nearby dispersal areas and to immediately start the process of collecting repairable aircraft and putting them back into flying condition. The 54th was also tasked to provide housing, transportation, and messing facilities for his pilots and mechanics once they arrived at the field. Everything was falling into place. There was only one more thing he had to tend to—find the Messerschmitt test pilots and factory mechanics without whose services the job would be immensely more difficult.

Captain Hubbard's 54th ADS moved into Lechfeld, including the adjacent Messerschmitt plant and offices, on May 4. The 54th went about inspecting Lechfeld the way they inspected every other exploitation target, with the additional task of supporting Colonel Watson in the recovery of German Me-262 fighter jets. Hubbard appointed Master Sergeant Eugene Freiburger to take charge of the Me-262 project. Freiburger, of German heritage and still speaking a fair Wisconsin German, picked eleven of his best and most suitable men to assist him—Staff Sergeant Medved, Sergeant Brumfield, Corporal Erickson, Corporal Zurliena, Staff Sergeant Higgins, Corporal Connors, Private Hallman, Private Dunn, Corporal Olsonoski, Private Strows, and Sergeant Baldachino. The first thing they did was to survey the sprawling airfield and factory complex to determine how many of the

Master Sergeant Freiburger and his men attached a rope to the nose gear of this photo-reconnaissance Me-262, intending to pull it into the nearby aircraft hangar. The gear promptly collapsed. (RB)

German jets appeared potentially recoverable. Then Freiburger selected a large aircraft hangar and went to work. They cleaned out the hangar and attempted to move their first enemy jet into the hangar's cavernous interior. The aircraft was a reconnaissance version of the Me-262 jet fighter, parked a couple of hundred yards outside the hangar. Freiburger and his men attached a rope to the aircraft's nose gear and tried to pull it into the hangar with a jeep. The aircraft promptly went nose down; the gear collapsed, too weak to withstand the strain. Scratch one good airplane. There had to be a right way to do this, Freiburger thought. That same day he received expert help and advice from an unexpected source—the Germans who had built, maintained and flown the Me-262s.

Only three days after Patton's troops swept through Augsburg on April 29, and before the 54th ADS settled down at Lager Lechfeld, Watson drove into the shattered town. He obtained a list of names and addresses of key Messerschmitt personnel from an AMG representative, and in his jeep he carefully picked his way through the rubble of the war-torn city using a prewar map. He was looking for Karl Baur, the chief Messerschmitt test pilot at Lager Lechfeld. This is how Isolde Baur, Karl Baur's wife, described the occasion. "Gerd Caroli, Karl's former colleague from the Messerschmitt Company, came running up the stairs in the morning. 'Karl, come quick. There is an American colonel downstairs who wants to fly the Me-262,' he yelled in excitement. 'You are kidding,' Karl responded. A look out of the window proved that he was telling the truth. 'Well, he knows that we have ships sitting in Lechfeld. He wants us to get the mechanics together and put the planes back into flying condition. If I understand him correctly,' said Gerhard Caroli, 'he is not allowed to come up to the apartment for security reasons. Also, he showed me paper from the High Command. I have the strange feeling he wants to take us as prisoners of war.' Together Karl and Gerd went downstairs. According to Karl this meeting was open and sincere: 'Hello, Colonel. I am Karl Baur. What can I do for you?' Colonel Watson handed the paper to him from the High Command while returning the greeting and introducing himself." The paper Watson showed to Karl Baur was his Eisenhower pass, which was impressive enough and instructed all those who read it in English, German, or French to provide whatever assistance he required. " 'Well, Colonel, I am not a military man,' " Baur replied. " 'I am a civilian. You cannot force me to work for you,' Karl stated while returning the paper to him with a faint smile. 'Well, if you refuse to cooperate then we have other means available to make you volunteer,' " Watson responded, also smiling.[3]

And so the issue was settled. Baur and Caroli rounded up a total of twenty-five mechanics and pilots. Baur was to function as the chief test pilot, assisted by test pilots Ludwig Hoffmann and Hermann Kersting. Gerhard Caroli, also a pilot, was reappointed chief engineer and director's assistant—positions he had held prior to Watson's

The proper way to tow an Me-262—a two-seat trainer that Freiburger christened Vera. June 1945, Melun, France. (RB)

arrival. Joseph Baur, Hans Brandt, and Andreas Sebald were rehired as technical inspectors, Karl Bayer as armament engineer, and Ernst Witte as hydraulics engineer. Hans Ebner, Heinz Lechler, Karl Schwenk, Konrad Berringer, Karl Stierle, Alfred Schillinger, and Georg Fauser were engaged as foremen or crew chiefs—*Meister, Obermeister,* or *Vorarbeiter.* The remainder of the men were *Monteure,* mechanics— Fritz Durrwanger, Fritz Hindelang, Richard Huber, Alfred Kapuczik, Ludwig Kleinmaier, Max Kohl, Reinhold Marutschke, Wilhelm Mann, Franz Nabholz, Joseph Rieger, and Wilhelm Wiedemann. Most of the Messerschmitt crew assembled each day at a designated pickup point in Augsburg where they were met by a 54th ADS truck and driven to Lechfeld, and then returned to the same pickup point in the evening. Hoffmann lived near the field, according to Freiburger, so Freiburger had him picked up in a jeep each morning. One of the very first things Gerhard Caroli taught Sergeant Freiburger was how to properly tow the Me-262.[4]

Prior to the arrival of the Americans, Messerschmitt mechanics had disabled the Lechfeld aircraft by removing their constant speed drives, carefully wrapping the drives in wax paper and burying them.

Caroli had the drives dug up for reinstallation in the aircraft which were selected for refurbishment. It quickly became a team effort between the mechanics of the 54th ADS and the German mechanics— a team effort with some reservations on both sides. There was one not-so-pleasant occurrence, noted Lieutenant Smith in the 54th ADS history: "Staff Sergeant Higgins discovered and neutralized a TNT charge, a fifteen pound booby trap under the cockpit seat of one ship."[5] That find put some strain on the budding German-American relationship, but no other booby-trapped aircraft was found, and in a short time the men overcame their distrust of one another and concentrated on the tasks at hand.

Baur described the Germans' attitude toward the Me-262 and their willingness to assist Watson this way: "The people of Germany had the right to know someday that during the darkest days of their existence something worthwhile was accomplished by their brilliant scientists and engineers."[6] With that attitude, to save their beloved jet airplanes for posterity, they worked hand in glove with their American conquerors. Watson left Sergeant Freiburger in charge of the Me-262 recovery effort pending the arrival of Lieutenant Strobell, but not without first instructing Freiburger that "any time I land here, I expect you to meet me at the aircraft in your jeep." According to Freiburger, he never failed to do so, and noted, "After one got to know Colonel Watson, he was truly one fine person."[7]

LAGER LECHFELD

On VE Day, May 8, 1945, an Me-262A jet fighter approached Lager Lechfeld, wagging its wings, a sign of surrender. The aircraft circled the field, recalled Sergeant Freiburger, then put on a stunning acrobatic display and finally came in low and slow, touching down tentatively. The Me-262A day fighter, painted in the green color scheme of JG 7, was flown by Leutnant Fritz Müller, who had found refuge in the last days of war at Königgrätz airfield near Prague. On the eighth of May, Müller decided to make one last flight, not to intercept enemy aircraft, but for himself. He, like others before him, had no intention of surrendering to the Russians and chose an American-occupied airfield for his destination.

Oberleutnant Fritz Müller was a Bf 109 pilot who flew with Jagdgeschwader 53, JG 53, the Pik As, Ace of Spades wing. By German fighter pilot standards, his tally of twenty-two victories was modest. But he was still alive, and that counted for something. German pilots, unlike their American counterparts, were rarely withdrawn from combat operations; instead, they flew until one fine day injury or death caught up with them. Müller amassed an impressive six kills in the Me-262 during the brief period he flew with JG 7. But on the eighth of May his mind was not on adding another American bomber to his tally; rather, it was time to escape the clutches of the Russian army just

Leutnant Fritz Müller's Me-262 on May 8, 1945, minutes after he flew into Lechfeld to surrender. The soldier in the cockpit is one of Freiburger's men from the 54th ADS. (DF)

outside the Königgrätz airfield perimeter. His own aircraft was out of commission, so Müller chose to fly an aircraft assigned to his friend and squadron mate, Oberfeldwebel Heinz Arnold, shot down a few days earlier while flying another jet. Arnold remained missing in action. Sergeant Arnold accumulated forty-two victories in the Bf 109 while flying with JG 5, then scored an additional seven kills in the Me-262—two P-47s, one P-51, and five B-17 bombers. Arnold's victory markings were painted on the left rear fuselage of the aircraft Müller flew into Lechfeld on May 8.

Karl Baur watched with amazement as the lone Me-262 jet put on an impromptu airshow above the field. Every GI was watching intently as well. Finally the pilot put down his landing gear and made a perfect landing. Dressed in his casual Bavarian lederhosen, Baur jumped into a jeep with Master Sergeant Freiburger at the wheel. Freiburger drove toward the enemy aircraft at full speed, dodging bomb craters as he went. By the time they got to the Me-262, Leutnant Müller had already opened its canopy and casually raised his hands above his head in a sign of surrender. Baur jumped out of the jeep before Freiburger brought it to a full stop, greeting Müller with a hearty "*Grüss Gott*," the traditional Bavarian greeting. One can only surmise how surprised Müller must have been to be greeted in this fashion. The uniformed and armed presence of Sergeant Freiburger made it obvious that the lederhosen-clad fellow was acting under American tutelage. Freiburger quickly disarmed Fritz Müller, confiscated his personal weapons, and turned him over to military police for interrogation and confinement in a nearby POW cage, as Americans jokingly referred to POW camps for Germans. Freiburger later recalled the incident. "I was pleased to get his aircraft in flying condition," he said. Then he added, "He was one of the most insolent and cockiest Krauts I had ever gotten a hold of." While Freiburger was busy with Müller, Baur removed Müller's flight gear from the cockpit of the Me-262. "I saved his flight gear which he had to leave behind," Baur wrote in his diary. "Seven years later—summer of 1952—I was able to return it to him when we had a wine-happy reunion with all former German jet pilots."[1]

In his history for the month of June, Lieutenant Smith of the 54th ADS noted that Freiburger's mission "was to learn as much as possible from the German mechanics about the new jet engines as well as see that everything operated smoothly in the reparation of the Me-262s, preparing them to fly." Learn they did. Noted Lieutenant Smith, "Sgt Brumfield, Cpl Olsonoski and Cpl Erickson, our own 54th ADS mechanics were taught by the German mechanics how to start and taxi the jet ships . . . certainly a thrill for men who had been away from engines for such a long time." As flyable aircraft began to roll out of his fix-it-up hangar, Freiburger had an idea. Why not give every jet a name? It would be much easier to keep track of them that way. The first operational jet was the one flown into Lechfeld by Fritz Müller, and Freiburger named it *Dennis*, after his young son.[2] Only four days later, on the twelfth of May, Karl Baur taxied *Dennis* to the end of

Lechfeld's concrete runway, by then repaired and swept clear of debris, and slowly brought the power up on the two Jumo 004 turbines. When the exhaust tail cones, the *Zwiebeln*, were in the right position, indicating to Baur that he had full power, he released the brakes and took the aircraft up for a twenty-minute test flight. The jet performed flawlessly. That may have been the first solo flight by a German pilot after war's end, four days after VE Day. Baur, the Messerschmitt test pilot, was flying a German jet with American markings above Augsburg, unmolested by American fighters. The war was really over.

The next aircraft to come on line was named *Wilma Jeanne* by Freiburger, after his wife. *Wilma Jeanne* was a Lechfeld test aircraft with "a 50 mm gun protruding from its propellerless nose," as the 54th ADS historian referred to it. It was still a strange experience for many to look at an airplane and not see propellers on nose or wings; an airplane just didn't look right without them. The Exploitation Division reported in its July 1945 status report that "Four types of 5 cm aircraft cannon have been in development by the Luftwaffe for installation in the Me-262. It is interesting to note that each of these automatic cannon [was] developed from single shot tank cannons. The weapons do not possess a high cyclic rate of fire, but are limited to between 30 and 50 rounds per minute. One complete installation has been flight tested at Lechfeld. The cannon mount, it may be noted, is an integral part of the fuselage. One of these cannon, together with complete plans for its installation, is being evacuated." There were actually three 50 mm cannons under development by the GAF specifically designed for use in the Me-262. "Documents . . . indicated that the ammunition would not be available before mid-1945, a rocket burning projectile with a cyclic rate of 300 rounds per minute." Although the plans were uncovered, an actual specimen was never found.[3] All in all, German aircraft gun development efforts showed no promise of being ready before the middle of 1945 at the very earliest. Additionally, the gun development effort made little practical sense, since the Me-262 was

Müller's jet, Dennis, *after it was Americanized. (DF)*

already successfully employing fin-stabilized unguided air-to-air rockets with devastating effect against American bombers. But then German scientists under the Nazis had little opportunity to exchange information, and as a result multiple similar developments were the rule, rather than the exception.

Freiburger said of *Wilma Jeanne* and its armament, "It only has one cannon, but the barrel protrudes six feet out of the nose. It is a 50 mm gun, carries thirty rounds, and the shell is about two and a half feet long. The recoil of the gun is hardly noticeable due to the hydraulic brakes. In the firing pit the aircraft would hardly move when you fired the cannon." The implication was that he and his crew fired the cannon at Lechfeld, although Watson never knew of this. And why should he tell Watson? Officers didn't need to know everything. Wrote Freiburger in a June 3, 1945, letter to his former employer, the Four Wheel Drive Auto Company in Clintonville, Wisconsin, "If the officers just leave us alone, we can accomplish more in one day than they can in a week. We use different methods than they do." Yes, he certainly fired that gun. It was just too much of a temptation for him to resist.

Vera, the two-seat Me-262B trainer, was used to train Watson's Whizzers. All Whizzers, except for Lieutenant Haynes, were checked out in Vera *by Karl Baur. (RB)*

Lieutenant Bob Strobell, who soon arrived on the scene at Lechfeld, said of the 50-mm-cannon-equipped aircraft, "It was in my book already obsolete. One of these same aircraft in our possession had the rocket racks under its wings. The rockets were far more effective than would have been the case with the cannon, because they could be launched out of range of the bomber's guns. To my great surprise, you could wave the cannon around like a sucker stick; it had no measurable effect on the performance of the airplane. You would think the airplane would be nose-heavy, but it wasn't. It flew just as well as the Me-262 fighter with the standard 30 mm gun armament. We were lucky this airplane and the rocket planes didn't get up in the air in 1943–1944. It would have been mass murder against our clumsy B-17 and B-24 formations."

Baur, as the Messerschmitt chief experimental test pilot, had flown the aircraft before, and he took her up again on May 14. When Watson saw *Wilma Jeanne* he decided it was his airplane. *Wilma Jeanne* was unusual and there was only one like it in existence. That did it for

Watson. He liked the Me-262 in general no matter what its configuration, but he took a real shine to *Wilma Jeanne*. The Me-262 "looked clean, had several innovative features that I had not seen on U.S. aircraft, and I was particularly interested in the Jumo 004 engines," Watson wrote about the German jet. "It was hard to believe that I was looking at the world's first high performance, combat qualified, turbo driven jet fighter," he swooned. "It looked sinister—but, at the same time—beautiful. It looked like a shark. And, from pilot reports, it could be as mean as a shark in combat. The Allied fighter and bomber pilot reports of encounters with the Me-262 indicated . . . that it was apparently one helluva airplane."[4]

Watson described the Me-262's major shortcoming as being "rather short-legged. It has a range of only 298 miles at sea level." This increased with altitude and reduced fuel consumption to about 500 miles at 20,000 feet. "So you see, from traveling at 520 miles per hour it has less than an hour's range." Its "initial climb is about 4,000 feet per minute at sea level. But at 30,000 feet it still has approximately 1,100 feet per minute rate of climb. We had nothing in our Air Corps for combat—or anything on the books to be in combat—with those performance characteristics." Watson was so enthralled with the Me-262 jet he felt he could "spend an hour or two [talking about] this airplane because it was one of my favorites—and it certainly was a thrill to fly."[5]

The third Me-262 to be declared flyable was *Vera*. *Vera* was an Me-262B two-seat trainer named after Freiburger's sister-in-law. *Vera* was flown on May 15 by Willie Hoffmann, Karl Baur's fellow test pilot at Messerschmitt. Willie's first name was Ludwig, but the Americans all called him Willie. Willie was liked by everyone, Germans and Americans. His manner was casual and he had a great capacity for storytelling once he had imbibed a drink or two. Compared to Willie, Karl Baur, although usually wearing his casual Bavarian short-legged lederhosen, appeared to be less approachable. At least that was the way the men perceived him. Both Karl and Willie were extremely competent test pilots, the major reason that Watson wanted them on his team. Sergeant Freiburger remembered Ludwig Hoffmann taking *Vera* up for its first check-ride. "It was surely a beautiful thing to behold, to see how fast the airplane traveled and how smoothly it made its maneuvers through the air. I was really impressed. After Ludwig Hoffmann landed, he refueled and gave Captain Ward, our squadron operations officer, a ride in *Vera*. Ward was the first American to ride in this two-seater jet." Other aircraft soon followed *Dennis*, *Wilma Jeanne* and *Vera*. *Connie the Sharp Article* was named by Master Sergeant Preston after his wife. *Connie* was a photo-reconnaissance aircraft with camera bulges on its nose rather than the standard four 30 mm cannons of the fighters. A remarkable aspect of the Me-262, Freiburger soon discovered, was how quickly it could be taken apart and put back together again. A nose section could be removed in a short time and replaced with another nose section, even turning a fighter into a recce aircraft or vice versa. Said Freiburger, "They came apart in sections—nose section, main fuselage, each wing came off as one piece, tail section, engine nacelles, and the turbines easily dropped off the wings. As a result we could swap bad parts for good parts" with ease.

While Willie Hoffmann was testing aircraft and advising Freiburger's mechanics, Karl Baur was summoned by Watson to Munich. On the morning of May 16, Watson's C-47 picked up Baur at Lechfeld and flew him to Munich-Riem airport, where Watson had found a fully operational Me-262A fighter left behind by Galland's JV 44 fighter squadron when they fled from Munich to Salzburg and Innsbruck in April. Baur ran up its engines, found all instruments in the green, took off, and flew the new acquisition back to Lechfeld. The former JV 44 aircraft received the name *Beverly Anne*. Freiburger had five jets ready to go. His goal was fifteen, and he really had no idea how he would get there. He and his men took another look at the fifty-some aircraft littering Lechfeld and the nearby forests. They found another

Wilma Jeanne *with its fearsome-looking 50 mm cannon at Lechfeld, June 1945.*
Feudin' 54th A.D. Sq. *was painted on the right side of the nose. (DF)*

five which could be made flyable. That was it. Patton's tankers had
done a thorough job on all the others.

Joanne and *Marge* were two photo-reconnaissance Me-262s to join
the growing stable of jets, and *Pauline* and *Doris,* two standard 30 mm
gun-toting day fighters, soon followed. Sergeant Freiburger, an inven-
tive man with time on his hands, had the squadron logo, *Feudin' 54th
A.D. Sq.,* painted on the right side of *Pauline* and *Wilma Jeanne.* He
continued to look for more jets, but could come up with only eight
flyable aircraft from the fifty wrecks littering Lager Lechfeld—*Wilma
Jeanne, Vera, Joanne, Marge, Pauline, Doris, Connie the Sharp Article,*
and aircraft number 3332. The eighth aircraft remained unnamed,
simply identified by the last four digits of its *Werknummer,* the manufacturer's serial number. A standard fighter version with rocket racks
under its wings, 3332 was not destined to go to the United States like the
others. Watson had different plans for it. *Dennis,* of course, had been

flown into Lechfeld by Leutnant Müller on VE Day and *Beverly Anne* came from Galland's JV 44 squadron at Munich-Riem. Those last two jets gave Watson the minimum of ten aircraft he had hoped for. He still wanted more. Karl Baur reflected on Freiburger's naming game and found it amusing. His wife noted, "One evening Karl came home chattering, 'Those Americans are like kids. . . . They gave each ship a girl's name and they actually refer to it by that name.' "[6]

The first Me-262 jet was delivered to the fighter evaluation section at Wright Field on May 21. It was the aircraft Hans Fay had flown to Frankfurt on March 31, which was disassembled by one of McDonald's ATI teams and shipped by "fast boat" to the ZI. It was the first German jet to reach Wright Field, but it was not the only Me-262 in the United States at the time. Another, also in a disassembled state, arrived in the belly of the U-234 submarine which surrendered at war's end and dropped anchor in Portsmouth harbor on May 17. The fate of that Me-262 remains a mystery. There are no records showing that this aircraft was ever flown at Wright Field, nor does Colonel Ken Chilstrom, a Wright Field test pilot and then chief of the fighter test section, remember such a plane.[7]

P-47 JUG PILOTS

On April 19, 1945, Brigadier General John G. Williams assumed command of the 1st Tactical Air Force Service Command (Provisional), headquartered at Vittel, France. Just five days later, on the twenty-fourth of April, Williams moved his headquarters from Vittel to Schwetzingen, across from the storied university town of Heidelberg. Schwetzingen was known near and far as a producer of high-quality asparagus. Most recently, however, the town had been much less interested in *Spargel* than in the manufacture of tanks. The senior officers of the 1st TAF headquarters staff, led by General Williams, flew to Schwetzingen the morning of April 24. The remainder of his staff followed by truck convoy and arrived later that evening. The entire move was completed in one day. General Williams moved his headquarters into what used to be a *Panzerschule*, a tank training school, at the outskirts of town, and his staff was billeted in several small requisitioned hotels. "On the arrival of the Americans in Schwetzingen, two camps of Russian and Polish slave laborers were liberated. As no arrangements were immediately available for returning them to their homelands, these laborers remained." The 1st Tactical Air Force Service Command history reports, "Some of the men and women went to work for the occupying American forces. Others just 'relaxed' with occasional sorties of pillage and looting against their former masters. American military police soon put a stop to this latter practice."

A message arrived from General Arnold, the chief of the Army Air Forces, praising the 1st Tactical Air Force and its Service Command for their accomplishments. Wrote the general, "My personal observations together with those of my staff during our European tour inspires this message of congratulations to you and all the men under your command for superb achievements in the destructive employment of air power. Having seen some of the results with my own eyes, I am profoundly impressed with your accomplishments and proud of the magnificent contributions you and your men have made and are making to the glorious history of the Army Air Forces." General Spaatz added to General Arnold's comments, "The achievements which have merited this message are the direct result of the courage and unstinting devotion to duty of you and the men under your command." Major General Webster, who replaced General Royce as commander of the 1st Tactical Air Force, in turn relayed the two messages to Brigadier General Williams and Williams passed them on to his men "with great pride." He knew, however, that this message read more like a funeral notice than a pat on the back. Sure enough, on May 16 the other shoe dropped. The message he had been waiting for arrived, activating the "provisional" caveat which had always been appended to the organization's title. He then issued General Order 125, Headquarters 1st Tactical Air Force (Provisional), announcing that the 1st Tactical Air Force would cease to exist as of midnight on May 20, 1945. "Personnel will be disposed of in accordance with orders to be issued by higher headquarters."

The history of the 1st TAF Service Command further reported that "morale of the men remained high despite the complete lack of many of the non-essential but pleasurable things to which the troops had long been accustomed" and of which Vittel had such abundance. The nonfraternization policy, with its curb on contact with enemy civilians, apparently didn't permit the large-scale flowering of such relationships in Schwetzingen, but of course there were still the DP ladies to whom the nonfraternization policy did not apply in all cases.[1]

The war was over, at least in Europe, and there was no further need for the 1st TAF. The First French Air Corps was on its own, and the P-47 and B-26 fighter and bomber groups once flying under the banner of the 1st Tactical Air Force were reattached to the 9th Air Force pending future disposition. For most of the airplanes the future meant the scrap heap or a needy Allied nation. For many of the men, it was a ticket home. Some stayed, however, to carry out "post-hostilities policies in Germany." Before its demise the 1st TAF performed one final act in support of Operation Lusty, publishing a general order assigning eight of its P-47 pilots to duty at Headquarters USSTAF. The assignment didn't mean that any of them would report to St.-Germain, but rather that they were at the disposal of Colonel Harold E. Watson, who soon let them know where he wanted them to go. In addition, ten P-47 mechanics were reassigned to report to Lager Lechfeld to become proficient in Me-262 operation and maintenance under the tutelage of German Messerschmitt mechanics. The arrival of the 1st TAF P-47 mechanics would allow Master Sergeant Freiburger and his crew to leave Lechfeld and rejoin the 54th ADS, which by then had moved to another location.

First Lieutenants Roy W. Brown and James K. Holt came from the 86th Fighter Group, as did Sergeants Ernest G. Parker and Charles A. Barr. The 27th Fighter Group volunteers in support of Operation Lusty were First Lieutenants William V. Haynes and Horace D. McCord, as well as Sergeants John G. Gilson and Donald J. Wilcoxen. From the 324th Group came Captains Kenneth E. Dahlstrom and Henry A. Nolte, accompanied by Sergeants Noel D. Moon and Edward J. Thompson. The 358th Fighter Group contributed Captain Fred L. Hillis, First Lieutenant Robert J. Anspach, and Staff Sergeants Charles L. Taylor and Robert H. Moore. And the 50th Fighter Group was tasked to provide Sergeants Archie E. Bloomer and Everett T. Box. Most arrived at

Lechfeld in dribs and drabs by jeep or weapons carrier; the pilots were flown in by their squadron buddies in a B-25 or B-26 bomber. When the final head count was taken at Lechfeld, McCord and Nolte were not among the chosen. Haynes would join the group at a later date in Melun, France. Anspach, Brown, and Strobell were seasoned combat pilots and volunteers, as were the rest of the pilots Watson chose for this special project. Only Anspach had seen an Me-262 in combat; Brown was the only college graduate among them; and Strobell, Brown, and Hillis had aerial victories to their credit.[2]

Robert J. "Bob" Anspach was a Milwaukee boy, his mother and father of Pennsylvania Dutch descent. Bob had been exposed to airplanes early in life. "I can remember Lindbergh coming back on a cruiser from Europe and all the talk about him. He was a true American hero. When my family moved from Wisconsin to Ohio, my father took me every year to the Cleveland air races. I recall seeing Ernst Udet, Jimmy Doolittle, Oscar Turner, and many other famous aviators. I went to the airport to watch planes taking off, and of course there were twenty-five-cent magazines, like *Battle Aces*, which I read religiously. Yet, I never thought I'd be flying an airplane myself. My family moved again, this time to Charleston, West Virginia. There I attended high school and graduated in 1940. The war was on and so was the draft. I wanted to join the paratroopers. My father took a dim view of my choice of service and suggested I take the Army Air Corps test instead. Nearly everyone in town who took the test flunked, so I didn't have high hopes of making it. "If you don't pass," my father promised, "I'll sign the papers so you can join the paratroopers." I passed.

"After graduating from flying school in class 43D I was sent to Bryan, Texas, for instrument training. From there we were sent to different flying training bases in the United States to set up instrument flying schools. I did that for a year, still flying BT-13s. That year I amassed a lot of flying time. I got the call to report to a fighter transition school for the P-47 Thunderbolt. Before I knew it, I was in Europe flying with the 365th Fighter Squadron, the Orange Tails, of the 358th Fighter Group. I was there for the Battle of the Bulge and ended the war in Sandhofen, Germany. For a fighter-bomber pilot I thought every mission was interesting, every mission different and exciting—firing my guns, dropping bombs, everything close to the ground. Once, though, I got shot up pretty badly. I was number three coming down on a target and as I pulled out German flak nailed me. I lost one wheel, had a wing perforated, and the engine was hit. I had an escort to the bomb line where he told me to bail out. I said, Naw, I'll get her back. At Toul airfield I bellied her in. The plane was ruined, but it made me feel pretty good about the P-47.

"One day I was flying cover for a group of B-26s in the Lechfeld area. I was P-47 element lead, when all of a sudden, as I looked down onto the flight of bombers, there was an Me-262 jet fighter sitting right behind and a little above them, flying formation with them. The bombers didn't even know he was there, or they would have been firing their guns. We immediately broke down toward him, and the Me-262 virtually thumbed its nose at us and shoved the coals to it and disappeared in a steep climb. He didn't shoot. He obviously wasn't going to shoot anybody down, because he sure could have with his four 30 mm cannons. The war was nearly over. The German jets were up there just to show us the superiority of their aircraft. You can't imagine what it was like to see something like that, to see an Me-262 jet fighter in that setting. Outside of the eight or ten of us P-47 jocks, who else had seen something like that in our fighter group? We'd heard about the Me-262 from our intelligence people, and we'd been told they were in our area, but no one in our squadron had ever seen one until that day. There he was, all by himself, totally superior to anything we had. To put it in perspective, imagine driving down the road in an old car at your maximum speed of forty miles an hour and have someone pass you at eighty—that's what it was like seeing the Me-262 climb away from us.

"I don't know how we were chosen, but one day during the morning briefing our operations officer mentioned that headquarters was looking for volunteers to fly captured German aircraft. The briefer didn't mention jets. I was young and had no entanglements, so I raised my hand. Fred Hillis was in my outfit too and he volunteered as well. There were several more, but only the two of us were selected. Once the selection was made, Hillis and I were flown to Lechfeld in a B-26. I don't recall talking to anybody the first day at Lechfeld. Some Army troops [Freiburger's crew] were moving airplanes around and they pointed to an empty tent. That's where we slept. All of us arrived within a day or two of each other. We saw some planes that looked like they were ready to fly. We didn't see Watson until a couple of days after we got to Lechfeld. The first person Hillis and I met was Lieutenant Bob Strobell who seemed to be running the operation."[3]

Roy Brown, another P-47 Jug pilot chosen to join Watson's growing group of American pilots at Lager Lechfeld, was born in March 1921, in the small river town of Spring Valley, Illinois. Roy was different from the rest of his fellow pilots in two respects. First, he was a college graduate, a rarity among fighter pilots at the time. Second, he was married. (Most of the young fighter pilots were single; at best they had sweethearts waiting for them back home, or they thought they did.) "I grew up in a house in the country. We were not farmers, but we had some cows. I did well in school, was pushed ahead by my teachers and graduated in 1935 from high school when I was fourteen. I went to a junior college because MIT at the time wouldn't accept anyone under the age of sixteen. So I entered the Massachusetts Institute of Technology as a sophomore. I graduated in 1940 at age nineteen with a degree in chemical engineering and went to work for Goodyear. While at MIT I completed Army ROTC, but I couldn't be commissioned until I was twenty-one. I turned twenty-one in March 1942, and was commissioned a second lieutenant in the coast artillery. When called to active duty I reported to an antiaircraft artillery unit at Camp Haan, Riverside,

California, right across the highway from March Field. Every day I watched the planes take off and land, and I decided that I would rather fly airplanes than shoot at them. I was young and foolish and craved some action. I wanted a piece of the war.

"I did my flight training in the Western Training Command and graduated in class 43I. All my training was in Arizona. I went through the usual primary, basic, and advanced phases, flying the Ryan PT-22, BT-13, and the AT-6. After graduation I was sent through instructor pilot training at Randolph Field near San Antonio, Texas, and upon completion of the course was sent back to Marana, a basic training field near Tucson. I instructed two classes in the BT-13, and once the students moved into the advanced phase I instructed them in aerobatics in the AT-6. While still in pilot training at Ryan Field, I met a coed, Frances Pickrell, who attended the University of Arizona in Tucson. Frances and I got to know each other pretty well and I talked her into marrying me while I was an instructor at Marana. We were planning our wedding when I got orders to report to a P-47 Replacement Training Unit near Baton Rouge, Louisiana. Fran and I moved our wedding up by a month, got married, and took off for Baton Rouge. It all ended too soon and Fran and I had to say good-bye to each other. I crossed the Atlantic to Naples, Italy, in a ninety-six-ship convoy. In Pisa we were quartered in a famous old school where Enrico Fermi received his advanced degree. Of course we all went up on the leaning tower.

"I was assigned an aircraft and named it *Pick*. My wife's maiden name was Pickrell; we called her Pick. I flew mostly close air support in the Po Valley. But there was one mission which was quite different from the rest. It was over San Remo. We were going after ships in the harbor. We sank a couple, then, I don't know what happened, suddenly my cockpit was filled with hydraulic fluid which coated everything including the windshield. There was no way to wipe it off, I had nothing to wipe with anyway, and I was coated by the stuff as well. I opened the canopy a little so I could look out the side for a landing. Fortunately

Roy Brown seated in his P-47 Thunderbolt, Pick, *prior to takeoff on a combat mission over Germany. (RB)*

I had gained a little experience landing that way when I was in the RTU at Harding Field. That was my first time landing, looking out the side of the canopy. It was good training for the real thing when it happened to me in Italy. But this stuff was on the inside of the windshield which made it even worse, but I managed to land without incident. In early 1945 my group was moved to France and assigned to the 1st Tactical Air Force. When the war ended we were flying out of Gross Gerau, a field located between Frankfurt and Darmstadt.

"I flew a total of eighty-four combat missions. On only one did I engage German fighters. That was very near the end of the war. We were flying in two flights of four, and two of us were flying rover, making a total of ten. As rovers we flew behind the two flights covering their rear. We were trying out a new leader. My wing man called me when he saw a group of FW-190s approaching. We warned the others, aborted our planned mission, and turned into the approaching enemy fighters. By the time the 190s got to us there were ten P-47s facing them head on. The long-nosed 190s came through us and shot down our new leader. It was a head-on shot. I happened to look down and saw him spin into the ground. I went after one of the 190s and got some strikes on him, but about that time one of our planes went by me with a 190 on his tail. I broke off the engagement and went after him. It was an interesting experience. The 190s were good planes, I knew that, and I didn't expect to be able to turn inside of one. But when the German pilot turned sharply to the left, I noticed that he stalled and snapped back to the right, which broke his turn a little bit. When I was overtaking him he did that twice, which allowed me to turn inside of him and shoot him down. The pilot bailed out." Colonel Hub Zemke, the commander of the 56th Fighter Group, the Wolf Pack, wrote about a similar encounter he had with an FW 190 on June 7, 1944.[4]

As good as the FW 190 fighter was, it had at least this one characteristic in a tight turn which could quickly turn fatal for its pilot if he let himself get involved in a horizontal dogfight. The 190's strength lay in the vertical plane. Kenneth O. Chilstrom, a retired air force colonel and test pilot, tested the FW 190 in the summer of 1944 at Wright Field. Said Chilstrom, "The FW 190 was an airplane all fighter pilots wanted to fly. Two captured 190s were delivered to Wright Field in early 1944. I was flying as a test pilot in the Fighter Operations Section after a combat tour in Europe. I was given the assignment to evaluate the 190's performance and handling characteristics. On the twenty-sixth of July, 1944, I flew both aircraft extensively and quickly discovered that the Focke-Wulf's rapid rate of roll was better than that of any other fighter I had ever flown, including the P-38, P-47, P-51, and the Spitfire. In the vertical plane the aircraft was nearly unbeatable: a pilot's airplane. However, in a horizontal turning engagement the FW 190 had a tendency to stall and opposite snap, allowing a Spitfire or P-47 to get inside its turn—a truly deadly situation for the Focke-Wulf pilot."[5] This was exactly the situation Roy Brown took advantage of when he shot down the 190 in April 1945.

"On the eighth of May, VE Day," Roy Brown recalled, "I was asked if I was interested in a unique assignment. My group staff would set up an interview for me in Frankfurt with some intelligence folks from General Spaatz's staff. We had nothing to do, so I volunteered. In Frankfurt I was questioned about my experience as an instructor pilot and the interviewers wanted to know if I knew anything about jet engines. Of course I didn't. At Gross Gerau we did little flying in those immediate postwar days. Life was boring and I was looking for something to do. Lots of celebrating was going on, of course, especially in the enlisted area." Notes the 526th Fighter Squadron history, "Someone discovered a large winery close to Worms that seemed to have an unlimited stock of wine and champagne, and for several days the fellows kept hauling it in until nearly everyone had at least one case. . . . Poker and drinking are the only diversions for the men, and they are both entered into wholeheartedly."[6]

"I don't really know how and why I was picked for the 262 program," Roy mused, "but one day in early June I received orders to report to Lechfeld. Jim Holt, another pilot in my group, had also volunteered for the assignment and was selected. My squadron flew me down to Lechfeld in a B-25. Bob Strobell was already there. Holt got there a day after I did. Not only had I never flown a jet, I had never flown a twin-engine aircraft or one with a tricycle landing gear—all that was part of the Me-262 jet fighter and new to me."[7]

Bob Strobell was the only pilot to have been personally evaluated and selected by Watson. All others were unknowns to Watson. He made his final selection based on personnel records and the recommendations of the interviewers. "It was mid-May 1945," Strobell recalled. "I had moved to Schwetzingen when I learned that, effective May 20, the 1st TAF would be no more. On the morning of the twenty-seventh Colonel Watson walked into my office, and in his usual direct manner said to me, 'Strobell, you are going down to Lechfeld.' In his hands he held a stack of papers a foot high that said Me-262 on it. He dumped the papers on my desk and instructed me to 'go down there and get as many Me-262s out of there as you can. I want at least ten. Remember— ten.' Fine. By that time I knew what an Me-262 was, but I had never seen one. I had no idea why I was chosen by him, but he must have had his reasons."

Bob Strobell was born in 1918 in Rutland, Vermont, and didn't know much about airplanes. "When I graduated from high school in 1937 I went to work at the House Scale Company filling production orders. When the war came along my buddy signed up for the Army and ended up in the Phillippines. Then a couple of other guys got drafted into the Army and the Navy, and I figured they were closing in on me. I decided I sure as hell didn't want to be walking around in the mud or drown at sea. So I decided to join the Air Corps. I knew about the aviation cadet program from my hunting and fishing buddies. I signed up and passed all the tests. I went through the South-East Training Command in Class 43H—BT-17s, the Vultee Vibrator, and then on to the AT-6 in advanced training. That was a hot airplane. Then I got a couple of flights in a P-40, and not much more in a P-47, before I was shipped overseas.

"I arrived at the 353rd Fighter Group at Metfield, England, in March 1944. Later on we moved to Raydon in Suffolk county. As a new guy I went through a transition period at the base—learning from the old timers how to fly the Thunderbolt properly. In a combat squadron they did things they never taught in training. They taught me all about instrument flying and navigation before I flew my first combat mission. I flew right through the invasion that June. The Luftwaffe just wouldn't come up for me. I flew mission after mission and never saw an enemy airplane—got shot at by flak, escorted bombers, and beat up the ground strafing. Finally, I got a couple of victories. I was flying wing to the flight lead, Captain Emery. I could hear my buddy Rupert Tumblin screaming on the radio, "Get this guy off my tail." When I looked down I saw the Focke-Wulf 190 and I knew my flight leader heard the same thing I heard on the radio. My flight leader didn't do a thing—just sat there. So I said, Breaking right, and went down and took that 190 off my buddy's tail. The 190 never knew I was back there when I hit him. At that point the pilots in the Luftwaffe were pretty thin on experience. A little later I got a Bf 109. That one I had to fight for. We pushed it up a couple of times. I came out on top and that was it.

"After I completed my combat tour I was transferred to London, to the Headquarters USSTAF aircraft contingent, to fly the big shots around. One plane was an L-4, another a Stinson L-5, there was an AT-6, a UC-64, a UC-78 twin-engine Bobcat, a C-46, a Beech C-45, and a big twin-engine Lockheed Hudson. When I looked at this strange assortment of airplanes I told them that the only one I had ever flown before was the AT-6. They just shook their heads and laughed. I told the crew chief who was assigned to me to get all the airplanes in top shape so I could check myself out in them. And by the way, I said to him, you are going along when I take my first flight in each aircraft. 'That's great,' the chief said. 'I love to go flying.' The Hudson looked so old I told the chief not to bother with it. I checked out in all the other airplanes just by using the technical manual and my crew chief. My approach to flying was to learn as much about an airplane as I could before I took it off the ground. I felt I needed to know the limitations of a plane and emergency procedures when critical functions didn't work. That's how you stay alive in the flying business. In October of forty-four I transferred along with the headquarters staff to the Paris area. From there I flew people back and forth to London, and ferried a few more of my aircraft over to France. On a flight from London to Paris late one afternoon darkness caught up with me. I made several passes over the pitch-black field when I got there, hoping someone would turn on the lights for me. A line sergeant was smart enough to put a jeep at the end of the runway and leave the headlights on so I could see enough to land. I set the thing down and thought that was the end of it. The next day I had about six officers on my neck asking me why I was flying at night into a place like that. Watson was one of them, I believe.

"Watson's instructions from the technical intelligence people in Paris were to collect every advanced German airplane he could lay his hands on. His instructions became mine. I didn't know it then, but he was already working with the air disarmament people and the AMG hiring Messerschmitt test pilots and factory mechanics to service the Me-262; that was in early May and the war wasn't quite over yet. Between Watson and the 54th Air Disarmament Squadron they assembled a team of 27 Messerschmitt mechanics and pilots. Gerhard Caroli, the shop steward, supervised the mechanics and was responsible for aircraft refurbishment. Those people were all in place at Lechfeld when Watson came to me, dumped his papers on my desk, and told me to get my butt down to Lechfeld. I arrived at Lechfeld on May 27, late in the afternoon on a bright and sunny day. As far as I could see nobody was on the field. I got out of the airplane. The pilot who flew me there never shut down the engines and immediately took off again. I stood there with a bedroll under my arm and a little ditty bag in my hand. I thought, What the hell am I doing here? There is no place to check in. No people in sight anywhere. Only lots of bomb craters and trashed buildings. It was obvious that this field had been bombed many times. I saw a big building to my left and decided to check it out. I found trashed offices. My mind-set was that I was in enemy territory and I didn't feel very comfortable about my situation. I was particularly intimidated by the fact that everything around me was destroyed and I had no transportation. I stepped outside that building again and saw what looked like a barracks. It was getting dark rapidly, so I headed for that building to see if I could find a place to sleep. There wasn't a square inch of the building that wasn't covered with glass shards and wood splinters. Bullet holes in every wall. I went upstairs, found a room, and swept an area clean to put down my bedroll. Then I proceeded to booby-trap the place, hooking up cans to some wire I found lying around, so if anyone

Watson posing with Hauptmann Hermann Kersting before an Me-262 jet fighter in early May 1945. Strobell soon fired Kersting. (RW)

came up the stairs it would wake me. I readied my .45 caliber pistol, tucked it under the bedroll and went to sleep.

"As soon as it got light I was up and out of there. Lechfeld was full of junked airplanes. The devastation spread out before my eyes was deeply depressing. I walked toward an airplane hangar on the far side of the field, and there I found three American sergeants and some Germans working on two Me-262 jets. By the first week of June all of us showed up at Lechfeld—ten American crew chiefs, twenty-seven German Messerschmitt pilots and mechanics, and six American pilots— counting myself."[8]

16

WATSON'S WHIZZERS

Watson visited Lechfeld before anyone else, right after Patton's troops came through and left their mark. It wasn't a pretty place to look at. Fortunately, the enthusiastic GIs hadn't destroyed every Me-262 they had come across, but they hadn't missed many. What the bombers didn't get, Patton's troops took care of, as Bob Strobell discovered on his first night there. Watson wrote that, after looking at a Messerschmitt jet for the first time, he knew he "needed some above average qualified pilots" to fly that plane. "This Me-262 was not a toy to be played with. German pilot reports indicated this airplane was a real killer" during training if not handled properly. He put Lieutenant Strobell "in charge of the operation at Lechfeld. He was a P-47 pilot—and a good one."[1]

Strobell was the man on the spot for the Lechfeld operation. Watson was far too busy doing other things, and only dropped in occasionally to monitor the progress of the 262 restoration effort. When Watson wasn't at Lechfeld he was at Munich-Riem, at Nürnberg-Roth, or Merseburg, where Captain Fred McIntosh was collecting the best of the Luftwaffe's piston-driven airplanes. Then it was back to Paris on occasion to confer with General McDonald and members of the intelligence staff. And of course there was time for an occasional discreet bit of civilized social life and the presence of beautiful women and the smell of perfume. Karl Baur wrote in his diary that Watson's men gave him "the affectionate title 'Grey Wolf,'" evidently believing that this had something to do with Watson's leadership ability and flying skills.[2] Watson was prematurely grey by 1945, with a flowing mane of carefully managed hair. "A handsome man" others said of him, a rare compliment paid by men to another man. But the "wolf" part of his name had little to do with the color of his hair and derived from skills other than flying and leading men, something Karl Baur wasn't necessarily attuned to. In a speech at the United States Air Force Museum at Wright-Patterson Air Force Base in March 1981, Watson talked about a Japanese four-engine bomber he had tested at Wright Field in late 1945, which was named Renzan by the Japanese and called RITA by American intelligence. Four of these aircraft had been built and one survived American bombing. After describing his experience test-flying the RITA, Watson said jokingly to his audience, "Now I want those 'he-men' among you to eat your hearts out. I got about three hundred letters from Ritas from all over—including one from Rita Hayworth. I suppose some wag among you is thinking 'The Silver Stallion rides again.'"[3] Grey Wolf or Silver Stallion, Watson was what people saw in him.

The morning of the twenty-eighth of May, after having spent a restless night in a demolished former German Luftwaffe barracks, Bob Strobell sat down for a breakfast of K rations in the Me-262 hangar with several newly arrived aircraft mechanics from the 1st TAF. "Is this all you guys are living on?" Bob asked, pointing at boxes of C and K rations. "Yeah," responded one of the sergeants. The others nodded their heads in agreement. "But we aren't really hurtin', Lieutenant," one of them said. "We've been out huntin' with Sarge Freiburger. Shootin' deer. We carve 'em up and split the meat amongst us. It really ain't bad. You should try it, Lieutenant."

"I thought I had to take care of that situation quickly," Strobell recalled. "So I set off and found the air disarmament people on the field, Master Sergeant Eugene Freiburger's bunch. They had full mess facilities at their end of the field. I told them to set up a mess tent at the hangar and provide our guys full meal service—morning, noon, and night. Then I met all twenty-seven of the German mechanics and test pilots. Gerhard 'Gerd' Caroli was the test engineer, also a pilot, and he supervised the mechanics—the *Monteure.* I had effectively two pilots at my disposal—Karl Baur, the Messerschmitt *Chefpilot,* and Ludwig 'Willie' Hoffmann, also a *Versuchspilot,* like Karl Baur. I didn't get many favors out of Baur because Watson stole him away all the time for his own projects. But Willie was mine exclusively and he was very helpful. Karl Baur was pure German in my book, what I call an elite, upper-crust kind of guy. Karl could work with Hal Watson, he couldn't work with me. I didn't really care what his social outlook was as long as he did the job I wanted him to do. I had good rapport with Watson, but not with Baur. On the other hand, Willie Hoffmann got along great with everyone, including me.

"I had a third German pilot, Hermann Kersting, he was a Luftwaffe pilot and I didn't like him. He didn't like me either. That was not why I fired him though. I fired him for not showing up to work when I needed him. When he finally did show up for work, after a prolonged absence, he was in his full Luftwaffe uniform with all his medals on, arriving in a sports car driven by his girlfriend. I said to him, You were supposed to be working here for the last five days. Where were you? He had some excuses. I told him bluntly, We don't need you anymore. Get back in the car and go away. He did. I had the other two test pilots, I didn't need this guy. But firing Kersting worried me. I didn't know whether one of the German mechanics was a friend of his and might try to do something funny, like booby-trap a plane to get even. Or maybe there was someone who just didn't like Americans, period. Interesting little things could happen to the airplanes."[4]

Strobell confided his fears to Roy Brown. "Sabotage was one of the things we were concerned about," Roy recalled. "There were precautions taken. When the mechanics got an airplane ready for flight,

Strobell or Watson, whoever was there at the time, wouldn't let anybody know who was going to fly it for the first time. It could be Baur or Hoffmann or one of us. The Germans didn't know who they were getting the plane ready for. But I am not aware of any incidents which would have indicated that there was a problem."

According to Watson, sabotage never became an issue. He wrote that German pilots and mechanics instead appeared anxious to save as many of the aircraft as possible to insure that the technology embodied in this airplane was not lost. When Watson interviewed Willy Messerschmitt in May 1945, he heard the same response to his questions — this airplane was something unique and different from any other, and not of Hitler's making. It represented the very best of German engineering under truly adverse circumstances. Of that achievement the Germans were justifiably proud.[5] Bob Anspach agreed with Watson's assessment. "I got the feeling that these people wanted to see us succeed. They were proud of that airplane. I never sensed that they wanted to do anything else, like carry on the war on their own. Of course our crew chiefs were there too, looking after us. The reason that we were ultimately so successful was that the crew chiefs, German and American, made the airplanes flyable and kept them flyable."[6]

Roy Brown and Bob Anspach spent more time with Baur and Hoffmann than Bob Strobell did, and therefore their views of the two German test pilots were shaped less by suspicion and more by the level of intimacy that developed between them as a natural by-product of their airplane talk. Brown, Anspach, Hillis, Holt, and Dahlstrom had nothing to do but learn all they could about this new and revolutionary airplane. Strobell, in addition to learning to fly the 262, had to deal with the management end of the operation, which allowed for less personal contact. "Baur and Hoffmann both were friendly," Roy Brown remembered. "Baur was more reserved than Hoffmann, more serious. He didn't really enter into conversation freely, while Willie was more outgoing and loved to tell flying stories. Willie had been a famous

A Bachem Natter (Viper), such as the one Willie Hoffmann claimed to have flown, photographed at Freeman Field. No American ever flew a Natter. (RW)

sailplane pilot before the war. He talked to us about flying inverted in a sailplane at one meter above the ground and doing a loop at one hundred meters. Willie told us about flying the Natter rocket plane which was launched from a rail, vertically. It had a nose cone with twenty-four rockets as armament. The idea was, according to Willie, to fly toward the formation of enemy bombers and shoot all the rockets. Then the pilot bailed out. The plane came down by parachute and was later recovered and reused, or that was the plan. Willie said that when he bailed out a metal fitting at the back of the chute hit his head and knocked him unconscious. Fortunately for him he regained consciousness before hitting the ground. Willie told a lot of flying stories like that and therefore we perceived him as being friendlier than Baur. Not that Baur was unfriendly, he just didn't mingle with the rest of us and remained reserved at all times."

"Willie liked schnapps," Bob Anspach recalled with a chuckle. "He was a lot of fun. I'd get a bottle of schnapps and that got Willie started talking about this or that from his never-ending repertoire of flying stories. I remember Willie coming in one morning and saying to me,

'You know who was at my house yesterday looking for me? Lindy.' We didn't want to believe it, but Lindbergh was in the area and took the time to look up his old friend Ludwig Hoffmann. They had flown together before the war."

Lindbergh left Washington on May 11, 1945, on a Navy aircraft and three days later arrived in Paris, the city of his prewar fame. Accompanied by officers of the United States Navy Technical Mission to Europe, Lindbergh toured through bomb-ravaged Mannheim and Munich and spent some time at Zell-am-See in Austria, where Göring and his air staff had been captured. Moving on to Oberammergau, Lindbergh met with Professor Dr. Willy E. Messerschmitt, who, as A. Scott Berg writes in *Lindbergh*, "had engineered many of Germany's most effective flying machines and had ushered aviation into a new age. His Me-262 was the world's first jet-propelled combat airplane, and his Me-163 Komet the first practical rocket-powered airplane—capable of speeds close to six hundred miles per hour. . . . Lindbergh learned the once-revered designer's large country house had been 'liberated' by American troops; and he found him living with his sister's family in a village farther into the country, reduced to sleeping on a pallet in a barn. Speaking through Messerschmitt's bilingual brother-in-law, Lindbergh conducted a technical conversation with the jet-age pioneer. Messerschmitt propounded the development of rocket-type planes for both military and commercial use and prophesied that within twenty years supersonic aircraft would need only a few hours to carry passengers between Europe and America. A visibly broken man, he told Lindbergh that he had been concerned about defeat as early as 1941, when he saw America's estimates for its own aircraft production. Lindbergh further learned that Messerschmitt had only recently returned from England, where he had been a prisoner of war. Both the British and the French had asked him to serve as a technical adviser. When Lindbergh asked whether he would be interested in working in America if an opportunity arose, he said he would have to hear the conditions. . . . Messerschmitt would remain in Germany, dying in 1978, never recovering financially or emotionally from the war."[7]

Like Watson, Bob Strobell was in love with the Me-262 from the moment he laid eyes on the airplane. "There were a number of things I really liked about this airplane. You could remove its nose in a few minutes and replace a fighter nose with a recce nose if you cared to do that, or if the aircraft had combat damage you could quickly exchange one nose section for another. A great capability to have in an airplane in wartime. You could also change an engine in almost nothing flat. The engines were plug-in types, which in a way made up for their short life. Pull the engine cowling off, and a mechanic could get the engine out in less than thirty minutes. How many hours could anyone put on one of those engines? That depended on whom you asked. The Luftwaffe people told me ten hours. Fifteen hours max. Flying beyond that was liable to result in a catastrophic engine failure. Gerd Caroli, our shop steward, told me twenty-five hours. I took that with a grain of salt. Maybe under ideal conditions that was achievable, but not in combat." In the early 1950s engine change time for America's first jet bomber, the Martin B/RB-45 powered by four General Electric J-47 engines, came after twenty-five hours of operation. The J-47 engine was continually improved, powering the Boeing B-47 six-jet bomber, and in time became a very reliable power plant. But the earliest models of the J-47 suffered from numerous problems, causing a number of B/RB-45 crashes and fatalities. Today, jet engine reliability approaches lifetime service of thousands of hours with no major overhaul required—something no one could have foreseen in 1945.[8]

"The process of repairing airplanes and bringing them up to readiness started before I got to Lechfeld," Bob Strobell noted. "Shortly after I arrived I went to Caroli and said to him, You got this two-seater airplane here. I need it for training my pilots. He answered me in good English, 'I can get it out for you today.' Great, I said to him, how many hours does it have on the engines? 'I don't know,' was Caroli's response.

What about the rest of the airplanes? 'I don't know that either,' Caroli answered honestly. Where are the records? I asked. 'We don't have any records.' I glared at him. Then you are going to take them all back into the shop and start from scratch. In my opinion there was no alternative. Caroli got right on it, but instead of getting the two-seater out first, he did that one last. Baur and Hoffmann checked them out one after another as soon as Caroli released an aircraft. In the meantime I put the guys to work 'hangar flying' while I waited for the first airplane to finish inspection.

"They were all Thunderbolt pilots. Never flown an aircraft using a tricycle landing gear or the metric system. So you have to figure out how you are going to train these guys. What I decided to do was to take an Me-262 that was not restorable to flying condition and I had it tethered to the ground outside the hangar. Then I asked all five of them—Anspach, Brown, Hillis, Holt, and Dahlstrom—to sit in the cockpit and go through the engine start, taxi, and takeoff routine. We'd go through the cockpit operation with this airplane tethered to the ground, run up the engines, and shut them down again. Then we practiced conceivable emergencies and what we would do. We didn't have any flight manuals to help us along. We could ignore the radios because they were German and we didn't have time nor a need to install American radios. And we were going to fly at ten thousand feet or less, so we didn't have to bother with oxygen. But everything else we had to know—cold.

"I knew that just having them do a cockpit checkout was not going to make them safe pilots in this airplane—and that's what Watson wanted me to do, turn out proficient and safe pilots. To be safe pilots they had to learn the idiosyncracies of the 262—what it did that the Thunderbolt didn't do type of thing. So I decided somewhere along the line somebody had to go first, and since we didn't have the two-seat trainer available to us I decided I was going to be the first one to fly the Me-262. When the first aircraft rolled out of the hangar for

Willie Hoffmann, the likeable Messerschmitt test pilot, checking out Lieutenant Haynes in Vera *at Melun, France, June 1945. (RB)*

flight test after the engine inspection I ordered was completed, I told Caroli I wanted Baur to fly the aircraft. Herr Caroli said, 'That's great.' Baur got into the aircraft, fired up the engines, and taxied out to the end of the runway and took off. Jim Holt, Bob Anspach, and I got in a jeep and drove over to the runway and waited for Baur to land. Baur flew around for about five minutes and then came in for a landing. As he rolled down the runway we hit the runway right behind him and followed him all the way down to his rollout. When he came to a stop I waved to Baur to get out. He got out and I jumped in. I taxied the airplane back to the hangar, refueled [fuel was an eighty-seven-octane gasoline and oil mixture; nearly any kerosene mixture would work in the Me-262] and taxied back to the end of the runway and took off. There was no sabotage, but I felt more comfortable doing it this way.

"The Me-262 was an honest airplane, a pilot can't ask for more than that. I made two or three pilot errors on that first flight. It's bound to happen, and better me than to any of the other guys. My very first error was on takeoff. I had the mistaken impression that when flying a swept-wing airplane [the Me-262's wing sweep was a little over eighteen degrees, while the F-86, patterned after the Me-262 and using many of its features, had a wing sweep of thirty-five degrees] I had to elevate the nose on takeoff perhaps a little higher than on the Thunderbolt. I had the nose up pretty high. Halfway down the runway, looking at the airspeed indicator, I noticed that it wasn't moving. I am going maybe eighty kilometers, but the airspeed indicator appeared to be dead. At that moment, I figured this thing wasn't going to take off, so I put the nose back down. The second the nose wheel touched the runway, up went the airspeed. I used six thousand feet of a six-thousand-foot runway to get that thing off the ground.

"Among the many things I really liked about this airplane was the fact that from a combat standpoint I was looking right over the nose of the airplane, down the bore sight of its cannons. In a Thunderbolt with the guns in the wings the pilot had to worry about convergence at three hundred yards. Where is three hundred yards in the air without reference points? But with the Me-262 you sat in the cockpit, feet forward, looking right down the barrels of the guns. Visibility from the cockpit was excellent. The first thing I heard and felt when flying the 262 were the leading edge wing slats which automatically opened at low airspeeds and retracted during high-speed flight. Neither Baur nor Hoffmann had told me about the slats. So I am watching these things popping in and out with the turbulence up there. What the hell are they? I thought. Are they supposed to be in or out? These things are going boom-bang, boom-bang. They were intended for low-speed flight only—changing the airflow over the top of the wing so it could be flown at a lower airspeed without stalling. Finally my speed picked up and they were shut, and I was happy. The next thing I noticed was that I was going about twice as fast as in the Thunderbolt and there were no vibrations. By my standards this thing was just screaming across the countryside, going like the proverbial bat out of hell. I felt a deep sense of exhilaration.

I flew it around for a little bit, then I entered the downwind leg, pulled the throttles back to idle, I was doing nearly five hundred miles per hour—and nothing happened. When I did that in the P-47 it was like hitting a brick wall. Nothing like that in the Me-262. About six miles beyond the airfield I decided this wasn't going to do it. I went back around, into the downwind leg again, pulled the throttles back and raised the nose. Climbing without the power on cut the airspeed. About the time I got down to the airspeed where I could lower the landing gear, I popped it out. The nose promptly went up and the thing pitched out on me. I needed some power to stay airborne. Before it was all over I am eight miles beyond the field again. I thought, to hell with this. I am going to climb, line up, and land. I made a gradual descent and brought her down. The two professional test pilots we had were not in the business of training other people. So, little details like how best to land this airplane didn't occur to them as being important to pass on to others. As a test pilot you just know how to do that sort of thing.

"When I came around and landed, Holt and Anspach sat at the end of the runway, still in the jeep. I taxied back to the hangar and shut down the engines. They pulled right up next to me and jumped on the wing. I opened the canopy and they grabbed my shirt collars and broke the props off my Army Air Corps insignia. Bob Anspach said to me, 'You don't need the props anymore. You are a jet pilot now.' That was one of the classiest acts anyone ever did for me. From then on it became a ritual. As everyone checked out in the aircraft, off came the props."[9]

"The next thing on the agenda," Anspach recalled, "was giving ourselves a name. Sort of an impromptu thing, just like snapping the props off our insignia. In one of our training sessions one of the fellows said, 'We should have a good time whizzing around the sky in the 262.' It struck me that obviously we pilots were Watson's Whizzers. So I proposed calling ourselves Watson's Whizzers. The name stuck. So we became Watson's Whizzers, and Hal Watson was as proud of that moniker as any of us."

The other five pilots learned much about takeoff and landing procedures from Bob Strobell's flight. Strobell talked to them as one P-47 Thunderbolt pilot to another—about what was different flying a jet and what was the same as flying the P-47. Hardly anything was the same. Once the two-seat trainer rolled out of the hangar, the checkout of Anspach, Brown, Holt, Hillis, and Dahlstrom went into high gear. "Karl Baur checked me out," Anspach recalled. "I got in the front seat, Karl in the back. We didn't have a radio, but we could talk and I could hear what he was saying. There wasn't that much noise in the cockpit, even when compared to American jets of a later period. I flew the F-86E and F models in Korea in 1952–53. For me at least the F-86 was the perfect airplane to fly, but it was noisier than the Me-262. It took until the early fifties for us to best the Me-262, which was a late-thirties design. One thing I remember Baur telling me as we sat at the end of the runway getting set for takeoff, 'When you rev up the engines, look at the engine nacelle and you'll see a cone emerging [German pilots referred to the cone as the *Zwiebel*, the onion]. It has marks on it. When it gets to this mark,' and Baur pointed to it, 'you have sufficient power and you can safely start down the runway.' Of course there was an RPM indicator on the instrument panel, but the *Zwiebel* was a more reliable indicator of thrust. Then Baur said to me, 'Your problem is not going to be taking off, or flying the airplane. Your problem is going to be landing.' He told me what to expect. 'Fly an extra-large pattern. Give yourself plenty of room. Get your flaps down and watch that tail cone. It's the easiest way to tell if you have enough power. Remember, once you cut the power you cannot bring it back up real quick. You will have to land if you want to or not. So you want to fly it hot.' We took off. I had never flown an aircraft with a tricycle landing gear before, and I don't believe anyone else had. Once we landed, Baur said to me, 'You did everything I told you to do. You will do just fine.' That one ten-minute flight was my instruction and checkout in the Me-262 jet fighter. Everything was by the seat of the pants."[10]

Jim Holt and Bob Anspach facing, Ken Dahlstrom with back to camera, in front of
Wilma Jeanne, *Lechfeld, June 10, 1945. (RB)*

The lack of a checklist providing start-up, in-flight, and shut-down
procedures for the Jumo 004B-1 engine could have been remedied easily had a knowledgeable person been able to screen some of the mass
of captured documentation forwarded to the Documentation Center
in London for processing. But confusion reigned supreme at the end
of a long war, and a checklist for jet pilots was an item of low priority.
However, in mid-June Bob Anspach and his fellow Whizzers made a
trip in Watson's C-47 troop carrier aircraft to Schleswig, a German airfield in the British zone of occupation just south of the Danish border.
Some of them continued on and flew up to Grove airfield in Denmark,
called Karup now. Grove had been home to the Arado 234 jet bomber,
which used the same engines as the Me-262. Their British hosts were
correct and friendly, but reticent in providing any captured items to
the curious and at times pushy Yanks. Anspach somehow managed to
locate a German Arado checklist. "I don't know how, but we got a hold

of one. I stayed up one night copying the flight manual." The checklist written for pilots and jet engine crew chiefs was brief and to the point, and provided instructions for engine priming, starting procedures, ignition, idling procedure after ignition, full power operation, engine shut down, and taxi and normal cruise operations. The checklist revealed to them for the first time how to properly initiate an in-flight engine start—below twelve thousand feet, not using the built-in Riedel starter used on the ground, but instead using the force generated by the windmilling turbine blades. Full power operation in flight was restricted to a maximum of fifteen minutes. Pictures illustrated each procedure, including rpm, temperature, and pressure settings for cruise and maximum speed operations.

Roy Brown recalled, "When I first arrived at Lechfeld we were pretty much on our own, spent our time in the cockpits of airplanes learning where the instruments and controls were located and what the functions of the controls were. Strobell had an Me-262 tethered near the hangar and we all sat in that aircraft, ran up the power and practiced our procedures. That was helpful, but it wasn't flying. For the final checkout in the tethered aircraft we closed our eyes, a blindfold check, locating every lever, button, and cockpit control. In an emergency there is no time to think, and reactions need to be near automatic. That is the way we trained in flight training, concentrating on developing conditioned reflexes. If I am flying along and something goes suddenly wrong, I don't always have time to think about the emergency. I may have to react immediately and instinctively and that requires training yourself to do the correct thing. Our blindfold checks served that purpose.

"I sort of sat back and listened when the others talked about engine problems due to abrupt flight maneuvers, or nose gear and braking problems. The aircraft had leading edge slats, something new to me. On the ground they were out. Around 150 miles per hour they retracted. The slats improved the airflow over the wing, lowering the aircraft's stall speed. The cockpit in the airplane was not crowded, at least I didn't find it to be that. The one thing I remember Karl Baur mentioning to us several times, 'When coming in for a landing keep the throttles forward a bit. Keep the turbines turning over at a pretty good speed. If you let the engines slow down to idle and you need power for a go-around, it takes a while for the jets to regain their power.' It's not like a prop job where the response is instantaneous, and all of us were used to flying that kind of an airplane. I remember on my check flight with Karl, I came in a little bit hot on landing, playing it safe. Once I came near the runway I pulled back on the stick a little to keep the nose gear off the runway, and once I touched down I dropped the nose slowly. I don't believe Baur ever touched the controls during my initial flight. For our subsequent ferry flight—after all, that was what we were training for—Baur reminded us that the auxiliary fuel tank was right behind the cockpit. Not long after takeoff you had to start transferring that fuel from the aft tank into the main forward tank in front of the cockpit. If you waited too long it was too late, the engines used more fuel than the pump could transfer.

"It is surprising that we had no problems checking out. Maybe it was because most of us had been instructor pilots, which made us more comfortable flying in a different plane. I think you learn a lot about flying when you instruct and it becomes easier to transition. Among the many nice things in the Me-262 was a true airspeed indicator. I was used to having to convert indicated airspeed, based on altitude, to true airspeed. True airspeed was the speed you were flying at, not indicated. I liked flying the Me-262. I thought it was an easy plane to fly, a very nice plane to fly—not noisy, not a lot of vibrations, the sort of thing I was used to in the Thunderbolt. As for Colonel Watson? I thought he was quite a person. He was something like a Steve Canyon type, the character in the comic strip. He was good looking and certainly we all knew that he was a very good pilot. He was articulate, could say what he wanted to say, and said what he wanted to say. I remember one time sitting in the cockpit of one of the 262s in the hangar familiarizing

In-flight starting procedure for the Jumo 004 engine, from a captured German Me-262/Ar 234 checklist. A helpful piece of paper for the novice P-47 pilots. (RA)

myself when he came up with a compass in front of the airplane and told me to tell him what the compass reading was. He was checking the compasses on all the airplanes. Like everyone else he was out there helping out wherever he could."[11]

Bob Anspach recalled that Watson "showed up briefly at Lechfeld, explained to us what we were doing and why, and otherwise he stayed pretty much out of our way. There wasn't all that much to this operation. We were there to learn to fly the airplanes, that was it. We were nothing in terms of an organization, just a bunch of pilots—Watson's Whizzers. But I do think that we were the first Army Air Forces jet pilots, and you could also say that we were the first operational American jet fighter squadron, although we flew captured enemy aircraft. We even had our own unit patch, which one of our crew chiefs designed and painted on the nose of every aircraft. We had plenty of time on our hands, there wasn't all that much to do to keep us busy. We'd eat in the mess tent Strobell had the 54th set up next to our hangar, and occasionally some of the guys would go down to the Lech River and throw in some grenades and kill some trout and we'd have a fish fry. There were also the mundane things to tend to, like laundry. Germans would stop at the fence by the field and try to talk to us. That way we met some of the local people. They were all very contrite. Victims of circumstances, I thought. On a walk through town I saw a woman and her daughter working in the garden in front of their house. I asked her if she would do my laundry. She nodded her head. I paid her in German marks, not worth much, and rations, which she was pleased to receive."

Although Karl Baur often was perceived as reticent, even arrogant, by the American pilots, in his diary he wrote of his admiration for them and for Watson. "Those Americans are excellent pilots," wrote Baur. "But, what impresses me most is the fact that they all have degrees in engineering [which was not true]. One checkout ride in the two-seater was enough to turn them loose. It is a pleasant experience to work with this group." Isolde Baur recalled that there were some advantages to working for the Americans. "All German personnel received meals, which was a very important factor, since food distribution to German civilians had broken down completely. Canned military rations were distributed. We learned to enjoy ham and eggs from dried eggs and canned ham. It was a 'heavenly' gourmet meal. Most men saved as much as they could to take home to their families, such as cookies and chocolate. What luxuries they were for us starving Germans! Also, 'Off Limits' signs were distributed to the workers for their apartments. It meant that our apartments were taboo for occupation by American military personnel, and we were spared having the former 'Guests of the Führer' [forced laborers] take over the possessions we had managed to salvage. Our apartment was inspected by military personnel the day they had occupied the City. It was declared unsuitable since we had no refrigerator, no central heating, and no bathroom entrance from the hall. We were among the fortunate people that had received glass to replace some of the broken windows. We had them installed so that we had some daylight in every room."[12]

Unlike the Soviets in their zone of occupation, Americans paid Germans for their services; payment had to be done in accordance with regulations issued by Headquarters, United States Army, European Theater of Operations, ETOUSA. Lieutenant Strobell quickly found himself confronted by the pay issue and asked Watson for advice. What were we paying the German pilots and maintenance personnel, and who was going to do it? Watson turned to Lieutenant Colonel Seashore, whose sole function at USSTAF headquarters was to support Watson. Seashore flew down to Lechfeld and hand-delivered the instructions to Bob Strobell. "Regarding payment of German nationals as pilots for the U.S., the following information is furnished," wrote First Lieutenant J. L. Whipple, assistant fiscal officer at USSTAF headquarters. Attached to Lieutenant Whipple's cover memorandum was a letter of instructions from ETOUSA, providing for the "Procurement, Administration and Payment of Civilian Labor in Germany." The instructions reminded Strobell that "Civilian personnel in Germany will not be engaged unless military manpower requirements demand that it be done. The greatest effort will be made to utilize military services units and civilian employees moved into Germany by the U.S. forces. Where these are unavailable, the first source of manpower in Germany to be exploited will be non-German civilians, particularly those who may have been imported into Germany by the Nazi Government. Enemy civilian labor will be hired only as a last resort." The instructions continued, "German civilians will be employed for the performance of menial tasks only where absolutely necessary and preferably where they do not come in contact with the troops. The most stern and rigid discipline must be preserved to prevent fraternization." Bob Strobell read the instructions with the attention a man gave things he knew he was going to ignore. Bob was a no-nonsense, get-the-job-done kind of guy, and stuff like this always made him wonder how the United States had managed to

Watson, flanked by two of his German Messerschmitt mechanics, posing in front of an Me-262 at Lechfeld, May 1945. The uneven skin of the Me-262 is clearly discernible in the picture. (RW)

win the war. The instructions did finally get down to what he was look-ing for—specific guidance on how to pay the Germans who worked for him. There was a schedule with rates of pay for male workers, and female workers were to be paid "from 70% to 60% of the rates for male workers." Strobell only had male workers to worry about.[13]

The twenty-seven pilots and aircraft mechanics Watson hired for the task of restoring ten Me-262 aircraft back to flying status were paid according to their positions within the organization and based on the size of their families. Karl Baur was classified as a chief pilot, *Chefpilot*; he had one child and was paid 3,300 marks monthly. Baur was the highest paid of the twenty-seven. Gerhard Caroli, as chief engineer, *Erprobungsleiter*, and pilot, with two children, received 3,000 marks; Ludwig Hoffmann, test pilot, *Versuchspilot*, with four children, received 2,500 marks. The mechanics' wages were set as high as 830 marks for a technical inspector, *Kontrolleur*, with two children, to a low of 460 marks for a plain-vanilla aircraft mechanic, *Monteur*, with no special skills and no children. The most important forms of compensation for all of the German employees were the meals served at their places of work and the access to Americans, which made it possible to pick up discarded food at the mess tent or to swap some family treasure for cigarettes, Hershey bars, or anything else American that could be traded on the black market for food.

THE MERSEBURG
FAN CLUB

In late April of 1945 Captain Fred McIntosh was called by the personnel section of the 65th Fighter Wing and asked if he would mind doing nine days of temporary duty, TDY, on the Continent. "Sure, why not," McIntosh replied. "The war was all but over and I didn't have a job anyway. When I picked up my orders they didn't read nine days, but ninety days. Maybe I had misunderstood, but it was too late to do anything about it. I left RAF Boxted for Paris on the fifth of May on one of our B-26 Marauders. I had no trouble finding someone to fly me to Paris once they learned where I was going. I checked in at USSTAF headquarters in St.-Germain. It was a beautiful location. Colonel Lloyd Pepple from the Exploitation Divison in the Directorate of Intelligence welcomed me and briefly acquainted me with my new assignment—Merseburg airfield, near the heavily bombed Leuna oil refinery complex. I was to receive detailed instructions in the next two days, including the necessary passports to allow me to function as a member of Colonel Dave Schilling's Air Technical Intelligence team. What a surprise. I thought Schilling was still at wing or 8th Air Force headquarters. He apparently maneuvered himself into this assignment to fly a German jet.[1]

"Colonel Pepple informed me that I had been billeted with a French family up on the palisades. After a day of briefings I wanted to get some sleep, but my French host family insisted that I go with them out on the palisades after dark. I thought they knew something I didn't. Pretty soon the palisades was like Times Square, packed with locals and a mixture of Americans. The night was jet black. All of a sudden there was a loud explosion and a single searchlight shone on the tricolor on top of the Arc de Triomphe. Boom—another search-light illuminated the top of the Eiffel Tower. And with that all hell broke loose. Lights came on everywhere. That was May 8, 1945, 11 P.M., the day and hour World War II officially ended for the western Allies. People were hugging, kissing, dancing, drinking—the merriment went on for three days.

"When I reported back to Colonel Pepple, I was passed a telephone message from Captain Maxfield at Merseburg. The message read, 'If you are not too busy having fun, Captain McIntosh, how about getting your ass up here to help me out.' That day I caught a ride on a courier plane to Merseburg. When I arrived, Colonel Schilling was no longer there. When Schilling first came to Merseburg he brought along his former squadron engineering officer, Captain Edwin D. Maxfield, and Sergeant Edmund Namowics. Maxfield wasn't a pilot, but he knew more about airplanes than anyone else. Sergeant Namowics, we officers called him Murphy, was a top-notch aircraft mechanic who spoke five languages. A good man to have around." Schilling's small ATI team was part of the larger aircraft recovery operation under Operation Lusty led by Colonel Watson.[2] "There were maybe half a dozen men in place at Merseburg, including Maxfield, Namowicz, and two pilots. Of the two pilots, one had sort of forgotten why he was there, a lieutenant colonel who was supposed to have been acting as Schilling's deputy. Instead, he requisitioned a chalet some distance from Merseburg and filled it with local lovelies. He had a radio to maintain contact with the airfield. So, if anybody of importance showed up, he would get the word to get out of bed and come to work. I met him once at his love nest. Maxfield took me out there. He said, 'I want you to see what you are up against. You are a captain, and he is a colonel.' Maxfield had talked to Schilling about the situation and pointed out to him that from a flight safety standpoint they needed someone who could act like an operations officer. 'You better get a pilot in here to run this operation or somebody is going to get killed,' Maxfield said he told Schilling. Schilling allegedly said, 'Fine. It's all right with me. If you know anybody, I'll requisition him.'

" 'Yes, I know somebody,' Maxfield replied. 'Your wingman.'

" 'Mac?'

" 'Yeah. He speaks some German. His stepfather is German.'

" 'If he hasn't gone home yet,' Schilling replied, 'get him.'

"Maxfield got on the horn with personnel, and that's how I ended up at Merseburg. Maxfield informed me that a Wright Field test pilot, a Colonel Watson, was taking over the Merseburg operation. 'He sent me a list of all he wants us to collect,' and Maxfield pulled the list from his back pocket and showed it to me.

" 'I guess we sit tight until this bird shows up, whoever the hell he is,' I told him.

"In Merseburg we lived in a requisitioned hotel, Der Alte Dessauer," recalled McIntosh. "It was convenient to the airfield and comfortable. The hotel had been taken over by doctors and nurses of an evacuation hospital which tended to American and British POWs being pro- cessed for release back to the U.S. and the U.K. Merseburg airfield was a dirt strip, like many German airfields, adjacent to the Junkers factory. Sitting on jacks in the largest hangar, we found a brand new Junkers 388. It was pressurized, had an ejection seat, and the typical bulbous Junkers glass nose. We immediately christened the plane *Old Venereal*." The Ju 388L used two BMW 801 turbo-supercharged engines and was one of forty or fifty aircraft built by Junkers for test purposes. It was intended as a high-altitude reconnaissance plane. Large-scale

The Merseburg Junkers 388L with its distinctive four-bladed props and bulbous nose at Freeman Field, Indiana, 1945. (RW)

production for the Ju 388 was scheduled to start in December 1945. "All the records for the plane were there. It had less than ten hours' flying time on it. Watson had heard about the plane and put it on the Wright Field want list. A note was attached to the list reading, I fly it when I get there. Signed, Watson.

"I didn't know who this guy Watson was, but if he ever got here, I thought, he would want some answers before he ever got into the airplane. Let's ground-check it, I suggested to Maxfield. Maxfield had devised an aircraft inspection checklist that we used to check out every airplane we intended to fly. 'I hate to fly,' I heard Maxfield mutter as we got into the aircraft—I soon learned he said that every time he got into an airplane. I started the engines on the Ju 388 and did some checking of the instrumentation to be sure I wasn't using the wrong numbers. This was the first time I had worked with instruments using the metric system. We did a taxi check. Everything seemed to handle all right. I said to Ed, Let's do at least one high-speed taxi check and see how it handles. Ed was sitting in a lower seat to one side. We taxied out. Ed said to me afterwards, 'I should have known what would happen next when you taxied clear to the back fence.' We came roaring down the field and Ed realized what I was up to. He looked at me and yelled, 'You bastard.' We lifted off and went around the field. I did a couple of stalls, basic stuff, then landed. Watson showed up a day later. We were having breakfast together, and he was talking about what he wanted us to accomplish. Then he said, 'I understand the 388 has been ground-checked. Is that correct, Captain McIntosh?' Yes, sir, I responded. Then he said, 'How does it fly?' Everybody looked at me. I thought I better be straight with him and said, Like a board, sir. He said, 'Good' and nodded his head. 'You and I are going to go and fly it together now.' "

Watson remembered the Ju 388 story a little differently. "I first heard about this airplane in late 1944 or early 1945," he wrote, "and it was well up on our list of priority targets. . . . It was my strict policy that no pilot on this project would fly any airplane without my specific approval. When I got back to Merseburg to check out this airplane I was amazed to find a couple of eager beavers, Captains McIntosh and Maxfield, coming in for a landing after an unauthorized flight. Although it would have been appropriate to raise a lot of hell, take them off the project, confine them to quarters, reduce their ration of beer—any of these would have punished me instead. McIntosh was a superb pilot with guts and Maxfield was a first-class engineering officer with unusual skill." So Watson chose to overlook the incident— a good decision. On May 20 Watson and McIntosh flew the Ju 388 to Kassel, since Merseburg was soon to come under Russian control.

McIntosh was impressed with his new boss. "Watson was a hell of a pilot. We hit it off good. I found it very easy to work with him. He knew what he was doing, and he knew what he wanted to be. He gave me the operation at Merseburg, and I had the pleasure of running the fan club. The pilot colonel with the requisitioned chalet just faded away; Watson took care of him. The other pilot unfortunately broke his back flying a German glider against my orders, so for a while I was the only remaining American pilot at Merseburg. I quickly learned that Watson had influence. He got me a C-47 transport from a troop

An L-5 observation plane like the one McIntosh referred to as his "beer wagon,"
which gives an idea of what they used it for. (JH)

carrier outfit, complete with crew. We also had what the guys referred
to as our 'beer wagon,' an L-5 two-seater observation plane, piloted
by a sergeant who came with the L-5. The L-5 sergeant pilot and the
radio operator on my C-47 soon turned into drinking buddies. I found
I had to keep them busy, otherwise they got themselves into trouble,
which they frequently did in spite of my best efforts.

"German women in the area did their washing in the nearby Saale
River. These two guys must have had a few beers too many because
they took the L-5 and flew over to where the women were doing their
laundry and landed right next to the river. Instead of leaving the airplane where they landed, they taxied it right up to the women at the
river's edge, trying to impress them. All the bridges in that area had
been blown, and the Army had thrown a Bailey pontoon bridge across
the river near this place. There were deep ruts left behind by tanks and
heavy trucks which had come through in late April. The two sergeants
got stuck, chewing up the wooden propeller on their L-5 in the
process. So I found this little personnel problem waiting for me when
I came back from a visit to the Zeiss factory in Jena. We had a lieutenant assigned to my team by the name of Horn, "Pappy," we called
him. He was one of the original ATI team members who trained with

The Fieseler Storch was a simple, rugged liaison plane. This Storch was forced down by Major Bennet, of the 14th Liaison Squadron, flying an L-5 near Freising, May 7, 1945. (JH)

the British and landed in France right after D-day. Pappy couldn't fly because of his glasses, but he was a very good private pilot. Pappy Horn was the one who solved the problem for me. At an airfield near Halle, Pappy found several gliders and Fieseler Storch liaison aircraft. With Pappy's help we managed to fly six of the Fieseler Storchs to Merseburg. Pappy took a Fieseler prop, redrilled it and put it on the L-5 and then flew it out. The sergeants? I gave them the expected chewing out, and hoped they would lay low for a while, which they did.

"The doctors and nurses living with us in the Alte Dessauer had put up the tents of their evacuation hospital in the middle of Merseburg airfield, right between the grass runway and the adjacent taxiway. This was a collection station for former American and British prisoners of war. Here they received a thorough medical examination before being shipped to a hospital or some other camp for final processing and release. Once or twice a week a bunch of C-47s showed up, loaded with the engines running, and quickly took off again. For some reason more former POWs showed up than the hospital folks could process and ship out. The waiting men wanted to get out of there and became restless and impatient. Pappy Horn saw the situation building, so he went over to the doctors and offered to give rides to the waiting GIs in our Fieseler Storchs. We had four pilots and could take up a total of eight passengers at a time, two per airplane. The doctors ran a lottery and the winners got to fly with us over the heavily bombed Leuna oil refinery, over Leipzig and other nearby towns and villages allowing them to get a bird's-eye view of the damage the air war had done to Germany. Pappy Horn's idea was a great success and took the edge off the situation. Soon the former POWs were all gone, and things quieted down.

"We didn't just collect German airplanes for Watson, but also went after other things on the Wright Field want list such as ground support equipment for the V-2 missile, submarine periscopes, radio-controlled bombs, antiaircraft fire control systems, Walther engines for the Me-163—that sort of stuff. We boxed up what we collected and sent it on to one of the collection points. We had several jeeps with trailers assigned, and teams of two to three people would go out to investigate when the disarmament people reported finding something that was on our want list. One day we were tasked to inspect a nearby textile mill. They made parachutes and lingerie—the coarsest brassieres I ever felt in my life. They also made high-quality cloth for the Nazi bigwigs' wives. So we helped ourselves to some of that fine cloth to take home to our wives and mothers, but of course we were there for the parachutes, not the cloth.

"I received a radio message from Watson to come down to Nürnberg. It was dusk when we got there, and Maxfield, who never liked flying anyway, was looking over my shoulder for landing lights. Suddenly I heard him saying, 'I won't go. I just won't go.' Ed, I hollered at him, what the hell are you talking about? He said, 'Look,' and he pointed at this large airplane sitting down there, a huge Junkers 290 four-engine transport. I turned to Ed and said, You are right, that's how we are going home. Watson wouldn't fool with that thing unless he had something in mind, and that thing wasn't on our want list."

The Junkers 290 evolved from the Ju 89/90 commercial aircraft pro-ject which was to have been the basis for a German four-engined strate-gic bomber. Instead, Ernst Udet's insistence that all bombers be able to dive-bomb, an idea he picked up on his prewar visits to the United States, among other considerations doomed the strategic bomber pro-ject and it was scrapped by the Germans as early as 1936. Udet saw the error of his ways too late after the shape of the Luftwaffe was pretty much cast in concrete, and he committed suicide in 1941.[3] Forty-one Ju 290As were built, nearly all in a reconnaissance configuration. They were based during the war at Mont-de-Marsan, France, with Fernaufklärungsgruppe 5, spotting Allied shipping for Heinkel 177 bombers and U-boats. After the Allied invasion of France in 1944, Fernaufklärungsgruppe 5 was disbanded and its aircraft were assigned to the Luftwaffe's special mission wing—Kampfgeschwader 200. KG 200 was formed in February 1944 and reported directly to the Ober-kommando der Luftwaffe, the German air staff, and flew an assortment of aircraft, including captured American B-17 and B-24 bombers.[4] The commander of the Ju 290 squadron of KG 200 was a thirty-year-old Hauptmann by the name of Heinz Braun. In early May 1945, Heinz Braun was at Königgrätz, Czechoslovakia, with orders to fly a group of Vichy French officials to safety in Spain. The French officials never showed up, and Braun instead chose to load his aircraft with German soldiers and fly to Munich to surrender to the Americans.

The Ju 290 was not unknown to Wright Field engineers. Among the over five hundred German and Italian aircraft captured in North Africa in May 1943 were three Ju 290 transports. One was captured at Bizerte and two at Tunis. All three were heavily damaged. "A feature of particular interest," noted Major Clayton Beaman in an interview on June 10, 1943, with the Assistant Chief of Air Staff for Intelligence in Washington, "is a ramp in the after part of the fuselage which can be lowered to the ground and over which small vehicles may be loaded into the interior of the fuselage."[5] Three Ju 290s had also been modified with extra fuel tanks inside the passenger compartment, allowing them to make flights across the Soviet Union to Japanese-occupied Manchuria to deliver jet engines and radars in exchange for critical raw materials. By the time the modifications were completed, however, the Wehrmacht no longer controlled the airfields from which they were supposed to launch their unique missions, and the Japanese expressed reservations as well about the feasibility of the project. So nothing ever came of it. One of the three modified planes survived and became an American war trophy—Colonel Watson's trophy. The Ju 290 had a less than impressive cruising speed of under two hundred miles per hour. What it lacked in airspeed it made up in endurance—an impressive twenty-two hours plus. In size the Junkers aircraft was more comparable to the B-29 bomber than to the state-of-the-art American C-54 cargo aircraft. Although the Ju 290, in contrast to the C-54, still used the old-fashioned tail wheel arrangement, its innovative hydraulically operated loading ramp, discovered by Major Beaman on his inspection trip to North Africa in 1943, gave it unusual versatility for a transport aircraft of its day. When the ramp was lowered, the tail of the aircraft raised up simultaneously, allowing palleted cargo or small vehicles to be rolled or driven on or off the plane.[6]

On May 8, 1945, the last day of the war in Europe, Watson was surveying Munich-Riem airport looking for Me-262 jets and other exotic German aircraft such as the Dornier 335 push-pull fighter. He was accompanied by his Wright Field friend and fellow airman Colonel George W. Goddard. Riem had been secured by a 130-man security detachment from the XII Tactical Air Command, a part of the 1st Tactical Air Force (Provisional).[7] Hal and George had known one another since 1940, when both served at the Materiel Division at Wright Field. Watson was elated because he had found one additional intact Me-262 jet fighter left behind by Galland's Jagdverband 44 when they hurriedly evacuated Munich-Riem in late April. Watson decided to have Karl Baur, the German Messerschmitt test pilot whom he had employed

Watson at Munich-Riem airport, May 8, 1945. Riem airport was almost totally destroyed. (RW)

only six days earlier, come down to Munich and fly the precious jet back to Lager Lechfeld. Watson looked at other aircraft at Riem and nearby Neubiberg airfield but found nothing he could use. A Dornier 335 fighter at Neubiberg was too riddled by bomb shrapnel. He definitely wanted a 335, but this one was not salvageable.

Watson and Goddard were standing on the tarmac at Munich-Riem, near the airfield's bombed-out operations building, when Watson thought he spotted an aircraft approaching. The strange-looking plane appeared to be flying very close to the ground with its landing gear down. "It's a strange-looking bird. Has to be German," said Goddard. Hauptmann Heinz Braun had departed Königgrätz earlier that morning with a load of seventy soldiers. He stayed at treetop level throughout the flight, hoping to avoid Russian or American fighters. The ride was bumpy and several of the soldiers got airsick. The plane reeked of

The Junkers 290 transport surrendered to Watson at Munich-Riem on May 8, 1945. It is shown here at Freeman Field in Indiana. (RB)

vomit. Watson and Goddard watched the huge Ju 290 land, then taxi toward them, shutting down two of its four engines, coming to a stop only feet away from them. Members of the XII TAC quickly appeared in jeeps and surrounded the aircraft, carbines at the ready. To Watson's and Goddard's surprise, the tail section of the aircraft slowly rose, a ramp lowered to the tarmac in the rear, and out strode the plane's pilot. Hauptmann Heinz Braun approached Watson and Goddard, came to attention, saluted, and in good English announced the surrender of his aircraft, crew, and passengers. A grinning Watson turned to Goddard and said, "My transportation to the United States has just arrived." Watson later wrote that "after the airplane had been cleaned up—all of which took a matter of hours—I got Captain Braun in the co-pilot's seat and I jumped in the pilot's seat. After a few minutes we took off and landed at my technical intelligence forward collection base in Nürnberg-Roth."[8]

"On May 30," Fred McIntosh recalled, "we received a message from the Exploitation Division at St.-Germain to vacate Merseburg not later than 2 June and relocate to Munich-Neubiberg.[9] Maxfield with the rest of my team drove to Neubiberg in our jeeps and trucks. I flew down to Nürnberg-Roth instead where we had accumulated a bunch of Focke-Wulf 190s for delivery to Cherbourg. Hauptmann Heinz Braun and three of his mechanics had been retained by Watson at Nürnberg to service the Ju 290, and Watson made Braun available to me whenever Heinz wasn't busy. Heinz spoke fairly good English and was an excellent pilot. He flew anything I told him to—the Ju 52 transport, Fieseler Storch liaison aircraft, Heinkel 111 bomber, and Focke-Wulf 190 and Messerschmitt 109 fighters. There was a Heinkel 111 on the airfield, flown in and surrendered by its German crew on May 8. The 111 was a Battle of Britain vintage plane and of no technical interest to us. I asked Heinz if he knew how to fly it and he answered, 'Ja, Herr Hauptmann, I know how to fly a Heinkel 111.' I needed to get back to RAF Boxted, my old P-47 base.

In early 1945 I was hit by German flak. Shrapnel shattered the canopy of my P-47 and shredded my parachute. I remember blood spurting from my ears. The cold air stopped the bleeding, but I couldn't hear. I pulled out of the formation, and, accompanied by another P-47, made it home. The doctors at the hospital in Boxted took out about a third of my teeth and put a temporary plate in my mouth. The war ended and I was in Germany, still with that temporary plate. I received a message from the dentist at Boxted just before we were to leave Merseburg that my plate had arrived. I better come and get it quickly, the dentist added, because he was packing up to leave for home. So Heinz Braun and I flew that Heinkel 111 over to Boxted. I chose the 111 because our airmen at Boxted had complained that they fought two and one-half years in the war and didn't even have a souvenir to show for it. So I told Watson that I would fly the Heinkel over so the men could field-strip it for souvenirs. He thought that was a good idea. After we landed in England I helped disconnect the batteries so the guys could begin stripping the airplane. My C-47 Gooney Bird then came over to pick us both up and flew Heinz and me to

Fred McIntosh and Heinz Braun flew a Heinkel 111 bomber like this one to RAF Boxted, McIntosh's wartime P-47 base. (RW)

Neubiberg. I remember the date well, it was the eighth of June, 1945, my twenty-seventh birthday.[10]

"Heinz Braun became an indispensable member of my group," said McIntosh. "Besides teaching me to fly the Heinkel 111, he checked out Jack Woolams, the Bell test pilot, in the fun to fly Fieseler Storch liaison plane. Later Heinz ferried Heinkel 219 night fighters, Bf 109s, and other aircraft from British bases in the north of Germany to Cherbourg-Querqueville. Without doubt, I believe, Heinz Braun's most memorable experience came when Woolams, he, and I set out to ferry three nearly new FW 190 fighters from Nürnberg-Roth to Cherbourg via St.-Dizier and Villacoublay. We took off from Nürnberg-Roth on a sunny June day, expecting to make routine refueling stops en route. Everything went fine at St.-Dizier. We landed, took on fuel, and took off again for Villacoublay, flying in a loose trail formation with Heinz in the number-three position. It was late afternoon when we got into the landing pattern at Villacoublay. Braun was having problems with the setting sun. Of course, I didn't know that because without radios we couldn't talk to each other. Heinz made two unsuccessful approaches and on the third he landed. Unfortunately, while concentrating on making his landing, he forgot to put down his landing gear. He bellied in and fire trucks and military police quickly appeared on the scene. Although Heinz wore an American flight suit, when the MPs got to him he was so rattled he forgot how to speak English. The MPs didn't know what to make of this German pilot in an American flying suit flying a German fighter, and before Woolams or I knew what was going on, the suspicious MPs threw Braun in jail. We wrote off the 190. As for Braun, Woolams and I decided to continue on to Cherbourg and leave Heinz behind and pick him up on our way back. While sitting in jail, Braun thought he was being punished for destroying the Focke-Wulf fighter. He was relieved when we showed up the following day, although he was quite unhappy with himself—forgetting to put down the landing gear is pretty embarrassing for an experienced pilot.

"I don't know if it made Heinz Braun feel any better, but shortly after his accident I totaled a nearly new FW 190 myself on landing at Nürnberg-Roth. Roth had a P-51 outfit assigned to it and they marked out a runway with oil drums on the grass field. That particular 190 I was flying had a defective propeller mechanism, leaking oil over the windshield. I couldn't see very well when I came in and was looking out one side of the cockpit trying to line myself up with the runway. I saw one row of drums, flared, and was just about to touch down when all hell broke loose. I had landed on top of the other row of oil drums. I was lucky not to flip over.

"As we pulled inspections on German planes," McIntosh recalled, "we always looked for booby traps. We discovered that a number of the FW 190s at Nürnberg-Roth carried explosive charges. When the pilot got out of the airplane he simply slid his hand up the back of his seat and activated the charge by removing a safety pin. Before flying the plane he reinserted the pin to safety the charge. It was a simple procedure. Maxfield had worked out an airplane acceptance checklist, and actuating the landing gear was one of the items on the list. When we

This Ju-87 Stuka dive bomber with missing wheel covers flew into Stuttgart to surrender on May 7, 1945. (RB)

put the first 190 on jacks and actuated the gear, a wing blew off. So we went over to the POW compound and found the pilot of that airplane. That's how we learned about the wing explosives and the safety mechanism. We also had a Ju 87 Stuka dive bomber. It was sitting on the field and still had bombs hung on it. General Quesada, who owned the P-51 outfit on the field and who had moved his headquarters to Nürnberg-Roth, warned me that the Stuka was his airplane, that he intended to fly it, and for me to stay away from it. I also wanted to fly a Stuka, at least once. When Maxfield and I looked at this thing we decided there were just too many wires near the bombs. Mechanics from the P-51 fighter group built a wooden cradle so we could drop one of the bombs by two inches. They tied a rope to the Stuka's bomb-release handle and to a six-by-six truck. Then we all hid behind a rise in the ground as the truck drove off, and, when the bomb dropped, the Ju 87 exploded. Booby traps were not a big problem, but it was something we had to be on the alert for."[11]

PROJECT SEAHORSE

No plan turns into action in an organization as large and hierarchical as the military without numerous "players" at ever-loftier organizational levels first having the opportunity to cross a "t" or dot an "i," to say yea or nay before that plan becomes someone's road map for implementation. Although cumbersome at times, the military coordination process largely ensures that the organization's goals are adhered to and that individuals don't work for their own accounts and turn into loose cannons. Operation Lusty was no exception to the rule. Watson never forgot how he fit into the larger picture and what his role was. One of the protocols he unerringly followed was to keep his bosses informed. He unfailingly passed information and suggested courses of action up his chain of command to Generals Knerr and McDonald, who then passed matters deemed sufficiently important on to General Spaatz. Spaatz made certain that General Arnold, the Commanding General of the Army Air Forces, was kept in the loop when he deemed that necessary.

By mid-May 1945, Watson had worked out his plan of action for the movement of captured German aircraft to the United States. In a May 16 message to the War Department in Washington, properly blessed by General McDonald and sent over the signature of General Spaatz, he outlined his accomplishments and a future course of action. In arcane military language the subject of the message was written as "Information On Mike Easy Two Six Two." In plain English this reads "Information on Me-262." Paraphrased in understandable English the message read:

> We have five flyable Me-262 aircraft and expect at least two additional to be flyable in a few days. These aircraft are special adaptations including one photo reconnaissance version, one bomber, three fighters, one fighter with wing racks for firing rockets, a two-seater trainer . . . and one aircraft with a 50 mm cannon mounted in a special nose. It has already been test flown. Three aircraft plus several other standard fighter models will soon be available for disposition. Our recommendation is to fly one standard fighter to the British and one to the French. Then fly the remainder to a port and load them on a flat-top for shipment to the United States. Reason—disassembly, crating and uncrating, will be certain to result in much damage under present field conditions. The Eighth Air Force would also like one flyable Me-262 if one can be made available. Also available are two Messerschmitt test pilots. These pilots report that the Me-262 is a superior aircraft, with good stall characteristics and very fast. 850 Km per hour is its standard high speed dash, the airplane is considered very safe, but requires a 6,000 foot runway for operation. Engines are removed and overhauled after twenty-five hours of operation. The airplane encounters the usual compressibility difficulties when flying over 1,000 Km per hour. A number of spare 004 power plants have been recovered and will be used to make a maximum number of aircraft flyable. Additional units will be shipped for spares if the above recommended allocation is approved. Request comments.[1]

Watson's message was exceedingly optimistic in its portrayal of the Me-262's performance. Under actual combat conditions engine changes were required after ten to twelve hours, although the German test pilots continued to cling to a twenty-five-hour change time, which in fact was probably achievable in an ideal flight test environment. The glowing portrayal of the Me-262 reflected not only Watson's own enthusiasm for the airplane, but also his desire to maintain a great degree of interest in his project at the highest levels of the War Department. The critical issue raised in his message was the use of an aircraft carrier to transport the German aircraft to the United States. Watson knew very well that only a few American escort carriers operated in Atlantic waters, and that most carriers were committed to fighting the war in the Pacific. He also knew that it would take some heavy hitters at the War Department to break loose a carrier from the Navy Department, even for such a high priority project as Operation Lusty. Whetting the generals' appetites for German technology, maintaining their interest when the war against Japan had moved to number-one priority on the agenda, was crucial to keeping his project on track. What Watson didn't want to happen under any circumstances was to have the German jets disassembled and stuffed into the holds of a bunch of Liberty ships. That approach had been tried before and found wanting. He also knew that airplane parts don't attract crowds, don't lead to press releases or high public visibility—the very circumstances needed to revive, even keep alive, America's own lagging jet program.

His proposed disposition of two aircraft to the British and French was a typical Watson good-will gesture. Building bridges and maintaining those bridges was second nature to him. Watson knew very well that he would need British agreement to obtain one or more Arado 234 jet bombers, and that those airplanes were only on bases in the British zone of occupation, in Denmark, and in Norway—also under British control. It was good politics to offer a 262 to his British counterpart and friend, Captain Eric Brown of the Royal Navy, even though he knew that the British had acquired a fair number of the German jets in their own zone. The French had been exceedingly accommodating and helpful to Watson ever since he set foot on French soil. It was payback time, but to do it right, higher headquarters needed to be involved and give the nod to proceed. While Watson could have simply flown a plane or two to the French and the British and no one would have been the wiser, such action would have been out of character. Not only that, but he would run the risk of being labeled a loose cannon, which invariably spelled the end of a military career. Watson was too smart to commit such crass errors. After all, Operation Lusty was General Spaatz's project, and Spaatz was his mentor and a much admired senior officer.

The 8th Air Force request for an Me-262 was a horse of a different color and probably owed its genesis to Colonel David Schilling, an ace and up-and-coming Air Corps officer with friends in high places. If it turned out that one extra aircraft became available, Watson saw no reason why the 8th, why Colonel Schilling, couldn't have his own Me-262. The big issue for Watson remained finding an aircraft carrier. Once he had his hands on a carrier, he knew everything else would fall into place.

General Arnold's people at the Air Staff responded positively to Watson's message. Disposition of three Me-262s to the British, French, and 8th Air Force was approved. The message continued, "Request remainder be shipped to Wright Field as proposed including all available Jumo 004 units. Advise Assistant Chief of Air Staff Intelligence of the date of shipment, name of the ship, expected date of arrival and Uncle Sugar [U.S.] port. Request glossy prints and any preliminary reports of experimental rocket-equipped version and model with fifty millimeter cannon be forwarded air mail to Assistant Chief of Air Staff Intelligence, attention Tactical and Technical Branch. Regarding test pilots, these not, repeat not desired in view of Hans Fay's availability."[2] Hans Fay was the pilot who had defected in a brand-new Me-262 to Frankfurt in March. In the interim Fay was brought to the United States for debriefing and to assist in assembly and testing of his Me-262 once it arrived at Wright Field. But instead of being made available to the Wright Field fighter test branch, Fay was diverted by the CPMB in Washington for a hard-ball technical interrogation, leaving the fighter test branch to fend for itself with a dramatically new airplane they knew little about. The result was all too predictable and the very thing Watson wanted to avoid. Fay's Me-262 nearly crashed on takeoff the first time it was taken up by Russ Schleeh, a Wright Field test pilot. Its guns had not been reinstalled when the Me-262 was assembled, and its CG, center of gravity, had correspondingly shifted aft. Schleeh barely got the airplane off the ground and only his great flying skill kept him from crashing.[3]

While the War Department message gave Watson permission to ship the German aircraft by carrier it didn't address the questions of where the flattop was to come from and how he was to go about getting it. It was obvious to Watson that without General Arnold's direct intervention his chances of obtaining U.S. Navy carrier support through normal channels were slim to none. Baur and Hoffmann, the two German test pilots Watson wanted to take back to the ZI with him, were obviously not wanted at this time, but he would keep on working that issue. He knew that in time he would get what he wanted. On May 30 an Exploitation Division Daily Activity Report mentioned that the "Eighth Air Force was informed that one Me-262 is now available for immediate delivery at Leck Airfield, Schleswig-Holstein," in the British zone of occupation. There is no record that the aircraft was ever picked up by the 8th Air Force, which had in the interim been tasked to prepare for relocation to the Pacific theater. The 8th moved its headquarters from Bushy Park to Okinawa on July 16, 1945. Colonel Schilling was much too busy planning the move then to be thinking about flying an Me-262.[4]

As soon as the Air Staff response to Watson's "Mike Easy Two Six" message arrived at St.-Germain, he put Lieutenant Colonel Malcolm Seashore to work. Seashore was the officer he had chosen to handle all the logistics and administrative details for Operation Lusty. His instructions to Seashore were simple and to the point—start moving equipment and aircraft to Cherbourg and prepare for the arrival of a flattop. Seashore, a nonflyer, had served with Watson at the 1st TAF in Vittel, France. Watson had picked him specifically because he knew how capable an officer Seashore was. Once Watson gave him his marching orders, Seashore moved out quickly. He took a small team of men to Cherbourg and inspected its port facilities and the nearby airfield of Querqueville. Cherbourg appeared to meet all requirements, providing anchorage for a large aircraft carrier and sufficient facilities to land, collect, and service many airplanes. Cherbourg-Querqueville airfield, designated A23 by the Army Air Forces, was still being operated by the 9th Air Force Service Command, which simplified everything from logistics support to providing security for the German aircraft once they arrived.

An operation of the scope Watson was orchestrating and Seashore was implementing had to have a code name just to keep things straight. The movement to the United States of Watson's German aircraft and literally tons of related equipment involved not only the Army Air Forces but also the U.S. Navy. The British soon played a very active role in the operation as well. It helped to have a code name to ensure that communications were delivered to the right individuals in Washington, at Wright Field, and in Paris and London, as well as to the remotest ATI team that would need to know if something had changed, been rescheduled, or added to their tasks. When Seashore raised the issue with Watson he replied, "Come up with something." Seashore did just that with an anagram of his own name—Project Seahorse.

Not only were airplanes beginning to flow into Cherbourg-Querqueville as soon as it was announced as the official assembly and shipping point for German aircraft, but the depots at Hanau and Kassel also had trainloads of category-one equipment ready to ship. Colonel Charles Tylor of the 9th Air Force Service Command called Colonel Pepple at the Exploitation Division on June 14, and told him that the 10th and 45th Air Depot Groups were assembling a train of "crated flyable aircraft and spare jet engines" and that ten railroad cars had already been loaded for movement to Cherbourg. Tylor was worried that it could take weeks for the cars to arrive at their destination. Pepple, the same colonel who had briefed Captain McIntosh as he passed through Paris in early May on his way to Merseburg, quickly allayed Tylor's fears. While Tylor held the phone, Pepple on another line called General Gray, who ran the Movement Division of the Transportation Corps, and straightened things out. "Keep on loading," Pepple told Tylor, "and assemble the train in Germany and make arrangements for a train escort with the 9th Air Force Service Command. Then move it out." Pepple then passed everything on to Malcolm Seashore. Seashore would not only have to load airplanes onto the deck of an aircraft carrier, but also stuff its belly with assorted jet engines, glide bombs, and rocket planes.[5]

The most significant issue remained the aircraft carrier—where to find one. On June 16 McDonald sent a memo to the USSTAF Command Section reminding the commanding general of the importance of the project and the need for his personal support to get the crucial flat-top. General Spaatz was reassigned on June 3 to plan the movement of the 8th Air Force to Okinawa and to take over the 20th Air Force in the Pacific, but on June 16 he was still at St.-Germain. Lieutenant General Cannon had taken his place as commander. McDonald wrote to Cannon:

> It is mandatory that if the available intelligence with respect to the certain already assembled items of German aircraft required by the "Category One" list, ATSC, Wright Field, is to be of use in the furtherance of the war against Japan, that a carrier be obtained for shipment of these aircraft and related items to the Zone of the Interior. There have been already assembled approximately fifty German aircraft, all in flyable condition, embodying the latest technological developments, in jet, rocket, and other advanced types. On 16 May preliminary notification was given the War Department with respect to the advisability of shipping six specific Me-262 jet aircraft to the United States. On 18 May the War Department approved the procedure, including the recommendation of a carrier, but did not make reference to whether or not coordination with Naval Chief of Operations had been effected. On 11 June, after coordination with this division, a message was sent by the U.S. Naval Technical Mission in Europe to the Naval Chief of Operations affirming

the desirability of shipment by carrier and requesting that a carrier be made available in the E.T.O. on or about 11 July, for a period of 11 days. To date no information has been received either from the War Department or from Naval agencies that the carrier requested will be made available. . . . Inasmuch as considerable preparation has already been made, and it is believed that the securing of a carrier is of utmost necessity if this material is to be exploited properly in the United States so as to be of most value in the war against Japan, it is urged that action be taken to ensure the securing of the carrier.[6]

The message clearly expressed the Exploitation Division's frustra-tion with the lack of support from Washington; they obviously wanted Cannon to take positive action to get the ball rolling again. If Cannon vacillated at all, his mind must have been made up to support his director of intelligence when a message arrived from General Arnold's people at the War Department suggesting that they, USSTAF, explore the possibility of shipping the fifty enemy aircraft "on five vessels such as the *John Love McRarley* which could be made available and having hatch openings 42½ by 23 feet. Request answer with dimensions of aircraft and port and date at which ready for loading."[7] Watson's worst fears were coming true. Not only did the chief of naval operations give them the cold shoulder, but their own people at the Air Staff appeared to be setting them up to use a bunch of Liberty ships.

Two days after receiving the "Liberty Ship message," Cannon fired off a message to General Arnold reminding him that shipment of the German aircraft is "necessary to ensure the technical superiority of our own equipment. . . . Disassembly and reassembly of flyable aircraft in the United States after normal shipment would result in damage to aircraft and loss of components thus making it advisable if not mandatory that an aircraft carrier be made available on eleven July for approximately eleven days. . . . Request coordination with Naval Chief of Operations to insure availability of carrier."[8] Cannon was onboard and pitching. A dialogue ensued between Air Force and Navy staffs in

Washington causing the Navy staff to inquire of its European headquarters in London how they assessed the situation. Navy London
supported Cannon's request for an aircraft carrier and in a message on
June 20 wrote back, "Strongly recommended U.S. CVE if available
because of nature and priority of these airplanes."[9] In spite of Navy
London's support, it was pretty clear to everyone that the U.S. Navy,
still fighting a war in the Pacific, wasn't going to come up with the aircraft carrier Watson so desperately wanted for his airplanes. The dialogue continued among the varied staffs in Washington, London, and
Paris. On June 22 relief appeared in the form of a terse, four-line message from the Chief of Naval Operations to the Commander, United
States Navy Europe: "No U.S. CVE's available. Understand several
British CVE's scheduled depart U.K. for U.S. in near future. Desire you
make arrangements with Admiralty to lift planes from Cherbourg to
U.S. in one of these CVE's. Advise."[10] Watson's carrier was "in the bag."

COMNAVEUR, the acronym for the United States Navy headquarters in Europe, sent a message the following day, the twenty-third of
June, to the British Admiralty requesting that *"HMS Reaper* be made
available to lift about 55 ex German planes from Cherbourg to the U.S.
This on U.S. Army and Navy account and at request of Commander in
Chief. Planes will be ready to load Cherbourg on 11 July."[11] The message
assured the British that their gesture of good will wasn't going to cost
them a penny; the U.S. Army and Navy were going to pick up all costs.
The British Admiralty promptly responded on the twenty-eighth of
June that *"Reaper* can be made available. Expected date of arrival
Cherbourg about 16 July." They also wanted to know about facilities
for loading the aircraft at Cherbourg and asked that all necessary
securing gear for the aircraft be provided, as well as a listing of aircraft
types and their dimensions.[12]

By early July, assisted by U.S. Navy representatives, Seashore had
made arrangements with the Cherbourg Port Authority for the arrival
of HMS *Reaper*. They worked out the loading process and brought in

a barge with a derrick strong enough to lift an aircraft from a Rhino barge to the deck of the *Reaper*. On July 3 Seashore accompanied a U.S. Navy team on a visit to HMS *Reaper* at its port in the United Kingdom. Seashore brought the requested list of aircraft, which the *Reaper*'s captain then forwarded to the Admiralty. The list provided for the loading of:

Me-262 (Jet fighters)	10
He-219 (Night fighters)	3
Do-335 (Experimental fighters)	2
FW-190 Long nose (fighters)	4
FW-190 Late type, not long nose	5
Me-109G (Fighter)	3
TA-152 (Latest version of FW-190)	1
Ar-234 (Jet reconnaissance bomber)	4
Me-108 (Trainer)	1
Ju-88 (Night fighter)	1
Ju-388 (High altitude recon)	1
Fl-282 Flettner Helicopter	2
Dh-243 Doblhoff Jet Helicopter	1
P-51 Photo reconnaissance	1
Total number of aircraft	39

The preliminary count of thirty-nine aircraft eventually changed to forty-one, with the addition of two FW 190 fighters. Additionally, fifteen Heinkel 162 single-engine Volksjäger fighters, each powered by a BMW 003 turbine, and ten Me-163B Komet rocket-propelled interceptors, all of which had arrived in crates by freight train, were also loaded on HMS *Reaper*. The P-51 added at the last moment was a reconnaissance aircraft with a unique camera configuration devised by George Goddard, Watson's friend, who wanted it returned to the United States for evaluation. Why Watson bothered to take three dated Bf 109G fighters to the United States is unclear, as is the inclusion of the Me-108 trainer. Perhaps the latter was an aircraft slipped in by Fred McIntosh

HMS Reaper, *a British escort carrier, anchored in Cherbourg harbor in France, with loading crane alongside. German aircraft are visible on deck. (RB)*

or Pappy Horn for his own use; both had made noises to Watson to that effect.[13]

Seashore prepared for the arrival of the British carrier at Cherbourg and coordinated various shipments coming in by rail, truck, and air. Security was provided, and people had to be fed and housed; although the 9th Air Force Service Command provided much of the infrastructure support at Querqueville airport, the details which made an operation a success fell squarely upon Seashore's shoulders. To assist him with the broad and complex task he obtained the services of Captain Orville Jenkins and six sergeants. On June 7, long before it was certain that an aircraft carrier would be made available, Watson sent Seashore a comprehensive "to do" list. It wasn't Watson's usual style to tell a man in minute detail what to do, when and where, but this was one time when he didn't want to leave anything to chance. His ego was definitely involved in this project, and he didn't want to be embarrassed by some avoidable oversight. The pressure began to show even on Watson.

"It is planned," Watson wrote to Seashore, "to ferry all flyable GAF airplanes to Cherbourg airport, A-23, for eventual loading on a Navy aircraft carrier." On June 7 the aircraft carrier issue was just beginning to be addressed and its outcome was far from certain, yet Watson moved ahead as if the matter had already been settled. He didn't entertain any other mode of transportation. "Aircraft will be loaded from ramp at southeast-end of field on NAVY RHINO barges which will transport them to Normandy Quay where they will be parked until loaded on flat-top. It is believed that at least 50% of the aircraft to be shipped should be on the quay before the arrival of the flat-top. After the airplanes arrive at A-23, hangar space should be provided to permit preparing the airplanes for overseas deck loading. This work should be accomplished before loading on the RHINO. To physically accomplish the preparation for storage, it will be necessary to secure a team of personnel equipped and trained to do this job from Burtonwood." Burtonwood was a supply depot in England which had the resources and skilled personnel to apply a covering of gel and plastic sheeting to protect aircraft stored in the open from the corrosive effects of salt air.

"In order to facilitate hoisting the airplanes from the RHINO to the dock," Watson continued with his detailed instructions to Seashore, "and from the dock to the deck of the aircraft carrier it will be necessary to have fabricated slings, fittings, etc., to suspend the airplane from proper jack-points. These jack-points will be properly marked at or prior to the arrival of these airplanes at A-23. It is believed first priority should be placed upon making available hanger space to store aircraft immediately upon arrival at A-23. Guards should be made available at this hangar to guard off sight-seers and all personnel not connected with the project. Further the airport military personnel should be advised that these airplanes will be arriving without radio communications. Green signal flares should be available for use. It should be kept in mind that airplanes now located at Villacoublay, Stuttgart and other collection points will be converging on A-23 starting Monday, 11 June. It is anticipated that within 20 days all of the flyable aircraft will be on A-23."[14]

"In addition to getting the Cherbourg facilities ready to receive HMS *Reaper* and up to fifty German aircraft, Watson tasked Seashore to prepare for his arrival at A-55C, Melun Airport, south of Paris, with ten German jets. Watson intended to put on an airshow for his mentor, General Spaatz, and the USSTAF senior headquarters staff. He knew the general was involved in getting the 8th Air Force to pack up and move to the Pacific theater of operations, so getting things moved out of Lechfeld to Melun-Villaroche assumed the highest priority for him. Watson had no idea when the general might be available for a static display of his collection of German jets, but whenever that was, sooner or later, he needed to be there with his airplanes. It was clear to him that he needed to move the jets from Lechfeld to Paris as soon as possible. Seashore got exactly three days' notice from Watson, on June 7, that he intended to fly the jets from Lechfeld to Melun on June 10, weather permitting, and that Seashore better have things ready.

"Messerschmitt 262 airplanes will be ferried to A-55," Watson instructed Seashore, "starting Sunday morning (June 10). It will be necessary to have available hangar facilities for 10 Me-262s and a working area for maintenance. Recommend one of the Blister hangars be secured from Colonel Williams [the commander of a troop carrier group assigned to Melun airfield]. Along with the Me-262s will be 10 American crew-chiefs and 7 American pilots who will have to be housed and fed at A-55. Further there will be approximately 15 German civilians (mechanics and pilots) who will have to be housed and fed. Arriving Monday or Tuesday will be 3 truck loads of spare parts which should be parked in the vicinity of the Me-262s, however it may not be necessary to uncrate or remove any of this material from the trucks. This material will eventually go on board the aircraft carrier along with the airplanes. . . . It is anticipated that five days will be the outside maximum length of stay at A-55. It will be necessary to have 6,000 gallons of diesel fuel stored at A-55 for servicing the Me-262s. This fuel should be stored in such a fashion that it can be readily pumped into the tanks of the airplanes."[15]

General Spaatz, Colonel Watson, and Brigadier General McDonald at Melun airfield inspecting a Jumo 004 jet engine, June 27, 1945. (RB)

Seashore managed to get everything ready for Watson's arrival at Melun. But it turned out that Watson was being overly optimistic—he would be at Melun considerably longer than the anticipated five-day maximum. Not until June 27 was General Spaatz ready to take a look at the fruits of Watson's labor. For Watson, that was the payoff for weeks of hard work and scrounging. He had promised the general in late 1944 that he was going to get the German jets for him—and now that he had them, Watson wanted Spaatz to see the planes with his own eyes.

MELUN-VILLAROCHE

Watson flew into Lager Lechfeld on May 29 to take a look at how things were going. He discovered to his surprise that Sergeant Freiburger and Herr Caroli had nearly finished putting ten airplanes into flying condition. Bob Strobell, who had arrived at Lechfeld only two days earlier, cautioned Watson that he personally didn't feel very comfortable with the situation. Caroli had no records to show how many flying hours each engine had accumulated since its last major overhaul. "Every engine has to be pulled and thoroughly gone over," he told Watson, "before we want to move any airplanes out of here." Watson had complete trust in Strobell's judgement and agreed with his recommendation. On Wednesday, May 30, Karl Bauer took Watson on a brief instructional ride in *Vera*, the two-seat trainer. Watson, who had flown the Bell YP-59 experimental jet at Wright Field, found the transition from prop to jet turbine uneventful, but he liked the feel of the Me-262. When he landed he told Strobell he was going to need an aircraft soon to check out the route between Lechfeld and Melun-Villaroche. The airplane Watson was going to fly for that purpose was an A-model fighter, the last one to be reconditioned out of fifty or so damaged Me-262s littering Lager Lechfeld and its nearby forests. What remained were hulks good for spare parts, but little else. Freiburger had not given this particular airplane a name yet, so its nose remained graffiti free. It was simply aircraft number 3332, the last four digits of its German manufacturer's serial number, the *Werknummer* 113332.

On Saturday, June 2, the 54th ADS redeployed from the Messerschmitt administration building at Lager Lechfeld to a new area of operation. Lieutenant Smith reported in the Unit History for the Month of June 1945 that "We were all quite happy to be leaving the large, drab, grey building in Augsburg. Living conditions were far from good, though we did have showers. . . . We departed from Augsburg at 0645 hours and arrived at our new destination in Mühlacker at 1530 hours the same day. Captain McGuire and M/Sgt Preston had everything quite in order when we arrived, having obtained local German labor to clean up the buildings for us." Freiburger and his men were released by Watson and accompanied their squadron to its new location at Mühlacker. But Freiburger returned on June 10 on his own initiative to watch the departure of the jets for Melun, France. He wanted to see "his" jets fly just one more time.

On Sunday, June 3, Watson took 3332 up for a brief test flight. It checked out fine. Gerhard Caroli had the aircraft refueled and gone over one final time, and on Monday morning, June 4, Watson took off intending to fly directly from Lechfeld to Melun-Villaroche.[1] His takeoff was normal, the plane climbing at 270 mph to 9,000 feet pressure altitude with full throttles. He encountered what he called "a rolling moment to the left" and corrected it by slightly increasing the power of the left engine. Once he got to his cruising altitude he applied full power for one minute, achieving a maximum speed of 500 mph, and then reduced power to normal cruising speed of 360 mph. This flight was Watson's first and only opportunity to check the airplane's characteristics before moving the remaining aircraft out of Lechfeld. If there was something to be learned he wanted to learn it then, when there was still a chance to pass information to his pilots. He checked the operation of the leading edge slats which extended when he slowed to between 240 and 260 Kph, depending on the angle of attack of the

Watson with Fred Hillis and Willie Hoffmann to his right, Jim Holt and Karl Baur to his left. L to R front: Dahlstrom, Strobell, Anspach, two sergeants, and Roy Brown. The picture was taken in front of Joanne, *the second aircraft in the nine-aircraft lineup. Lechfeld, June 10, 1945. (RW)*

airplane. "At no time did engine exhaust temperatures exceed 650 degrees Centigrade," he noted in his postmission report. "With wheels extended and full flaps and engines throttled to 5,000 RPM at 5,000 feet" at 125 mph the airplane exhibited normal stall characteristics. Watson continued to check various power settings and fuel consumption at different altitudes. He found the Me-262 to be an honest airplane with no apparent hidden characteristics which could spell doom for an inexperienced pilot. Watson understood that all of his pilots, no matter how much time they had in the P-47, were inexperienced jet pilots. As he approached St.-Dizier, A64, Watson realized he had a problem on his hands. He was running low on fuel.

A six-hundred-liter auxiliary fuel tank was located directly behind the pilot in single-seat versions of the Me-262, and fuel transfer to the main forward tank had to be initiated soon after takeoff. The auxiliary tank's fuel pump was too slow to supply sufficient fuel directly to the two engines, so the procedure was to top off the main forward fuel tank during flight. Either the fuel pump had failed or Watson had forgotten to turn it on soon enough; the latter seems more probable since he had no way of knowing that the fuel transfer pump was unable to keep up with the demands of the engines. The result was the same. He had to land at St.-Dizier, a former P-47 Thunderbolt base he was familiar with from his days with the 1st TAF. The landing was uneventful, and a local combat engineer unit provided standard truck diesel fuel to allow him to continue his flight to Melun. At Lechfeld the airplane had been serviced with J-2 jet fuel; he learned that truck diesel fuel worked just as well, or was in fact the same as J-2 jet fuel. As a result of his experience, Watson decided to make St.-Dizier a refueling stop for the transfer of the nine Me-262s from Lechfeld to Paris. Here he would also position a mixed German-American maintenance team, in case an aircraft had a problem that couldn't wait until it got to Melun. Once at Melun Watson wrote up a detailed report of his flight, including a pilot's cockpit procedure, engine starting procedure, notes on flying characteristics, approach and landing procedure, taxi procedure, and a procedure for stopping engines. With his report finished, he immediately started to plan for the quick transfer of the remaining nine aircraft to Melun-Villaroche.[2]

During the first week of June, Strobell, Baur, and Hoffmann gave ground and flight checks in the Me-262 to Holt, Hillis, Dahlstrom, Brown, and Anspach. Watson had settled on June 10, a Sunday, as the day when they would try to move the aircraft out of Lechfeld. Both Baur and Hoffmann were to fly an aircraft, since there were only seven American pilots and nine airplanes to be moved. Watson would fly *Wilma Jeanne*, of course, the jet with the 50 mm gun. "That's my plane," he told Strobell when they first met. It was the most unusual looking of the nine aircraft, and everyone knew that Watson would want to fly that one. Out of the twenty-seven Germans Watson hired, he planned to take ten mechanics along to Paris, as well as Caroli, the chief engineer and technical supervisor, and Hans Brandt, the technical inspector. The Germans were to be flown to Paris in his C-47 via St.-Dizier, but were not told of their impending transfer until the day before. Watson continued to play things close to the vest. He didn't feel like the war was over yet, although it really was for the Germans.

"Captain Hillis arrived at our apartment on the morning of June 9th," wrote Isolde Baur. " 'You are ordered to ferry one of the Me-262s to Cherbourg, France,' he said to my husband Karl. 'Do I have time to finish breakfast and pack an overnight bag?' Karl asked. Captain Hillis nodded, 'Of course,' and accepted Karl's invitation to sit down."[3] After Karl Baur finished his breakfast and packed a change of clothing, he and Fred Hillis drove to Lager Lechfeld, where the other mechanics who were to accompany Watson to Melun were already assembled. There they were fed and put up for the night. Strobell asked Watson, "What if Willie or Baur has an emergency en route and they have to land somewhere? We need to give them a pass." Watson provided a brief memo for the two German pilots: "To whom it may concern: The pilot of this airplane has been hired by the U.S. Government to fly this airplane to St. Dizier and thence to Melun. Contact nearest U.S. Government office. Signed: H.E. Watson, Colonel, Air Corps, AC."

On the morning of June 10, a bright sunny day filled with sounds of distant church bells calling worshipers to Sunday services, nine Me-262 jet fighters lined up nose to tail on the Lechfeld runway for the first leg of their trip to Paris. *Vera*, the two-seat trainer, was to be piloted by Willie Hoffmann. Willie was scheduled to be the first one to leave that morning. *Joanne*, a photo-reconnaissance aircraft, was Captain Hillis's bird. He would depart after Hoffmann. Next in line was *Pauline*, which was assigned to Lieutenant Bob Anspach. Then came *Dennis*, the combat-tested veteran which was to be flown by Lieutenant James Holt; Captain Kenneth Dahlstrom would fly *Marge*, another photo-reconnaissance aircraft; and *Connie the Sharp Article*, a third photo-recon aircraft, was assigned to Lieutenant Roy Brown. *Doris*, a day fighter, was Karl Baur's ship, seventh in line, and Bob Strobell selected *Beverly Anne* for himself. *Wilma Jeanne*, with its big 50 mm gun sticking out of its nose like a swizzle stick out of a mixed drink, was the last one in line. All but Willie Hoffmann in *Vera* and Roy Brown in *Connie* were to fly from Lechfeld to St.-Dizier for refueling, and then continue on to Melun. Willie's two-seater did not have an auxiliary fuel tank like the others, making his aircraft very short-legged since he had to stay below ten thousand feet. Strobell and Watson did not choose to use auxiliary belly tanks for *Vera*, so Willie was ordered to fly from Lechfeld to Stuttgart, refuel in Stuttgart, then continue on to St.-Dizier for a second refueling stop before proceeding to his final destination of Melun-Villaroche. As for Roy Brown, he was an engineer and in doing his meticulous flight planning he determined that he had sufficient fuel to fly directly to Melun without an intermediate refueling stop—as long as he got up to ten thousand feet cruising altitude quickly and began his fuel transfer from the auxiliary tank immediately after level off. After listening to Roy's proposed flight plan, neither Bob Strobell nor Watson had any strenuous objections and gave their approval. Watson cautioned Roy that if at any time the fuel situation looked questionable, he was to exercise conservative judgement and divert to St.-Dizier.

The flight from Lager Lechfeld to Melun was a special occasion for everyone, Americans and Germans alike. Was it not the first American jet squadron to take to the air, even if it was composed of former enemy aircraft and flown by both American and German pilots? Although Watson's Whizzers were not carried on any official table of organization, for a brief moment in time they were a de facto Army Air Forces flying unit with its own name and squadron patch. Many pictures were taken that sunny Sunday morning in May of the nine Me-262s lined up nose to tail on the runway at Lager Lechfeld. Willie Hoffmann in the first aircraft started his engines at 0925 and was followed by the others in fifteen-minute intervals. By spreading out the departures of his aircraft, Watson was trying to preclude any chance of an accident tying up the runway at St.-Dizier. His plan worked well. Watson, the last to leave Lager Lechfeld, landed safely at Melun at 1915 hours that evening. In his after-action report, Watson wrote that "very little difficulty was experienced with the Jumo-004 engine. Two failures of the two-cylinder starter motor clutch were experienced necessitating changing of these starter units, consuming approximately 30 minutes at St.-Dizier. One exhaust cone was found slightly cracked. Considerable main gear trouble was had due to excessive use during the first three landings by newly trained pilots."[4]

"When I took off from Lechfeld," recalled Roy Brown, "I was concentrating on seeing where I was. The speed of the plane was more than I was used to. I was impressed with my progress over the ground and had to change from one map to the next very soon. They were very good maps, even the shapes of wooded areas were shown accurately. I have to admit, I knew pretty well where I was most of the time because I had flown in this area in the war. But the last half hour or so I wasn't quite sure, it was new terrain. I found myself looking for landmarks. Finally I saw Melun coming up on my left and I breathed a sigh of relief. I flew over the field, lined up with the runway to check for signals from the tower, then circled back to the left for a gradual descend and landing. I touched down gently, leaving plenty of runway ahead of me to minimize the use of brakes. Normally when I landed a P-47 I came in hot and low, peeled up to the left in a steep climb and circled back around, using the brakes frequently after landing to steer the P-47. I did nothing fancy in the Me-262. I didn't know enough about this airplane, and Watson had impressed on us the importance of getting the Me-262s to the United States in a flyable condition. We were conscious of this at all times. At least I was. A 'follow-me' jeep met me at the end of the runway and led me to my parking place. Then I learned that I was the first aircraft to arrive at Melun."

Nine reconditioned Me-262 jets lined up on the Lechfeld tarmac, ready for takeoff, June 10, 1945. (RB)

The first thing a jubilant Watson did the day after arriving in Paris was to send a memo to Colonel Sheldon, the chief of the Exploitation Division, to inform him that "the project of ferrying 10 Me-262s from Lechfeld, Germany, to A55 has been completed. These airplanes are being serviced and maintained at A55 [Melun] and will be flown to A23, Cherbourg, for preparation for overseas shipment prior to loading on Navy flat-top." The tenth aircraft Watson was talking about was the one he had flown to Melun the previous Monday, June 4. Then Watson briefly reiterated what he had accomplished while at Lechfeld:

a. Assembling the 10 Me-262s by former Messerschmitt German employees.

b. Training 10 airplane crew-chiefs on airplane and jet engine maintenance.

c. Determining maintenance history of the Me-262 airplane and engine and securing 5, 2½-ton truck-loads of spare parts, maintenance tools, and special purpose maintenance equipment.

d. Training 6 American pilots in the operation and performance of the jet airplane as well as giving each pilot a flight test in a two-seater Me-262 trainer.

e. Establishing refueling points and emergency landing fields along the route from Lechfeld to A-55.

f. Personally flying the first Me-262 from Lechfeld along the proposed route to Melun to definitely establish the feasibility of project and to secure range and performance data on the airplane to enable training of American pilots.

Watson mentioned to Colonel Sheldon that three additional pilots were undergoing training at Melun. Actually only one additional pilot would be trained to fly the Me-262, Lieutenant William Haynes. The other two opted for an early return to the United States. Then Watson listed by name the Germans he had brought along, mentioning that two of them were "Messerschmitt's best test pilots." Watson knew very well that this information would be briefed to the commanding general, whoever it was at the time, at the following morning's staff meeting, and he was making a subtle pitch for Hoffmann and Baur, whom he still intended to take back to the United States. Finally Watson recommended to Sheldon that "the Me-262 airplanes along with the 10 trained crew-chiefs and pilots be shipped and transferred to Wright Field or other research centers in the United States as a unit in order to accomplish performance and flight testing and comparative analysis with similar American equipment. From the experience gained while carrying out this project by the undersigned, it is believed that research centers in the Zone of the Interior would profit considerably should this project be carried through as outlined above." Watson was right, but the political pressures to "bring the boys home" now that the war in Europe was over made his suggested approach impractical. Three of his own Whizzers would choose to separate from the Army upon their arrival in the United States—Roy Brown, Ken Dahlstrom, and Fred Hillis.[5]

Watson attempted to nail down a date on General Spaatz's calendar to have him come out to Melun to inspect the German jets. That was easier said than done. They were suddenly playing musical chairs in the command section at Headquarters USSTAF. Lieutenant General John Cannon, a fighter pilot by trade, replaced Spaatz the bomber general on June 3, the day before Watson ferried the first Me-262 from Lechfeld to Melun. Watson's contacts quickly allayed his concerns and informed him that General Spaatz wasn't leaving just yet. Spaatz intended to remain at St.-Germain for the immediate future to clean up some loose ends, and to prepare for his next assignment as commander of the 20th Air Force in the Pacific. "Be patient," Watson was told by insiders. "He knows you want him to come out to Melun." Only ten days later, on June 13, Cannon stepped aside and Spaatz resumed command. Watson must have breathed a sigh of relief. He had no idea what was going on at the top, but he knew that Spaatz's resumption of command was only temporary. There was no better time to get the general's attention. Watson stopped by the command section at every opportunity to check on the commander's availability. "We'll let you know, Colonel," was the polite reply to his nervous inquiries. Watson could only hope that when and if he finally got on the commander's calendar it would still be Spaatz, or that at least Spaatz would still be around for the occasion.

While Watson was fretting about his air show, his pilots decided they had lived long enough with Sergeant Freiburger's airplane graffiti. These were their airplanes now; they decided to have a little fun of their own and came up with new names. By unanimous vote of the Whizzers, *Vera* was rechristened *Willie* in honor of their ever-jovial and story-telling Messerschmitt test pilot, Ludwig Hoffmann. They had come to like Willie and this was their way of saying, "You're one of us." Willie was indeed flattered by the generous gesture of his American pilots. The war was finally over for all of them. As for the other planes, every pilot named his own. *Joanne* was renamed *Cookie VII* by Fred

Hillis; it was his daughter's nickname. Fred had gone through a string of Jugs during his combat days, and this was his seventh aircraft. *Pauline* became *Delovely*, so named by Bob Anspach after the song lyrics "it's delicious, it's delightful, it's delovely," and the name *Feudin' 54th* vanished forever from its side. *Dennis* became *Ginny H*, named for Jim Holt's girlfriend. (Ginny would meet her beau in New York upon his return to the United States on HMS *Reaper* to get married.) *Marge* was renamed *Lady Jess IV* by Ken Dahlstrom, and *Connie the Sharp Article* became *Pick II*. *Pick I* had been Roy Brown's P-47 Thunderbolt, which had taken him all the way from Italy to France and finally into Germany with the 86th Fighter Group. When Baur was asked what name he would like to give *Doris*, the plane Karl had flown to Melun, he exhibited a superb sense of humor by suggesting that they name it *Jabo Bait*. Jabo was the German abbreviation for *Jagdbomber*, referring to aircraft like the P-47s flown by the American pilots who were now Baur's flying buddies. The Me-262 was, of course, "bait" for the P-47s— so *Jabo Bait* it was. Bob Strobell remembered "screaming" across the countryside at Lechfeld on his first flight in an Me-262 and changed *Beverly Anne* to *Screamin' Meemie*. Finally, Hal Watson was asked what name he would like to give *his* aircraft, *Wilma Jeanne*. Watson chose *Happy Hunter II*, Hunter being the name of his only son. *Happy Hunter I* was a P-47 Watson acquired while he served at the 1st TAF and used as a runabout. Not only did all the aircraft receive new names, but one of their sergeants came up with a squadron patch as well, and the new patch was painted on the nose of each jet. Maybe Watson's Whizzers were not an officially recognized squadron of the Army Air Forces, but the pilots did everything to make it look like they were.

On June 25, shortly after returning with Karl Baur from Grove airfield in Denmark with two coveted Arado 234 jet bombers, Watson received word that the air show and static display would be held on Wednesday, June 27. He also learned that General Spaatz intended to fly to Melun for the event. Watson was elated, and tasked Captain

Snafu I, *an Arado 234 jet bomber, on the ramp at Melun, being readied for inspection by General Spaatz, June 27, 1945. (RW)*

Hillis, who had been appointed operations officer for his Whizzers, to prepare a formal order for the event. Operations Order No. 2, dated June 26, 1945, ordered in precise military language:

> There will be a military review of all German jet aircraft now stationed at A55 at 10:30 Wednesday 27 June 1945. After the review there will be a demonstration formation flight of 3 Me-262s for the reviewing party. The sequence of the review and demonstration flight will be in the following order: The reviewing party will be met by representatives of the permanent party of A55. The reviewing party will be directed to the aircraft to be inspected. Pilots and Crew Chiefs will be standing by their respective aircraft to receive the reviewing party and answer inquiries that might be made. After all aircraft have been inspected, the three aircraft to be flown will be towed to the runway to be used. Two spare aircraft will also be towed out to stand by for a failure to start of one or two of the first three aircraft. The reviewing party will be driven to the starting point to witness the starting of the jet units. As soon as the first two jets have been started, the reviewing party will be driven to the middle of and 100 yards away from the runway to be used to witness the take-off, flight, and landing of the demonstration aircraft. The direction of the reviewing party from this point will be at the discretion of the permanent party of A55.

The "permanent party" referred to by Fred Hillis was General Beach, commander of the 53rd Troop Carrier Wing, who as the senior officer on the station was the official host. The second most senior officer was Colonel Williams, the commander of a troop carrier group operating out of Melun. After outlining the procedures to be followed for the display and flyby, Hillis provided specific instructions for aircraft positioning and what pilots, crew chiefs, and others were to wear and do. After all, they were being honored by a visit from the man who had run the air war in Europe. "Officers to be reviewed will be dressed in blouses, pinks, and service caps. Crew Chiefs will be in O.D., slacks, shirts and service caps. Pilots of the aircraft will stand two paces in front of the nose of their respective aircraft. Crew Chiefs will stand two paces to the left and two paces to the rear of the pilots. Where there is no pilot [in the cases of Hoffmann's and Baur's aircraft and the two Arado jet bombers] and only a crew chief, he will align himself with the other crew chiefs. When the inspection party gets within six paces of the ranking person of each aircraft, this person only will render the military salute. . . . Captain Dahlstrom will join the reviewing party before they drive to the point of vantage for watching the flight. He will be prepared to answer any inquiries that may arise during the rest of the demonstration." No detail was too small, nothing was left to chance. Watson wanted the review to come off perfectly.

Captain Dahlstrom may have been appointed to answer questions, but in fact Watson was going to be at the general's side for the duration of the visit and would answer whatever questions the general might have. In addition to their new names, the ten Me-262s received new numerical designators for the purpose of the review. Fred Hillis didn't think it was quite right to include in a formal military order the names the pilots had bestowed upon their aircraft. Watson's 50-mm-cannon-bearing aircraft became 000. *Screamin' Meemie*, Strobell's airplane, was 111, and Ken Dahlstrom's *Lady Jess IV* became 222. The number 333 was assigned to Bob Anspach's *Delovely*, and Roy Brown's *Pick II* became 444. Willie Hoffmann's *Willie* was assigned the number 555, and 666 was given to Fred Hillis's *Cookie VII*. Lieutenant William Haynes, the newly checked-out pilot, was to stand in front of Karl Baur's *Jabo Bait*, which had the number 777 added to its nomenclature. The JG 7 veteran *Dennis*, now named *Ginny H* and piloted by Jim Holt, became 888. Those were all the named airplanes from Lechfeld. The solitary unnamed aircraft 3332 kept its number. Finally, there were two additional Me-262s acquired only days earlier from the British and flown into Melun by Bob Strobell and Willie Hoffmann. *Ole Fruit Cake*, an Me-262 night fighter, was given the number 999, and 101 was assigned to *What Was It?*, a second two-seat trainer. By the early morning hours of June 27, all twelve Me-262s were in their assigned positions, as were the two newly acquired Arado 234 jet bombers, *Snafu I* and *Jane I*. *Jane I* became 202, and *Snafu I* was assigned number 303 for purposes of Fred Hillis's operations order. Everything was ready.[6]

The morning of June 27 was not bright and sunny; rather, a low stratocumulus cloud deck defined the limits of the air show Watson's pilots would be able to put on for the visiting dignitaries. General Spaatz and his small entourage arrived a little before ten o'clock in a UC-45 Beech twin-engine transport; its designated parking place was on the taxiway near the static displays. As the C-45 slowed, its pilot opened a side window, and out popped a small red flag with four gold stars on it—General Spaatz had officially arrived at Melun. As the general alighted from his aircraft he was greeted by General Beach, Colonel Williams, and Colonel Watson. General Spaatz was relaxed and pleased to see Watson and he showed it. Spaatz and Watson shook hands after the general had greeted everyone else. General George McDonald, Spaatz's long time intelligence chief, and Colonel Donald Putt, who had only recently returned to Paris from directing the exploitation of the Hermann Göring Research Institute at Völkenrode, accompanied the general, along with the usual train of sergeants and aides-de-camp. After a brief exchange of pleasantries the group walked directly to the static display area to begin the inspection of "Watson's loot." Spaatz took his time looking at the jets, talking to pilots and crew chiefs alike, having his picture taken with the men. Hal Watson remained glued to the general's side—guiding, explaining, introducing. Bob Anspach remembered that day well, Watson leading the general from plane to plane. "He was a handsome-looking man," Anspach recalled. "He looked the epitome of the fighter pilot. He wasn't one, but he looked it."

"When Spaatz finished looking at all the airplanes," said Strobell, "Watson escorted him to the reviewing area next to the runway where three of our airplanes were ready to go. I was the lead ship of the formation. Holt and Hillis were the other two. The crew chiefs, ready and waiting in their jeeps, pulled the three aircraft out on the taxiway. We got in and fired them up. We had a low overcast and we could only get up about two to three thousand feet. We did a rat-race line astern type of thing and Holt and Hillis were numbers two and three. We made several high speed passes in front of the reviewing stand. From three thousand feet you could actually get into a shallow dive to pick up almost full speed. We were crossing the airfield at a pretty good clip cruising near five hundred miles per hour.

"On one of the passes Fred Hillis's gear popped out and he couldn't get it back up, so he left the formation and landed. Holt and I made a couple more passes, and then I did something stupid. After I went across the airfield on the last pass, I pulled the damn jet up and rolled it. The reason I say it was stupid, it didn't add a damn thing to the demonstration and I was risking an airplane on top of that. The Jumo 004 engine didn't like radical air-intake changes. Doing a maneuver like that could upset the air flow and have it flame out. The Me-262 was not a dogfighting airplane like the F-86 was later on. So Holt and I landed after that last pass. No one ever said anything to me about my impromptu maneuver. But you know how it is—you remember your mistakes in life for ever and ever."[7]

Years later Watson wrote about this June day in 1945. "We received word that General Spaatz's staff wanted to inspect these Me-262 airplanes and, if the weather was right, to have a flight demonstration. . . . This was General Spaatz's first view of the world's first combat qualified turbo jet fighter. Of course, General Spaatz's concern and enthusiasm was the highlight of the day! He was not a vocal person, but following the inspection and flight demonstration we walked, sort of arm-in-arm, to his car, and he kept saying over and over again, 'Wicked, wicked, wicked.' A couple of days later I had a call from General Spaatz and he asked if a friend of his could be flown in a twin-seated Me-262. It turned out to be Alexander de Seversky, the President of Republic Aviation, the builder of the P-47, and prior to that the P-35. . . . Mr. Seversky was a famous Russian pilot during World War I. This was a milestone in his illustrious career. His first flight in a combat-qualified jet aircraft. That afternoon we took off and flew for about thirty to forty minutes and, incidentally, he had control of the airplane from the rear seat. My chore was to restrain him from doing things that I didn't want the airplane to do at this point—but we had one helluva ride."[8]

It is somewhat curious that Seversky didn't pick up on the swept-wing idea at that time. The initial versions of the F-84 Thunderjet didn't even come close in performance to the nimble and sleek Me-262 of a much earlier vintage. In contrast to the popular and robust P-47 Thunderbolt flown by every Whizzer pilot, the Thunderjet, even in its later swept-wing F-model incarnation, renamed Thunderstreak, remained for many pilots a flying nightmare. "The 84 had lots and lots of foibles that you more or less lived with," wrote Wright Field test pilot Bill Reed. "Trying to sort them all out would have been a full-time job and, let's face it: pilots didn't fight to fly the F-84 like they did the various F-86s we had. The one reason I was in this kite . . . is that I happened to be current in it. Many of the fighter jocks deliberately went 'uncurrent' in the 84 so they wouldn't be available when one needed flying."[9]

Watson's Whizzers at Melun-Villaroche, June 27, 1945. L to R: James Holt, Robert Anspach, Harold Watson, William Haynes, Kenneth Dahlstrom, Roy Brown, Robert Strobell, Fred Hillis. (RA)

The Melun airshow generated the first of many news releases that the German jets, and especially Watson as the flamboyant and intrepid jet pilot, would inspire in the future. Trumpeted a June 30 news release, datelined 436th Troop Carrier Group: "Three jet pro-pelled Messerschmitts owned by the AAF demonstrated the capabili-ties of jet aircraft to Gen. Carl A. Spaatz, Commanding General of the USS[T]AF, and his staff recently. Taking off shortly after a rain from airstrip A-55, commanded by Col. Adriel Williams of Shelbyville, Ky., the jet planes flew so rapidly that they blasted the fallen rain into walls of spray. As soon as they left the ground, they attained a speed so great that an A-26, flying overhead, seemingly stood still. They climbed almost straight, trailing twin streaks of black smoke. . . . Details of the craft are still secret, but they are believed to be the fastest man-carrying machines ever built."[10]

20

ROAST DUCK AT AALBORG

By the seventeenth of June, Fred McIntosh was back at Villacoublay to pick up a Ju 388, the same airplane which he and Watson had flown in May from Merseburg to Kassel. He flew the 388 to Cherbourg-Querqueville. His arrival at Querqueville was timed to coincide with the arrival of Germany's strangest-looking aircraft—two Dornier Do 335s from Nürnberg-Roth. The Do 335, called *Pfeil* (arrow), was a heavy push-pull fighter with one engine in the front and another in the rear. It was still in the development stage when the war ended and never saw combat. Wrote Watson, "It looked less like an arrow than anything I've ever seen. Apparently some Germans thought so too because they called it *Ameisenbär*, anteater."[1] According to Watson the Do 335 was equipped with two twelve-cylinder Daimler-Benz liquid-cooled engines, rated at 1,750 horsepower each, and cruised at 425 mph at 23,500 feet altitude. German test data, however, claimed a speed in excess of 470 miles per hour for the fastest piston-driven aircraft in the world. The Arrow was equipped with an ejection seat. Prior to ejecting, the pilot had to push three buttons in the cockpit. "One would jettison the rear propeller using an explosive device, the second button blew off the upper vertical tail surfaces, and the third armed the seat." The Do 335 "typifies German creativity," Watson wrote, "and tests showed that it was tops in speed for a piston type aircraft."[2]

An ATI team had located one 335 at Neubiberg airfield. Watson took a look at it in early May when he was in the area, but it was too heavily damaged by bomb fragments. Four others, however, were located at the factory in Oberpfaffenhofen, a few miles west of Munich. It was two of those factory aircraft Fred McIntosh was expecting at Querqueville airport. The third and fourth airplanes Watson gave to the British. The French had acquired several Do 335s in their zone of occupation, but for some reason wouldn't release even one to their American ally. Earlier in June, Flugkapitän Hans Padell, one of Germany's best test pilots who had previously worked at the *Erprobungsstelle* in Berlin-Rechlin, the German equivalent of Wright Field, led a flight of two 335s from Oberpfaffenhofen to Nürnberg-Roth. Watson had obtained their services in the same manner he acquired the services of Karl Baur and Willie Hoffmann. On the seventeenth of June, Hans Padell and the other Dornier 335 test pilot were supposed to be on their way from Nürnberg-Roth to Cherbourg with a P-51 escort.

"I had made arrangements with the P-51 outfit across the field to escort the two 335s from Nürnberg-Roth to Cherbourg," McIntosh said. "After they landed, I looked up and saw the 51s coming over the field. They dipped their wings, we waved at them, and they went home. The 335s and the 51s never got together. Hans Padell later explained to me that they shut down one engine and cruised on the power of the remaining engine to give the 51s a chance to catch up, but they never did. I hooked up with that airplane again when we got them ashore in Newark, after they were degunked and cleaned up. One of our maintenance men working on one of the aircraft set off part of the ejection mechanism. The lower fin of the airplane blew off as well as the propeller. Those explosive charges on the airplane were never properly explained to us. Then Jack Woolams and I worked on the other one to make it flyable. I personally greased the wheels and did all the cockpit

*The shrapnel-riddled Dornier 335 Watson found at Neubiberg in early May
1945. (RW)*

checks. No decision had been made as to who was going to fly the airplane. When the day came I proposed to Jack that we match coins to
see who would take the thing up. I wasn't too wild about flying this
machine. I won the flip. I said to Jack, I won. You fly. Something told
me to stay out of that airplane. Watson called and told us to get a bird
out to Freeman Field in Indiana. 'Stop in Pittsburgh to refuel if you
have to,' Watson added. Woolams taxied out to the end of the runway.
He got a red flare from the tower. He sat there for a while, until finally
the tower gave him the green light. His rear engine began to run hot,
and when he accelerated, just at the point of rotation, he lost that
engine and he had to feather the prop. I saw the gear coming up. He
came around and I noticed his nose was a little high. He sideslipped
the aircraft down to the runway and just before touchdown popped the
gear. You had to be a test pilot and have nerves of steel to do that. The
aircraft banged down on the concrete, he threw out the flaps and went
down the runway with the fire trucks chasing him. As soon as he slowed

down enough, he went over the side. What happened? A screen had been installed backwards and the rear engine overheated. After that debacle Watson told us to ship the aircraft by truck or rail. I don't know if I could have done as well as Jack, probably not. Letting him fly the airplane most likely saved my life."[3]

Why didn't Watson use Hans Padell to supervise maintenance on the complex Dornier 335, and why didn't he have Hans Padell fly the two aircraft from Newark to Freeman Field? The questions remain unanswered. A June 20, 1945, memo on the status of Project Seahorse stated, "German Civilian Test pilot of Dornier 335, Hans Padell, to be taken to States."[4] Most likely, Padell, like Hans Fay, the Me-262 test pilot, was a ward of the CPMB in Washington and being interrogated. Padell had no problems flying the Dornier 335, but it was just too complex a machine for any pilot, even a test pilot, to "throw on a saddle and ride it into the sunset," as borne out by the dismal results.

Soon after the arrival of Watson and his Whizzers at Melun-Villaroche on June 10, Watson renewed contact with his "French connection" and arranged delivery of an Me-262A fighter, *Werknummer* 3332. At this point the French had only one other 262, and they appreciated Watson's generous gesture. It was a quick trip from Melun to Corbeilles, where he spent just enough time to check out Colonel Badre, a French test pilot. He quickly returned to Melun.[5] At Melun Willie Hoffmann checked out First Lieutenant William V. Haynes in *Vera*, the two-seat trainer. Bill Haynes was a P-47 pilot from the 27th Fighter Group, and joined the Whizzers on their arrival at Melun on June 10. It was the usual ten-minute ride for Haynes. Haynes was the last American pilot to check out in the Me-262. Haynes also was the last to become a part of Watson's group of raiders. The group was as large as it was ever going to be.

In addition to a couple of C-47 transports, Watson also had a P-47 Thunderbolt fighter at his disposal, which the Whizzers used to fly here and there as needed. All were P-47 qualified combat pilots, so it was the ideal machine for them to move around the country. Early on Saturday morning, June 16, Roy Brown "strapped on" their P-47 and flew it up to Schleswig. Watson had finally received permission to go up into the British zone of occupation, as well as to visit former German airfields in Denmark and Norway. Roy's task was to find out what was available at Schleswig, and to see if any Arado 234s were at Grove and what condition they were in. Brown called Watson from Schleswig and from Grove and reported his findings, then flew back to Melun. Watson didn't wait for Brown to return—he took off as soon as he heard from him that not only were Me-262s available at Schleswig, but so were Arados at Grove. Watson loaded most of his crew into his trusty old C-47 Skytrain and headed for Schleswig airfield in the far north of Germany.

A number of requirements on the Wright Field want list remained to be filled—highest among them the Arado 234 jet bomber. Using the C-47's radio, Watson managed to track down McIntosh and told him to fly up north to Schleswig as soon as he could. "Bring all of your pilots," Watson told Mac. All of his pilots was a total of three, counting himself, the other two being Jack Woolams and Heinz Braun. On this foray into new territory, in addition to the jets, Watson hoped to find at least one flyable TA 152H fighter, the final version of the versatile FW-190. He also was looking for three Heinkel 219 Uhu night fighters. Because of the separately negotiated surrender on May 5, 1945, for Schleswig-Holstein and Denmark, not only did most night fighters end up in the British zone of occupation, but most undamaged aircraft did as well. There were several Uhus at Lechfeld, but they were damaged. Watson much preferred to take aircraft which were in fly-away condition. After a long flight across the war-scarred cities and towns of France, Belgium, and Germany, Watson's aircraft touched down at Schleswig.

Schleswig was crowded with German aircraft. As usual the British were forthcoming and helpful, having already identified a number of aircraft at Schleswig, Flensburg, Sylt, and other nearby German air

Willie Hoffmann wearing his customary floppy hat and standing on the wing of What Was It?, *an Me-262B two-seat trainer, at Schleswig airfield. Willie later flew the aircraft to Melun. (RB)*

bases for transfer to the United States, if Watson wanted them. Watson gratefully accepted an Me-262B two-seat trainer which his enlisted men quickly named *What Was It?*, as well as another Me-262B night fighter. The night fighter was christened *Ole Fruit Cake* for its mottled camouflage. Both aircraft had British colors painted on their fuselages and vertical stabilizers. Watson had his German mechanics and American crew chiefs remove the British roundels from the two jets and replace them with American stars and bars. Before Watson departed for Grove, where a complete German air defense installation had been surrendered intact to the British on May 5, he directed Bob Strobell and Willie Hoffmann to fly the two 262s back to Melun. Hoffmann was the instructor pilot, so he was given the two-seat trainer; Strobell took the night fighter.

On Tuesday, June 19, Strobell and Hoffmann took off from Schleswig, flying a loose trail formation heading for Twente airfield, near Enschede, Holland. They intended to refuel and then proceed to Beauvechain-Le Culot in Belgium, with their final destination Melun-Villaroche. "Well, I had been briefed at Schleswig that the runway at Twente was on the short side," Strobell recalled grimly, "so I planned to put her down at the very end. That's what I did. The only trouble was, I was about a foot too low and that translated into about fifty feet from the end of the runway. There was a berm in front of the runway, and I took its top off. The impact broke the wheel-scissors on the right side. When I hit the tarmac that wheel whipped around forty-five degrees to the runway and I was dragging it sideways. I wiped out the entire right side of the airplane. I was able to hold it on the runway, opened the canopy when it came to a stop, and climbed out. There was no fire. A trip that should have taken a few hours turned into four days. I should have made a hotter approach, that's what Willie and Karl always preached to us—keep that power up, keep that power up! Willie saw what happened to me, refueled, and kept on going. He arrived at Melun without my help. I made a few phone calls and had some of our crew chiefs go down to Lechfeld in a Gooney Bird and collect the parts—a wing and gear assembly—and put me back together again. Although such severe damage would have consigned most other aircraft to the scrap heap, the Me-262's modular construction made it a relatively simple matter to replace the damaged wing and landing gear. On the twenty-third, a week after leaving Melun for Schleswig, I finally made it back."[6]

Watson and the remainder of his crew meanwhile had moved on to Grove, an airfield about forty-five miles south of Aalborg in Denmark. In contrast to Lechfeld, which had been heavily bombed, Grove was in perfect condition. It had been the home of *Kampfgeschwader* 76, KG 76, which flew the Arado 234 jet reconnaissance bomber, as well as a night fighter unit, *Nachtjagdgeschwader* 1, NJG 1, which flew the Heinkel 219. At Grove, Watson and his entourage were met in the usual courteous manner by the British and presented with several war trophies. One was a large colorized picture of the Führer of the Third Reich, Adolf Hitler, and a similar picture of Hermann Göring. Both pictures had once decorated the Grove officers' mess.

Watson, on the right, presenting Major General James P. Hodges, Assistant Chief of Air Staff, Intelligence, Headquarters AAF, with a picture of Adolf Hitler. (RW)

Another trophy acquired on the sly by Bob Anspach was a 9 mm Luger pistol. "Watson was, of course, there to get Arados," Bob Anspach reminisced. "None of us had ever seen one, much less flown one. Watson tasked me to see if I could get hold of a flight manual, a checklist of sorts, anything that would be of help flying the airplane. I don't know how we did it, but we obtained that sought-after flight manual and I stayed up all night copying it—how to start the engines, how to taxi, takeoff and landing procedures, and so on. The British didn't seem anxious to part with any of their Arados, so everything was a little clandestine. I befriended one of the Brit officers. That evening he came by to see me and asked if I would like to see something. I didn't know what he had in mind, but I went along. He took me to a storage building, unlocked the door to a room, and to my astonishment, the room was filled with hundreds of pistols—Walther P-38s and 9 mm Lugers. 'Would you like one, Yank?' he asked. He handed me one and I brought it home and gave it to my brother."

A Heinkel 219 Uhu night fighter without its canopy at Grove, in Denmark. The two-man crew of pilot and radar intercept officer sat back to back. Ejection seats are clearly visible. (RB)

McIntosh—never one to cool his heels—continued to move around the countryside looking for loot. The British offered up several Me-410s from Sylt/Westerland. The 410 was an improvement on the ill-starred Bf 110 Zerstörer, but never really found its niche in Luftwaffe operations. Watson had no particular interest in that aircraft and it wasn't on the Wright Field want list anyway, so McIntosh turned down the offer with thanks. However, Mac gladly accepted three FW 190s from Flensburg, a late model Ju 88G night fighter from Grove, and three He 219 Uhu night fighters, also from Grove. There was in fact a late model Ju 88G night fighter in perfect condition at Lechfeld, but McIntosh may not have known about it since he had little to do with the Lechfeld operation. "The 219 was a twin-engine airplane," McIntosh explained, "with a high aspect wing. A hell of a fine airplane to fly." The only operational German aircraft with an ejection seat, it looked ungainly but turned into a terror of the night skies for RAF Bomber Command. Its four 30 mm and two 20 mm cannons augmented by the Lichtenstein or

A TA 152H at Freeman Field, 1945, with crudely reapplied German markings. British colors applied at Tirstrup, Denmark, are still visible just above the FE 112 designator. (RW)

Neptun radar spelled a fiery death for its victims. Every World War II night fighter was an improvisation with the exception of the Northrop P-61 Black Widow and the Heinkel 219 Uhu. According to Captain Eric Brown, "This unattractive creation had acquired the reputation of being the most effective nocturnal interceptor employed operationally by any of the combatants."[7] McIntosh, Woolams, and Heinz Braun ferried the three Heinkel 219s to Melun, and eventually from there to Cherbourg.

The really good news was that the British were willing to part with a TA 152H high-altitude fighter sitting at Aalborg, where it had been flown by them from Tirstrup to undergo maintenance. McIntosh and his crew—Woolams, Maxfield, and Braun—flew up to Aalborg in their trusty C-47 Gooney Bird as soon as they finished up at Schleswig. Watson flew in as well from Grove. "When we arrived at Aalborg we immediately took a look at the promised TA 152 fighter," wrote Watson. "The engine in this TA 152 . . . had to be replaced. Captain Maxfield took on this task immediately with some of our crew, while the rest of us tried to settle in for the evening." The TA 152 was the final version of the FW-190 series and named in honor of its designer, Professor Kurt Tank.

"I am the only one of our team who flew the TA 152," McIntosh recalled with pleasure, "and it was one of the best airplanes I have ever flown. I flew it a couple of times out of Aalborg against a P-51 and both times I ended up on the tail of the P-51. It was a very good airplane with all the kinks of the 190 worked out of it." Captain Eric Brown of the Royal Navy, Watson's counterpart, tested the TA 152 as well and wrote, "In my view, the Ta 152H was every bit as good as any of its Allied piston-engine counterparts and, from some aspects, better than most. It was unfortunate for the *Jagdflieger* but undoubtedly fortunate for the Allies that it arrived on the scene too late to play any serious role in the air war."[8]

"There was a small lake behind the British officers' club at Aalborg," McIntosh recalled with glee. "I was told by my British escort that absolutely no firearms were to be discharged in the area. I noticed a fair number of ducks happily swimming around the lake. Then I remembered that we'd been living on K rations and much too much Spam for far too long. I mentioned the ducks to Jack Woolams. Somehow Woolams got hold of a .22 caliber rifle and shot five ducks. The Brits, of course, heard the shots, even though the .22 isn't very loud. They quickly came over to investigate. 'We told you no hunting,' the military policeman lectured us in an agitated voice, looking somewhat ridiculous in his white gloves, white spats, white hat, with a large sidearm on his web belt. It must have been obvious to the Brits that we Yanks were guilty of something, because the duck population on the lake had suddenly taken a downward turn. The Brits became even more frustrated with us after they couldn't find any evidence of our wrongdoing after a time-consuming search. Finally I said to one of the MPs, Come and search our quarters. I don't have time for this. I have things to do. They actually came and searched every room including the toilet. I followed them around and noticed when we were in the bathroom that one of the airmen was a bit fidgety. The Brits finally left; not happy, but they left. I turned to the man and said, What the hell is going on here?

L to R: Strobell, Holt, Watson, Hoffmann, and Dahlstrom at Schleswig doing some informal flight planning. (RW)

He walked over to the toilet, picked up the cover of the water tank, and there were five ducks wrapped in paper. Our enlisted cook cooked up all the ducks and we had a grand dinner, with schnapps, of course. Watson was with us and had a good time talking to the airmen. But the ducks were tough. Oh, were they ever tough."[9]

Watson remembered this incident a little differently. "There appeared to be a bag of white feathers hidden in the back of our C-47—but we thought someone was saving them for a pillow that would be more comfortable than a rolled-up flight jacket. When dinner was announced it was obvious" [where the feathers had come from]. "Who could complain about duck roasted in proper style with fresh potatoes, fresh peas, a great salad, and to top it off, strawberries and cream! All of this on a blanket under the wing of our C-47. . . . Hiding plucked ducks in the water closet behind the john was, for my money, first class!"[10]

21

THE ARADO 234 CAPER

Although Watson was pleased to obtain one of the few TA 152Hs for his growing collection of German aircraft, what he really wanted from the British were several Arado 234 jets, the German twin-jet bomber and reconnaissance aircraft. None were found in flyable condition on the many GAF airfields occupied by American forces. The British, however, came across seven flyable Arados at Grove and one at Schleswig. While usually forthcoming and ready to share their booty with their American ally, on this occasion the British appeared reluctant. In later years Watson expressed understanding for their behavior, saying, "The British were perfectly correct in not assigning to us any of the Arados ... until they had discovered what they really had." Eventually, two Arado jets were set aside for the Army Air Forces, designated USA 5 and USA 6. As soon as Watson got word that the British had allocated to him two of the coveted Arados, he hustled his crew back to Grove and set to work inspecting the two aircraft and getting them ready for flight. In the process both Arados acquired new names—*Jane I* and *Snafu I*. The first Arado was ready to fly on June 20. Karl Baur took it up on a test flight the same day. He test-flew the other Arado three days later, on June 23. On the twenty-fourth of June,

Watson and Baur departed for Melun with an en route refueling stop at Le Culot—Watson flying USA 5 (*Jane I*) and Baur flying USA 6 (*Snafu I*).

The British made it a practice to give a USA number to each aircraft allocated to the AAF. USA 1 through 4 were Me-262 fighters of which Watson chose to accept USA 2, the night fighter named *Ole Fruit Cake,* and USA 3, a two-seat trainer named *What Was It?* Those two aircraft had already been flown from Schleswig to Melun by Bob Strobell and Willie Hoffmann. Both Arado 234 jet bombers and the Me-262B night fighter were new additions to Watson's German aircraft collection, and featured in the show-and-tell he put on for General Spaatz on June 27. USA 8 through 10 were the three Heinkel 219 Uhu night fighters, which had also been accepted, and USA 11 was the prized TA 152H fighter.[1]

The "Arado 234B was the world's first jet bomber and the world's first high altitude jet reconnaissance aircraft," Watson wrote. "When I first heard about this aircraft in October 1944, while at General Spaatz' headquarters, I looked forward with great anticipation to seeing one. But never in my wildest dreams had I ever thought we'd capture one intact and be able to fly it." At Grove, Watson came face to face with the Arado 234B jet, and he fell in love with it just the way he had with the Me-262. "My first view of this airplane was—simply put—breathtaking!"[2] Watson was more than right to feel that way; there was nothing quite like it anywhere else in existence. Wrote Captain Eric Brown, who flew the Arado many times in 1945, "It was a magnificent aeroplane of which no real equivalent existed in the Allied order of battle, so it may be said without fear of contradiction that the Blitz was truly in a class of its own." It "seared across the skies above Normandy and British East Coast harbors like greased lightning, performing its reconnaissance missions with complete impunity. The Ar 234 appeared truly *blitzschnell* to Allied fighter pilots assigned the impossible task of intercepting this turbojet-driven interloper; they had about as much

Jane I *and* Snafu I, *designated USA 5 and USA 6 by the British, then numbered 202 and 303 by the Whizzers at Melun, were Arado 234B jets from Grove, in Denmark. Here shown at Melun-Villaroche on June 27, 1945, awaiting inspection by General Spaatz. (RB)*

chance of bringing their guns to bear on the elusive German new-comer to the air war arena as they had of knocking it from the sky with a volley of profane oaths. At the speeds and altitudes at which it normally performed its reconnoitering [450 + mph and 30,000 feet] only mechanical malfunction could bring it down."[3]

"I knew," Watson wrote, "there was nothing planned, or on the drawing board at Wright Field, or, as far as I knew, in the mind of anyone that resembled this airplane, which had already performed several operational missions. . . . I fully appreciated that at last I was looking at something that justified my view that the Germans were well advanced in science and technology and aerodynamics and manufacturing capability under the most difficult situations. . . . Unfortunately for the Germans, and fortunately for the Western Allies, when the war ended they had produced about 210 of these aircraft and less than half. . . had gotten into operation, due to shortage of engines and fuel."[4] Captain Brown shared Watson's sentiments: "This aeroplane looked right and in my experience this was always a good omen with regard to flying qualities. With its slender shoulder-mounted wing, slim underslung engine nacelles and smooth fuselage profile, it exemplified careful aerodynamic design."⁵

A Headquarters USSTAF Exploitation Division report noted that as of June 20, 1945, the following aircraft were on hand for Project Seahorse: "11 262s; 2 335s; 6 Long nose 190s; 1 TA-152; 1 JU-388; 3 HE-219s; 6 Late type FW-190s, not long nose; 2 Arado 234s; 1 JU 88 night fighter; 15 Me-162s crated; 10 Me-163s crated."⁶ The report was actually premature and was counting chickens before they hatched. "Allocated" would have been a better word choice than "on hand." Only ten Me-262s had actually arrived at Melun—Strobell was still up at Twente with his heavily damaged night fighter, not knowing if it could be made flyable again, and Watson had already turned over one of the 262s to the French. So there were really only ten aircraft on hand. The two Arado 234 jets were still at Grove and wouldn't arrive at Melun until four days later.

Watson wasn't satisfied with just two Arados. He knew that half of whatever he brought home was supposed to go to the U.S. Navy, and he wanted to take at least two of the Arado jets back to Wright Field for testing. The British held onto the other six jets at Grove and Schleswig, and there was no indication formally or informally that they were going to let go of any more. To emphasize their determination to hold on to the Arados in their possession, the British began to move Arado jets from Grove and Schleswig to Farnborough as early as June 6. The day after Watson and Baur flew USA 5 and USA 6 to Melun, Eric Brown led a flight of two additional Arados to RAE Farnborough. It became obvious that the Grove connection was drying up as a future source of Arado 234s.⁷ At first only a rumor, McDonald's intelligence people soon confirmed that the British had captured an entire squadron of Ar 234B jets at Sola airfield near Stavangar, Norway. When German forces capitulated in Denmark on May 5, one squadron from *Kampfgeschwader* 76 flew its aircraft from Grove to Sola. The withdrawal most likely was a defiant reflex reaction, the German airmen not wanting to surrender just yet. The Germans made this one final futile flight to Stavangar, where they surrendered their aircraft in perfect flying condition to the British five days later, on May 10. When Watson heard that nine additional Arados were at Sola he knew he had to act quickly. "Time was running short," he wrote, "and there was very little time for proper paperwork." HMS *Reaper* was loading at Cherbourg and had a sailing date of July 12. At the very best, Watson had two weeks to come up with two additional Arado jets and get them stowed on the deck of HMS *Reaper*.

Watson must have thought, What if I just went up to Sola and picked up two of the German jets? Who is going to stop me? I am well known to my British friends; I've been up to Grove and Schleswig just recently to retrieve several aircraft from them. Everybody knows about me; I'm no stranger to them in this business. Who is going to challenge me if I just show up at Sola with my Eisenhower passes in my pocket and some forged papers and pick up a couple more airplanes? Watson must have had thoughts along those lines and run his plan past his people at USSTAF. No one there would tell him not to proceed; nor would anyone tell him to go ahead, either. But tacit approval would be good enough for him. Whatever Watson's thoughts might have been, on the first of July, accompanied by his sidekick, Karl Baur, and a mix of American and German maintenance people, Watson flew his C-47 from Melun north to Sola.[8]

Watson continued to feel insecure in his relationship with the German pilots and maintenance men working for him, in contrast to his crew of P-47 pilots, the Whizzers, who by this time had formed comfortable, even close relationships—not to mention Fred McIntosh, Jack Woolams, and Heinz Braun, who were probably the closest of them all. Maybe it was the fact that Watson had never been in combat and faced death, as all of his Whizzers had, which made him overly cautious. Whatever the reason, he never quite managed to shake a certain sense of discomfort and continued to play what he referred to as his "shell game."

"We were constantly concerned about the sabotage of aircraft that U.S. pilots and crews would be flying," Watson wrote. In the case of the German ground crews at Sola this scepticism was appropriate. "To say that the German ground crew at Sola . . . were disgruntled about their prisoner of war status would be a gross . . . understatement," Watson wrote. But those of "the German crew members that I took to Sola airfield . . . were at this point quite reliable, as they had been with us for some time and we had promised them everything—including a trip to the United States. . . . We played what I guess one would call 'the shell game.' Once the Arado 234s were prepared for flight I decided at the last minute which airplane would be flown by me . . . leaving the other one to the German Messerschmitt test pilot Baur." The ground crew never knew which airplane their countryman was going to fly.

Watson picked out two Arados at Sola with the assistance of his British hosts, who had not yet been notified by their own authorities to identify additional aircraft for the Americans. Watson seemed to have all the necessary paperwork. Of course, they knew of him, so there didn't seem to be any reason not to let him have the two aircraft he said he had come to pick up. Watson noted that "the British people on the base were most helpful." The two Arados were inspected and their compasses swung, and Baur took each one up on a brief test hop. Then Watson bade his British hosts farewell, thanked them for their hospitality, and disappeared with Baur into the overcast. Watson's German-American maintenance crew boarded their C-47 and headed south to France. The Yanks were gone as quickly as they had arrived.[9]

It was about an hour's flying time from Sola to Le Culot, Belgium. Watson wanted to refuel there and then press on to Melun. Although he had flown with Baur many times before, Watson didn't give Baur any navigation charts for the flight. Watson had charts, but he apparently feared that Baur might use the opportunity to defect to neutral Sweden. Watson should have realized that this man who had flown on his team for two full months had no reason for such a foolish act, and would certainly never have abandoned his wife and infant son, who lived in Augsburg. Wrote Karl Baur in his diary, "From Stavanger we ferried two of the twin-engine Arado 234 jet bombers. . . . 'Stay on my wing' was the order from Colonel Watson for the flight to Melun, via a refueling stop in Le Culot. Of course Watson did not know that I knew this area like my hip pocket from numerous prior flights during the war. After making a perfect 'spot landing' in Le Culot I did not spare my compliments for a job well done. At one time—we had no radios then—when he was checking on me I had the feeling he was surprised that I was still with him, and enjoying myself."[10]

After takeoff from Sola, Watson circled above the cloud deck and waited for Karl Baur to show up. Once Baur was tucked in on his wing they headed south. They flew strictly dead reckoning, time and distance, following the compass needle toward their destination. The charts Watson carried were of no use in this environment. "It's a little over an hour's flight from Stavanger. . . When time was up, to the second, we circled and, by the grace of God, there was the airfield below us, — visible through a break in the clouds. We landed, refueled, and . . . took off" again.[11] Watson had called Fred McIntosh prior to his departure from Sola and instructed him to be at Le Culot at twelve o'clock sharp with fuel and food. "My radio operator on the C-47 got a call from Watson early that morning telling me, 'Have jet fuel at the end of the runway and a sandwich available not later than 12:00 hours.' So we're out there and the fuel is in barrels and we use chamois cloth to strain it. Out of the overcast, at exactly twelve o'clock, came these two Arados. They touched down and taxied over to us. We filled them up. Watson and Baur had a sandwich and a beer, and after Watson finished he said, 'Got to go.' They got back into their aircraft and off they went" to Melun.[12] Watson and Baur flew the Arados from Melun to Cherbourg on July 5, where they were cocooned and loaded on HMS *Reaper*. These were the last two aircraft acquired by Watson. The deck of HMS *Reaper* was filled.

In later years Watson recalled that "this airplane was a real joy to fly," and had excellent visibility. He thought it was quite comfortable too, as comfortable as any seat could possibly be in a combat aircraft, but he wondered how you would get out of it in flight if you had to abandon it. Without equivocation Watson felt that the Arado was a remarkably advanced aircraft for 1944. "One additional item of considerable interest," he observed, was that "the Arado 234B was equipped with a braking parachute to shorten the landing run. It was the first aircraft in the world . . . to have this as a standard fitting."[13]

There were no official repercussions from Watson's Sola caper. Watson told McIntosh at Wright Field in 1946, just before Mac returned to civilian life, that he had heard through the grapevine that the British learned of his Arado heist almost immediately after he left Sola. There was considerable "heartburn" over the matter among some of his British colleagues, one even suggesting sending fighters after them and shooting them down. What fighter would have been able to catch an Arado 234 jet is unknown. The comment was certainly made in jest, but revealed British anger and frustration over the behavior of their trusted Yankee friend. As for Watson, once the episode was behind him, he focused on the future, as was his nature. His job in Europe was done: it was time to plan his trip home in "his" Junkers 290.

22

SO FAR, SO GOOD

Within a period of two weeks, Watson had pulled together more than fifty Americans and Germans to do his bidding. On May 2, 1945, when he showed up at the doorstep of Karl Baur's apartment house in Augsburg, he was pretty much a one-man operation. With Karl Baur came twenty-six former Messerschmitt company employees. Then Watson acquired Freiburger's group from the Feudin' 54th, the P-47 Thunderbolt pilots who volunteered to fly German Me-262 jets, and Colonel Schilling's fledgling ATI group at Merseburg. Captain Fred McIntosh soon joined the Merseburg operation, and later became Watson's key man at Nürnberg-Roth, while Lieutenant Strobell performed a similar function at Lechfeld. On May 8, Hauptmann Heinz Braun landed his Ju 290 at Munich-Riem airport, and Watson added him and his flight engineers and mechanics to his group of "raiders," as well as Hans Padell, the Dornier 335 test pilot, and several other German pilots as they became available. Then the industrious Lieutenant Colonel Seashore and his small group of logisticians joined Watson. Watson, with his usual light touch and ever-present smile, provided the focus and the glue that held this disparate group of individuals together as a functional organization—if not an organization in the traditional sense, then a team of men working together toward a single objective, which was to save Germany's aeronautical treasure.

Watson wasn't interested in organizational structure. He was after results, and quick results at that. He needed flexibility and the ability to push ever downward the tasks which came his way. Watson couldn't afford to let himself get mired in detail. Fred McIntosh, Bob Strobell, and Malcolm Seashore gave him the option to remain unencumbered. These men were his anchors. They ensured that he retained his freedom of action. By late June 1945 his mixed crew of American and German pilots was flying varied captured German aircraft from Nürnberg-Roth and Melun-Villaroche into Cherbourg-Querqueville, where Seashore's team was busy preparing them for their trans-Atlantic voyage. Surprisingly, there were very few aircraft accidents or incidents to mar a nearly flawless two-month operation. This was all the more surprising, because the American pilots were flying aircraft with instrumentation very different from what they were used to, not to mention transitioning from reciprocating engines to the new jet with tricycle landing gear. Watson attempted to minimize the potential for trouble by stipulating that his jet pilots have at least a thousand hours' flying time, including combat experience, and if at all possible that they had flown as instructors prior to coming to Europe. He checked out key personnel like Bob Strobell on his own, or insisted that no one else fly an airplane type before he had flown it at least once. In the case of the Arado 234, Watson kept American pilots other than himself out of the cockpit entirely. Only he and Karl Baur flew the Arado jets, and by doing so he minimized the inherent accident potential lurking in this operation. Yet the very nature of his loosely knit group of pilots, operating under minimal control and direction, bore within it the seeds of potential calamity.

Karl Baur wrote in his diary about Watson's American pilots, "One checkout ride in the two-seater [*Vera/Willie*] was enough to turn them loose. It is a pleasant experience to work with this group."[1] Baur saw the Whizzers from the perspective of a German who had worked with German pilots. The Americans, in contrast to their German counterparts who had received mostly hurried training late in the war, survived the very best pilot training program in the world. The Americans had an air of quiet confidence about them. The Whizzers were typical small town American boys—polite, low key, always underplaying their hard-earned skills. Where they came from, showing off was in bad taste. Bragging or arrogance wasn't part of their makeup; it wasn't part of their culture, civil or military. Wearing their crushed wheel hats, brown leather flight jackets, rumpled GI pants, and high-topped combat boots, they looked every bit the competent and confident American warriors they were. It was the aura projected by these young men that captured Karl Baur's imagination.

Initially, Watson kept a tight rein on his jet operation, understanding that one or two spectacular accidents could endanger the entire project. But he clearly used a different standard for McIntosh and his "fan club," which had much lower visibility with him and others. For instance, there was Heinz Braun's belly landing in an FW 190 at Villacoublay on June 13, resulting in the loss of the aircraft. Heinz forgot to put the gear down—pilot error. McIntosh ruined an FW 190 as well by landing on a row of fuel drums at Nürnberg-Roth, something that could clearly have been avoided if Fred had paid a little more attention to what he was doing. Having some oil smeared across the aircraft's windshield wasn't all that unusual an occurrence for piston-driven fighters, and Roy Brown coped with two such situations. In each case, Roy brought his airplane down safely. Roy, a disciplined engineer, flew differently from how the treetop-chewing P-47 pilot Fred McIntosh did. There is no evidence that Watson took notice or ever talked to McIntosh about either accident. It was a failing that was to have consequences.

Bob Strobell's accident at Twente in the Netherlands was of a more serious nature and should have elicited Watson's immediate attention; it didn't. The accident was clearly avoidable, pilot error, a fact that Bob Strobell readily admitted. Bob forgot what he had been taught and let his attention wander. He got behind the proverbial power curve and promptly lost control of his airplane—excusable because of his lack of experience in jets, yet avoidable. Strobell, a first-rate pilot, knew that and didn't like his slip of concentration one bit. The FW 190s Fred McIntosh and Heinz Braun totaled were no great loss to the operation; there were plenty more where they came from. The Me-262B night fighter Strobell dented at Twente was the only one of its kind in Watson's inventory. There were few of them around. A replacement aircraft was unlikely. That it was quickly repaired was a tribute to the 262's maintainability, which was lucky. There was another incident when Karl Baur lost the canopy of the Arado 234 he was piloting into Melun on June 24. All in all, Watson's flyers, American and German, preserved a good safety record in this early and potentially most dangerous period of their operation. Yet enough had happened to have elicited Watson's concern. So far, so good. All there was left to do was to fly the jets from Melun to Cherbourg. That should be "a piece of cake," as airmen were apt to say.

On June 29, Watson and Baur flew *Jane I* and *Snafu I* from Melun to Cherbourg-Querqueville. Watson chose to fly *Jane I* again, Baur following in trail in *Snafu I*. Watson and Baur quickly returned to Paris and then moved up north to Sola to pick up the two additional Arado 234s. Heinz Braun, Jack Woolams, and Fred McIntosh—drinking buddies at this stage—in the meantime had brought in three He 219 night fighters from Grove and were back in Schleswig-Holstein getting more airplanes. Seashore's boys at Querqueville were kept busy preparing airplanes for their sea voyage to the United States.

On June 30, three days after the air show and static display at Melun, Bob Strobell was going to move eight of the Me-262s from Melun to Cherbourg, again flying them in relays rather than in formation. Watson rightfully believed that this was a safer way of moving aircraft from place to place. If they flew in a large formation and one of them crashed on the runway, closing the field, the others would quickly find themselves running out of fuel. So, it was one at a time from Lechfeld to Melun, and again one at a time from Melun to Querqueville. With Watson and Baur unavailable, Bob Strobell had eleven airplanes to move and eight jet-qualified pilots. *Willie*, the two-seat trainer, remained behind at Melun because Watson needed it to give Seversky a ride at the request of General Spaatz; the other trainer acquired from the British also stayed at Melun as a backup, as did *Ole Fruit Cake*—all three two-seaters. Strobell assigned Willie Hoffmann to fly *Happy Hunter II*, Watson's prized 50-mm-gun-toting aircraft. Hoffmann was the most experienced pilot of the eight, so Strobell decided he should fly Watson's prized airplane. He didn't want anything to happen to *Happy Hunter*. What should have been an uneventful transfer of aircraft flying straight and level, "a piece of cake," turned into a comedy of errors with plenty of drama.

"We agreed to fly below ten thousand feet," recalled Bob Strobell. "Anspach decided all on his own to take her up a little higher. He flew time and distance, dead reckoning, and when he came back down through the overcast he couldn't see anything but water. Bob had overflown his destination to a considerable extent and was out over the Atlantic heading for blue water. Seeing nothing but water ahead, Anspach did a 180, and an island came into view off the nose of his aircraft—it was the British Isle of Jersey. On Jersey there was a primitive grass landing strip. Anspach didn't know where he was, but he could see that airstrip and he was running low on fuel. So he panicked a little and put her down, not knowing if the grass fild was long enough to take him. He apparently did a great job putting her down, because he and the airplane survived. When he finally got in touch with me a couple of days later—the island had no modern communications and had been occupied by the Germans during the war—I got our Gooney Bird, loaded it up with a couple of fifty-gallon drums of kerosene, and sent it over to him. I thought, you got yourself into that mess, you get yourself out. And he did. I never ordered him to fly the bird out. I felt only he could make that decision. It was indeed a short runway, and grass at that."²

"I took her up to fifteen thousand feet," recalled Bob Anspach, "just for once, to get the feel for that airplane at that altitude. On descent into what I thought would be the Cherbourg-Querqueville area, when I broke through the cloud deck, to my great surprise all I could see was water. I was getting low on fuel and had no real idea where I was. I have to admit that I was getting a bit frantic about this time. I did a quick 180 and saw an island in the distance. When I got over it I could see a landing strip. Grass, not concrete. It was the Isle of Jersey, I learned after landing. Grass or no grass, I had to bring her in. It turned out I had forty-three hundred feet of grass strip on which to put down the Me-262, which as far as I knew needed five to six thousand feet of concrete. The strip looked very short—but I quit thinking and just began doing. I made one pass over the field, and God was with me, I got her down on the second try. I brought her to a stop near the end of the field, at the edge of a cliff looking down on the English Channel. Somebody had seen me come in for my landing and later told me that on my approach I headed straight for the steeple of their church at the approach end of the field. He thought I was going to take off the steeple. Instead, he said, 'That steeple went right between your landing gear.' So I was cutting things really close. That was my third flight in the airplane. Karl Baur and I talked about my experience a few days later and he said to me, 'If you asked me if you could put that plane down on that strip, I would have told you, no, you couldn't do it. But you did.' Baur was really amazed at what I did.

"After landing on Jersey, I was incommunicado for forty-eight hours. I couldn't get through to the outside world. Strobell had no idea what happened to me. He must have thought I crashed somewhere and killed myself. The people on Jersey were really nice and helpful, but there was no way to communicate with anyone off the island. They put me up in their finest hotel situated on a cliff with a beautiful view of the sea. Finally, after two days, I got hooked up with Bob Strobell over radio, and he said, 'We'll get you out, Bob.' He sent a C-47 with a couple of barrels of kerosene accompanied by Lieutenant Colonel Seashore. Seashore, not a pilot but a damn good organizer, looked at the field and shook his head. 'It's your decision, Bob,' he said to me. 'I'm not going to tell you to fly out of here. If you don't want to do it, we'll just leave her here.' Flying out of there became a matter of pride for me. I figured if I could get her in, I could get her out. I knew I was the one who got myself into the situation, and I didn't want it to cost us an airplane. I had that drop-off at the end of the field, and if I didn't pick up enough speed I figured I could drop down a little and pick it up that way. I got into the cockpit, fired her up, and came out of there as slick as a whistle. It wasn't me who did it, it was the airplane." It was a big relief to everyone to see Bob Anspach land his errant jet at Querqueville.

On July 3, the same day Bob Anspach flew his 262 off the Isle of Jersey, two of the remaining three jets from Melun, *Ole Fruit Cake* and *What Was It?*, were flown to Cherbourg. Once Seashore arrived at Querqueville in the C-47 from Jersey, all of the pilots jumped onboard the aircraft and headed back to Paris, leaving Seashore behind to tend to the loading of HMS *Reaper*. On Friday morning, July 6, Anspach flew *Vera/Willie*, the last remaining jet at Melun, to Cherbourg. Bob stayed below ten thousand feet, took up a heading of 290 degrees, and flew straight to Cherbourg. There was no cloud deck that day to obscure his visibility, and twenty minutes into the flight he saw the Querqueville runway coming into view. "Everything looked just fine to me as I made my approach," Bob recalled. "I put my gear down and concentrated on setting her down. Then, as I began my rollout, the nose dropped on me. Not another one, I thought. I slid along the concrete nose first, starting a small fire in the nose section. The nose gear hadn't come down and I didn't know it. The tower didn't shoot a red flare indicating that anything was wrong with me. We had no radios. The instruments on the aircraft weren't all working anyway. The only

General Spaatz at Melun looking at the cannon carried by Happy Hunter II.
Watson is standing attentively behind his general. (RB)

instruments we cared about were the flight instruments—airspeed,
compass, altimeter, fuel. Someone took a picture of the aircraft as it
sat on the runway nose down with flames shooting up the right side of
the nose. It looked like the aircraft would be a total loss. The emergency
crew showed up in a hurry and put the fire out quickly. I took a Gooney
Bird with some of our maintenance people down to Lechfeld, we
picked up a new nose section and a couple of engine nacelles, and
a couple days later *Willie* was in perfect condition again."[3]

While Anspach got disoriented on his flight to Cherbourg, Willie
Hoffmann, the jovial Messerschmitt test pilot, had to deal with a true
in-flight emergency. Watson had flown *Wilma Jeanne/Happy Hunter II*
from Lechfeld to Melun-Villaroche. And he would have flown *Happy
Hunter II* to Cherbourg, but he was busy giving jet rides to VIPs and

getting a couple more Arados out of Norway. So Willie was chosen by Bob Strobell to fly *Happy Hunter*. "When Willie Hoffmann left Melun," Bob Strobell recalled, "everything seemed to be going just fine. He got up to cruising altitude. I don't know what altitude he was flying at, but it was below ten thousand feet, I presume, when he lost an engine. According to Willie it literally shook the airplane apart. In the process of the emergency the violent vibrations put the trim on the airplane in a downward mode. You can't override the trim with a control stick on this airplane. So Willie was cruising at five hundred miles per hour, loses an engine, and the nose starts going down on him. He shuts down the other engine and fights to control the airplane, but he can't get a hold of the trim-tab to pull it back. He knew he had to bail out. He opened the canopy, undid his seatbelt, and he was probably the only guy who would have done that, rolled the airplane upside down and let go of the stick. The airplane went one way, he the other. He made one grievous mistake; he thought he was close to the ground and pulled the ripcord. The resulting jolt blackened and blued him from his ears to his knees. His whole body was one huge bruise.

"When Luftwaffe pilots were shot down or bailed out for some emergency, they nearly always returned with their parachutes under their arms. Apparently that was standard operating procedure in the Luftwaffe. And typical Willie, he had his parachute in his room when I got there. That parachute had six-foot rips on each side, and he broke six shroud lines. A shroud line on a parachute is unbelievably strong, but he broke them when he opened his chute at too high an altitude. What probably saved his life was the force of the opening shock being dissipated by the ripping chute and the breaking lines. What happened next? People in the upper echelon of the technical intelligence program tried to court-martial me for Willie's accident. Willie was working for us, but someone was looking for a more sinister reason than just an accident, and since I ran the Me-262 operation, I was it. I went to Watson and we talked. I said to him, Colonel, anybody who wants to court-martial me, ask them one question, would you please? He said, 'Sure, Bob.' Ask them if they would have rather lost one of our American boys in that airplane, or was it all right that we lost the airplane with Willie in it? After that I didn't hear another thing about a court-martial. If that engine had disintegrated on me or one of my guys, we would have never rolled the airplane upside down. We were not test pilots. Willie was. We weren't even ready to think about doing something like that. The reason Willie was flying that particular airplane was because I knew Watson wanted it back to the States, so I put my best pilot in it. How could you foresee that it had a bum engine? A year or so after that accident the American sergeant assigned to service that aircraft came forward and admitted that he didn't inspect the engines at Melun. 'I know all the rest of the guys inspected theirs,' he said, 'but I just didn't inspect those engines as I was supposed to.' Had the sergeant inspected the engines he would have probably caught the crack or something strange looking on one of the blades and we wouldn't have lost the airplane. It was standard procedure to visually check every engine before flight. He just didn't do it that day." The 50 mm cannon from *Happy Hunter II* was later recovered and is on exhibit in the United States Air Force Museum at Wright-Patterson AFB, Ohio.

Bob Strobell's good judgment, and a little bit of luck, put an experienced test pilot in the seat of *Happy Hunter*, or very likely the operation would have suffered its first fatality. As it was, Watson's group was lucky that things had gone as smoothly as they had up to this point. But that was not the end of the Whizzers' streak of bad luck. On Tuesday, the third of July, Bob Strobell was back at Melun to ferry *Ole Fruitcake* to Querqueville. The flight to Cherbourg was uneventful. The next day Bob grabbed their P-47 Thunderbolt and flew to Sandhofen airport, Y79, near Ludwigshafen. Sandhofen was the last base Bob Anspach had flown out of, and Bob Strobell had stored some of his belongings there. "After the war ended the Army Air Forces classified many aircraft as war weary," Strobell explained. "War weary meant that the aircraft had the number of engine and airframe hours on it making it marginal to fly under maximum conditions. We were allowed to fly these aircraft as long as we didn't fly combat maneuvers. The P-47 we used as a runabout was one of those. Nearly every one of us flew that airplane at one time or another. I was picking up my personal belongings from Sandhofen airport to take back to Cherbourg. I was scheduled to return to the States on HMS *Reaper*. I poured the power to it, took off—and it blew the induction manifold while I was at maximum power. The engine was filled with raw, vaporized gasoline. When that happened you either shut the switch off and got the hell out of there, or try a 180 and dead-stick her into the airport. I reached up to turn the switch off, intending to take her back to Sandhofen, when she backfired. The engine blew up in front of me. I barely got out. Made about one oscillation in my chute and hit the ground. What hurt the most was that I lost about twenty rolls of film I had taken in the Me-262 program. People at the airport saw me bail out but didn't see the chute open. Scratch one American, they thought. I remained in the hospital for forty-five days. HMS *Reaper* sailed without me. When I got out of the hospital I received orders to report to Wright Field to Building 89, which held much of the 'stuff' we had brought over from Germany. Watson was at Wright Field at this time and had me transferred there."[4]

THE CONQUERING
HERO

Just a day after Bob Strobell bailed out of his P-47 fighter over Mannheim, Colonel Harold Watson and Flugkapitän Karl Baur ferried the last two Arado 234s from Melun-Villaroche to Cherbourg. The last Me-262 was delivered on July 6 by Bob Anspach. Although damaged on landing because of a nose-gear malfunction, the jet was quickly restored with parts flown in from Lechfeld. After that, Karl Baur and the Messerschmitt mechanics who had accompanied Watson from Lechfeld to Melun and then to Cherbourg were released and returned to Augsburg in Watson's C-47. Versuchspilot Willie Hoffmann was recuperating from his injuries in an American military hospital in Paris. Hauptmann Heinz Braun, after making his last aircraft delivery to Cherbourg, was sent by Watson to Paris to work on "his" Ju 290 transport—the same Ju 290 Braun once piloted as a member of KG 200. Watson had promised Braun he would take him and his three mechanics along to the United States. On July 10 the Russians moved into that portion of their occupation zone once occupied by their American ally—Merseburg would remain under Russian control for many years to come. The boundaries for postwar Germany were set.

Lieutenant Colonel Malcolm Seashore's crew at Cherbourg was busily cocooning Luftwaffe aircraft and transferring them to the deck of HMS *Reaper*. This is how Bob Strobell described the operation: "They rolled the cocooned airplanes from the nearby airstrip out onto a jetty. A barge-mounted derrick then lifted them onto another barge which took them out to the aircraft carrier anchored in deeper water. The German planes then were lifted by crane up to the deck of the *Reaper*." In addition, several Liberty ships anchored in the harbor were loaded with boxes of disassembled Me-163 aircraft, machine tools, missiles, jet engines, and all the varied paraphernalia Wright Field engineers had put on their want list. Most of that "stuff," as Bob Strobell referred to it, would end up in Building 89 at Wright Field, inventoried and sitting for years gathering dust.

On July 7, General McDonald signed off on a USSTAF Exploitation Divison memo giving approval for the Whizzer pilots and ten enlisted crew chiefs "to accompany the aircraft carrier to the Zone of Interior to be utilized as pilots and maintenance personnel for the jet aircraft being delivered." The memo was in line with Watson's earlier proposal of June 11, when he suggested that the "trained crew-chiefs and pilots be shipped and transferred to Wright Field or other research centers in the United States as a unit in order to accomplish performance and flight testing and comparative analysis with similar American equipment." The memo also authorized Colonel Seashore to return home on the *Reaper*. The officer and six enlisted men who worked for Seashore on the Seahorse project were released for reassignment. "It is not believed," stated the memo written in the usual stilted military English, "that the 6 EM and officer presently working for Col Seashore are essential to the operation upon arrival in the Z of I. . . . It is believed that adequate arrangements can be made at whatever port the ship docks at to furnish necessary unpacking and re-assembling personnel without shipping additional people from this theater." The memo concluded, "Col Watson, two officers and six enlisted men are

Cocooned German jets strapped to the deck of HMS Reaper *in Cherbourg harbor, July 1945. (RB)*

planning to fly a Ju 290 bomber to the Zone of Interior on or about 20 July to meet this shipment at the other end and make such arrangements as are necessary at Wright Field."[1] The Ju 290 was not a bomber, but people continually referred to it as such.

Only days before the *Reaper* was to "set sail," its stateside destination was still in limbo. A 26 June Navy message suggested Naval Air Station Quonset Point as the unloading port, since "jet planes require 6000 foot runways," and Quonset Point met that requirement.[2] The final destination for HMS *Reaper* turned out to be Pier 6 in the Bayonne Military Ocean Terminal, just down from Ellis Island and the Statue of Liberty, and across from Newark airfield, but that decision was not reached until shortly before the flattop departed Cherbourg. On July 12 the loading of HMS *Reaper* was completed, but the carrier remained in port for another week, not departing until Friday, July 20. There were a number of reasons for the delayed departure, one of which was an awards ceremony for Colonel Watson and his Whizzers.

On the deck of the *Reaper*, cocooned and securely tied down, sat an assortment of forty German aircraft, the result of Watson's foraging operation—ten Messerschmitt 262 fighters, trainers, and reconnaissance jets; two of the strange-looking Dornier 335 push-pull engined fighters; one Focke-Wulf TA 152H high-altitude fighter; one Junkers 388 twin-engine high-altitude reconnaissance bomber; a Junkers 88G twin-engine night fighter; three Heinkel 219 night fighters; and four Arado 234 twin-jet bombers. Nine Focke-Wulf 190D/F fighters were scattered about the deck, including three of the long noses, airplanes with in-line engines and two-stage superchargers and gyrostabilized gunsights. The three older Messerschmitt 109G fighters looked somewhat out of place, as did the two Bücker 181 trainers and one Messerschmitt 108 utility aircraft. One Doblhoff jet-propelled helicopter and two Flettner 282 helicopters completed the diverse array of German airplanes on the *Reaper*'s deck. A lone P-51 reconnaissance aircraft with a new camera suit sat among the forty German aircraft being sent to the ZI for test and evaluation.

On July 17, Watson and his Whizzers—Captains Dahlstrom and Hillis and First Lieutenants Brown, Anspach, Holt, and Strobell—were summoned to the USSTAF headquarters at St.-Germain to be honored for their part in the recovery of the German Me-262 jet fighters. Strobell had to take a rain check, whiling away his time in a Mannheim hospital bed instead. Lieutenant General John K. Cannon, again the commander of the United States Strategic Air Forces in Europe, pinned the Distinguished Flying Cross on Colonel Watson's tunic and presented the Air Medal to the six captains and lieutenants for "meritorious achievement in aerial flight." Watson's DFC citation read, "*For extraordinary achievement in aerial flight while serving with Exploitation Division, A-2, Headquarters, United States Strategic Air Force in Europe, during the period 3 June 1945 to 11 June 1945.*" This period took in Watson's test flight on June 3, 1945, and his June 4 flight from Lechfeld to Melun in the unnamed Me-262A, *Werknummer* 3332,

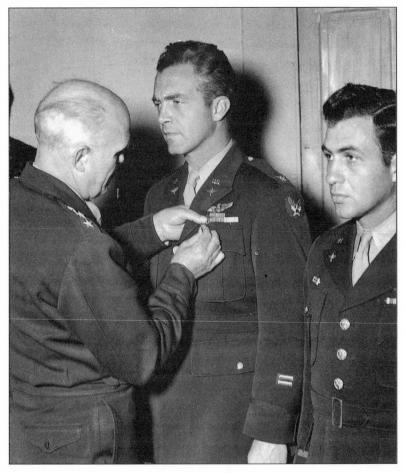

Lieutenant General J. K. Cannon, USSTAF commander, pins the Distinguished Flying Cross to Colonel Watson's blouse. Captain Dahlstrom is standing next to Watson. (RW)

which he subsequently delivered to the French, as well as the delivery of the remaining nine aircraft from Lechfeld to Melun-Villaroche on June 10.[3]

Watson was pleased with the award of the Distinguished Flying Cross, the nation's fourth-highest combat decoration, after the Medal of Honor, Distinguished Service Cross, and Silver Star. A "slick chest" at war's end was an embarrassment for many a senior flying officer.

Although Watson served his country well at the Wright Aircraft Engine Factory and in the laboratories at Wright Field, at the bar of an officers' club, where rank carried little weight, lieutenants and captains with bemedaled chests that revealed their wartime exploits were apt to make unkind remarks to senior pilots with no more than a row of service ribbons on their tunics. The award of the DFC made Watson "one of them." It was the twelfth award of the Air Medal for Dahlstrom, the fifteenth for Hillis, the seventh for Brown, the sixth for Anspach and Holt, and the fifth for Strobell. All of them had also earned one or more awards of the Distinguished Flying Cross while participating in combat operations. Haynes joined the group too late to be considered for an award. McIntosh was "only" flying piston-driven aircraft, so he wasn't considered for an award, although he too earned the DFC and a number of Air Medals while flying the P-47 Thunderbolt as a member of the Wolf Pack. As for the Germans who flew the Me-262s alongside their American captors and, most recently, their employers—they were happy to have enough to eat and a little food left over at the end of the day to take home to their families.

After the DFC presentation, Watson gave a dinner party in Paris. Fred McIntosh was invited as one of many guests, French and American, and recalled that "an attractive and obviously affluent French lady, a friend of Watson's, acted as his hostess. It was a going-away and thank-you dinner wrapped all in one. I remember Watson saying to me, 'Shave and be on your best goddamn behavior, Mac,' meaning, don't get drunk. We all had a good time that evening." On July 14 General Eisenhower announced the closing of his headquarters at Versailles— SHAEF. Things were changing rapidly now that the war in Europe was over. New priorities appeared, and the drawdown of American military personnel began in earnest. The days for Headquarters USSTAF at St.-Germain were also numbered. For Watson and "his boys," change was in the cards. On July 20, three days after the medal ceremony at St.-Germain, HMS *Reaper* lifted anchor and set sail for

Newark, New Jersey, accompanied by Watson's Whizzers, sans Strobell. The day before, on July 19, McIntosh and Braun had flown the Ju 290 from a repair depot at Le Culot to Paris-Orly. At Le Culot they had installed American radios and a navigation compass and added survival kits for a crew of ten. "Maxfield checked the engine screens after we landed," Fred McIntosh recalled, "and found metal shavings in the one engine we didn't change in Nürnberg-Roth. Maxfield grabbed a truck and Braun's three mechanics and drove from Paris to the Bayrische Motorenwerke in Munich to find another engine. We tried a C-47 first, but the engine and its dolly wouldn't fit on the aircraft. So, truck it was. I had to give the Germans credit for being practical. They built up their engines on roll-arounds, so they were easy to move. Maxfield and his three helpers rolled the engine on the six-by-six and drove all the way back to Paris. After the engine change I took her up with Heinz Braun. It was the twenty-sixth of July and high time for us to get out of there if we wanted to arrive in the ZI before HMS *Reaper* got there. The airplane tested fine, its engines ran smoothly. I also swung the newly installed navigation compass. A rail line ran from Paris straight south for a stretch. I used that railroad track to verify the accuracy of our compass. Once I had done that, I felt we were ready to go. After we landed, Maxfield checked the engines again for metal shavings and found none. When I told Watson that we were finally ready to leave, he replied, 'Let's get this show on the road and get my ass back to New York.' "

Of course, that airplane had to have a name just as the German jets did. Watson asked McIntosh what he thought they should call it. "*Alles Kaputt*," said Mac, which means "everything is broken"—a truism for Germans and Germany alike, a phrase uttered by nearly every German man, woman, and child at the time to describe their situation. When *Alles Kaputt* was painted on the nose of the Ju 290A by Watson's crew chief, he did it with a flourish, in large flowing letters. Victory was sweet. They had won the war; they were going home; they were entitled to a little levity.

Side view of Watson's Ju 290, A3+HB, at Orly, France, revealing its heavy defensive armament. A B-26 Marauder is kicking up dust in the background. (RB)

Watson personally put together the crew to fly his airplane back to the United States. He would pilot the aircraft; there was never a question about that. After all it was he who had accepted its surrender at Munich-Riem from Hauptmann Heinz Braun. Even with the stars and bars replacing the Nazi swastika on its tail and the *Balkenkreuz* on the fuselage, the Ju 290 still looked fiercely sinister and every bit the war prize it was. In addition to *Alles Kaputt* on the left side of the nose, the aircraft had an FE number painted on its two vertical stabilizers and rudders; FE 3400 was just another among many names and numbers assigned to captured aircraft by various organizations and individuals. The Me-262s carried the name first given them by Sergeant Freiburger and later changed by their American pilots at Melun. Again at Melun these same airplanes were assigned numbers for the Spaatz review, and subsequently received FE numbers assigned to foreign equipment by the Wright Field Foreign Equipment Laboratory. If the aircraft came from a British-controlled airbase, it would carry a USA number as well. So there was no lack of numbering, tracking, and subsequent confusion. Since neither the British nor anyone else had a chance to play around with Watson's Ju 290, it was simply *Alles Kaputt* and FE 3400.

Flying the Ju 290 to the United States was to Watson more than just a matter of exhibiting his aviator skills and technical competence. Above all it reflected the man—his own sense of bravado, which pervaded his entire life, from the women he attracted and chose, to the college he attended, to the aircraft company he went to work for, to the manner in which he chose to serve his country. Returning to the United States as a conquering hero wasn't all bad; what better way was there to arrive than in one of the enemy's war planes, and a very unusual one at that? He didn't mind the publicity that was sure to follow. Watson was not shy in that respect and appreciated its potential value to him as well as to the Army Air Forces at large. As for the rest of the crew, Watson wrote, "I had with me my two unruly eager beavers, Captain McIntosh, who was copilot, Captain Maxfield, who was engineering officer on many of the airplanes for Project Lusty . . . and Captain Maxfield's assistant—a liberated Dachshund known as Schnapps." It wasn't very difficult for Watson to find a competent navigator with an excellent record, First Lieutenant George A. Brock. In the post-VE Day world, aircrew were in abundance and readily volunteered for a quick ride home. Maxfield's backup, also named Brock, was a technical sergeant who flew on the crew as a second flight engineer. (The two Brocks were not related.) The rest of the crew were sergeants, including a radio operator, a crew chief, a mechanic, an instrument technician, and an electrician, for a total of ten, the same number as the German crew that once flew this plane into Munich-Riem airport. This time there were no gunners on board.[4]

Watson released Heinz Braun and his three mechanics, Oberfeldwebel Burow and Unteroffiziere Mosblech and Titschkus. The job was done. He no longer had a need for them; Heinz Braun had served Watson well, more so than any other German pilot. Watson had promised to take Braun and his mechanics to the United States, and he recalled that Braun "was somewhat put out when we left without him." It appeared that Watson's promise was a ploy to buy Braun's loyalty, or at least Watson thought he had to use such subterfuge. As long as they thought they were going to be flying on this aircraft to the United States, Watson felt, Braun and his men wouldn't try anything to sabotage the plane—not that there was ever an indication that they would do that. Yet, interestingly, when the Ju 290 was finally scrapped at Wright Field in December 1946, after many test and public relations flights, "a booby trap hidden in the right wing" was found. "Fortunately, it turned out that there was a defective activating pin."[5] McIntosh remembered Watson calling him, "one cold December day, we were both at Wright Field and I was working for him again. 'I got some wonderful news for you,' Watson said to me over the phone. Then he told me about the booby trap on the 290. Somebody put a packet of plastic explosives in a wing next to a fuel cell and a rib. The ignitor was set to go off on takeoff. The explosive wasn't discovered until the engineers chopped up the airplane wanting to learn how the Germans engineered that big wing. When they peeled back the skin of the right wing they discovered the plastic explosive. When we learned of this, Watson and I initially thought it had to be Heinz Braun and his people. But after the engineers examined the explosive charge and its activating mechanism they determined that the device was set by someone before Braun surrendered the airplane to Watson. The Germans used foreign labor extensively, including for aircraft maintenance, and possibly during its last overhaul someone implanted the explosive in the wing. We both were glad that it didn't turn out to be Heinz Braun, and of course everyone who flew on that airplane was very lucky."[6]

Once Watson released Braun, he and his mechanics were picked up at Orly by American military police and escorted to St.-Germain les Loges and put up in the École d'Éducation de la Légion d'Honneur.

Karl Baur noted in his *Tagebuch* that it was "a fancy sounding name! Only it turned out to be an MP station and jail for GIs! We joined a number of German scientists who had been here already a couple of days. Above our quarters were the jailed GIs who had committed all sorts of crimes." Baur was there with other German scientists and test pilots waiting to go to the United States under the auspices of Project Overcast. "Captain Braun," Baur wrote, "stayed here with his mechanics for one night. They had repaired a Ju 290 for Colonel Watson in Orly and were released now." It must have been especially grating for Heinz Braun to hear from Baur that he was on his way to the United States to assist Colonel Watson.[7]

"The day before we took off," Watson wrote, "Colonel Goddard, a friend of mine for many years, approached me with a box under his arm and asked if I would mind taking a doll back to the States for his daughter. Of course I was happy to do so. Then George took a tour through the airplane and left for Paris with the box still under his arm. Need I say more about George Goddard's appraisal of our chances of getting back to the States safely?" But Watson was not intimidated by his friend's negative assessment of his chances of making it across the Atlantic. On Saturday morning, July 28, Watson's Ju 290 roared down the runway at Paris-Orly and headed for the Azores, their first planned stop on the way to Wright Field. After nearly nine hours' flying time, Watson and McIntosh discerned the cloud-shrouded outline of eight-thousand-foot Pico Alto sticking through the undercast, the only still-active volcano on the Azores island group. They headed for Santa Maria, southeast of Pico Alto. Watson made a standard instrument approach through the cloud layers, guided by his navigator, Brock, and when their wheels touched the runway, Lieutenant Brock entered nine hours and ten minutes' flying time in his log for the first leg of their Atlantic crossing.[8]

That same July afternoon one of three C-54 transports assigned to support the presidential party at the Potsdam conference also landed

Watson and his crew posing before the Junkers 290 Alles Kaputt just prior to their departure from Paris-Orly airfield on July 28, 1945. Watson is third from left, standing. (RW)

at Santa Maria. The ongoing conference was attended by Stalin, Truman, and Churchill. President Truman arrived at Antwerp on July 12 on the cruiser *Augusta*, which was escorted by the *Philadelphia*, another cruiser, forming Task Force 68. The *Sacred Cow*, the president's personal C-54 aircraft, then flew him and his entourage from Antwerp to Gatow airfield, near Babelsberg, the one-time German movie capital. The British had an election on July 5, the results of which were not announced until July 26, and the voters threw the incumbent rascals out and installed Clement Attlee as their new prime minister. Effective the twenty-seventh of July, Clement Attlee was in, and Winston Churchill was out. General Arnold, who also attended the conference, had been released by President Truman and arrived in his C-54 at Santa Maria soon after Watson landed in his captured German behemoth.[9]

That night the Santa Maria airbase commander hosted a dinner for General Arnold. "A hell of a big party," McIntosh recalled. "I don't know if Watson was invited or not, but the party didn't break up until the early morning hours. That day 'Hap' Arnold and a bunch of hangers-on toured our aircraft. Watson personally escorted General Arnold through the Junkers 290. It was quite obvious that Arnold knew Hal Watson, because throughout the tour of the German aircraft it was Hal this, and Hal that. That was the time when they were having tire problems on the C-54s, and on the ramps wherever they could park them there sat grounded C-54s because they couldn't get tires for them. Those are the things you remember. The other thing I remember was that we were traveling presumably on a secret clearance. And the next morning on the bulletin board in base operations there was an item from the *New York Times* that told about our trip, the airplane and the crew."

What McIntosh didn't know, and Watson may have, was that the Associated Press had released a story on their upcoming flight datelined Paris, July 22, six days prior to their departure from Paris-Orly. Quoting the Associated Press, the *Hartford Courant* reported, "Germany's largest land plane, a four-engine Junkers transport, which Yank aviators have flown with 98 passengers and 11 crewmen aboard, soon may be seen in America. Army men believe that only two such planes are flying, the British having the other one. The ship in possession of the U.S. Army was captured 20 miles south of Nüremberg. Officials are considering an attempt to fly the plane non-stop from the Azores to Dayton, O. It has a wing span of 138 feet." The news release was less than accurate. Several Ju 290s other than Watson's survived the war. The reference to the ninety-eight passengers and eleven crew flown on the Ju 290 was something that Heinz Braun, its one-time German pilot, had written about in a statement he gave to the Exploitation Division about the aircraft's operation while in Luftwaffe service. It was late in 1944 when Heinz Braun flew ninety-eight sick and starving German soldiers from the isolated Greek island of Rhodes, off the Turkish coast, to Wiener Neustadt in Austria. But the reference to eleven Yanks flying ninety-eight passengers would be a recurring theme in numerous American newspaper articles following Watson's flight to the United States.[10]

The day of Watson's actual departure from Paris, July 28, the *Hartford Courant* reported in its July 29 edition:

Farmington Pilot Flying German Plane to America

Colonel H. E. Watson of Farmington, Conn., an Army test pilot, took off today in a Junkers-290, Germany's largest land plane, from Orly airfield outside Paris on an attempted one-stop flight to Wright Field, Ohio. The German plane, comparable in size to the B-29 Super-Fortresses, was scheduled to stop only briefly at the Azores for refueling. The Army made no estimate on how long the flight to Wright Field would take. This type of German plane has flown with as many as 98 men and a crew of 11 aboard and has a range of 3200 miles. Its cruising speed is only 175 miles an hour, considerably slower than the B-29. Watson took a crew of nine with him. A test pilot for five years at Wright Field before coming overseas, Watson has been testing German aircraft for the last four months. The Junkers was captured intact near Munich three days before E-Day. It will be tested for features which might prove valuable to the Army Air Force.[11]

Fred McIntosh may have thought there was some secrecy about their flight, but obviously the publicity mill at Headquarters USSTAF saw things differently, and the flight was public knowledge by the time they touched down in the Azores.

On Monday, July 30, both General Arnold's C-54 and Watson's Ju 290 departed Santa Maria. General Arnold's aircraft headed for Bermuda, Watson for Wright Field. The weather in the Azores was clear, and the forecast called for no unusual weather en route. Watson's plan to fly directly to Wright Field was stretching even the limits of the Ju 290 with its extra fuel supply, as the prevailing winds in the northern latitudes generally blew west to east and did not favor Watson's plan of establishing speed or distance records. Soon after takeoff Watson encountered radio problems which convinced him to head to Kindley Field, the American airfield on Bermuda. Although Watson departed the Azores after General Arnold's C-54, he arrived in Bermuda an hour before him.

"Flying with Watson was a delight," McIntosh recalled fondly. "We sat side by side, he on the left, me on the right in the copilot's position. We had a 'Tokyo tank' in back with enough fuel to make it to the ZI. Maxfield was flying the engineer's position between and behind us, monitoring engine instruments on takeoff and in flight and controlling the flaps. When we started down the runway I controlled the power. Watson had the wheel in both hands steering and flying the aircraft after liftoff. I could either do the gear on Watson's order or I could tell Maxfield to raise the gear. We had to hand-fly it all the way because somebody stole the autopilot control back in Paris."

Twelve hours later, Watson and his tired crew landed in Bermuda. After a meal and a brief rest they took off again, heading for Patterson Field, just down the road from Wright Field. That was to be their shortest leg and only lasted six hours and thirty minutes. "We intended to remain in Bermuda overnight," said McIntosh, "but our quarters were near the maintenance area and the constant engine noise kept all of us from going to sleep. So we decided to take off early and get it over with. We landed at Patterson Field on July 31, the day I learned that three days earlier two lieutenant colonels had flown a B-25 bomber into the Empire State Building. We went through customs at Patterson Field, our port of entry, and on the following day, August 1, we flew her to Freeman Field in Indiana, our final destination. That last flight was only a short ninety-minute hop."

The Air Technical Service Command, commanded by Major General Hugh Knerr, headquartered at Wright Field, controlled the Wright Field laboratories and foreign exploitation activities of T-2,

Technical Intelligence. ATSC acquired Freeman Field, a former flying training base, near Seymour, Indiana, on June 15, 1945. The commander of Freeman Field was tasked to "receive, identify, preserve, assemble, restore for engineering evaluation, display, and store for scientific use, such foreign aircraft, engines, and related equipment as may be allocated by higher authority; and to receive, restore, and preserve for museum purposes selected and important models of aircraft and related aeronautical equipment used by the AAF and foreign air forces." The Commanding General of Technical Intelligence was Colonel Donald L. Putt, who was waiting to put on his first star, and was tasked by ATSC to exercise "Policy direction and staff surveillance over the activities of Freeman Field dealing with foreign aeronautical equipment for technical intelligence evaluation."[12] Colonel Putt in effect owned Freeman Field and had full authority over everything that went on there. Watson's Ju 290 was parked at Freeman Field, and nearly all of the aircraft which arrived on HMS *Reaper* would end up there. Wright Field just didn't have the space.

Watson's trip across the Atlantic in the giant German Junkers aircraft generated a flurry of press reports. "Col. H. E. Watson Makes Paris-Dayton Two-Stop Flight In German Plane," one headline read. Another article with a Wright Field, Ohio, dateline proclaimed, "German Plane Flown to ATSC For Evaluation." The *New London Evening Day* proudly announced, "Pilot of German Plane Is Son Of Local Woman." Its article read, "Col. H. E. Watson, pilot of the captured German Junkers plane . . . is the son of Mrs. Louise Watson of Ridgewood Park, Waterford. . . . He has come here often to visit his mother and has many friends in this vicinity." They arrived home to much fanfare and jubilation.

On October 16, 1945, Colonel Harold E. Watson was awarded the Air Medal for flying the Junkers 290 across the Atlantic from France to the United States. "For meritorious achievement in aerial flight while serving as a Pilot of a Ju 290 aircraft in a difficult Trans-Atlantic

With its Nazi insignia reapplied, Watson's Ju 290 was a frequent performer at air shows at Freeman Field and Wright Field. (RW)

flight," read General Order 136, issued by Headquarters, United States Air Forces in Europe, the former USSTAF. "The superb flying ability and keen judgement exhibited by Colonel Watson on this occasion are in keeping with the finest traditions of the Army Air Forces. By Command of Lieutenant General Cannon."[13] That was Hal Watson's first and only Air Medal, awarded on the personal initiative of General Cannon, USAFE's commanding general. Now Watson had one of each—a Distinguished Flying Cross and an Air Medal—and was no longer a slick-chested senior officer. On August 7, 1945, Headquarters, United States Air Forces Europe, USAFE, the former USSTAF, assumed command over all U.S. air forces in Europe and North Africa. General Arnold's vision was implemented and USSTAF was no more. By September 27 the headquarters staff completed its transfer from St.-Germain to the picturesque spa town of Wiesbaden, Germany, on the banks of the Rhine River.

Watson didn't beat HMS *Reaper* home to the United States after all. The aircraft carrier docked in New York harbor on July 31, across from Newark airfield in New Jersey. The *Reaper*'s American contingent of officers and enlisted men was just as happy to be back in the United

States as the Ju 290s crew—some of them maybe even more so. The pastime activities of the men crossing the Atlantic on the *Reaper* had been quite different from those of the men who flew across the Atlantic. On the *Reaper*, American airmen and British sailors quickly became friends over many a shared bottle of beer, and it was said that some of the American sergeants had been especially adept in relieving British sailors of their money in long-lasting poker games.

24

THE FOCKE-WULF 190 TRAGEDY

Wright Field had been testing captured German fighters and bombers since 1943 to determine their strengths and weaknesses. Whatever the Wright Field test pilots learned about those aircraft was passed on to the men fighting the Luftwaffe. One of many test pilots at Wright Field was Kenneth O. Chilstrom. Ken was assigned to the Fighter Section of the Flight Test Division of the Army Air Forces Technical Service Command. His assignment was a fighter pilot's dream. Flight test was what every hotshot pilot aspired to, and Ken thought of himself as a hotshot pilot. Dick Johnson, a Wright Field test pilot, described this feeling of being the best of the best, of having arrived in fighter pilot heaven: "We all knew that, for an aviator, Wright Field was the greatest place on earth.... At Wright Field, one was privileged to fly seven days a week.... Aviator Heaven? It was indeed!"[1]

For young Chilstrom, flying was a dream that came true with the advent of World War II. Born in 1921 in Zumbrota, Minnesota, Ken started building model airplanes soon after entering grade school. One week out of high school, Ken and two friends went to the Army Air Corps recruiting office and enlisted. They wanted to become pilots, but they didn't have the two years of college required to enter the aviation cadet program. So he and his friends enlisted and were sent to Chanute Field, Illinois, where they became aircraft mechanics. Ken attended night school to gain the needed college credits for pilot training. By 1941 the world situation had changed dramatically, and he was allowed to enter the aviation cadet program without the previously required two years of college. He graduated in Class 42I at Lake Charles, Louisiana, and as a freshly minted second lieutenant pilot was assigned to the 58th Fighter Group at Bolling Field, Washington, D.C., on the banks of the Potomac River. The mission of the 58th was to guard the nation's capital. In February 1943, Ken and his fellow 58th Group pilots took a train up to the Curtiss Airplane Factory in Buffalo, New York, and picked up brand-new P-40 Warhawks and flew them to Norfolk, Virginia, where they then embarked on the aircraft carrier USS *Ranger*.

About one hundred nautical miles off the North African coast, the 58th pilots were told to strap on their P-40s and get ready to launch for an airfield near Casablanca. "I was number thirty-five when we launched off the USS *Ranger*," Ken recalled, "somewhere in the middle. They had turned the carrier into the wind and got her up to maximum speed to get as much wind across the deck as they possibly could. As I sat there with the prop turning I never saw anyone else fly off. Everyone went off to the left of the carrier and disappeared. I didn't know if they made it or not. We didn't lose anyone, I later learned, but I didn't know that as I sat there sweating in my P-40 cockpit wondering what awaited me. After I launched and dropped off the side of the carrier, I quickly discovered that as I got near the water I picked up additional lift from the ground effect and I flew on just above the wave tops.

"Something had happened to our airplanes at Norfolk which we pilots were not aware of until we launched off the *Ranger* toward Casablanca. When we landed in Norfolk, coming from the Curtiss factory in Buffalo, we had to taxi our new planes a couple of miles to get alongside the *Ranger* to be loaded. In the process we wore out our brakes. None of us realized that until we sat on the deck of the *Ranger* getting ready to launch. The deck controller would give the wind-up signal with his hands. The pilot whose turn it was then applied power, the brakes wouldn't hold and the plane began to eke forward. As soon as the controller saw him moving forward he gave the signal to launch. Like all the others before me, when my turn came, all I could do when my P-40 began to slide forward because of the bad brakes was to move the throttle to full power and pray. The whole thing was a little disconcerting, but all of us survived. Subsequent air groups launched in this manner off a carrier lost some planes and the practice was discontinued.

"We got to North Africa soon after the disaster at Kasserine Pass. The 33rd Fighter Group, which had preceded us, lost most of its airplanes when Rommel's troops overran their airfield. Because their pilots had some combat experience and we had none, they took our planes. We sat around for a while until a batch of A-36 attack aircraft was delivered. It was the earliest version of the P-51 fighter. It was a better airplane than the P-40, at least I thought so. The A-36 carried two five-hundred-pound bombs and six .50 caliber machine guns. I dive-bombed and strafed myself through the North African campaign, into Sicily and up the boot of Italy as far as Naples. I was sent home in November 1943 with eighty combat missions to my credit, a Distinguished Flying Cross and eight Air Medals. I was the first of my group to come home.

"In the aircrew redistribution center near Miami they tried to send me to a P-40 RTU, a replacement training unit. That was the last thing I wanted to do. I went to see my commanding officer, a major, and told him that I wanted to go to Wright Field and be a test pilot. I didn't know anything about being a test pilot and what it involved, but that's what I wanted to be. My CO ordered his adjutant to check with personnel if there were any openings in Flight Test at Wright Field. A couple of days later the answer came back—no. I said to the major, You let me go to Wright Field and I'll get a job. To my great surprise he issued the orders sending me to Wright Field. I took the train to Dayton, Ohio, and walked into the Flight Test section. Major Chris Petrie, the chief of Fighter Test [he was killed in an aircraft accident only a few months later on May 7, 1944], told me that he didn't have a job for me in Flight Test. But, he added, 'I need a maintenance officer. Can you do that?' I lied, 'I'm a good maintenance officer, sir.' That's how I got my foot in the door. Flight Test was just in the process of expanding. A good time to be there. Industry was producing numerous prototypes, some good, some bad, all had to be tested at Wright Field. A lot of airplanes were built, one or two of a kind, and eventually I got to fly them all. Most never got into production. I wore a flight suit all day long going from one airplane to another. Out at Vandalia, now the Dayton airport, we opened a test pilot school and I went through the second class with Glenn Edwards. Glenn and I were roommates. Glenn crashed on June 5, 1948, testing the YB-49 flying wing, and perished along with four others from the Bomber Test section—Dan Forbes, Chuck LaFontaine, Claire Lesser, and Ed Swindell. Muroc Field in California was later renamed Edwards Air Force Base, and the one-time bomber and reconnaissance base near Topeka, Kansas, was named after Major Daniel Forbes.

"Being a test pilot in those heady days of aviation exacted a heavy price at times. I lost many friends," Ken added, sadness coloring his voice. "But for a guy who wanted to fly everything with wings on it, Wright Field was beyond belief. The ramp was always filled to near overflowing with airplanes. I got to fly everything. And there was great camaraderie among all of us test pilots, regardless of what we were flying, and we shared each other's thrills." In 1943, as a result of the North African campaign and the Allies' advance into Italy, several captured German aircraft showed up at Wright Field. "Two Me-109Gs, two FW 190s, and a Ju 88 twin-engine bomber were the first to arrive. The first two Me-262 jet fighters arrived in the spring of 1945, and by the time Watson brought his German airplanes back to the

Captain Ken Chilstrom, after surviving eighty combat missions over North Africa and Italy, has just gotten word that he is going home. November 1943. (KC)

United States we already had twenty-four German and Japanese aircraft sitting on our ramp. I got to fly all of them," said Chilstrom. "The fact that I got to know and fly many different types of airplanes forced me to keep the basics in mind. As a test pilot you quickly get familiar with what is critical on an airplane—the fuel system. You have to keep that engine running to have a long and happy life, and to keep it running you have to understand the fuel system of whatever airplane you were flying. Then you can learn about a plane's handling characteristics, and fly it conservatively in the beginning, until you become familiar enough to push the envelope.

"Another important thing to a test pilot's survival is to know an airplane's center of gravity. Watson brought in a couple examples of

One of two Dornier 335s being hoisted onto the deck of HMS Reaper *in Cherbourg harbor. (RB)*

a new and unusual German aircraft, the Dornier 335, with a push-pull engine arrangement. It was in the fall of 1946 when the plane was supposedly ready for flight test over at Freeman Field. Chuck Yeager was in my Fighter Test section then, and when I learned that the 335 was finally ready, I said to Yeager, Why don't you and I go and fly that airplane? We took a B-25 and flew over to Freeman Field. The German airplane was absolutely huge for a fighter. I talked at length with the mechanics and engineers and they couldn't convince me that they knew where its center of gravity was. Well, the center of gravity is one of the key elements as far as control of an airplane is concerned, and in this particular airplane knowing the CG appeared to me to be especially critical. Yeager and I never did fly the Dornier 335. I don't believe anybody flew that airplane after Watson brought it over, except for Jack Woolam's brief and nearly catastrophic flight at Newark.

"We damn near lost Russ Schleeh due to a CG problem on the first Me-262 we got. Russ was a pilot in Bomber Test, one of the few bomber pilots I ever knew who loved to fly fighters. Schleeh took a year off to fly with us in Fighter Test, and while he was in the fighter section with me, we put together that first Me-262 over at Vandalia. I watched Russ make his first takeoff. He used the whole length of the runway because he didn't have enough elevator power to overcome a CG problem he encountered on takeoff. We hadn't installed the guns in its nose, and taking guns out of an airplane that is designed to have guns installed changes its CG aft, and its handling characteristics become very different. We hadn't given that fact sufficient consideration. I remember standing there watching his takeoff roll and wondering, Boy, is he going to make it? He finally got it off the ground and immediately headed for Wright Field and landed. He said to me when I got back to Wright Field, 'Ken, you can have this project.' That was the last time Schleeh flew the 262. I then gave the project to Walt McAuley. You are willing to take a certain amount of risk in the flight test business, but you want to do it with understanding and for a good reason.[2]

"One characteristic common to all German airplanes was poor brakes. On a jet-powered aircraft the RPM, exhaust gas temperature (EGT), and fuel flow were the three most important things. If all of those were in the proper ranges then you knew you were getting sufficient thrust. [German test pilots like Hoffmann and Baur simply used the *Zwiebel*, the position of the exhaust cone, as their thrust indicator because of recurring instrument failures.] We had problems with the 262's instrumentation, reflecting the proper tailpipe temperature, for instance. Often they had to tow me back when the EGT gauge failed and I had only two indicators for thrust—fuel flow and RPM. When I was ready for takeoff I ran up the engines and gave the sign to pull the chocks. I'd start out slow. Typically the aircraft would start drifting left or right, and to keep it centered on the runway I had to change the thrust on one of the engines, because the brakes usually were ineffective. As a steering mechanism the rudder didn't become effective until I got up to fifty or sixty miles per hour. So we always had to work around the bad brake situation on all of our German airplanes.

"I spent much more time testing the Focke-Wulf 190 fighter than any other. For one thing, it became available to us fairly early." Ken Chilstrom's Form 5, an airman's official flying record, revealed that the first time Ken strapped on a Focke-Wulf 190 was on July 26, 1944. That day he flew the FW 190 twice. Between then and February 26, 1945, Ken flew the 190 for a total of fourteen hours on eighteen separate occasions to determine the airplane's handling characteristics. Another pilot who spent a considerable amount of time testing the FW 190 was Gus Lundquist. Lundquist wrote, "Although not quite in the class with our P-51, I found the FW 190G, nevertheless, to be a first class fighter plane. Like the P-51, it was a 'pilot's airplane' with an excellent cockpit layout, good visibility, excellent control response and maneuverability."[3] Yet the FW 190 had a couple of potentially lethal flaws which were not corrected until the TA 152H came along late in the war. If the pilot didn't take them into account when engaged in air-to-air combat, the results were invariably catastrophic. Ken Chilstrom became very proficient with the airplane, yet it was one of those systemic flaws which nearly killed him.

"It was my tenth flight in the FW 190 on February 24, 1945, that came close to being a disaster. I was performing a functional check flight after some adjustments had been made to the engine controls. That day I had been up to twenty thousand feet and was satisfied with the engine's operation, so I returned for a landing at Wright Field. It was the custom for all fighters in those days to come down low, approximately fifty to a hundred feet over the end of the runway, and peel up in a tight, left-hand, 360-degree turn without any power. It was the mark of a good fighter pilot that once the peel up started you would not use engine power before touchdown. This required skill in gauging distance, trading off speed by sideslipping, and the use of flaps while aiming for the end of the runway. I was comfortable in my approach to the runway and was heading north and parallel to the flight line. I had a good tight pattern and was down to maybe two hundred feet in a turn with the power off. When I adjusted the tail plane trim switch to relieve some of the forward stick pressure, the stick came back and the airplane pitched nose up. This is a bad situation to be in close to the ground, and I immediately tried to get the nose down and added power for a climbing recovery. My unusual maneuver was seen by my boss, Colonel Albert Boyd. After regaining control I went up to several thousand feet to experiment with the trim switch. Then I discovered that it was a runaway switch which went to either nose full up or full down. I chose the nose-down position, which I could manhandle for a landing. I made a straight and level approach with great caution and landed without incident. After taxiing in and shutting down the engine, the first person to meet me at the airplane was Colonel Boyd. Wearing his usual sober expression he said, 'Ken, I saw that first approach you made and don't understand what you were doing up there. What's the problem?' After I told him about the runaway trim switch he understood my situation and said that he was glad to see me down safe. This experience didn't change my mind about the FW 190 as one of the best fighters of World War II. But this particular airplane had an electrical problem in its trim switch and it had nearly killed me."[4]

Many such problems were encountered in flight testing and a test pilot was expected to be able to deal with them. Some occurrences, such as the runaway trim switch on the FW 190, were not necessarily recorded and passed on. It was, after all, only a malfunctioning switch. The problem with that kind of rationale was that it was a systemic problem in the switch design, and Ken's experience wouldn't be the last time an American pilot would have to deal with such a situation. Ken couldn't have known he had experienced and survived one of the Focke-Wulf 190's fatal flaws.

August 1945 was a busy month for Watson and his men, a group significantly reduced in number with the loss of its German contingent.

They were busy unloading the *Reaper* under the supervision of Lieutenant Colonel Seashore, and degunking the airplanes as they were delivered to Newark Field. Of the original group of nine Whizzers, only three remained. Willie Hoffmann was still in a Paris hospital recovering from his nearly fatal ejection. Karl Baur, accompanied by one of his mechanics, was lost somewhere in a bureaucratic maze on his way to the United States. Bob Strobell still lay in an Army hospital in Mannheim. Roy Brown, Ken Dahlstrom, and Fred Hillis had decided to take advantage of their high point count and got out of the Army Air Corps soon after arrival in New York. That left Watson with only four jet-qualified pilots, not counting himself—Bob Anspach, Jim Haynes, Jim Holt, and Jack Woolams, the Bell Company test pilot. To ferry the propeller aircraft from Newark to Freeman Field, Watson also had Fred McIntosh.

Other world shaping-events soon overshadowed the arrival of the Junkers 290 and HMS *Reaper*. On August 6 the first atomic bomb was dropped on Hiroshima, followed by a second bomb on Nagasaki three days later. Six days later Emperor Hirohito announced to his people in a brief radio address Japan's unconditional surrender. August 15 became Victory in Japan Day, VJ Day, and World War II was finally over, at least as far as the fighting was concerned. On September 2, the Japanese delegation signed surrender documents on the deck of the battleship USS *Missouri* anchored in Tokyo Bay. While these momentous events ran their course half a world away, Watson began to move his aircraft from Newark to Freeman Field in Indiana. Watson again laid out a route, as he had done for the Me-262 flights from Lechfeld to Melun, this time funneling all of his aircraft through Pittsburgh, where they were to refuel before proceeding on to Freeman Field.

Two of the Arado 234s, *Jane I* and *Snafu I*, one Dornier 335, and five of the Me-262 jets—*What Was It?*, *Lady Jess IV*, *Screamin' Meemie*, *Willie*, and *Delovely*—were picked up by U.S. Navy pilots and flown or trucked to Patuxent Naval Air Station in Maryland, leaving Watson with five Me-262s and two Arado 234 jets to fly out of Newark. On Sunday,

August 19, he was ready. He decided to pilot *Pick II*, Roy Brown's former aircraft, while Jim Holt was to fly *Cookie VII*. They took off from Newark at midafternoon and arrived at Pittsburgh airport around four o'clock. They still didn't have working radios and relied on the airfield control tower operator to use standard light signals or flares in an emergency. Watson made a shallow approach to the field, landed, and promptly experienced problems with his brakes. He managed to control the aircraft and bring it to a safe stop. Holt was on final approach coming in hot; catching some air under the wings, he floated for about five hundred feet above the runway before finally getting the bird to touch down. When he applied his brakes, "There were none." At the end of the runway was a steep drop-off, something Holt was not aware of. His aircraft sped off the runway, continued on the over-run, and hurtled across the ditch. When he hit the opposite slope, the landing gear and the engines tore off the hapless Me-262 and the fuse-lage broke in half. The aircraft was a total loss. Holt was unharmed.[5] While Holt's inexperience flying jets was a factor in the accident, the failing brakes did the rest. Watson continued on alone to Freeman Field in *Pick II*.

The remaining three Me-262s at Newark were undergoing degunking and a thorough going over. They would not be flown out for several more weeks. In the interim all available pilots, including Watson, ferried the "fan jobs" to Freeman Field. "There was an FW 190 that was ready to be moved, so I offered to fly it, inasmuch as there was no one else available at the time. So on September 12, off I went heading for Pittsburgh where I intended to refuel. It was a really good flying air-craft," Bob Anspach remarked. He never quite forgot his two previous incidents flying German aircraft, and he was expecting number three to come along every time he made a takeoff. Bob was making a gradual descent over Pennsylvania heading for the greater Pittsburgh area, when he reached over to make a slight trim adjustment. His world suddenly turned upside down. When he touched the electrically operated

Roy and Fran Brown and Ginny and Ken Holt at the Café Zanzibar in New York City, August 1945. (RB)

horizontal trim control, it cycled to a full-up position and the Focke-Wulf fighter responded by pitching violently nose up and over. Bob had never heard that the Focke-Wulf 190 had a problem with its trim actuator, and he wasn't a test pilot like Ken Chilstrom. He soon discovered just as Chilstrom had that the trim could not be manually overridden. He pulled the power back and struggled to find a power setting allowing him to make forward progress and still fly straight and level. Once Bob felt he had control of the aircraft he tried once more to adjust the trim, but it was frozen in the full nose up position. He looked around for a place to land. He saw a small dirt strip and headed for it. It was Hollidaysburg airport, just south of Altoona. Bob's approach was rough, nose high, dragging his tail. It was a very short strip and he was coming in with a lot of forward momentum. He touched down and applied the brakes; the right brake failed immediately, pivoting the aircraft to the left, and with that movement the Focke-Wulf's landing gear collapsed. Next the propellers dug into the soft ground, and then the

Bob Anspach's hapless FW 190 in a Pennsylvania cow pasture. The propeller assembly spun off on contact with the ground and ended up hanging on the wall of a local flying club. (RA)

entire propeller assembly spun off and away as the aircraft slid to a stop on its belly. Bob slid back the canopy as the aircraft was still moving and scampered out of the cockpit the instant it came to rest on the grassy surface. There was no fire, every airman's greatest fear, and he discovered that he was not injured.[6] Upon hearing of Anspach's debacle Watson sent an aircraft to Hollidaysburg to fetch him back to Newark. The Focke-Wulf was hauled away for scrap. Neither of the two aircraft accidents were picked up by the press. It was just as well; it wasn't the kind of publicity the Air Corps needed at the time.

Lieutenant William Haynes flew one more FW 190D from Newark to Freeman Field on September 13, also stopping in Pittsburgh for refueling before proceeding to Indiana. Haynes was going to fly this same aircraft on Saturday, September 22, for a German aircraft exhibition and air show sponsored by the Air Technical Service Command. Watson, with the help of the public relations office at Wright Field, had extended an open invitation to members of the Institute of Aeronautical Science, the United States Congress, the press, and local officials.

Many aces also attended—Gabreski, Schilling, Gentile—to explain to the press and congressional delegations the role of airpower in defeating Hitler's Wehrmacht. A subtext was to drum up support for the lagging American jet program. Jets were portrayed by some as inefficient, mere toys, and General Arnold, struggling to get the P-80 jet program off its tottering feet, needed to educate the public and gain their support. German jets, American jets—it was all the same. Jets were mysterious and exciting to the public, and few had ever seen one. Merely mentioning a jet at an air show raised the public's interest and drew a crowd. At this time Watson had only one operational Me-262 at Freeman Field, and that aircraft was used strictly as a static display. A flyby of the German jets was planned for a subsequent exhibition scheduled for September 28 and 29. A large aircraft exhibit open to the public was also scheduled at Wright Field for October 13 and 14.

Freeman Field, the Foreign Aircraft Evaluation Center, was a former Flying Training Command airfield which had been declared surplus, and, because of its relative proximity to Wright Field, only an hour's flying time away, it had been taken over by ATSC for the purpose of storing and evaluating foreign aircraft. One of the reporters present for the air show wrote, "This field, in southwestern Indiana, is a 'ghost town' as large as Dayton's Patterson Field. At the height of its service, more than 5,000 cadets were training there to fly twin-engine planes. Now only a few hundred officers and enlisted men operate the field." Some of Freeman Field's hundreds of mostly open-bay barracks were used to house the invited air show visitors, and they were fed in what one press release called "GI chow lines." It didn't appear that anyone minded the Spartan military lifestyle.[7]

On Saturday, September 22, the first day of the two-day air show, the highlight was the flyby and demonstration of German aircraft. Captain McIntosh flew the Ju 388 that he had liberated at Merseburg. The Heinkel 219 and Ju 88 night fighters, as well as a number of other conventionally powered aircraft, were put through their paces to the delight of the audience. Bill Haynes was to put on a demonstration in one of the remaining eight FW 190s. It was the aircraft he had flown from Newark to Freeman Field. He was thoroughly familiar with it, or so he thought. After taking off, Haynes made several high-speed, very low-level passes by the reviewing stand. He was at the end of his flying routine, at about three hundred feet above ground level and preparing for landing, when suddenly, for no apparent reason, his airplane appeared to pitch up and roll over, bellying into the ground nose up. The aircraft was destroyed and young Lieutenant Haynes killed. A hastily convened accident investigation board reviewed the scene of the crash and the wreckage of the aircraft and determined that Lieutenant Haynes had attempted a wingover maneuver to impress the watching spectators. Not having enough altitude to complete the maneuver, he dived his aircraft into the ground. The board's finding was "pilot error." A wingover maneuver occurs when the pilot from level flight pulls the nose of the aircraft up until he is nearly in a vertical position, rolls the aircraft sideways 180 degrees until it is pointing straight down, and levels off after regaining flying speed. The board felt that Haynes was much too low to have attempted such a risky maneuver. The accident board didn't know about the trim switch wiring problem in the Focke-Wulf 190.

Roy Brown, one of Watson's Whizzers who fought the FW 190 on more than one occasion and downed a "long nose" in an engagement near the end of the war, wrote about Lieutenant Haynes's accident.

> Nine of the planes brought to this country were FW 190 propeller-driven fighter planes. This plane was well designed and had a good reputation as a fighter. What turned out to be a particularly acute problem for the 190 was the electrically controlled, horizontal stabilizer trim tab. This trim control allowed the pilot to reduce the force he had to apply to the control stick in order to climb or dive. It was well designed but a serious problem could result from improper wiring. On February 24, 1945, Ken Chilstrom had experienced a failed trim tab situation in an FW 190 he was putting through its

paces, and Bob Anspach had a similar experience on September 12, 1945, while ferrying an aircraft from Newark to Freeman Field. Both survived their experiences. Anspach had sufficient altitude, and Chilstrom, although at low altitude, was an experienced test pilot. Curiously, the only instrument found intact in the wreckage was the horizontal stabilizer trim indicator; its setting was tail-down. It seems very likely that Lieutenant Haynes attempted to adjust the trim control while on the base leg of the landing pattern and the control switch ran away to a full nose-up setting. Before he could react to get the nose down he lost flying speed and stalled. The tail section hit the ground before the forward part of the fuselage. In the accident report the investigating officer stated that Haynes was performing a wingover from an altitude too low for a combat fighter type aircraft. To assume that Haynes was trying a wingover maneuver at a relatively low speed and at low altitude in the traffic pattern is doubtful. He was an experienced P-47 combat pilot, and a good one. To me at least his accident can only be explained by the failure of the horizontal trim control.[8]

AIR SHOWS AND
AIR RACES

In the 1940s airmen died all too frequently exploring the frontiers of flight. There was still much to learn, and the equipment they were flying had a diversity of problems. As for the aircraft Colonel Watson retrieved from Germany, they were beset by their own unique problems, some the result of the early state of technology, such as the turbines powering the Me-262 and the Arado 234, and others due to the lack of natural resources available to the Third Reich. There were the low-quality synthetic tires—the Arado 234s suffered from frequent tire failures and as a result were seldom flown—and the bad brakes, characteristic of all German aircraft, which caused accidents or exacerbated emergency situations, such as the experience Jim Holt had when he attempted to land an Me-262 at Pittsburgh airport and the brakes failed just when he needed them most. Lieutenant Haynes's death in a Focke-Wulf 190 fighter unfortunately was just another tragedy among many. The air shows continued.

The second air show was put on at Freeman Field on September 29 and 30 for writers and photographers of the press, for radio men (as radio announcers were then called), and for the usual bevy of politicians and senior military officers. On display was an array of captured

German aircraft—the Focke-Wulf 190 and Bf 109 conventionally powered fighters, the Heinkel 219 and Ju 88 night fighters, the Me-163B Komet rocket plane, an Me-262 jet fighter (which was always the main attraction at an air show), the Arado 234 reconnaissance bomber, and the Bachem Ba 349 Natter, a liquid-fueled rocket plane with twenty-four air-to-air rockets in its nose. Watson's Ju 290, with its logo, *Alles Kaputt*, prominently painted on the nose, was always included either as a static display or to fly invited guests around the airfield perimeter. The Ju 388 high-altitude reconnaissance aircraft, and others, completed the static display and flybys.

The Me-262s Watson desperately needed for his planned flyby at Freeman Field weren't ready at Newark until Saturday the twenty-ninth—the first day of the show. The weather was lousy. Still, Anspach, Watson, and Woolams flew *Doris/Jabo Bait, Dennis/Ginny H,* and *Ole Fruit Cake,* the Me-262B two-seat night fighter, from Newark to Pittsburgh and then on to Freeman Field. The spectators at Freeman Field watched with awe as the German jets landed, and Watson gave a press conference immediately after their arrival. He had cautioned both Anspach and Woolams to leave the talking to him, which they did. The reports published in the following day's Sunday editions across the country were everything Watson could have hoped for. "Farmington Pilot Flies Nazi Jets," wrote one correspondent. "Colonel H. E. Watson Tests German Me-262 Rocket Planes. In a breath-taking flight from the East Coast, Colonel H. E. Watson . . . led a flight of three German jet propelled Me-262 planes to Freeman Field. Landing at Pittsburgh on their way here, the planes averaged almost 400 miles an hour. . . . According to German documents the Me-262 is capable of a top speed of over 500 miles an hour. . . . Colonel Watson pointed out that the Me-262 jets composed Germany's chief threat to our Air Forces from March 1945, when they appeared in combat, to the finish of the European war. Unofficial proof of the planes' effectiveness is shown by the fact that on the plane piloted by Colonel Watson [*Dennis/Ginny H*] was a score board indicating that this particular jet airplane with its four guns had shot down 42 Russian and seven American planes, a high score considering the short time the Me-262 was in actual combat. . . . In common with all jet engines the plane flies with a peculiar high pitched scream that reminds the listener of a locomotive whistle in the distance."

Dennis was the Me-262 surrendered at Lechfeld by Lieutnant Fritz Müller on VE Day. The victories shown on its fuselage were the total victories accumulated by Oberfeldwebel Heinz Arnold, whose plane it was, not victories creditable to that particular airplane. But it made for a good story. Another press report noted, "On the ground during taxiing and run-ups, the jet engines emit a loud whistle that makes talk in the immediate vicinity impossible, while the blast from the rear of the engines will scorch and blow away anything not fastened down."[1] Jets, whether German or American, excited the imagination of press, radio men, and public alike, and every favorable report published was helpful to General Arnold in his struggle to get his own P-80 jet program funded and off the ground. Skeptics about the jets were aplenty in the halls of Congress and among the titans of industry. The reciprocating engine, after all, was to many of them the ultimate achievement in aircraft propulsion. Like the defenders of the horse cavalry in 1945, they weren't about to give in to a screeching newcomer without a fight.

Karl Baur, after an eight-week journey that began on July 21 in Augsburg, arrived at Wright Field on September 24 accompanied by Andreas Sebald, one of the Messerschmitt mechanics. On September 27 Captain Boesch flew the two to Freeman Field, and Baur and Watson finally met again late in the afternoon of the twenty-ninth in the Freeman Field Officers' Club bar, after Watson's press conference. It was a pleasant reunion. Watson teased Baur about his mustache. Baur responded, "You are lucky I did not grow a beard."[2] They were soon joined by Colonel Gabreski, the third-highest-scoring American ace of the war, Colonel Dorney, the Freeman Field base commander, and

Watson making a very low-level, high-speed pass in Jabo Bait *past the reviewing stand at Freeman Field, September 30, 1945. (RW)*

many others wanting to meet Watson and his German sidekick, Karl Baur. Whizzers Holt, Strobell, and Anspach stopped by as well.

The following day, Sunday, September 30, Watson gave an evidently spectacular performance in *Jabo Bait*, passing in front of the reviewing stand of assembled dignitaries at nearly rooftop level. Wrote one correspondent, "High spot of the air show was the 400-mile-an-hour flying of the twin jet engine Messerschmitt 262. The low-winged fighter was flown by Col. Harold C. [*sic*] Watson of Farmington, Conn., who probably has piloted more German planes over a longer distance than any other American pilot. . . . He 'buzzed' the field at terrific speed, bringing the sleek ship down to within 20 feet of photographers." No modern air show would permit high-performance aircraft to come that close to spectators—but this was 1945 and the spectators loved every minute of it.

The sense of wonder at the German jets also elicited practical thoughts of what it all meant. "Demonstrating need for uninterrupted development of aviation, Air Technical Service Command showed 300 U.S. writers, photographers and radio men here today what Germany had done with its air force before allied might fell on Hitler's head. Topnotch U.S. Army Air Forces' pilots flew German planes in a two-hour demonstration. Many of the aerial weapons were aloft for the first time for field visitors. . . . Flight of the 'hottest' German planes and inspection of Nazi aviation equipment were a preview of what the public will see Oct. 13 and 14 at Wright Field, when the ATSC and AAF stage a huge 'Army Air Force Fair.' That program also is intended to stress the need for U.S. maintenance of supremacy in the air. The event here and the later Dayton show are likely to make Americans more aware that appropriations for aviation research and development are good investments." The reporter got it absolutely right as far as Watson was concerned. It was the type of press coverage General Arnold and the Army Air Forces desperately needed to keep the P-80 program from stalling out. Watson's air shows played no small part in convincing reluctant legislators where to put their money.[3]

With the war totally over, the United States continued the process of unilateral disarmament begun in the summer of 1945. Funding for even the most essential Army Air Corps projects was in jeopardy. One of those threatened projects that was dear to aviators' hearts was the P-80 jet. Watson's air shows were not just staged to entertain the masses, but had the more important and serious aim of educating and persuading the voting public and key politicians of the necessity to continue funding the Army Air Forces jet program. By 1946, when the P-80 finally overcame its safety-of-flight problems, the Air Corps followed Watson's earlier lead and began to give its new jet fighter much needed public exposure. "We put on air shows; we tried to set all the speed records in the world with the P-80; we tried to break everyone else's record," Ken Chilstrom recalled. The shows put on were often no more than one pilot heading into the American heartland over a weekend and thrilling local crowds. Pete Everest, a Wright Field test pilot wrote,

"Several times a month, usually on weekends, one of us would head out somewhere to put on an air show. . . . Amazingly enough, years later young AF jocks would come up to me and ask if I remembered putting on an air show at such a place, and upon responding in the affirmative, they would say that my show inspired them to work toward becoming a fighter pilot. That always gave me a warm feeling."[4]

Dick Johnson, another Wright Field test pilot, thought of these impromptu air shows as "a delightful assignment—to cross the country with a P-80, stopping here and there to do aerobatic demos; it was indeed good fun and experience. During a visit to Sioux Falls, South Dakota, the air show attendees, as usual, were allowed to quiz the 'jet pilot.' A rather large group, mostly young men, indicated that they had arrived too late to see the jet fly—could it be done again? I told them refueling was done by a hand crank pump from drums of fuel and that it was a lot of work. They immediately volunteered and lined up for a turn at the pump. This went on about every two hours all day."[5] Men like Pete Everest and Dick Johnson not only inspired the nation's young men, but also helped put the idea of an independent air force over the top. Their air shows for mom, pop, and the kids inspired an entire nation. To those watching the intrepid jet flyers, jets were the future. Watson played his part in all of that in 1945. He introduced jets to the American public, to politicians, radio men, and the press when the United States didn't have any jets of its own to fly.

In addition to air shows, national air races were held, such as the 1946 races at Cleveland, where America's newest jet plane was shown off. The P-80 broke every record, and Ken Chilstrom remembers how his buddy Gus Lundquist, whom he described as the most experienced fighter test pilot at Wright Field, stole the race from him. "During the war," Ken said, "we had a couple of Spitfires which we modified for the Brits to give the plane a little more range. The Spitfire was very short-legged. We installed wing tanks in these two Spits and Gus Lundquist flew one of them over, accompanied by Charlie Able, who flew the other one. When Gus got to England he wanted to fly some combat. He had never fired a gun in anger before. On his third or fourth mission he was promptly shot down and spent the rest of the war in a German 'rest camp.' The Germans, of course, had a dossier on every American pilot and they were totally stumped when Gus showed up and they found that they had nothing on him—and he wouldn't give them anything. When Gus was released after the war, the Air Force sent him to school and he got a master's degree in aeronautical engineering. Gus was a kind of guy who excelled at everything and he was liked by everyone. After he got his master's in 1946 he came back to flight-test at Wright Field. I had been prepping three of our new P-80s for at least a month for the Cleveland races. Jack Sullivan, Gus, and I were going to fly in the race. The 1st Fighter Group at March Field, California, headed by Robin Olds, also sent three guys. Well, Gus looked at the three airplanes and then he said to me, 'Ken, I think I'll take that one,' and he pointed to my airplane. Gus outranked me, so I flew his airplane instead.

"As we raced down the track we were wing tip to wing tip. Going into the third turn, I was indicating about 515 miles per hour, right on the deck, full throttle at 101 and ½ percent, the boost goes out on me. I couldn't move the stick, and I'm in a turn. All I could do was pull back, and I was out of the race. I knew what happened. The early P-80 models had an electrically driven hydraulic pump, and the pump shorted out. Later they changed it to an engine driven pump. I could land the airplane, but not much else. Gus won the race. Robin Olds, who was a fierce competitor, turned off the engine regulators on his planes and flew his engines at 109 percent. Gus and I flew by the book. Olds was right on Gus's wing. It was like they were flying formation. But Lundquist won the race. Not one of those engines that came from the 1st Fighter Group could fly back home. They over-temped their engines and ruined the blades. When Robin Olds landed his P-80 he flamed out right after touchdown. He couldn't even taxi in—he had run out of fuel. He flew at a higher RPM and burned more fuel than our planes.

Ole Fruit Cake, *the Me-262B night fighter here shown at Melun, was frequently flown by Watson at his air shows. Watson used the aircraft to give rides to many, including Mrs. Dorney, the wife of the Freeman Field commander and the first American woman to fly in a jet aircraft as a passenger. (RB)*

Olds retired as a one-star. A great guy."[6] Air races provided an incredible amount of publicity and good will. With its new jet, in September 1947, the Army Air Forces became the United States Air Force and the P-80 became the F-80. Even then, there were influential people who still thought jet airplanes were nothing but fancy toys.

Freeman Field was commanded by Colonel Dorney. After the second air show on September 30, 1945, Watson flew the Ju 290, always a crowd pleaser, over to Wright Field for the next event planned for October. He returned to Freeman Field on Monday morning. Karl Baur and Andreas Sebald had gone over the two-seater night fighter, *Ole Fruit Cake*, to get it ready for Watson. Watson wanted to show his appreciation to Dorney for all the support he provided during the two air shows and offered to give Mrs. Dorney a ride in *Ole Fruit Cake*. Mrs. Dorney was willing, so he outfitted her with a flight suit, strapped her into the back seat, and off they went. Watson wrote, "Mrs. Dorney . . . became the first woman in the U.S. to fly in the back seat of a Me-262—or any jet aircraft." Then Colonel Dorney, Major

Meiersberger, and Lieutenant Stanley received rides in *Ole Fruit Cake*, all expressing their enthusiasm for the plane upon landing. At the October air show at Wright Field Watson again flew the Me-262, pleasing the large crowd of Daytonians, as well as Orville Wright. Watson proudly recalled that Wright "gave me an autographed picture" following the flight demonstration of the world's first combat qualified turbo jet fighter—forty-two years after he had flown his Wright Flyer.[7] Orville Wright died in Dayton, Ohio, on January 30, 1948. He was seventy-six years old.

26

THE BIRTH OF
PROJECT OVERCAST

A former Heinkel 177 pilot, Franz Hausmann, recalled, "In late April 1945 I found myself at Parchim airfield in Mecklenburg, flying the Ju 88 twin-engined medium bomber. We were sitting in the officers' mess, talking about what we should do, where we should go to surrender, when someone said, 'I am just going to walk out of here.' Several of the officers got up from the table, went to their quarters, changed into civilian clothes and walked off the airfield. I pulled my crew chief aside. He and I had been together for a long time in both Ju 88s and Heinkel 177s. I trusted him. I said to him, Why don't you and I just fly out of here? His eyes lit up. 'That's a fantastic idea,' he said. 'Where to?' West, of course, I said, just you and me. Keep your mouth shut. There were still some devout Nazis around and if they found out about our plans they would have shot us. Tomorrow morning, before first light, I told him, you run up the engines as if you are getting the aircraft ready for a mission. Then taxi out to an open area from which we can take off. I'll tell the tower that you are doing a maintenance check. I'll then come out to where you are, engines running, and we'll just get out of here as fast and low as we can.

"It worked. Once airborne, I headed for Belgium, not France. We had heard that aircrews who landed in France had been attacked by French farmers with pitchforks. I flew very low, it was still dark and raining. I had my eyes glued to the horizon. I didn't want to fly into the trees, but neither too high where someone might spot us and fire on us. I flew just barely above treetop level. I came to an area that looked familiar, put down the flaps and made a perfect belly landing the way I had been taught in flying school. I remembered at the moment before touchdown to take my hands and feet off the controls and to put my arms in front of my face. If I held on to the yoke it would break my arms as it slammed back and forth in a belly landing. Before the aircraft came to rest, I slid down the right side and took off on a run. My crew chief slid down the left side and disappeared in the opposite direction. Unfortunately we hadn't discussed what we would do once we landed. I am sorry we didn't, because I never saw him again. After the war I tried to locate him, but no one ever heard from him again. Maybe an irate farmer got him after all.

"I was walking through the forest when I came to a road. I followed the dirt road and at an intersection I saw an American soldier standing guard. He looked liked any soldier looks who has to perform a dull, unpleasant task—rifle slung over his shoulder, hands in his coat pockets, smoking a cigarette, bored. When the soldier saw me he said in a casual, matter-of-fact tone of voice, 'Where did you come from?' I just belly-landed my airplane not far from here and want to surrender, I said. 'Have you had breakfast yet?' he asked politely. I never will forget this experience. I soon found myself standing in the chow line in an American mess tent, a German Luftwaffe officer in full uniform with all my medals on. My English was acceptable, not great. I could answer questions and have a simple conversation with curious GIs. I was absolutely flabbergasted at the cordial reception. We all sat down together at a table to eat and talk. It turned out that I was the first German soldier they had captured. It was a field artillery unit, getting ready to ship out to the Pacific. I stayed with them overnight, slept in a tent all by myself in the comfort of an American sleeping bag. It all seemed too easy. During the interrogation the following morning I revealed that I had experience with remotely controlled flying bombs, the Hs 293, launched from the He 177 bomber I had flown out of Istress near Marseille, France."

Hausmann's interrogator must have thought he fit the profile for people identified under such varied projects as Eclipse, Alsos, and Safehaven—projects which identified requirements for German scientists to be shipped to the United States for further interrogation and exploitation. Of course, the interrogator made a mistake. "I was just an operator of weapons, not a scientist who developed them. After several days I and fifteen others were transported in an open truck to Antwerp where we boarded a troop ship along with hundreds of GIs bound for the Pacific. We slept in hammocks among the GIs, packed in like sardines. When we arrived at the Brooklyn Marine Terminal and the local commander saw us uniformed Germans coming off the ship along with the GIs, he exploded. 'Who the — got these Krauts on board this ship?' he screamed. He continued to bellow and gesticulate with his arms, venting his rage on his subordinates. I couldn't care less what he was shouting. I was alive, well fed, and had escaped the Russians, that's all that mattered to me. I was put on a train, heading south, with about forty other German prisoners of war, accompanied by ten guards. We were served our food in a dining car where the tables were set with white linen table cloth, linen napkins, and silver place settings. I ended up in Tampa, Florida, in a POW camp on the site of what now is MacDill Air Force Base, an officers' camp, where I was thoroughly interrogated. I stayed until October 1945. By then I wore an American Army officer's uniform and had all the gear an American Army officer would have had—canteen, web belt, my own sleeping bag, and so on. Then someone decided that we were of no further use to them and we were shipped back to Antwerp. I was turned over to the Brits, who relieved me of my

American gear and uniform, except for my sleeping bag, and issued me a British uniform dyed dark brown with a large yellow disc painted on the back of the jacket and on the knees of my pants. The yellow disk indicated that I was a POW. I worked as an auto mechanic until March 1946 when I was released to my hometown of Vienna, Austria."[1]

Franz Hausmann, the Austrian Luftwaffe pilot, found himself on an American troop ship heading for the United States before he fully understood the meaning of the term "prisoner of war." During his brief interrogation by his American captors in Belgium he had dropped the term Hs 293, and as the interrogation report made its way up the chain of command someone decided that this man was wanted by the United States Navy. Hs 293, the guided air-to-surface glide bomb, was on the Navy's Black List, a high-priority item, and it became Hausmann's ticket to the United States. The U.S. Navy didn't want Franz Hausmann; it wanted Dr. Wagner, the designer of the Hs 293. When Wagner was located, he and several assistants were stuffed into an airplane, and while Franz was crossing the Atlantic by ship, Dr. Wagner and his staff of technical assistants passed overhead in flying comfort to be ensconced in a lordly estate on Long Island. In an environment of peace and quiet Wagner could unravel the secrets of his radio, wire, and TV-guided flying bomb for the U.S. Navy. The error which took Franz Hausmann to the United States was soon rectified, and after a few months of tranquil "vacation" in the Florida sun, he found himself again returned to Belgium, where he had surrendered in the first place.

Hausmann's and Wagner's stories are representative of the carte blanche mode of operation the military enjoyed in wartime and for a few days thereafter when the demands to defeat the one remaining enemy, Japan, continued to provide sufficient rationale to transport enemy aliens to the United States for further interrogation. Those men brought to the United States were essentially prisoners of war, even if they were civilians, with very limited rights and privileges.

Hans Fay, the Me-262 test pilot, was shipped to the United States within days after his landing an Me-262 jet at Frankfurt airport on March 31, 1945. He soon learned that he was a ward of the Captured Personnel and Materiel Branch, the CPMB, of the War Department's Military Intelligence Service, MIS, and his treatment was less than cordial. By August 1945 the military had lost its carte blanche authority, which under the guise of national security allowed it to move men and equipment at will between Europe and the United States. The need, as perceived by senior military officers, to bring Germany's leading scientists to the United States for detailed interrogation and exploitation had just begun to be understood when the doors slammed shut.

While Watson was busy collecting German jets in the summer of 1945, and Colonel Putt was leading the exploitation of the LSF at Völkenrode, it sank in to many in the military community that collecting hardware, no matter how advanced and sophisticated, was just a beginning. What was really needed to redress the United States's scientific backwardness were the men who had designed and built the jets, missiles, and wind tunnels. Those scientists, those men of vision, needed to be brought to the United States to make up quickly for years of missed opportunity and neglect. Only they had the know-how to move the United States forward quickly and allow it to acquire the technological expertise to produce what, in the minds of many military officers, would define the second half of the twentieth century: missiles with intercontinental range and jet planes flying beyond the speed of sound.

In the spring of 1945, as the demise of Nazi Germany became obvious, McDonald and Putt, as well as General Knerr, began to express their opinions ever more forcefully. They needed a vehicle for bringing German scientists to the United States for "temporary exploitation." If nothing else, they wanted to keep the scientists out of the hands of the Russians. To them it was clear that in the near future the Russians would at the very least become a competitor, if not an adversary. In faraway Washington that perspective had few adherents. Washington was not very focused on the need for bringing German scientists to the United States. Why not exploit them in Germany? That seemed to be a rational approach. After all, the Germans, no matter how smart, were really Nazis, and bringing Nazis to the United States was to many an abhorrent idea.

Major General Hugh J. Knerr, then Deputy Commanding General Administration at Headquarters USSTAF as well as Commanding General USSTAF Air Service Command, was keenly interested in transferring German scientists to the United States. He wrote to his boss, General Spaatz, and recommended that the Army Air Forces "make full use of the established German technical facilities and personnel before they were destroyed or disorganized." Knerr continued, "It is considered essential that their immediate dependent families accompany them. Such a realistic arrangement will guarantee willing cooperation and maximum contribution to the program of aeronautical development that we must expedite if we are to come abreast of and attempt to surpass those of other countries. And if my recommendations are implemented, these men should be paid a good salary and in nowise [be] treated as prisoners or slave workers. The scientific mind simply does not produce under duress. . . . Occupation of German scientific and industrial establishments has revealed the fact that we have been alarmingly backward in many fields of research. If we do not take this opportunity to seize the apparatus and the brains that developed it and put the combination back to work promptly, we will remain several years behind while we attempt to cover a field already exploited. Pride and face-saving have no place in national insurance."[2]

Knerr raised the same issue with the Honorable Robert A. Lovett, Assistant Secretary of War for Air, who was on a visit to the ETO in April. Knerr pointed out to Lovett that time was of the essence in getting the Germans moved to the United States to keep their research teams from being scattered. He presented to Lovett his concept of a workable plan, which he had outlined to General Spaatz earlier and which was to transport the most valuable scientists, together with their families, to the United States; keep them segregated and watch them with all due precaution; determine their individual scientific and personal qualities and characteristics; and extend citizenship to those qualified, returning the unqualified to Germany, but meanwhile thoroughly exploiting their knowledge and experience without delay. In his own words, "It was desirable to take the families not only for the mental stability it would give the men to know they were safe, but to prevent the possibility of their being taken hostages in the scientists absence."[3] The possible hostage takers were the Russians.

Knerr, Putt, McDonald, and Watson—all came from Wright Field, the location of Air Technical Services Command, which had under its control flight testing, engineering, and numerous laboratories. The Engineering Division of ATSC soon learned from Colonel Putt that he had under his control at Völkenrode three experts on supersonics. That revelation piqued the Wright Field engineers' interest. They agreed that the "temporary services of certain eminent German scientists would unquestionably be profitable to the Army Air Forces research and development program." On May 14, 1945, the Director of Intelligence, Army Service Forces (ASF), expressed his interest in bringing German scientists to this country as well. He had his eyes on Wernher von Braun's group and a hundred or more V-2 missiles on their way to Fort Bliss in Texas. Writing to his counterpart at the War Department General Staff, he flatly stated, "General Somerwell [the commanding general of the ASF] and several of the Technical Services are desirous of transporting selected German scientists to the United States to assist in research and development agencies of the Army Service Forces in perfecting types of equipment to be employed in the war against Japan. War Department approval is asked." Attached to the ASF memorandum to the War Department was a long list of names of scientists wanted for exploitation, in effect the greater part of Wernher von Braun's V-2 rocket team of over four hundred scientists. Only three days later, on May 17, General Somerwell himself repeated the same request in a letter to the Chief of Staff of the War Department. The War Department at least seemed to be waging a more or less coordinated campaign to achieve its aims to bring the Germans to the United States.[4]

Meanwhile Donald Putt was diligently working away at Völkenrode, at night secretly shipping sensitive laboratory equipment to the United States using his small fleet of B-17 and B-24 transports, during the day lobbying to ship German scientists to the ZI. He wrote to Major General Wolfe at Headquarters ATSC, Wright Field, "There are five scientists here who would be of immense value in the jet engine and airplane development program, who I think should be sent to the U.S. However, it seems to involve policy on such a high level, that no one will move." Putt not only let his frustration at the slow pace of development hang out all over, but bypassed his own chain of command at USSTAF, although McDonald and Knerr were aware of what Putt was up to and gave their trusted subordinate much latitude. Putt continued, "If you could cable a request to SHAEF for the following five men to be sent to the U.S. it would be applying pressure from all sides." Putt then listed Professor E. Schmidt, chief of engine development at the LFA, and Professor Busemann, "Germany's No. 1 man on compressibility and supersonics. Karman considers him much superior to John Stack at NACA." The issue was important to Putt, and no one was going to hold him back if he had anything to say about it. Then he listed Professor Zobel, "another aerodynamist who has developed a method of photographing airflow around wings and turbine blades which is most helpful in their design." And last on his list were Professors Lutz and Nöggerath. "Both of these men are foremost in the development of fuels, particularly rocket fuels, and nitrous-oxide injection for engines." He ended his letter by again invoking von Karman's name: "I have talked to all of these men and we can lay our hands on them at a moment's notice if someone will say the word. Von Karman would particularly like to get the first three to the U.S. Von Karman estimates that at this one place there is information immediately available that will take us at least two years of research in the U.S. to obtain. Also enough here to expedite our jet engine development [which wasn't going well at all] program by six to nine months."[5]

Although Putt never received a reply from Wolfe, he soon heard from General Knerr at USSTAF. "I had a discussion with Severski on experimental and development matters in which you are currently interested," Knerr wrote from St.-Germain on May 30, 1945. "As you no doubt know, I am taking over the Technical Command in the near future. I have asked General Eaker to make you available as head of the technical information organization at Wright Field on completion of your survey of the German establishment [Völkenrode]. I have noted your suggestion that one-half dozen outstanding German scientists be shipped to U.S. for use in our development program. I would like to get your ideas of the most effective way of accomplishing this. It occurs to me that we could get the most out of them by making them comfortable. Therefore, they could be handled in the best fashion by organizing them as a unit in charge of a project officer for transportation to Wright Field. At Wright Field they could set aside a block of houses over in the Osborn Development [NYA barracks] for their use, rather than scatter them in the community or by having them locked-up like caged animals. In addition, it might be well to consider the possibility of sending their wives with them. Will you give this some thought so when I see you we can send a cable outlining the proposal."[6]

Obviously Knerr and Putt saw eye to eye on the matter of bringing key German scientists back to the United States, and Knerr didn't mind Putt going over his head and dealing with issues directly. They had no lust for revenge, no emotional axes to grind; all they saw was an intellectual resource that had fallen into their laps and they wanted to put it to use as quickly as possible to the benefit of the Army Air Forces and the nation as a whole. Knerr and Putt were a powerful minority, in time cutting through the red tape of the Washington bureaucracy, but not without first experiencing some setbacks. General Eaker was not a supporter of Knerr's and Putt's ideas. He much preferred to leave the Germans where they were, but he released Putt when Knerr asked for him. Eaker pointed to a demonstration project of the School of Aviation Medicine at Heidelberg, to show that it really wasn't necessary to bring the Germans to the United States. At Heidelberg, thirty-five incomplete German research projects dealing with biophysical, physiological, and psychological aspects of aviation medicine were being completed under the supervision of American scientists. The project was terminated in October 1946 on the direction of General Clay. Neither Putt nor Knerr was impressed with the experiment or felt it had any relevance to what they were trying to do.[7]

Knerr's lobbying with Robert Lovett and Putt's incessant memos and cables from Völkenrode to anyone who would listen, in which he asked people to make a decision and get off the dime, finally had results. On May 21, 1945, the chief of the Interrogation Branch of the office of the Assistant Chief of Staff (AC/S), G-2, of the War Department General Staff, wrote the Assistant Chief of Air Staff (AC/AS), Intelligence (A-2): "The Assistant Chief of Staff, G-2, WDGS has charged CPM Branch MIS with the responsibility of immediately implementing and setting up an organization which will cover the handling of subject personnel re: acquisition and transportation from ETO to Zone of Interior, quarters and subsistence, pay, security and all other pertinent details. As soon as all details have been cleared with State Department, Justice Department and other interested agencies, subject personnel, upon request, will be brought to a 'central pool' for interrogation and exploitation of the AAF, AGF [Army Ground Forces] and ASF [Army Service Forces]. Subject personnel may also be moved to other parts of the Zone of Interior for further exploitation. Subject personnel will not be handled as prisoners of war."[8]

The memo was a classic of bureaucratic jargon but plainly stated that, OK, we are about to move out to bring the German missile experts, von Braun's group, and the aerodynamicists, Putt's group, to the

United States. We'll put them up in a central place and you can then pick them up from there and do with them whatever you please. Happy now? The plan still needed the go-ahead from the secretary of war or his designated representative. Fortunately that approval had already been obtained verbally and came in writing the following day, May 22, designating the CPMB as having primary responsibility for the return, control, handling, and disposal of enemy personnel involved in this temporary exploitation plan. The word "temporary" kept cropping up.[9] But writing a plan acceptable to the Washington military and political community proved exceedingly difficult. Even within the War Department there was open animosity toward the idea of bringing Germans (Nazis) to the United States. In such a hostile environment, a plan requiring extensive coordination not only within the War Department but also within State and other agencies was faced with obvious delays, if not slow demise. Additionally, the British had to be consulted and their nod of approval obtained, because it was to be a unified response, not one ally appearing to grant privileges another was not prepared to offer. That, however, proved to be no obstacle because the British were as interested in securing German cooperation as Wright Field and Fort Bliss were anxious to get to work on their jet and missile programs. The actual plan was finally announced on July 20, 1945, with an effective date of July 19. The announcement was made by the Joint Chiefs of Staff, who assigned the program the secret code word "Overcast." Overcast was described as a "Project of exploiting German civilian scientists, and its establishment under the Chief, Military Intelligence Service, on an island in Boston harbor at a camp formerly known as Fort Standish."[10] Fort Standish was actually Fort Strong.

Project Overcast conferences among various parties came up with a draft policy on "exploitation" by July 6, 1945. The draft listed a number of principles and procedures to guide the process, including the stipulation that only those specialists whose actual physical presence was essential would be brought to the United States. Stating the obvious in such complex negotiations is a way of keeping on moving forward. How to define such imponderables as "essential" is often best left alone, or no progress can be made. Lists of names of scientists desired for exploitation in the United States would be submitted to the AC/S, G-2, WDGS, by military agencies. Fort Strong would be used for "housing and feeding and for exploitation other than that necessary to be accomplished in laboratories or similar installations," and "since personnel will be returned to Germany eventually, they will be exploited and controlled in such a manner that their ability to become acquainted with United States knowledge and techniques will be kept to a minimum." Additionally, Project Overcast provided for an "initial quota of 350 scientists, who were to be volunteers, not listed as war criminals; employment under Civil Service Regulations A-1-7 was authorized, and the rate of pay established. Dependents and immediate families were to be afforded protection in Germany during the scientists' absence." On July 27, Project Overcast instructions were sent to the field.

Meanwhile the folks in the field were trying to hold onto German scientists by the thousands, keep scientific teams together, and find some way to get the process off dead center. The British and the French also were interested in obtaining the services of German scientists and actively recruited them, but the United States's greatest competitor by far were the Russians. The Russians were quick to exploit an ever-deepening German famine by offering food and other attractive benefits to scientists who would switch sides. To thwart the Soviet recruiting effort, German scientists were being signed up for employment in the United States in anticipation of an Overcast agreement which it was hoped would look something like the plan General Knerr proposed to Mr. Lovett in April. On July 12, General Cannon, the commander of the United States Air Forces in Europe, now headquartered in Wiesbaden, sent a memorandum to General Arnold announcing that "eminent German scientific personnel now awaiting shipment to the U.S. together with their immediate families have been cleared with Air Ministry. . . . Urge this Hq be advised at once as to progress of this project."[11] The advice sought for came promptly, stating that the release of a policy was expected immediately, and according to the policy "scientific persons only and not members of families will be returned." Overcast, as formulated, made no allowance for German scientists to stay in the United States on a permanent basis; it was not considered that they would ever become U.S. citizens, nor were provisions made for their families to join them. All of these limitations left those most interested in the development of a workable plan and process, the American military engineering and scientific community, with no more than a foot in the door. Fort Strong was transferred on July 16 to the War Department to accommodate Project Overcast scientists.[12]

While Washington bureaucrats pondered Overcast and its related issues, at Völkenrode, Colonel Putt tried to deal with his own problems and frustrations in his usual direct manner. He didn't want to lose his people, and he knew he was soon going to leave Völkenrode. So he promised the six candidates he had selected for movement to Wright Field that he would fly them there directly, and their families as well. He told them that there was housing ready for them at Wright Field, and that once they were there, it was "very likely that permanent residence in the U.S.A. could be made possible, if desired."[13] In mid-May when negotiations in Washington were beginning to look promising, Putt told the Germans to get ready for an immediate departure, settle their affairs, get rid of furniture and anything else they owned, and pack only essentials for travel by air to the United States. Putt planned to put the scientists and their families on one of his B-24/B-17 aircraft and fly them directly to Wright Field. He sent them all to Bad Kissingen, in the American zone, where they were put up in the hotel Wittelsbacher Hof, which was used to accommodate German detainees. The scientists and their families remained there for thirteen weeks,

B-17 bombers, such as this one shown at Naples, Italy, with its armament removed, made excellent cargo aircraft. Colonel Putt used demilitarized B-17s and B-24s to haul his loot out of Völkenrode under the unsuspecting eyes of the British. (RB)

waiting for direction, having almost no clothing or anything else to support their prolonged stay. Putt's private airline vanished when he returned to Wright Field in August. Not until mid-September did Nöggerath, Zobel, his two assistants, Rister and Bök, and Dr. Braun get flown to Paris. Their families stayed behind.

What Don Putt couldn't and didn't anticipate wrecking his plans to move Zobel and the others to the United States was powerful opposition from Dr. H. P. Robertson. Robertson was Chief of the Scientific Advisory Group to General Eisenhower (Field Intelligence Agency Technical, FIAT), "and Robertson bluntly expressed the opinion [to von Karman] that the removal of German scientists to the United States for any period of time would, in the end, imperil various phases of scientific development underway there." In a November 3, 1945, letter, McDonald, the chief of Intelligence at Headquarters USAFE in Wiesbaden, confessed to General Knerr at Wright Field that "it now becomes apparent why difficulties have been raised in the return of scientists that have been selected by Don Putt. . . . Dr. H. P. Robertson and his Group in USFET have been in a position to interfere . . . and I am convinced that the objections have, in a great measure, been raised because the American scientists believe that the return of a number of eminent German scientists may jeopardize their own professional status."[14]

Once in Paris, the German scientists were put up in the Chateau du Grand Chesnay in Versailles, a relatively luxurious environment. They were in the company of Karl Baur, the Messerschmitt Me-262 test pilot, and his assistant, Sebald, also on their way to Wright Field, and Dr. Wernher von Braun and a few of his missile engineers and scientists, who were heading to Fort Bliss. Not until the twenty-second of September did the Germans finally arrive at Fort Strong, the first group of German scientists to arrive in America under the auspices of Project Overcast. If they were frustrated by events, so were their American sponsors.[15] Major General Knerr, who assumed the position of commanding general, Air Technical Service Command at Wright Field, upon his return to the United States, did not buy into the War Department's short-sighted solutions. Knerr was aware of the fact that Germans were reluctant to accept family separation, and even if they did sign a contract to come to the United States, there were no arrangements in place to assure them of the welfare of their families. As early as July 14 Knerr wrote to his War Department counterpart, "Arrangement to return German scientists without their families is not a satisfactory arrangement from our point of view. Intangibles of a scientist's daily life directly affect the quality of his product. It is urged that our original arrangement to bring complete family to live in a segregated area now available at Wright Field be adhered to." Knerr didn't get anywhere. The canned response from Washington was that Project Overcast was an interim measure. Therefore, it didn't make economic sense to bring families to the United States. The family issue obviously needed resolution, but not until late in September 1945 was a housing area established for dependents of German scientists at Landshut, Bavaria, forty miles northeast of Munich.[16]

Wright Field submitted requirements to Washington for sixty-seven German scientists. Under pressure from the top, that number was quickly reduced to fourteen. Along with the name list, Wright Field also submitted an outline of an exploitation plan which envisioned the use of a seminar approach in which the Germans would first present lectures in their respective disciplines, then submit to a question-and-answer period, which would culminate in visits to Wright Field laboratories. Instead of the expected fourteen, only six scientists signed contracts under Project Overcast and departed Europe in mid-September for Wright Field. They were given assurances that their families would be taken care of and settled in the new housing area at Landshut. Once the six arrived at Wright Field, the seminar idea did not prove practicable. The quality of the scientists was of such high caliber that Colonel Putt, who by then had been appointed by General Knerr as the commander of Technical Intelligence (T-2) for ATSC, proposed that the Germans be assigned to work on projects requested by the Wright Field laboratories. That approach worked well because the Germans were men whose whole world was the laboratory.[17]

On the family side, events developed in the opposite direction. Word filtered back to the six Germans working at Wright Field that indicated "failure on the part of military authorities to carry out contract terms concerning housing, food, and fuel" for their families at Landshut. Their morale plummeted to the point where General Putt, who had recently been promoted, wrote a letter to Major General Echols at the Office of the Military Government of Germany allowing him to send an officer over to personally view the status of the Landshut project. Permission was granted. The Landshut housing project for Overcast dependents was administered by four military officers and six enlisted personnel, augmented by a large staff of

German helpers who took care of routine maintenance. Eventually even a medical doctor was added to the staff. Problems seemed to have arisen especially during the start-up phase of the Landshut project, which had been established in a former German army compound. "Families were not in any way forced to move to Landshut; and, by the same token, they were free to leave there if they so desired. Those families choosing not to live at Landshut were authorized to receive salary payments and mail and were given letters of identification to protect their property against confiscation. They were not, however, entitled to supplementary rations. . . . The matter of supplementary rations for these dependents remained a problem and, to a considerable degree, a controversial issue. . . . In spite of repeated attempts to obtain permission to furnish extra food and fuel for dependents living outside the housing area, very little could be done to alter existing conditions, not only because of contractual restrictions but because the Office of Military Government advised against such action in view of the widespread resentment that would naturally result and possibly cause political repercussions."

In the winter of 1945–1946 living conditions in Germany deteriorated substantially. Outright hunger was the norm. The privileges granted to German families living in the Landshut project elicited resentment and hostility from Germans living nearby who were not so fortunate. The privileges enjoyed by the Landshut Overcast dependents were substantial when compared to the entitlements of other Germans. An Overcast dependent was entitled to twelve hundred grams of fats per month, versus three hundred grams for other Germans. An Overcast dependent received twice as much bread and sugar per week, seven rather than two eggs per month per person, three times as much meat, and generally more than twice as much cheese and marmalade. Landshut residents received nearly half a pound of real coffee per month and an assured supply of cigarettes, items highly tradable on the black market. The normal German living in Landshut received only ersatz coffee made from cereal grains, and low-quality German cigarettes were a matter of availability. All food and fuel for the Landshut project was provided by the government of the state of Bavaria. The contract called for the provision of a minimum of twenty-three hundred calories per day for Overcast dependents residing at Landshut camp, if not available from German sources then to be supplemented by the United States government—a condition which never had to be implemented. Regarding wood for cooking and heating, as well as clothing, the Overcast dependents again fared much better than the general population. "It is also interesting to note that no restrictions were imposed on the use of gas and electricity at Landshut." Finally, "Residents of the housing project were allowed to have two pairs of shoes resoled per family per month; German citizens outside of the project were allowed one pair of shoes resoled per person per year. The scientists' dependents fared much better than other German citizens in the matter of general clothing also." The winter of 1945–1946 was difficult for everyone, and by spring and summer most problems at the Landshut project had worked themselves out—except for the continuing resentment of less fortunate Germans toward the camp's residents.[18]

Project Overcast, a program of a temporary nature offering short-term, six-month employment contracts, was never able to transition to something more substantial and was finally scrapped. On September 3, 1946, President Truman approved a follow-on to Overcast—Project Paperclip.

27

PROJECT OVERCAST AND ONE MAN'S EXPERIENCE

Karl Baur was one of two mainstays of Watson's Me-262 recovery program; Ludwig Hoffmann was the other. From the day Watson arrived in Augsburg on May 2, 1945, until the last Me-262 was delivered to Querqueville airfield, Karl had been there to provide assistance and advice. Not only that, but Karl was the only other pilot besides Watson to have flown the Arado 234. Watson knew that he needed expert support at Wright Field to keep his fleet of German jets in flying condition, and Baur was his choice. He had intended to take Willie Hoffmann as well, but Willie was in the hospital recuperating from the injuries he sustained when bailing out of *Wilma Jeanne*. When asked which mechanics Baur wanted to take, Karl chose Fritz Hindelang and Andreas Sebald.

Watson released Karl Baur immediately after the delivery of the last Arados to Cherbourg, on July 5. Only two weeks later, though, an American sergeant stood at Karl's front door encouraging him to hurry up and get ready to go. Karl found himself again abruptly wrenched away from his family to begin an odyssey that would take him first to Paris, then to the United States. Project Overcast had been implemented two weeks earlier, and American military officers moved quickly to transport German scientists, and others like Baur and Padell, the Do 335 test pilot, to waiting laboratories and test centers in Ohio, Maryland, and Texas. Isolde Baur wrote, "We threw Karl's only suit, some faded underwear, shirts and mended old socks in a suitcase, while the sergeant was waiting impatiently. Karl wore his Bavarian leather shorts, his everyday summer outfit—the only thing left to wear after being bombed out several times. No time for big farewells. I picked up my infant son and together we watched from the window. Karl jumped into the jeep—and off they went."[1] Baur, Hindeland, and Sebald were escorted onto the daily Munich-to-Wiesbaden shuttle, a war-weary C-47 transport from the 302nd Transport Wing. In Wiesbaden they transferred to another aircraft which took them to Paris-Villacoublay. Their first day's travels ended with a truck ride to St.-Germain, where they were put up in a school housing both GI prisoners and German scientists on their way to the land of the *unbegrenzten Möglichkeiten,* the land of unlimited opportunities.

At the École d'Éducation de la Légion d'Honneur, Karl met some old friends and acquaintances also on their way to Wright Field: Professor Dr. Ernst Hertel, Ernst Zindell, and Hans Grobler, all three from the Junkers Company; Dr. Alexander Lippisch, the renowned aircraft designer; Dr. Rudolph Götherd, a respected aerodynamicist; and Dr. Friedrich Ringleb. They spent their time mostly in long discussions and playing *Skat,* a favorite German card game similar to Hearts. On July 28, Hauptmann Heinz Braun and his mechanics showed up to spend a night. They had worked for Watson at Orly airfield until that morning, when Watson and his crew of nine departed in the Junkers 290 for the Azores. Braun wasn't too happy. Colonel Watson had promised to take him to the United States and didn't keep the promise. The following day Braun and his mechanics flew back to Germany.

Nothing much happened until the first week in August when Karl and his two mechanics were transferred to more amenable quarters in the Chateau du Grand Chesnay, an old estate in Versailles. There "we had more freedom and were allowed to walk in the park without an MP on our tail," Karl wrote in his diary. A nearly endless procession of senior German military officers, scientists, and engineers passed through the chateau detention and interrogation camp. There was little to do but take endless walks, smoke cigarettes, play more *Skat*, and talk about the war that had been lost. On September 14, two months after leaving Augsburg, Baur and his mechanics were presented with a contract which they quickly signed. The contract was a standard format developed for German nationals coming to the United States under the provisions of Project Overcast. It read: "In consideration of the service to be rendered by the individual named in Section I, above, hereinafter referred to as the Employee, in the position indicated in Section I, above, for gross pay in the amount shown in Section I, above, the following contract of employment is entered into by such individual and the War Department, hereinafter referred to as the Employer. The Employer hereby offers and the Employee hereby accepts employment subject to the conditions herein set forth." The conditions of employment provided for a six-dollar-per-day per diem, the remaining salary to be "paid in marks bi-weekly by the Finance Officer to the bank or dependent named by the Employee"; a baggage allowance of 65 pounds for those traveling by air to the United States, 175 pounds for those traveling by water; no physical restraints, "but must agree to remain in the area selected by the Employer unless specific authority is granted to leave the area." The established tour of duty was defined as forty-eight hours per week, eight hours per day, six days per week. Employees would be housed in temporary construction similar to that furnished junior officers, and food would be furnished through Army-operated messes. Dependents would not accompany the employee to the United States and would be furnished adequate housing [meaning the camp at Landshut]. "When a diet of 2,300 calories per person of reasonable variety and minimum fuel requirements are not available, the Employer will supplement food and fuel," the contract read. Further, "after the initial employment period of three months this contract may be extended for an additional period not to exceed nine months. If at the end of the 12 months the Employer desires to continue the employment for an appreciable period of time, and conditions at the time make it practicable, an effort will be made to permit dependents to be moved to the United States."[2]

That last caveat was a huge concession and provided hope for many that eventually they would be reunited with their families, either by returning to Germany or while still working in the United States. Karl expected to go to the United States for three months only, but one never knew what the future held in store. The annual salary scale for Project Overcast employees provided for the payment of 24,000 to 31,200 marks to a professor or an individual holding the title of Doktor. Senior Doktor engineers were paid 15,000 to 23,999 marks, junior Doktor engineers between 8,700 and 14,999 marks, engineers 8,700 to 11,399 marks, and skilled laborers or master mechanics from 4,800 to 8,699 marks.[3] A question remained unanswered: what could one possibly buy with the nearly worthless reichsmark? Without ration cards, the reichsmark was only so much paper. After the contract signing, Karl and his two mechanics underwent a thorough physical examination which revealed Hindelang's leg wound suffered early in the war. Hindelang was promptly sent home, his contract terminated. Karl was disappointed, because his other mechanic, Sebald, spoke little English. The two men gave copies of their contract and personal letters to Hindelang, who promised to drop them off to their wives.

That same September day, Karl Baur met Dr. Wernher von Braun, the famous designer of the V-2 ballistic missile. Braun had arrived the night before with six of his engineers and revealed to Karl that he intended to bring at least another 115 members of his V-2 development team to the United States once he settled in at Fort Bliss. On Tuesday, September 18, a rainy Paris day, Karl Baur and Andreas Sebald boarded a bus for Orly airport, along with Dr. Theodor Zobel, Dr. Rudolph Edse, Dr. Wolfgang Nöggerath, Dr. Gerhard Braun, all from the Hermann Göring Research Institute, and Dr. Wernher von Braun with his six engineers. At Orly they were given an opportunity to exchange the nearly worthless reichsmark for coveted dollars at a rate of ten to one and headed for the officers' club for a good meal. Baur wrote in his diary, "Boarding a military transport plane—C-54—during pouring rain at 10:00 P.M. Quickly, the plane moved through the clouds and a beautiful, clear sky with bright moonlight greeted us. For the first time—I cannot recall the number of years—I enjoyed a flight as a passenger. The final lights of Europe diminished at the horizon after about two hours. Everyone picked up some blankets and we all lay down on the floor to catch some sleep." At dawn on September 19 the C-54 "touched down at the Azorian island of St. Maria. We bought the first good cigarettes and had breakfast. The C-54 was filled and ready for takeoff at 9:00 A.M."

After a long and boring flight across the Atlantic, with a refueling stop at Gander, Newfoundland, the passengers finally saw the lights of New York City appearing on the dark horizon. "What a sight!" wrote Karl. "After living five years in darkened cities we were overwhelmed by that illumination. It took our breath away! What an experience! We landed at night at the New Castle Airport in Wilmington, Delaware. Tired of sitting on hard benches, we had hoped that this would be our final destination. Wrong! After [customs] duty inspection we boarded again—about 3:00 A.M.—this time a C-47 with comfortable seats, to reach our temporary destination—Boston." From Boston's Logan Field the group was driven in Army sedans to Boston harbor where a waiting boat took them out to Long Island, the site of Fort Strong, one of a string of forts built in the early 1800s to protect the east coast of the United States from British invasion. "The barracks in which we stayed were clean and the meals were excellent," wrote Karl. "We used the time on our hands playing volleyball and walking around the island. The passing boats with the silhouette of the city's skyscrapers in the background were most picturesque and we did not get tired of looking at them. And once more we had to prove to the doctors that we were healthy specimen. The police registered our fingerprints, just in case we might try something 'funny.' German POWs kept our quarters in tip-top shape and did our laundry too. None of them had any complaints, except that they would rather be back home in Germany. Some people around here don't like the idea of my walking around in my leather shorts. I explained to the officer that this was the only thing I had to wear besides one suit, which I had to save for official occasions such as going out to dinner. He finally agreed to see what he could do to get some clothing for me. I had no coat and my only pair of shoes showed the wear and tear openly." But it was only a brief stay at Fort Strong. On September 24, Baur, Sebald, and the four German scientists, Braun, Nöggerath, Zobel, and Edse, departed in a C-47 for Wright Field.

Watson was not there to meet Karl when he arrived; he had just finished putting on his first air show at Freeman Field for the press and assorted civilian and military dignitaries. Baur didn't know that. Baur also didn't know that Lieutenant Haynes had been killed on the twenty-second in the crash of an FW 190. On Thursday, September 27, Captain Walter Boesch, who was in charge of Germans under Project Overcast at Wright Field, flew Baur and Sebald in a C-46 transport to Freeman Field. Watson wanted them to help him get ready for the next air show scheduled for Saturday and Sunday. That evening Baur and Watson finally met at the bar of the officers' club. The next few days were taken up getting airplanes ready to fly for the air show.

After the second air show at Freeman Field, Captain Fred McIntosh and Karl Baur flew to Newark Field, where a number of German

planes were being readied for transfer to Freeman. That first weekend
in October, Karl accompanied Captain Maxfield, the engineering officer, into Manhattan to see its fabled skyscrapers. The unauthorized
side trip had consequences; it upset Captain Boesch. Boesch, the son
of German immigrant parents, was Baur's official keeper, and he liked
to have everything neat and tidy. Walter Boesch certainly didn't like
the feeling of having his authority challenged by a German. But there
wasn't much he could do to Karl Baur without tangling with Colonel
Watson, so he let it go for the time being. In the future, at Wright Field
and at Freeman Field, Boesch would restrict Karl's freedom of movement to the point where Karl finally couldn't go into town at all, even
when other Germans were allowed to do so. Watson would have taken
care of the situation quickly had Karl complained, but Karl didn't.

It rained most of the time while Karl was at Newark. On October 9
the weather improved, and Jack Woolams flew in. Karl briefed Jack on
the Arado 234 and Jack enthusiastically proposed that he fly the Arado
to Wright Field, with an intermediate refueling stop in Pittsburgh.
When Woolams got near Pittsburgh and tried to put down the landing gear, there was no response. He had to pump the gear down by
hand. When Karl arrived and took a look at the wounded Arado,
he found a broken hydraulic line. He wished he had brought his
mechanic along, so he spent the next day installing a new hydraulic
line hastily flown in from Freeman Field. That evening he went over
to the Red Cross station at the field and "was served a delicious
barbeque sandwich at no cost—my supper for that night." Karl kept
learning about America's habits and people; he found it a strange yet
appealing land. It began to grow on him, as it had on thousands of
others before him. Most people were friendly, he discovered, even
though the war between Germany and the United States had ended
only weeks earlier.

The next day Woolams told Karl he could fly the Arado to Wright
Field. Woolams said he had some pressing business to attend to.

More likely Woolams had had enough of flying the Arado after wrestling with its failed hydraulic system. "Since the runway was somewhat short for the Arado, I barely cleared the ground at the end of the runway. Unfortunately, not enough to make it over that darn hill which was located . . . [at] the end of the runway." It was the same hill into which Captain Holt had crashed his Me-262, *Cookie VII*, on August 19 when his brakes failed on landing. Karl managed to maintain control of his aircraft with great difficulty. It was touch and go. He was only feet off the ground, his glasses knocked off his face by flying objects; he had one hand flying the aircraft and the other cranking up the gear. Finally, he made it up to nine thousand feet, his planned cruising altitude. Karl had no useable radio with which to let anyone know he might need assistance on landing at Wright Field. But luck was with him. First, the aircraft had not been structurally damaged, and second, "Major Meiersberger, who had taken off after me in a P-51 in Pittsburgh, saw what had happened to me. He had radioed the tower in Wright Field to make sure all preparations were made for an emergency landing of the Arado 234. He had followed me all the way from Pittsburgh. International pilot-comradeship in action!" Karl touched down at Wright Field, and, "while taxiing, I saw the fire engine and an ambulance. Mentally and physically exhausted I opened the cockpit and was greeted by the whole group of German scientists" and others. "What was all the excitement?" After the close call with the Arado at Pittsburgh, Karl decided to quit flying unless someone bought him an adequate insurance policy. "I made it clear to my superiors that I would not fly in the future without someone paying a casualty insurance policy for me. It was impossible to do that by myself from the $6.00 a day allowance. After staying alive through all the years of hair-raising flying experiences, I had no intention of sacrificing my life now, leaving my wife and son without financial protection." After being flown back to Freeman Field that night, Karl decided to celebrate his "final flight as a test pilot. So, according to 'German Rule' I soaked down the day's experiences with the best whisky the country club had to offer and as much as my $6.00 allowance allowed me."

Baur and Sebald soon became bored with their lives. There wasn't enough work and they had no contact with their families, both situations cumulatively depressing. But the pace quickened again. They departed for Patuxent Naval Air Station in Maryland to assist the Navy in their efforts to rebuild several of the aircraft allocated to them from HMS *Reaper*. "The Air Force," Karl wrote, "had given the two worst-looking Arado 234s to the Navy." Karl later wrote a memo to that effect which greatly upset General Putt, who put the clamps on any further communications of that nature by his German guests. At Patuxent, "what a surprise they had in store for me! Two POWs greeted me—Mr. Bringewald and Mr. Ruff—from the Messerschmitt Company. The two engineers were on the way to Japan via German submarine, when they were captured by the U.S. Navy. . . . I stayed with them overnight—a pleasant break in their boring routine." Then it was back to Wright Field, and life became more and more monotonous and depressing—Karl just wanted to go home and be with his wife and son. There was nothing for him or Sebald to do at Wright Field. There was nothing for the German scientists to do either, who were vegetating in their barracks. "All scientists had hoped to continue their particular research here. Instead, no money was provided for the simplest equipment. Everyone was sitting, gaining weight and became mentally depressed," Karl confided to his diary. Again he asked to be allowed to go home. Colonel Belvin, one of the officers Baur worked with, promised to relay Karl's wishes to General Putt.

On November 15, "Lt. Kasperek took us into Indianapolis," Karl wrote, "in an 'official car.' It was getting colder now. We needed warm winter clothing to wear. The prices were reasonable enough, so I could afford a coat, a suit and one pair of shoes. Driving through the countryside I realized the corn still had not been harvested. Kasperek filled me in: the American farmers are independent businessmen. Such was difficult for me to picture since all the years in Germany, German farmers had to produce what the Government asked them to produce. The farmers here can keep as much cattle as they want, the type they want. They can sell when they want or can hold it back, just as they please or the business demands."

A week later Baur and Sebald were informed that their travel orders to return to Germany were ready. It was the twenty-third of November. "At 2:00 P.M. we were ready to leave with our hands full of written recommendations and warm farewell wishes from all officers. . . . Most of them felt sad about our departure and we promised each other to stay in touch by mail as soon as the circumstances would allow us to do so. We left with a feeling that we had been well liked. . . . Captain Boesch still carried a grudge against me. Apparently about my independent traveling around New York without escort. He refused to let me join the others for a shopping trip into Dayton. So I made a big list for my friends to do the shopping for me." The final evening Karl spent with Albert Lynch, a German-speaking bachelor who lived with the Germans in the Wright Field compound housing Karl and the German scientists. They went to a German restaurant in Dayton, Lynch drinking his favorite vermouth *mit Zitrone*, Karl opting for whisky with Coca-Cola. They talked about "Salzburg, Austria, Bavaria and the Gemütlichkeit which the United States does not offer."

Baur and Sebald soon found themselves back at Fort Strong, which they referred to as Devil's Island, not because of any particularly bad treatment they or anyone else received there; it was more a reflection of their helplessness and inability to determine their own futures. Fort Strong was filled with engineers and scientists on their way to Wright Field or to join Dr. von Braun at Fort Bliss, Texas. The great majority of the engineers were flown out on November 27. The weather was stormy and Baur's and Sebald's departure was delayed. They played Monopoly, the capitalist's game, to pass the time. "Nobody was in a good mood," Karl wrote. "You optimists! You'll never be home by Christmas!"

their friends teased them. But Karl and Andreas refused to listen to the voices of gloom. On the fifth of December Karl and Andreas were informed they would be leaving the following day—by boat. They were given one last opportunity to go shopping in the post exchange. They had to buy extra suitcases to carry all their purchases, "luxuries no one had seen in Germany since years: chocolate, coffee, tea, canned foods, fancy underwear and stockings for the ladies." On the sixth of December, they stepped on a small cutter and departed Devil's Island. The waves were high and their small boat nearly capsized, or at least Karl thought so. Once on the mainland they were driven to the pier where the *Kokomo Victory*, their home for the next several days, lay at anchor. They arrived in Le Havre ten days later, on December 16, and were driven to Paris, where they caught a train to Germany. "The train did rumble through Saarbrücken when I woke up during the predawn hours. I realized how hopeless it looked for our country. Grotesque house ruins along the railroad tracks in a dull drizzly rain. Depressing! The bombed-out railroad station was still filled with debris; only a couple of tracks had been cleared for trains passing through. The few people I could see looked worn out, pale and hungry." On December 23, 1945, Karl Baur and Andreas Sebald were back in Augsburg. Project Overcast and Wright Field were only memories. It was a good feeling to be home in spite of everything, and it felt good "being a 'real' Santa Claus," Karl recorded as his final diary entry. Karl Baur and Andreas Sebald had made it home by Christmas after all.[4]

FROM OVERCAST TO PAPERCLIP

By October 1945, after the last air show for the year at Wright Field, Watson relocated all of his German aircraft to either Wright Field or Freeman Field. Ninety-six freight cars loaded with everything from air-to-ground guided antiship missiles, such as the Hs 293 and the Fritz X, to V-2 ballistic missiles, and a plethora of parts, pieces, documentation—what Lieutenant Strobell liked to refer to as "stuff"— began to accumulate at Wright Field, much of it never to be looked at again. Watson went to work as the chief of the Collection Division of Technical Intelligence, T-2, commanded by his longtime friend and Operation Lusty coexploiter, Colonel Donald Putt. Both Watson and Putt worked for Major General Hugh Knerr, commander of the Air Technical Service Command.

Watson's Collection Division had the responsibility for the exploitation of foreign military aircraft and related technical materiel, including all of the German aircraft he brought back from Germany. Upon Strobell's release from the hospital in Germany, Watson found a job for him managing "stuff" that had been stored in Building 89 at Wright Field. Watson took care of Fred McIntosh as well, finding a position for him in his division. The past bound all of them together; they looked after one another, took care of one another, and proceeded to finish the job they had begun in Europe. All of them, from General Knerr down to First Lieutenant Strobell, were coming from an environment of plenty—plenty of men, plenty of airplanes, plenty of everything. By late 1945, with the war definitely over, as the lyrics of a popular song proclaimed, there suddenly was "plenty of nothing"—money for nearly any military purpose dried up like rain falling on parched desert sand.

The United States entered a disarmament frenzy of unprecedented proportions. Jet propulsion, radar, the ballistic missile, and above all, the atomic bomb, irrevocably changed the emerging postwar world. In Washington, however, the primary concern was getting the boys home, transitioning to a peacetime economy, putting money in places other than the military. There was no vision of what the postwar world might look like, no inkling of what the war's scientific breakthroughs might portend. Knerr, Putt, and Watson were forced to struggle with unaccustomed funding shortages, a shrinking military, and the con- troversial influx of German scientists into the Wright Field engineer- ing community.

"I guess, having made so much noise about it before I left Germany, when I got to Wright Field I was put in charge of the German scien- tists," Don Putt recalled. "You know, if you complain about the soup, you wind up in the kitchen."[1] He assumed the position of Deputy Commanding General for Intelligence at Wright Field on September 4, 1945, less than three weeks before the first German scientists arrived from Völkenrode, the very people he had handpicked while still there. General Knerr, the first to return from Europe to Wright Field in mid- summer, immediately took the initiative to get housing and messing facilities ready for an expected initial group of fourteen German sci- entists. The general's wishes to get things ready were noted by his staff, but in the ever more austere budget environment of 1945 no one knew exactly who was going to pay for housing, bed linens, laundry services, and all the other things people needed on a daily basis. Payroll costs and expenses associated with operational aspects of Project Overcast were charged against research and development funds. No one had yet addressed the question of who was going to pay for more mundane items such as food, laundry, and lodging.

Three cottages and five one-story barracks in a thirties-era labor camp lying between Wright Field and Patterson Field, referred to as the Hilltop, were identified for refurbishment. The barracks contained from ten to sixteen single rooms, a lounge, a separate toilet, and a shower area. One of the cottages contained four bedrooms, the other six, and each cottage also had a lounge and two baths. Who was going to pay for refurbishing the Hilltop barracks and cottages which had stood empty for years? Someone got the bright idea that a good source of funds would be the Wright Field Officers' Open Mess. On July 23, the officer in charge of the Wright Field Officers' Club was directed to "equip 4 buildings in the NYA Area in order to house 18 German nationals." He was further directed to employ a civilian cook and civilian housekeeper.[2]

Captain Shurley, the club officer, proceeded as directed and employed a cook and a housekeeper at a cost of three hundred dollars per month, and had the quarters painted and furnished at a cost to the officers' club of five thousand dollars. Food stocks for the kitchen were provided by the officers' club, which was also made responsible for laundry services and incidentals required by the expected German guests. This was indeed a strange approach to paying for a program directed by the government of the United States. By late July, a Project Overcast report noted that "all arrangements were completed; living quarters were in readiness, and a civilian and his wife had been employed to prepare meals and attend to housekeeping details." Nothing happened until late September, when, instead of the expected fourteen, only six German scientists arrived. "By April 1946 there were thirty-five, and by the fall of that year, almost ninety. Additional barracks had to be repaired and furnished as the group became larger but considerable difficulty was encountered because of a change in the original financial arrangements."

The Wright Field judge advocate, Colonel R. C. Harmon, received an informal request to review and interpret article 5 of the short-term contract for the employment of German nationals under Project Overcast. Article 5 dealt with quarters and subsistence. No one said who made the request for a legal opinion, but it most likely was a concerned club officer, Captain Shurley, who wasn't convinced that what he was doing was legal. Colonel Harmon informed Captain Shurley that "It is the opinion of this office that: The Government, and not the Officers' Club, is obligated to furnish housing and incidental services under Article 5a of the contract. . . . The Government, and not the Officers' Club or Mess, is obligated to furnish food." Then the judge advocate recommended that "The furniture purchased with Officers' Club funds should be removed from the buildings . . . and Government-owned furnishings should be secured. . . . The practice of securing food from supplies of the Officers' Mess and of paying the cook from Officers' Club funds should be discontinued" and "an effort should be made to collect from the German nationals the amounts which they would have been obligated to pay had housing and food been furnished by the Government."[3] On the basis of Colonel Harmon's legal opinion, Captain Shurley canceled the officers' club's support for Project Overcast and asked for the club to be reimbursed for expenses incurred. The caretaker and his wife were fired; the scientists were asked to take care of their own quarters and were fed at the mess hall for enlisted men. "The scientists protested vigorously," because the caretaker and his wife had done such an excellent job taking care of their charges. The scientists had to do things for themselves, something few had any experience with.[4]

Colonel Putt recalled that when he was handed the job of "mothering" the German scientists, "I put a German-born chap in charge of the camp, an army captain who had been in army intelligence during the war, by the name of Walter Boesch. Walter just loved this cloak-and-dagger and spy work, and he could understand how they thought because he was one of them, so to speak."⁵ Boesch promptly went to work to resolve the mess Colonel Putt handed him. First, Walter thought the Germans had been "spoiled by the civilian couple, who had, out of kindness and generosity, done far more for the men than it had been intended they should."⁶ Boesch turned to a source of free manpower he was familiar with—German POWs. There weren't any at Wright Field, but he quickly fired off a memo to the AC/AS Intelligence in Washington to get the ball rolling. Then he followed up and went to Washington personally to make his case. Before long his request elevated to the general officer level, and the CPMB of the War Department was requested in a formal memorandum to provide thirty-five German prisoners of war to act as translators and cooks for the German scientists. "Technical translators are very necessary to the success of the OVERCAST project and are extremely difficult to obtain through Army and civil service channels. The cooks are desired in order to reduce the expense of feeding the scientists. It is desired that the Provost Marshall General relax the restrictions ordinarily imposed on PW so that these particular PW may be housed in the same area as the German scientists on Wright Field, rather than in the usual PW stockade, with double barbed wire fence. It is planned to quarter some American EM in the same area who will act as guards and escorts." The memorandum to the CPMB concluded that "Captain Boesch would like to interview the German PW . . . at their present places of confinement before they are sent to Wright Field.⁷

General Weckerling at the War Department replied gruffly, "It is not considered advisable from a security standpoint to permit selection of German prisoners at random from PW camps for the purposes outlined in your undated note. Furthermore, should it become necessary to make any such selections, this should be done by trained interrogators from the CPM Branch only." Clearly, Weckerling wasn't going to have

Boesch mucking around in his preserve. But after that mild rap on the fingers, the general continued in a more conciliatory note, "There are a limited number of PWs who have proven themselves anti-Nazi and cooperative still under control of CPM Branch. It is believed that a sufficient number can be chosen from this list to provide cooks and orderlies." As for the translators, the general had little faith in the skills of German prisoners and instead suggested "loan[ing] you on temporary duty a number of these enlisted translators to assist you in your present problem. . . . If the above meets with your approval, every effort will be made to furnish you with as much help as possible and with minimum delay."[8] Captain Walter Boesch's problems were resolved.

Complaints and protests by the German scientists ceased abruptly when German prisoners of war arrived to act as cooks, waiters, orderlies, and firemen. A POW subcamp was established at Wright Field, "making it possible to restore the rapidly declining morale" among the scientists. "A school bus and driver were assigned to the NYA Area to transport the scientists to and from the offices of the Foreign Exploitation Section, and a time schedule for meals was established. Thus, the pattern of daily routine again became fairly well formulated."[9] The one problem Boesch had yet to resolve was how to reimburse the officers' club. Boesch solved that problem by having the scientists, who continued to increase in number, pay $40 each into a "mess fund" out of their $180 monthly per diem allowance, which was established contractually at six dollars per day. Boesch used the money to repay the club debt in installments and to pay for services still provided by the officers' club laundry, which continued to wash bed linens and towels for the *Wissenschaftler*. As for personal laundry, Boesch contracted with a Dayton commercial laundry for a weekly pickup and delivery, again paid for out of the mess fund.

The POWs worked out very well, and as the scientist population increased, more and more German prisoners of war were provided by the CPMB, until by spring 1946 there were several hundred POWs at

Wright Field. These POWs lived in a regular barracks-type environment and had access to the post exchange and the movie theater as long as they were accompanied by an American officer. Other than Captain Boesch, there were no sticklers for authority around, and life went on in an uncomplicated way for the POWs and the scientists. The prisoners not only tended to the German scientific community, but were also used to make up for shortages of maintenance personnel at Wright Field. The "gravy train" came to a halt when the secretary of war ordered that all German POWs would be released by June 30, 1946. "Translators, interpreters, cooks, orderlies, firemen and laborers," it is recorded, "left Wright Field one day during the first week of April, on a special train bound for . . . Columbus, Ohio."[10]

The transition proved a little rocky, until twenty American enlisted men were assigned to the NYA area and billeted there with the *Wissenschaftler*. "They quickly restored operations to normal, and maintained a degree of service that was satisfactory to exploitation administrators and scientists alike. The scientists in particular were relieved when they could once again have meals in their own mess hall." The work hours for the enlisted personnel were longer than the generally accepted tour of duty. "To compensate them in some measure for these extra hours and also to maintain morale, they received a reasonable cash payment from NYA funds each month. Rent collections from the increased number of resident scientists reduced the balance due the Officers' Club to a point where one third of the total collected could be set aside for the enlisted men, to be divided equally among them. From that point on, no major changes were required in the NYA Area 'housekeeping' arrangements until a complete rearrangement of living quarters was necessitated in December 1946 when some of the scientists' dependents began to arrive at Wright Field."[11]

The housekeeping and quality-of-life aspects of Project Overcast as implemented at Wright Field in 1945 and 1946 were at best informal and unconventional, at worst illegal, but clearly not worthy of prosecution.

Whoever heard of using officers' club funds to finance a government operation, or paying soldiers from a communal "kitty" for extra hours worked? Such practices obviously wouldn't work in today's overly legalistic environment, but they worked then and not to anyone's detriment. The Overcast program at Wright Field, in spite of its muddled start, worked out quite well for everyone—for the American GIs who supported the German scientists, for the scientists themselves, and for the Army Air Forces and the United States of America.

Until December 1946, dependents of German scientists were housed in the Project Overcast housing area at Landshut, Bavaria. Project Overcast contracts for the German scientists were of six months' duration and for a total period not to exceed twenty-four months. Under the short-term Overcast contract no families were permitted to come to the United States, and all payments for the scientists' services were made in reichsmark, payable only to their dependents or a bank in Germany. The only funds the men had access to was the six-dollar-per-day per diem paid to cover personal expenses. By winter of 1945–1946 about 103 families, 320 persons, resided in the Project Overcast housing area in Landshut. The families were there for one reason only—they were waiting to be reunited with their husbands and fathers. The family separation issue was without a doubt the greatest single factor contributing to low morale among the scientists at Wright Field. Contact between families and scientists was initially nonexistent. Neither family members nor husband and father knew what was happening to the other. There was no mail service, even though postal regulations were issued by USFET in October 1945 providing for mail service between the United States and Germany. The USFET procedures were nullified by security instructions from War Department Intelligence, G-2. "Communication with persons in the United States other than those directly concerned with their exploitation is not authorized," stated the G-2 directive. "Communication with persons outside the

United States will conform to such regulations as apply to enemy aliens." While the "contract said 'yes'; security regulations said 'no.' "[12]

Putt's operation at Wright Field was faced with an ever more serious morale problem which rapidly threatened the entire Overcast project. The situation got bad enough that Putt decided to send one of his men to Europe to determine what was happening with the families at Landshut. Colonel McCoy, who during the war had worked at USSTAF Headquarters (Rear) in London, reported after his return from Landshut that "all of their families were exceptionally well taken care of." A rumor making the rounds among the scientists at Wright Field was that Germans working for the British at Völkenrode received much better treatment and compensation than they did. Reported Colonel McCoy, "Contrary to information given by the Germans at Wright Field, it is reported that the Germans remaining at Völkenrode are very unhappy. They have a bare subsistence. The British . . . pay for the scientists at Völkenrode only averages about one fifth as much as the U.S. pay of the Wright Field families. . . . In addition they only get the 1,100 calorie per day food issued compared to the 2,300 calorie diet guaranteed by our contract. The situation is extremely bad for the Germans who had been bombed out of their houses in Braunschweig, because the British are doing absolutely nothing to help them out."[13]

This firsthand information from Colonel McCoy alleviated many of the concerns of the Wright Field scientists, and a certain amount of Schadenfreude, gloating, occurred about their colleagues who chose to work for the British. An arrangement was also worked out with WDGS Intelligence allowing for doubly censored letters to be delivered between scientists and their families. It still took six weeks for a letter to reach its intended recipient. Packages could not be sent by the scientists until June 1946, and then only if the families lived in the American zone of occupation. A request for an exception to allow the scientists to "send small Christmas packages to their families" was denied. All this occurred in spite of the fact that general mail service between Germany and the United States reopened on April 1, 1946.

The Overcast project continued to flounder in other ways as well, as more and more scientists arrived at Wright Field. The salaries contractually agreed to were received by families in Landshut months late. The delays occurred because the hours worked by the scientists had to be certified, and then the time sheets had to be forwarded for processing. Weeks passed as payment vouchers made their way through the red tape. Family separation, pay problems, and lack of mail service were not the only issues leading to low morale among the scientists; a lack of meaningful employment was also a contributing factor. They wanted to work. After all, they were scientists, the cream of the crop, the very best Germany had produced. For a number of reasons, the staff at the Wright Field engineering laboratories could not decide how best to use their intellectual war booty. Captain Boesch had met with the laboratory chiefs as early as July 1945 to work out a first approach for utilization. He suggested having a seminar program in which the scientists would provide lectures in their areas of expertise; these would be transcribed by bilingual stenographers and be followed by round-table discussions leading to laboratory visits. Boesch, echoing his boss's sentiments, also suggested "that the best results were obtained by treating these people decently and being courteous to them. He also found that these people are much happier if they are kept busy and not left just sitting around."[14]

"It was somewhat amazing and embarrassing too," Colonel Putt recalled, "because all they wanted was an opportunity to work. . . . They asked for drafting machines and drawing boards to put into their living quarters so they could work at night. They were just that glad to have something to do."[15] But the scientists would have to wait; they were kept busy with make-work projects such as writing their professional histories, preparing reports on their past work, and putting down their desires regarding what they would like to work on. "Review of these gave evidence of the high-caliber work that could be anticipated, and also confirmed previous estimates of the value to Wright Field's research and development program that could be realized through exploitation."[16] Boesch's seminar program quickly ran into trouble. There were not enough bilingual stenographers or translators around, and few wanted to relocate from New York to Dayton, Ohio. Security instructions began to loom large as a problem area as well—how to guarantee custody of the scientists at Wright Field. Who could participate in the proposed seminars? Could contractors be included? Putt, finally tiring of the bureaucratic nonsense, proposed the establishment of a board of technically qualified officers from the engineering laboratories to review work projects and prioritize them. To show how serious he was about finding a solution, every member of the new board was a full colonel.

"Although more than enough work projects were requested by Engineering Division laboratories to fully utilize the scientists' services, Wright Field was not equipped with adequate laboratory facilities to enable its scientists to complete their work, and use of the facilities existing in private and institutional research organizations was prohibited. It was indeed embarrassing that one of the scientists, for example, was forced by these circumstances to rig up his own laboratory apparatus—highly sensitive and fragile measuring instruments and reflectors—in the corner of a warehouse, devising mounting platforms from empty cartons and crates."[17] The man referred to was Dr. Zobel, whose breakthrough scientific processes made airflow in supersonic wind tunnels visible and photographable.

Although Wright Field senior managers were highly supportive of Project Overcast, cooperation at lower levels was less than enthusiastic. There appeared to be misunderstandings about the program, including isolated instances of "political convictions so strong as to result in open manifestations of animosity toward the German scientists and the exploitation program as a whole." More important, inertia at higher echelons in Washington was a serious threat to the survival of the program. The air inspector at Headquarters ATSC noted in a January

1946 report: "There has been no definite policy issued by Washington or this Headquarters regarding the exact extent and procedure to be followed in handling this project. Without knowledge of what authority and responsibility the using agencies were expected to assume, it was impossible to determine what should be done, or if what was being done by necessity met with approval."

Putt had enough. He wanted the program to succeed. He had invested too much of himself into the Overcast project to watch it die at his feet. First, he had the program explained to the rank and file, listing the German scientists' names and their experience and scientific qualifications. Second, he went to the Chief, Air Staff Research and Development, and pointed out in his usual direct manner that an opportunity was being wasted "for advancement in research in the field of solid fuel rockets." The opportunity "was being seriously hampered, if not entirely wasted," Putt pointedly asserted, "because scientists could not be exploited in such a manner as to obtain the highly valuable information that they were known to possess." Slowly things began to move off dead center. Wright Field got the green light to go ahead with its proposed seminar program, including industrial interviews, the latter shaken loose by General Curtis E. LeMay, who inquired of Air Staff Intelligence what action they had taken on the matter. None, of course. Suddenly the Pentagon action officers got cold feet, knowing that General LeMay was a comer, and found the incentive to move out smartly.

"The first industrial interview took place in March 1946 with representatives of the Airplane Division of Curtiss-Wright Corporation. . . . By mid-July 1946, over eighty conferences had been held by the German scientists with representatives of research organizations and industry. . . . Praise and enthusiasm were expressed by aircraft manufacturers, research laboratories, and universities, and this interest was further confirmed by requests from at least twelve organizations that they be given the earliest possible opportunity to engage the services of certain of the scientists." It was the dawn of things to come, when the scientists would actually become employees of American corporations. That was not something envisioned by the drafters of Project Overcast, but American business nearly always got what it wanted. "Requests from industrial agencies for at least temporary assignment of individual scientists to their organizations became more frequent and more urgent."

Restrictions and security measures at Wright Field became less and less intrusive for the scientists as well. They were not treated as POWs but rather, as stated in "Instructions to German Scientists," they were "in the category of employees of the U.S.A. and will therefore be accorded corresponding courtesies and privileges." For purposes of identification each scientist was "photographed, fingerprinted, and issued a regulation Wright Field pass." They were allowed to attend the movie theater on post, to visit the post exchange (PX) and purchase any items except uniform articles, and to move around freely within the boundaries of Wright Field. Additionally, Saturday shopping tours to Dayton were arranged, as well as visits to the YMCA. In August 1946 scientists were permitted "to visit neighboring localities unescorted provided the scientist does not remain away from the station overnight and is English speaking or accompanied by an English speaking scientist." Eventually, all that was required of them was to sign in and out when leaving the NYA area and record their intended destinations.[18]

The marked improvement in the quality and type of work the scientists were allowed to participate in was a definite morale lifter. Increased freedom of movement was also appreciated, yet the family issue remained. There was one other matter which begged resolution, and it was complex and drove at the heart of Project Overcast itself—the men at the NYA camp were no longer willing to sign the short-term employment contract. They were no longer willing to endure indefinite family separation, and they wanted to know their immigration status. Whether they had the opportunity to become American citizens or not became a frequently asked question. By late 1946, most Overcast contracts were expiring. Either the program would have to undergo a major facelift or a mass exodus of scientists to Germany was in the offing. "Most of the scientists had proved their potential value to United States research and development, and it was desirable to retain their services."[19]

Words written in late 1945 by Colonel Putt to Major General Elwood R. Quesada, then serving on the air staff in Washington, in a "Dear Pete" letter had an eery echo a year later: "It is the feeling of General Knerr and myself," Putt wrote Quesada, "that unless there is some change in the program . . . it will be doomed to failure and we may as well stop now before we get anymore people over from Germany. . . . I think you will agree that the thing has been badly managed and since we are competing with the British and Russians for the voluntary services of these people, we are now in a very poor bargaining position."[20] It seemed that since October 1945 conditions had not progressed significantly beyond those of a year earlier. What got things moving in a new direction was a British plan to use German scientists on military as well as civilian projects with a view toward allowing them to settle in Britain and obtain citizenship. The JCS ordered the implementation of a plan paralleling the British plan in April 1946; by that time there were 155 German scientists in the United States. The Joint Intelligence Objectives Committee (JIOC), consisting of representatives of the War, Navy, State, and Commerce Departments and other interested agencies, was reconstituted, and it was "anticipated that entry into the United States would soon be made possible for scientists whose entry with their families would be in the interest of national security." The JIOC requested lists of names from using agencies and established procedures for entry into the United States, only to see its efforts dashed to the ground by its own State Department representative, who suddenly surfaced major security problems—not then, but "fifteen years hence." With State's position it became obvious to everyone that Project Overcast was doomed. A totally new approach needed to be devised to save the program, and it had to be done with some alacrity. "Delay by the

United States in consummating contracts, furthermore, had resulted in the acceptance by many scientists of reputedly liberal contracts offered by the French and Russians. . . . Nine months of inactivity, due to the prohibition against continuing their previous studies, had engendered extreme unrest among the scientific group, and many of them had filtered into other zones of Germany to seek employment." Under continuing pressure from agencies using German scientists and with the full support of the secretary of war, the War Department general staff finally moved out on its own and came up with a new plan. Project Paperclip was to take the place of Project Overcast. Paperclip was approved by the secretary of war on July 31, 1946, and promptly forwarded to the State-War-Navy Coordinating Committee (SWNCC). Surprisingly, State went along with the Paperclip plan and submitted it to the president for approval. On September 3, 1946, President Truman by executive order approved Project Paperclip for implementation.[21]

The War Department public relations division rather quickly emerged with a press release announcing "More German and Austrian Scientists to Aid Army-Navy Research Program." The carefully worded release trumpeted, "It is planned within the next several months to bring to the United States additional volunteer Austro-German specialists to join the more than 200 brought over since the end of the war in Europe. . . . It is emphasized that those found to be active Nazis, war criminals or suspected war criminals are arbitrarily eliminated from the entire program. . . . Upon completion of their work for the Army and the Navy they will be made available to American industry through auspices of the Department of Commerce after a further thorough screening and investigation to determine their eligibility for status under immigration laws."[22] Although the press release did not reveal the project's code word, which was classified, in its November 11 issue the magazine *Newsweek* reported, "Operation Paperclip is the new name given the program under which the U.S. Army and Navy are quietly recruiting German scientific brainpower."[23] The War Department got out ahead of speculation by announcing on November 12, 1946, that Wright Field in Dayton, Ohio, and Fort Bliss in El Paso, Texas, would make "available to press, radio and pictorial services" German scientists who signed contracts to work in the United States. "Interviews and photographs will be permitted."[24] To make the matter more palatable to the public, the Army public relations staff spoke of Austro-German specialists, although among the hundreds of scientists brought to the United States there were only sixteen Austrians.

The response by press and radio was positive. The *Dayton Daily News* on Wednesday, December 4, 1946, featured interviews with and pictures of Dr. Alexander Lippisch, the designer of the Messerschmitt Me-163 rocket fighter and the Lippisch glider and a "leading authority on flying wings, transonic and supersonic aircraft design"; Dr. Rudolph Hermann, "specialist in supersonic wind tunnels"; Dr. Theodor W. Zobel, "former chief of the high speed aerodynamic section at Brunswick"; Fritz Doblhoff, "inventor and designer of the Doblhoff jet-propelled helicopter in Vienna"; Dr. Rudolph Ammann, "designer of the BMW-801 aircraft engine used in the Focke-Wulf 190 fighter"; Dr. Heinz Schmitt, "largely responsible for the development of the Junkers 004 jet engines used in the Messerschmitt-262"; and Dr. Helmut Heinrich, "specialist in ribbon parachute research at the Graf Zeppelin Institute near Stuttgart."[25]

Under the new Project Paperclip plan, authority was provided to bring dependents of scientists to the United States, increase the scientists' maximum annual salary to ten thousand dollars, raise the total number of scientists allowed entry into the country from 350 to 1,000, and offer the scientists a long-term employment contract. "Although a contract for long-range employment was drafted in October, it was not in final form and approved as legally and fiscally acceptable until January 1947."[26] The scientists at Wright Field were elated and promptly signed the new contract when it was offered. It was Article 20—Visa—which settled the morale issue, reading, "Upon signature of this contract and provided the personal conduct and political background of Contractor justify such steps, the Government will make immediate efforts to obtain an immigration visa for the Contractor and his dependents."[27] The families could be reunited, and, most important, there was an indication that in time they would have the opportunity to become American citizens.

The commanding general at the Air Materiel Command (renamed AMC from ATSC in March 1946) at Wright Field, Lieutenant General Nathan F. Twining, who replaced General Knerr, was informed on November 1, 1946, that "In conformity with Section II, paragraph 16b of the contract now in force, this headquarters has been informed by the Director of Intelligence, WDGS, Exploitation Branch, that the families of the following scientists have been alerted for evacuation to the United States during the last week of November 1946: Dr. Gerhard Braun, Dr. Theodor Zobel, Dr. Rudolf Edse, Mr. Albert Patin, Mr. Hans Rister, Mr. Otto Bock. It is requested that each of the above named scientists be provided with a copy of this communication."[28] The families of the first six scientists arrived in New York in early December 1946. In the NYA area of Wright Field, refurbished housing was ready and waiting. Within days the six families were reunited. It was the beginning of a new and enduring relationship between the men of science of a former enemy and their Wright Field mentors and employers.

The *Dayton Daily News* reported on December 12, 1946, "The Dayton Daily News learned Thursday through sources other than the Army that 'several' families of German scientists now stationed at Wright Field have arrived in Dayton and are currently being quartered in housing units in the former National Youth Administration project at the field. The News also learned that the families of other German scientists are expected to arrive soon and that renovation of several buildings in the NYA Area is now being carried out to provide further housing facilities."[29] With the arrival of spring, Wright Field personnel struggled with the completion of "ponderous case histories required by the State Department for consideration of visa clearance, and at that time no prediction could be made of the future trend that immigration matters might follow, or of the length of time that might elapse before issuance of visas would be an accomplished fact."[30] As a result, the transfer of German scientists from military to civil employment was a dead issue "until such time as they might be granted immigration visas." No visas, no civil employment. The secretary of war again inserted himself, reminding all parties that "The value of this presidentially approved program to the nation as well as to the naval and military services warrants full support of the War Department. . . . I desire that all War Department agencies fully and expeditiously implement all pertinent phases of this project which fall within their jurisdiction."[31]

Frustration with the halting progress of anything related to Project Paperclip was evident at every level of government, both military and civilian. Rules and contracts might change, but in the end people made things happen or not, and many still harbored resentment, if not outright opposition, toward anything German. On top of that, a small anti-German-scientist movement emerged that spring. The *Dayton Daily News* reported on March 24, 1947, that "The Federation of American Scientists urged today that the German scientists brought to this country for work on military research projects be denied jobs in private industry or education. Their return to Germany 'as soon as possible' also was suggested in a letter to President Truman."[32] What finally broke the logjam was a young P-38 fighter pilot, Captain Lloyd Wenzel, a Texan of German heritage and an ETO combat veteran. Wenzel didn't know about bureaucracy, politics, and hate. He had a job to do, and nothing was going to stop this bright-eyed young Texan from doing just that. Wenzel had prevailed in the hostile skies over Europe, and he had no intention of failing at a job where no one was even shooting at him.

HOW CAPTAIN WENZEL MADE AMERICAN CITIZENS OUT OF ENEMY ALIENS

The first four German scientists destined for Wright Field—Doctors Braun, Edse, Zobel, and Nöggerath—had accompanied Karl Baur in September 1945 on his flight via the Azores to the United States. Dr. Rister and Mr. Bock, assistants to Dr. Zobel, joined them two days later. The six men were promised that their families would soon follow and that their short-term contracts would be changed to a long-term basis. But things dragged on. Their morale hit rock bottom. First, there were no quarters at Wright Field for the families; then a hassle developed over the term "dependent"—who was and who wasn't. By the time all of these time-consuming issues were debated and resolved to everyone's grudging satisfaction, the contracts of the six scientists at Wright Field were running out and temporary extensions had to be negotiated. When Baur and Sebald returned to Fort Strong, in late December, things looked bleak for the six men at Wright Field. Karl Baur recalled, "Most of the scientists envied us for going home. Dr. Zobel also had in mind to cancel his contract—which was due for renewal on 18 December—in case he would not be allowed to do any productive work. However, I recommended to him it might be better for him to sit it out a while longer."[1]

Another year passed before Dr. Zobel's wife and two children were able to join him at Wright Field. Mrs. Zobel traveled on November 22, 1946, by train with her two children from Landshut to Bremerhaven, the American enclave in the British zone of occupation. There, she and her children boarded the USNS *General Henry Gibbins*, one of several Liberty ships plying the North Atlantic between the United States and Germany. Frau Zobel *und Kinder* were accompanied by Frau Braun and her two children and by Frau Patin, the wife of the industrialist and inventor Albert Patin, whose autopilots were sought in May 1945 by Bill Jack, of Jack & Heintz. The families arrived in New York on December 4, having experienced en route an American Thanksgiving with turkey, cranberry sauce, sweet potatoes, and all the trimmings. In New York, they were met by Captain Lloyd Wenzel, who escorted them on their final leg of travel by train to Dayton, Ohio.[2]

By March 1947 a total of "338 German scientists were in the United States under military exploitation," with 149 arriving at Wright Field and at the Army Air Forces School of Aviation Medicine in San Antonio, Texas. All of the AAF exploitees were under the control of Air Materiel Command, under General Putt's supervision. Conditions had improved by that time to a point where some of the scientists worked on military projects away from Wright Field in industries with contracts with the War and Navy Departments. Families of fifty-one scientists had arrived in the United States, living in either military or civilian housing procured by the War or Navy Departments. At Wright Field the families were quartered in renovated barracks in the segregated NYA area—safely hidden away from the outside world.[3]

It wasn't yet smooth sailing. Many in the American Jewish community were not thrilled about the presence of the German scientists, nor were some of America's scientists. An influx of the former enemy's "brain trust" could only mean more competition in an already tight job market. On March 24, 1947, the *Dayton Daily News* reported that the executive secretary of the Federation of American Scientists wanted nothing to do with German scientists in this country, saying that "Any favor extended to such individuals even for military reasons represents an affront to the people of all countries who so recently fought beside us, to the refugees whose lives were shattered by Nazism, to our unfortunate scientific colleagues of formerly occupied lands, and to all of those others who suffered under the yoke these men helped to forge."[4] The nascent opposition never organized into a political force, the drum America marches to, and the protests vanished quickly.

As for political Washington, it was in the midst of transitioning the nation from a war-based economy to a civilian economy. World War II was rapidly slipping into the past, and Project Paperclip was of little interest to most, except for a few men who understood the changing world they lived in. These men felt that there was little time to prepare for a possible future conflict that had the potential to be far more dangerous than Hitler's unsophisticated mass armies had ever been. German scientists played a major role in the calculations of men such as the young and relatively unknown political analyst Paul Nitze. Bringing American science up to where it should have been all along was fundamental to the calculus of survival. Captain Lloyd Wenzel, a P-38 fighter pilot, suddenly found himself deeply involved in a program no one wanted to explain when he was first assigned to it—he was told that he didn't have the necessary security clearance. It was this company grade officer without the necessary security clearance, a combat flyer, not a politician, who turned the final corner for Project Paperclip. Perhaps what Captain Wenzel had going for him was that he was young and unbiased, had experienced war, and, not least, was a Texan, raised in a land where one could stretch one's arms without touching another person, and where earth and sky merged on a distant and untrammeled horizon.

"I was born in June 1922, in Seguin, Texas, a small town thirty miles east of San Antonio. Seguin, named after Juan Seguin, a Mexican who sided with the Texans against General Antonio López de Santa Anna, sits on the line where the black soil of the north meets the sand of the south. Germans who settled this area picked the black soil for their farms to grow cotton. Seguin had a big German community when I was a boy. Then you were either a German, or you were a 'raggedy,' that's what they called non-Germans. The Germans were very neat and kept their barns and houses painted. Other places, to them at least, looked raggedy compared to their own. My paternal grandmother was six years old when her family emigrated from Germany, shortly after Texas broke away from Mexico. They settled in the little town of Waldeck, about sixty miles from Austin. The local authorities were eager for farmers to settle the land. My grandmother's father was made a very attractive land offer, bought a farm near Waldeck and started to grow cotton. When my grandmother was still in her teens she married. Soon after her wedding, her fellow rode off to fight in the Civil War. The guy had one of his legs shot off and died on the way home.

"My paternal grandfather too came from Germany, but as an indentured servant. A Texas farmer paid his way over and he had to work for the man for three years to pay him back. That man's farm happened to be right next door to the farm of the young widow whose husband lost a leg in the war and died. The two married and had five sons. My uncle Albert, as the oldest, inherited the farm; Uncle Gustav and Uncle Otto became carpenters; Uncle Adolf became a blacksmith. My dad, Robert, the youngest, wanted to go to college to become a schoolteacher. When he told the old man about his plans, his father locked him in the corncrib and told him to shuck corn until he got that foolishness out of his head. My dad had severe hay fever and nearly died shucking corn. That night my grandmother dragged him out of the crib and saved his life. The old man finally relented, even letting my father ride his horse to school. Dad never did get a college degree, but he got enough college to teach school in Seguin for fifty years. Actually, he retired by the time World War II came along and the school board called on him and said, 'Robert, you've got to teach again.'

"My mother was half German, half English. Her parents too were farmers. I have a sister eleven years older than I, she taught me to speak German. Randolph Field was about fifteen miles from Seguin and my dad and I would ride out there occasionally and look at the airplanes. When they officially opened the field, General Pershing came down from Washington for the occasion. I went over to watch the ceremony. It was all very exciting for a young lad. Once an airplane made a forced landing on my grandfather's farm and we got to look at that broken-up plane. My grandmother made refreshments for the pilots until someone came to pick them up. I felt awed by the flyers. Maybe some day I could be a flyer, I thought. My best friend and I frequently rode our bicycles to Randolph Field, right into the hangar, and looked at the airplanes and kicked the tires. There were no fences or guard posts. A couple of times I sat in the lap of a sergeant when he ran up the engine. It was a BT-8, a single-engine trainer. Soon I was building model airplanes, and in the Boy Scouts I went after the aviation merit badge. I sat around for hours with my friends talking flying. Airplanes became and remained an exciting part of my life.

"I spoke German like nearly everybody else. As a boy you couldn't work in a grocery or drygoods store in Seguin if you couldn't speak German, there were just too many people who only spoke German. Willie and Lena Voss were my folks' best friends. They were on the school board. Willie passed away while I was away in the war. When I came home in June 1945, my father and I went to see Mrs. Voss. My German was so rusty, I spoke in English to her. When we left, my dad said to me, 'What's the matter with you, Lloyd? Don't you have any

A Severski BT-8 with a Pratt & Whitney engine, possibly one of the airplanes young Lloyd Wenzel admired at Randolph Field in Texas, June 1936. (RW)

manners? Speaking English to that old lady and putting that burden on her. You should have spoken German.'

"I attended Texas Lutheran College in Seguin with the intent of getting enough credits so I could apply for aviation cadets. You had to have two years of college to get into the program. When the war came, my mother was intent on not letting me go, but when I turned twenty in June of forty-two I applied anyway. On August 13 I went to take my test at Fort Sam Houston in San Antonio. I passed the written, but flunked the physical. I had an undescended testicle. 'If you don't have that corrected it can become malignant,' the doctor said. I must have looked so disappointed that he said to me, 'You really want to fly, don't you?' I said, Yeah. I've always wanted to fly. 'Listen, boy,' said the doctor, 'I'll put your file up here,' and he stuffed my folder among some books on a shelf above his head. 'You remember where it is, because I will examine thousands before you get back. Have the thing removed and if you can get back here in two weeks I'll continue to process you. Otherwise, you'll have to start all over again.' I phoned my doctor at home from the major's office and set up surgery for the next morning and had the damn thing taken out. After I could walk again my friends accompanied me to Fort Sam Houston and carried me up the stairs to the doctor's office so I could get sworn in. Because they cut me open in the groin I wasn't supposed to walk up stairs yet and had to be carried up. I used to tell people that it cost me my right ball and sixty-five dollars to join the Air Corps. My fellow cadets gave me the nickname 'Stud.'

"It wasn't until February 1943 that I received a pilot training class assignment, 43K. I thought I would be going to a cadet training center in San Antonio, but they threw me instead on a train and sent me to Santa Ana in California. I wanted to be a B-17 pilot because my scoutmaster flew B-17s. He was highly decorated and came home on military leave from the Pacific before I went off to California. I listened to his war stories and wanted to be just like him. But once I got to California I saw the P-38 fighter and that changed everything for me. The P-38s would come in low, dive toward the end of the runway and then peel up and over, doing a complete vertical 360-degree turn, and land. In the early P-38s they had the coolers for the turbochargers in the leading edges of the wings, and there were two little square holes near the tip of each wing allowing the air to escape. In the high humidity of California those P-38s would pull two big streamers off each wingtip as they went up and over and came in to land. I decided, to hell with the B-17, I want to be a P-38 pilot.

"In flight training I first flew the PT-17, a beautiful Boeing biplane, and then the BT-13, known as the vibrator for all the noises it made. Next came the AT-9, a twin-engine high-performance aircraft, and then the RP-322. The RP-322 was a twin-engine P-38 ordered by the Brits before the start of Lend-Lease in early 1941. Once Lend-Lease came into effect the Brits canceled their order and those airplanes were converted to American specifications and configured as trainers.

I got about ten hours in that airplane. After I was awarded my pilot wings I was assigned to a P-38 RTU in California. I found the airplane to be a high-performance beast and if you didn't pay attention it would kill you quicker then the Germans could. I was lucky, the training outfit I went to had a bunch of North African campaign veterans from the 82nd Fighter Group, guys who had combat experience flying the airplane in North Africa against Rommel's Afrika Korps. I remember one of them, Captain Albert Wolfmueller, from Fredericksburg, Texas, another German. He was strafing and didn't see some high-tension lines. As he pulled up, a line caught his tail and flipped him over on his back at about ten feet off the ground. He controlled that airplane and recovered. Quite a feat. Albert was the son of the owner of the Wolfmueller bakery in Fredericksburg.

"We finished training in March 1944 and were outfitted for deployment to the Pacific. Everything was hush-hush. When we arrived in San Francisco they had us turn in all that Pacific stuff and we drew European stuff instead. We got on a train to New York and crossed the Atlantic on the liner *Mauritania* in five days. There were only three P-38 groups in England—the 474th, the 370th, and the 367th. I was assigned to the 474th Fighter Group. We were in the IX Tactical Air Command, IX TAC, of the 9th Air Force, commanded by Lieutenant General Hoyt S. Vandenberg. Major General Elwood R. Quesada commanded the IX TAC. All P-38 groups were slated to convert to P-51s or P-47s. Because of its longer range they wanted the P-38s in the Pacific. My group petitioned General Spaatz to let us keep on flying the P-38. Spaatz approved our request. We were the only group to fly P-38s out of England onto bases in Germany.

"November of forty-four was colder than hell. I had fifty-two missions by then. We were in Florennes, Belgium, and experienced heavy losses. On one mission we lost eight out of twelve aircraft. Most of our losses were due to antiaircraft fire. By D-day, the Luftwaffe was pretty much beaten down, but the ground fire was fierce. The 88mm

P-38 fighter pilots, December 1944, Belgium. L to R: Lieutenant Rankin (the Kid), Lieutenant Holt (the Holt), Lieutenant Wenzel (the Stud). Holt and Rankin were killed in action soon after this picture was taken. (LW)

radar-directed gun was a mean gun and could shoot you at thirty thousand feet. My squadron, the 428th, was authorized fifty-five pilots and twenty-five airplanes. We lost twenty-eight pilots in less than a year. We sustained the heaviest losses in the 474th Fighter Group. The 430th squadron had the least; their commander had combat experience in North Africa and flew a little less aggressively than we did. Near the end of the war it was announced that a fighter tour in the IX TAC was seventy missions. We moved to Euskirchen, then to Langensalza— deep in what would become the Soviet zone of occupation. After I flew my seventieth mission my group commander wanted to see me. I trotted into his office and he said, 'You've got five months in grade, Wenzel. In a month I can promote you to captain, if you stick around, that is.' I said, No sir. I want to go home. 'No,' he said, 'I won't let you go home. You stay.' Well, if I stay I want to fly. He looked at me, shook his head, and said, 'Wenzel, you are through flying combat. You can run an orientation for our replacements and teach them formation flying and tactics, but your combat flying days are over.' I was kind of glad he said that. I didn't want to fly any more combat. I was sick of it.

"Once I got back to the States, in June 1945, I had orders to go to the Pacific. Two days before I was to ship out for San Francisco they dropped the atomic bomb. I was at home on leave and right near Fort Sam Houston. I reported to Fort Sam and they told me, 'Things have changed. If you want to get out you can, but you have to decide right now.' So I phoned my wife; we had married the day I got my pilot wings at Williams Field, Arizona, in 1944. We talked and agreed for me to stay in. I was ordered to Luke Field near Phoenix. All of my old friends were there. At Luke there was nothing to do but hang around. For reasons unknown to me I was selected to go to the Air Technical Service Command at McClellan Field in Sacramento overhauling B-26 Marauders. On July 29, 1946, I received orders issued by the Sacramento Air Materiel Area directing me to report at once to 'Wright Field, Dayton, Ohio, for duty with Intelligence (T-2).'[5]

"I asked, what is Intelligence? Nobody knew. Personnel phoned Wright Field, and nobody had an answer. At that time Project Overcast, renamed Project Paperclip on September 3, was pretty well classified and no one who knew anything about it talked. So I got to Wright Field before I knew what I was going to do. I checked in with First Lieutenant Paul Robiczek. Robiczek spoke excellent German and clued me in about my job in Intelligence. Project Overcast, Robiczek said to me, was a very hush-hush operation. My place of work was a camp built in the thirties by the National Youth Administration, referred to in short as the NYA area. The camp was self-contained and included barracks, recreational facilities, and mess halls. The facility was fenced and located in an isolated part of the field. That was where the German Project Overcast scientists lived. Robiczek, a bachelor, chose to live there as well. Also, a strange Mr. Lynch lived with the Germans in the NYA area. Albert Lynch was a civilian. Nobody seemed

to have requisitioned him nor knew exactly where he came from.
[Lynch was actually assigned to the Analysis Division of Technical
Intelligence, T-2, and worked for Colonel Putt, serving as Putt's eyes
and ears, but, of course, Lloyd Wenzel couldn't have known that.]
Mr. Lynch spoke perfect German and we speculated that he must
have been from counterintelligence or something like that. Whenever
I went to see Mr. Lynch he'd insist that I join him in a vermouth
mit Zitrone. Robiczek and Lynch spent all their time with the German
scientists, twenty-four hours a day, seven days a week.

"Since I was married, I lived in town. My office was in the administration building in the NYA compound. Eventually we ended up with
a little short of two hundred *Wissenschaftler*, not quite half of them at
Wright Field; some worked in private industry, others at the school
of aviation medicine in San Antonio. Among the first ones that came
was Doktor Ingenieur Habilitatus Rudolph Hermann and his group
of wind tunnel experts from Peenemünde. Dr. Hermann ran the wind
tunnel tests for the V-2 for Dr. Wernher von Braun, who was working
with his group of missile experts at Fort Bliss, Texas. We had to treat
them all as enemy aliens, which meant that there had to be restrictions. We put a sentry at the gate of the NYA area, not to keep the
Germans in, but to keep people out. I served as administrative officer
for the scientists and eventually took over the entire camp operation.

"Over the four years that I was to spend at Wright Field on Projects
Overcast and Paperclip, I did just about everything that had to do
with the German *Wissenschaftler* under Air Force control. I picked up
their families at the port of New York when they began arriving and
escorted them to Wright Field. I met newly arrived scientists, usually
at Rome Field in New York State, and shepherded them and their baggage
to Wright Field. I even became their paymaster in June 1947, being designated a class A agent finance officer for purposes of making periodic
payments to them. In those days we paid people in cash, and at times
I carried as much as fifteen thousand dollars around with me—quite

a considerable sum of money in 1947.[6] Many times I traveled to Rome Field or Mitchell Field on Long Island, both in New York State, to pick up laboratory equipment for use by our scientists. In 1947, when Captain Barnett left the program, I was appointed Chief of the Foreign Scientist Office, T-2. With that appointment I had the whole nine yards under me. Problems were quick in coming, principally related to contract administration, income tax, and, of course, immigration issues.

"The German scientists worked all over Wright Field. To show that I had at least some control over them I had them come into my office every day and sign a roster, a quite informal affair. On weekends we allowed them to go into town alone to go shopping. They bought things for their families in Germany with their six-dollar-a-day per diem which they were paid under the provisions of Project Overcast. That per diem ended when Paperclip came into being and they received regular salaries paid in American dollars. We always notified the laboratories of new arrivals and their specialities. The labs would then schedule interviews and find a place for them. Initially, I detected a certain reluctance by the labs to use the scientists. That problem resolved itself in an unexpected manner. Dr. Rudolph Gothert was an aerodynamics engineer, a wind tunnel expert. He ran the three-meter wind tunnel at Völkenrode, it was his design. About the second day he was at Wright Field we took him to our ten-foot tunnel, which wasn't running well at all. Every time they tried to run it, it flung the model off the stand and mashed it against the wall. Gothert walked in and looked at the setup and said, '*Ach*, you must have a turn here, and a this-and-that there.' And soon the wind tunnel ran like clockwork. That really put us over the hump using the Germans in the Wright Field laboratories. The word quickly spread, 'That German solved our ten-foot wind tunnel problem with the snap of his fingers.'

"Another fine man was Dr. Theodor Zobel, formerly from the LFA Hermann Göring at Völkenrode. He was the interferometer expert who developed the concept of changing a mirror's spectrum without having to go through the expense of regrinding it. We had Dr. Alexander Lippisch and Dr. Ringleb. Lippisch was the Me 163 Arrow rocket plane designer, and Ringleb was his mathematician. We had Opitz the Me 163 test pilot and Professor Dr. Busemann, an authority on compressibility and high-speed air flow, as was Dr. Guderley. Dr. Braun was an infrared guy, and of course there was Dr. Hans von Ohain, the inventor of the axial flow jet engine, and many, many more. The talent we had at Wright Field was extraordinary."[7]

Among the "many, many more" was the former Generalmajor, Brigadier General Walter Dornberger. Dornberger recruited Professor Dr. von Braun in the early thirties and between them they initiated what became known as the A4 (V-2) ballistic missile project. In November 1945 Brigadier General George McDonald, the Director of Intelligence at Headquarters USAFE in Wiesbaden, wrote to his friend General Hugh Knerr at Wright Field, "I am sending you a list of the German scientists that have been shipped to the United States, those that have signed contracts and are awaiting shipment, and those that had been selected but have refused to sign. . . . Some of the reasons for refusal to sign have been based by the Germans upon the belief that after a short period in the United States . . . they will be returned to Germany and forced to re-start in life." McDonald noted with distaste, "In compiling the list of German scientists, the name of the administrative leader of the Peenemünde group . . . Walter Dornberger was included. His name was not submitted by any agency in the theater as far as I have been able to determine. . . . Monitored conversations between Dornberger and fellow inmates of detention centers, leave no doubt as to his untrustworthy attitude in constantly seeking to turn ally against ally, and he is an exceedingly glib fellow who would go to any length to achieve his ends. I believe that his name should be deleted from the list, because, as an individual he cannot be trusted, and would be a source of irritation and future unrest among the Germans if he were to be returned, in fact, we may

trade him to the Russians for a dish of caviar. Sincerely, George."
It was patently clear to Knerr that his friend George cared little for
Walter Dornberger—yet, for his own reasons, Knerr kept Dornberger
on the list, and he came to Wright Field as one of the "many, many
more" *Wissenschaftler* Captain Wenzel was charged to ride herd on.[8]

"Shiploads of scientific documentation began to arrive," Lloyd
Wenzel recalled, "which had been collected under Operation Lusty.
The documents were unsorted and packed in huge boxes. We had the
Germans go through the piles of paper and throw out the trash and
assemble what remained into a technical library. Colonel Watson
was the chief of the collection division in the Technical Intelligence
Directorate, T-2, commanded by General Putt. Watson recognized the
value of the captured documents and set up the organization which
then systematically exploited these papers for use by the Wright Field
laboratories, industry, and academic institutions. Nearly three hundred people worked on the task by the time Watson departed Wright
Field in September 1946 to attend the first class of the Industrial
College of the Armed Forces in Washington, D.C.

"Another aspect of the exploitation program was to provide
American industry the opportunity to come in and talk to the Germans.
At first only companies with War Department contracts were allowed to
participate; later this opportunity was expanded to include companies
which had contracts with any government department. One of the first
scientists let go by us to work for industry was an engineer who had
worked on heavy metal presses in Germany, Dr. Hans Meier. Dr. Meier
went up to Lowey Hydropress in New York. By early 1947 we had five
German scientists working at Lowey. Of course we had to set up some
sort of surveillance for them—after all, they were still enemy aliens and
we had to treat them as such. Surveillance didn't amount to much,
though. Occasionally I went up there to make sure they were still there.

"Colonel Watson was a close friend of General Putt's [Putt had
exchanged his eagles for a star on February 5, 1947]. I heard about

Watson and what he had done when the war ended, but never met him. I also didn't know the crucial role General Putt played in bringing the German scientists to this country. I was just a fighter pilot thrown into this thing because I spoke some German. In June 1947, after completing senior service school, Watson was assigned to the Office of the Assistant Secretary of War for Air in the Pentagon, the Honorable Kenneth C. Royall. I don't remember exactly anymore the contractual issue that arose at about this time but it was of a critical nature and I found myself right in the middle of the Paperclip mess."

The issue that was gumming up the works dealt with the fact that the War Department had an obligation to keep all the scientists in limited military custody until such time "as they might be granted immigration visas, constituting a parole of these persons by the Justice and State Departments to the War Department until legal entry to the United States was firmly established. ... At this particular time there were indications that no additional scientists would be ordered after 30 June 1947." State was adamant about not issuing visas to enemy aliens in this country. Relations within the War Department on Project Paperclip issues, and between War, Justice, and State remained testy. The Germans at Wright Field and other places were clearly enemy aliens. The question of how anyone could even consider issuing immigration visas to such people was a recurring theme among War Department staffers, reminiscent of the Overcast days. To put it in aviators' terminology, things began to stall out again. But Project Paperclip was a presidentially sanctioned program, and the secretary of war, keeping a jaundiced eye on progress, or the lack thereof, was finally forced to remind people in a strongly worded memorandum "to all services, departments, and agencies concerned with exploitation" that "The value of this presidentially approved program to the nation as well as to the naval and military services warrants full support of the War Department. In order to expeditiously conclude Project Paperclip, and to complete the ordering of these specialists by 30 June 1947, I desire that all War Department agencies fully and expeditiously implement all pertinent phases of this project which fall within their jurisdiction."[9]

In spite of the secretary's memo, negotiations between various State and War factions dragged on. But the secretary's words didn't leave any doubt in Putt's and Watson's minds that this was an opportunity to jump on the wagon and change its direction. Both clearly understood that they needed to take the initiative and move quickly. Captain Wenzel suddenly found himself in the awkward position of having to write a legal position, a contract, that would result in the implementation of what Paperclip had already stipulated, terms of reference and implementation which would eventually make American citizens out of enemy aliens. General Putt had Wenzel up to his office and told him, "You're in charge, Wenzel. The Germans are your people. Write a contract and get it signed by the secretary or his authorized representative. And I need to remind you, do it fast."

Wenzel continued, "I actually ended up writing a contract because nobody in the contracts section of the Air Materiel Command at Wright Field was cleared for Paperclip access. So I, a fighter pilot, took an old supply contract and spread it out on my living room floor. I cut and pasted and made a contract out of it, and into the contract I wrote the terms of Project Paperclip: that we would get them immigration visas, how we would go about doing it, and that we would bring their families over, and so on. Then it came time to have the contract approved in Washington. It was a personal services contract, and personal services contracts had to be approved by the secretary of war himself or by his designated representative, such as the assistant secretary of war for air. Watson was the executive to the assistant secretary of war for air. I reviewed the contract with General Putt, and he had some of his officers take a look at it, but they didn't really know what they were looking at. Putt was looking for certain things in the contract I had drawn up, and he felt that what I had was 'good enough' to get things moving. On my final visit with him he said to me, 'You have to go to Washington and get the assistant secretary for air to sign this thing. If you get into trouble call this guy,' and he handed me a piece of paper with Colonel Watson's name on it, his room number in the Pentagon, and phone extension.

"I put that paper in my pocket and went to Washington with my 'raggedy' contract in my briefcase. My first stop in the Pentagon was with a major in the Women's Army Corps, a WAC. She was a contracts specialist who had been cleared for Project Paperclip and was to review my contract. She had very little compassion for my half-assed effort. She was thinking along the lines of the Armed Services Procurement Regulations or whatever regulations contracts had to comply with in those days. She finally said, 'I know what you are trying to do, Captain. But what you have here doesn't even qualify as a contract. Why don't you go back to Wright Field and find somebody who knows how to write one. Now get out of my office, I don't have any more time to waste with you.'

"I went down the hall and got on a phone and called Colonel Watson. General Putt already spoke to him. Watson said to me, 'Come on down to my office right away. I'm in a hurry.' I went to his office. I started telling him about the contract when he interrupted me, 'That sounds good, Captain. What do you have to have to get out of here?' I have to have the secretary's signature, I said. Watson said, 'Where?' I opened up the contract and said, Right here, sir, pointing at the place where I wanted the secretary to sign. He said, 'Come with me,' and we went in to see the secretary. 'Mr. Secretary,' Watson said, 'this is Captain Wenzel from Wright Field on that German scientist program. He has drawn up the contract for the Germans. It's very critical that we get them on contract so we can proceed with their employment and get them out of that enemy alien status. We need your approval.' The secretary said, 'What do I have to do?' 'Sign here,' Watson said, handing the secretary a pen and holding the signature element in front of him. The secretary signed and I returned to Wright Field. That was it. Without Watson we would have never moved forward on this. There were just too many people dragging their feet. All but one of the German scientists took us up on our offer and signed the contract.

"Still, we didn't get much sympathy from the State Department in our efforts to obtain visas. At the time there were limited quotas for people to enter the United States, and the Jewish community fought us tooth and nail when they learned that we had come up with a way to let our *Wissenschaftler*, in their opinion no more than a bunch of Nazis, legally immigrate and become American citizens. Again, if we hadn't had men like General Putt and Colonel Watson and Harry Truman we probably would have lost the fight, it was such a complex issue. We had to keep the Russians from getting these people, and we didn't want the British to have them either. No one seemed to understand that, or didn't want to understand how important these people were to our national security. The British really wanted some of these guys to pump up their economy, and we spirited them away from under their noses. They were not too pleased with our Yankee manners.

"I had a couple of real fine young women working for me who kept track of the details and kept the immigration visas coming. For each man there had to be a piece of paper half the size of a regular dining room table which had to be filled in by the applicant. None of them, of course, had the things you needed. And if a document was missing we would have to go back to State with a message asking them what we could substitute for a birth certificate, for instance. We had to get statements from other sources in Europe to assure that none of these men were really the ones who killed anyone, or gave the orders to do so; that in fact they were scientists working in their respective fields. It was a tremendous administrative task. Once we figured out what State wanted, we pursued things with vigor. Each scientist ended up with a dossier a foot thick. The main thing we had to prove was that they were not Nazis.

"When their families began to come over and join them, either I or Lieutenant Robiczek would go to New York to meet the boat. We stayed in the Hotel New Yorker, downtown. We usually reserved a Pullman car on the Spirit of St. Louis for the trip to Dayton. I remember Dr. Rudolf Hermann's wife came over with a little baby boy, his name was Siegwulf, a name favored by the Nazis. I will never forget that trip. Siegwulf had a bad cold. Mama didn't know what to do to calm the baby. I ended up holding Siegwulf to give her a chance to go to the dining car and get something to eat. Siegwulf kept on crying, runny nose, the whole thing. I remember thinking, what am I doing here? I'm a fighter pilot, not a babysitter. When I told Robiczek about my experience, he said, in jest, 'You should have thrown the little bastard off the train.' We did what we had to.

"Once immigration visas were issued to a scientist and his family, they had to leave the country to shed their enemy alien status. They remained enemy aliens until they were readmitted to the United States. So we took them up to Niagara, New York, drove with them across the border into Canada, we had everything cleared with our embassy, and the Canadian authorities stamped their papers. Then we turned right around and had them readmitted to the United States, this time as legal immigrants. Lieutenant Robiczek was the first one to make one of those trips. I made several such trips to Canada, as did Captain Fred McIntosh. In 1948 the NYA camp pretty much shut down. We let those who wanted to move out, move out, and most of them wanted to leave the camp, of course. All of the *Wissenschaftler* had several job offers. Some, like Dr. Hans von Ohain, went to work for the government, but the great majority accepted positions in academe or private industry, usually industries with defense contracts in their speciality.

"I had few problems with the *Wissenschaftler* during my three years with them. They were learned men and not difficult, if at times somewhat lacking in common sense. I recall one of our scientists getting very ill. I took him to the hospital where they determined that he had a severe case of food poisoning. I went to his room and found a half-eaten can of sardines sitting on the windowsill. These guys were used to having servants and didn't know how to deal with the simple things of life. The sardines had ripened in the warm Ohio air. He nearly died eating the half-rotten sardines. Another scientist hung himself, Dr. Willie Merte, the optics genius. I didn't even know he was unhappy. Later some of the people told me that he had been pining to go home. After that incident I kept my eyes open for signs of depression, but nothing like that recurred.

"Dr. Werner von der Nuell, the supercharger expert, what a wonderful guy he was. He came from the AVA, the Aerodynamische Versuchsanstalt in Göttingen. He was among the first we released to work in industry. There was a time when I got real worried about von der Nuell because we didn't have anything to do for him. All the things he specialized in were contracted out to private industry. He was bored. One of the other Germans told me how downhearted he was. I was afraid he might do something to himself, like Dr. Merte, or quit the program and go home. I found out that one of his best friends was working at the school of aviation medicine in San Antonio. Of course, my parents lived in nearby Seguin. So I proposed to fly him down there while I got to spend a couple of days at home. I offered my idea to my boss, Colonel Klingerman, who said, 'A hell of a good idea, Wenzel.' I took an old C-45 and put von der Nuell in the right seat. He was just overjoyed. I got him a pile of maps and had him do the navigating from Dayton to San Antonio. I even took him home to meet my folks. He eventually went to work for a large electronics company in California.

"Those scientists who continued to live in the NYA area thought I should go back to school. We got to know each other rather well and they knew I only had two years of college. They kept on saying, '*Ach*, Herr Hauptmann, you must go back to school.' These people who were urging me to return to school had such titles as Professor Doktor Ingenieur Habilitatus. The 'Habilitatus' meant that they had postdoctoral university teaching qualifications. Simply stated, they were the very best people in their fields and allowed to sit on the committee that awarded doctorates in their discipline. They told me that they would help me get started. 'We'll get you going again, Herr Hauptmann,' they said. And they did. When I left the Paperclip project in August 1949 I remained at Wright Field as a third-year student at the Air Force Institute of Technology. AFIT, as it is commonly referred to, is a postgraduate school, but at that time they modified their program to allow two-year college types to obtain degrees. I didn't really think I could hack it. But the German professors tutored the hell out of me in the evenings, and I graduated in 1951 with a degree in industrial administration, a degree the Air Force wanted for its procurement officers—my next assignment.

"Before I could leave the Paperclip program to enter AFIT I had to clear my accounts. In 1948 I had been appointed property officer for Account Number 14, German scientists, vice 1st Lieutenant Paul Robiczek.[10] Robiczek left the program to return to civilian life, and I took over his account. I never gave it another thought. I should have, because I was responsible for every table, chair, spoon, towel, or bedsheet issued to the Germans. The first scientists who brought their families to the United States were moved with their families into converted barracks and I had signed for all the stuff those guys had—their furniture, linens, dishes, and so on. When it came time for me to leave the program, my replacement did an inventory, something I should have done when Robiczek left, and discovered that, among other things, I was short a thousand towels. I learned that the German women had taken the towels, dyed them, and made window drapes or throw rugs out of them. With a little understanding on the part of several officers I was able to get around my towel deficit and cleared my account without having to pay for my shortages. The remaining Germans left Wright-Patterson Air Force Base in 1950. Dr. Hans von Ohain stayed on, becoming the chief scientist of the Wright-Patterson

Air Force Base laboratories. Dr. Ohain died at the age of eighty-six at his retirement home in Melbourne, Florida—an American."

By 1950 World War II was only a memory for many. German science and its *Wissenschaftler* had been well integrated into America's future. With the outbreak of the Korean "police action," as it was then referred to by politicians, the United States began a period of active confrontation with a onetime ally—the Soviet Union. The Cold War entered a new and dangerous phase.

THE WAY THINGS CHANGED

"It was in the Battle of the Bulge. We were cowering in our foxholes when my sergeant called out, 'Here come the Krauts.' And I was looking up for airplanes, but I couldn't hear the sound of motors. And then I thought, What on God's earth is that? One of the new German jets passed right above me, didn't have a propeller in front. Didn't fire on us. He was going to bomb somewhere behind us. The Germans are so far ahead of us, I thought, and still they are losing the war. Later that morning I saw some B-17s high above us. Then two of them seemed to drop out of the formation of about forty, a wing came off one, then they disappeared from sight. Weeks later I got a V-mail and my mother wrote that my cousin, a B-17 bombardier, had been killed over Germany. I wondered if it was my cousin's plane I saw going down. I wondered if I would ever make it out alive." Private Robert Drew did make it out alive and he had every right to wonder why the Germans seemed to be so far ahead in their technology.[1]

In March 1946, in an address to the Dayton, Ohio, Civitan Club, Colonel Harold Watson asked a question similar to the thought that crossed Private Drew's mind when he looked up from his cold, soggy foxhole in the winter of 1944 to see an Me-262 jet fighter passing overhead at treetop level. "Germans flew the first jet propelled airplane before the German army marched against Poland," Watson said to his listeners. "Revolutionary developments in aeronautical engineering were in progress in Germany for a long time before we fired our first shot against the Nazis. Yet, a long time after that shot—after we had managed with considerable difficulty to gain the upper hand over our enemies—there we were, out in no-man's-land, scrambling around for the secrets of Nazi airpower while Nazi bullets whistled in our ears. Why were we out there then? Why hadn't we learned those secrets before that late date? We wouldn't listen to the few people who told us we were wrong. We wouldn't listen to Charles Lindbergh. We wouldn't listen to Eddie Rickenbacker. We wouldn't listen to the foreign correspondents who told us in newspapers and magazines and books that Germany was cooking up something that was treacherous. . . . Of course we won the war, but we must remember that we had a great deal of pure luck on our side." Watson concluded his presentation by asking his listeners, "Do we want to trust to luck again?"[2] Not if Watson had a say in the matter, and he did.

As chief of the T-2 Collection Division at Wright Field, Hal Watson was instrumental in the establishment of the Analysis Division within T-2 late in 1945. He wanted to ensure that the nearly one thousand tons of captured German documents, films, blueprints, and detailed drawings were properly examined and analyzed and that the findings were put to the best possible use, not only in the Wright Field laboratories, but also that they were made available to private industry—a partnership he felt strongly about and deemed essential for America's security. Referring to the captured German data, Watson said, "If we can evaluate this information and disseminate it properly and promptly, we can cut years from the time that our own engineers would devote to research on problems which have already been scientifically investigated."[3]

The second initiative Watson pushed was the creation of ATLOs, Air Technical Liaison Officers, who would be located at selected embassies throughout the world to report on developments in air and missile technology. Watson's idea fell on fertile ground and was readily supported by his peers and friends who sat in key positions at Wright Field and in Washington. Only two months after his presentation at the Dayton Civitan Club, in May 1946 Headquarters Army Air Forces informed Lieutenant General Nathan F. Twining, the commanding general of the newly established Air Materiel Command at Wright Field, that the "plan for attaching ATL Officers to selected embassies and legations has the complete support of the Assistant Chief of Air Staff Intelligence [General McDonald] and action has been initiated . . . for the implementation of this plan."[4] Watson's initiatives significantly expanded T-2's responsibilities and laid the foundation for what in later years would become the Foreign Technology Division, which played a major role in the analysis of the Soviet threat during the Cold War years.

Dr. Vannevar Bush, one time vice president and dean of engineering at MIT and head of the Carnegie Institution of Washington, headed the Office of Scientific Research and Development (OSRD) in World War II. Dr. Bush was largely responsible for the direction of America's scientific effort in the war years—the results of which Private Drew, standing in his cold foxhole in 1944, intuitively perceived as odd and puzzling. Watson's take on the situation was that OSRD was relying on luck. Luck it was, although coldly calculated. At the request of his friend President Franklin D. Roosevelt, Bush formed and chaired the OSRD and did a remarkable job of harnessing American scientific resources to the needs of a wartime economy, something the Nazis were never able to do successfully. By 1945, thirty thousand scientists of all disciplines were working on America's weaponry, focusing largely on applied research to provide the fighting men with the weapons needed to prevail on the field of battle.[5] It became a matter of producing rugged, effective, and compatible weapons and support systems in great numbers to prevail and conquer. From numerous factories across the nation, fleets of B-17 and B-24 heavy bombers, thousands of medium B-25 and B-26 bombers, and even more thousands of P-38, P-39, P-40, P-47, and P-51 fighters emerged. The Luftwaffe, and with its demise, Germany, was literally beaten into the ground with America's massed technology of the past. Vannevar Bush's plan proved to be a successful marriage of the nation's productive capacity with its scientific resources. The development of the atomic bomb and the proximity fuze were the two prominent exceptions of basic research applied to the war effort. The remainder of the American effort was largely a matter of applying yesterday's scientific insights to today's perceived requirements. As a result of the emphasis on yesteryear's technology, there were no American jets flying over Private Drew's head in late 1944.

Although the chosen course of action proved to be successful, it carried with it substantial risk—the risk of dated technology employed en masse becoming irrelevant in the face of much superior technological innovation. Wrote Vannevar Bush in hindsight, "They never built a proximity fuze." If they had, "they could have stopped our bombing. They would have stopped our bombing. We could not have stood the attrition they could have caused, from either a moral or a material standpoint." Combined with the effective employment of radar and jet aircraft, the air war in Europe could very well have taken a quite different turn.[6] Colonel Watson grasped the problem intellectually as he roamed around a defeated Germany in May 1945 gathering up Germany's jet aircraft.

As a result of the nearly exclusive focus on applied technology, jet and missile development in the United States languished and was even viewed with skepticism as to its utility—toys more than tools, prominent engine manufacturers averred. Vannevar Bush justified the chosen direction toward the development of a jet plane by writing that it tended to throw the advantage to the defense and "we did not acutely need jets and therefore did not bring weight to bear on their development."[7]

As for the V-1 cruise missile, Bush explained that "It was a much more important weapon to the Germans than it would have been to us, for they had the target." The target, if properly chosen, would not have been the cities of London or Antwerp, but the massed invasion fleet off the coast of Normandy in June 1944. "We had a blind spot," Bush wrote, "on this whole affair, and it will do us little harm to admit it."[8] The cruise missile blind spot, unfortunately, persisted for many years. "Unlike the V-1, this was a true rocket," Bush wrote of the V-2 ballistic missile. "It was a guided missile in a certain limited sense. . . . Development and production of the V-2 called for the very skills, facilities, and materials that could have been used to much greater advantage in the program of jet pursuit aircraft, which, if thus used, could have been embarrassing indeed to our progress in bringing Germany to her knees."[9] All in all, Bush justified the chosen course of action for the United States by saying that we had little to worry about, that the Nazi scientific effort had been "quite completely bungled."[10] Bush was absolutely correct in that assessment, but to rely on one's enemy's bungling to prevail on the field of battle was at best a tenuous strategy not conducive to long life and happiness. The end of World War II revealed that we had gaping holes of knowledge in key scientific fields and little understanding of the implications of jet and ballistic missile technology on the future course of the nation. These holes in our scientific repertoire needed filling quickly. That was clearly understood by General Arnold and his scientific advisor, Dr. von Karman, and down through the ranks to generals and colonels like Spaatz, Knerr, Putt, and Watson.[11]

Filling those critical scientific voids, however, was not the first change that faced postwar America; it came second, after bringing the boys home. "The arrival of Marshal Stalin from Moscow was delayed," wrote President Truman, "because of a slight heart attack which he had suffered. . . . I took advantage of this unscheduled delay in the opening of the [Potsdam] conference [in July 1945] to make a motor tour of Berlin. Our motor convoy left Babelsberg early in the afternoon and soon turned onto the famous autobahn, heading north for what was left of the German capital. About halfway to the city we found the entire American 2nd Armored Division deployed along one side of the highway for my inspection. We stopped, honors were rendered by a band and honor guard, and I left the sedan in which I had been riding and entered an open half-track reconnaissance car. In this I passed down the long line of men and vehicles, which comprised what was at that time the largest armored division in the world. Men and tanks were arrayed down the highway in front of me as far as the eye could see. The line was so long it took twenty-two minutes to ride from the beginning to the end of it."[12]

By the end of 1945 President Truman, citizen soldier Robert Drew, and Colonels Watson and Putt were home again, as were most of the men of the 2nd Armored Division. Its tanks, half-tracks, and trucks were largely left behind; given to needy allies, some served as village victory monuments, while others ended their service in scrap yards. At Landsberg, a former Luftwaffe airfield, B-26 bombers of the 1st Tactical Air Force (Provisional) were lined up by the hundreds to be burned and turned into scrap by Germans who only weeks earlier had tried hard to shoot them down. Most of the 1st TAF's P-47 Thunderbolts were simply stripped of their instrumentation and destroyed. The same thing happened to many of the aircraft of the 8th, 9th, and 15th Air Forces. Said Colonel Marion C. Mixson, a B-24 pilot and squadron commander with the 15th Air Force, "All those B-25 and B-17 bombers in Italy at the end of the war were destroyed. None were sent home. For a while I flew a brand-new B-25. German prisoners took the armor out of it, stripped the paint, and polished the airplane to a high gloss. Although I had orders to turn the plane in, to be destroyed like all the other bombers, I kept stalling for about two months. Finally I got a message that if I didn't turn in the plane I was going to be court-martialed. So I flew it down to the Pomigliano depot; my buddy came down in a C-47 to take me back. By the time we finished filing our clearance for our return trip, they had drained the gas out of that beautiful B-25, cut the engines off, cut holes in the crankcase and into the propeller blades. That airplane was completely smashed in about an hour."[13]

As the hardware and the manpower vanished, so did the organizations they once filled out. The famous 8th Air Force officially transferred its headquarters from Bushey Park to Okinawa in July 1945, its planes dispersed or put into storage. The 9th, 12th, and 15th Air Forces were inactivated by December 1945. The United States Air Forces in Europe, USAFE, with a strength of 315,000 men and 10,000 aircraft deployed on 109 airfields at its inception in August 1945, at the end of 1946 was down to a strength of 75,000 officers and men and a mere 2,300 aircraft, most of them noncombat aircraft such as AT-6 trainers, L-5 observation aircraft, and war-weary C-47 transports. The fleets of fighters and bombers which only months earlier had defeated the Luftwaffe and devastated Germany's cities were no more. By December 1947 the full impact of America's unilateral disarmament had reduced USAFE to a shadow of its former self, leaving it with 45,000 officers and men and 458 aircraft of all types deployed on 13 permanent air bases. All that was left was one fighter group equipped with 52 P-47 combat aircraft.[14] The first change that took place after war's end was the dismantling of America's military power. Men shed their uniforms as quickly as ships and planes could bring them home, and much of the equipment was left behind, given to European allies needing to rebuild their decimated military inventories. Much more was simply buried, burned, smashed, twisted, chopped up, or melted down to be turned into the proverbial pots and pans.

As for the Japanese who had been privy to many of the German technological advances, they were unable to do much with the new knowledge they had gained before they were overcome by larger events in August 1945. The Japanese did build their equivalent of the

These 186 B-17 bombers at Holzkirchen, Germany, were scrapped. GIs removed the radios and batteries, then placed one-and-a-half-pound TNT charges in the cockpits and blew them up. (JH)

Me-262, the Kikka. "They built two of these and made one flight in the first one," wrote Colonel Watson. "The second was scheduled for flight two weeks later but the bombing raids caused them to cancel. Their Kikka was smaller and the turbo engine had less thrust, because of metallurgical problems, than the German Jumo 004. However, the performance was about equal to the Me-262. Production lines were being set up but, again, the air raids demolished them." The Japanese also attempted to build an Me-163 rocket-powered fighter, the Shusui. "But here again," Watson reported, "its performance was not up to Dr. Lippish's design." The Kikka and the Shusui were the two major examples of German technology applied by the Japanese to their war effort. It all came too late for the empire of the rising sun.[15]

As 1945 came to a close, Colonel Watson, again assigned to Wright Field, had put on his last air show and display of captured enemy aircraft for press, radio, photographers, military brass, and the public. His daringly acquired German jets were scattered—some remained at Wright Field and Freeman Field for test purposes, others were retained as museum pieces, many were given to universities and engineering centers for study. Watson's German jets and the wide press coverage they received did raise the level of public awareness for jet aircraft, building visions in the eyes of the American public of exciting new things to come, creating what might be called a Buck Rogers atmosphere, which was vehemently decried by Dr. Bush as comic strip fantasy. To the American public in 1945 little seemed impossible.

By 1946, not only had the Germans been thoroughly disarmed, but all that was worth getting out of Germany had arrived in the United States for further exploitation. The 9th Air Force Service Command, in a final Record of Accomplishment of Air Disarmament, reported that 1,894 tons of new or secret German air force equipment of research or experimental value had been shipped back to the United States, including:

1. V-1—jet propelled weapon;
2. V-2—rocket weapon;
3. Messerschmitt 262—jet propelled aircraft;
4. Henschel 293—remotely controlled, jet propelled flying bomb;
5. Messerschmitt 163—rocket propelled aircraft;
6. Viper—piloted flak rocket;
7. Natter—remotely controlled flak rocket;
8. Horton 8 and Horten 9—Flying wing and jet propelled flying wing;
9. Fritz X 1400—remotely controlled bomb;
10. Arado 234—twin engine, jet propelled bomber.

Noted the report proudly, "These and other similar items returned for study and experiment are contributing greatly to the advancement of Air Force research in new and improved aircraft for civilian and military use as well as other weapons of war." The writer of the report appears somewhat confused—items 6 and 7 actually refer to the same aircraft, the Bachem Natter, Viper in English, which was not an antiaircraft rocket but a piloted interceptor. Disarmament squadrons, the report continued, visited and neutralized 9,132 separate GAF-related installations in the American occupation zone alone, including:

1. 248 Airdromes, landing grounds and glider fields;
2. 1,192 Factories producing for the GAF;
3. 112 Research and experimental stations;
4. 1,395 Depots, air parks and storage sites;
5. 4,896 Flak installations and gun sites;
6. 1,289 Miscellaneous targets (GAF hospitals, schools, headquarters, false targets, radio and radar sites, etc.).

"Not included in the above figures," it was noted, "are an additional 4,000 targets in the British, Russian and French Zones of Germany upon which primary disarmament was accomplished by American disarmament units. The Hannover, Brunswick, Magdeburg areas in the present British and Russian Zones were especially rich in important German Air Force targets, including large aircraft assembly plants and research installations. Before they were forced to withdraw, disarmament teams extracted a great deal of new, experimental equipment, documents and other tech intelligence information from this area." Finally, the report noted that 180 tons of documents were screened and extracted from the thousands of tons of worthless material processed by Air Disarmament Document Centers and forwarded to London and Wright Field.[16] The air disarmament squadrons, groups, and wings, the former combat crew replacement training units, had done an outstanding job completing an unfamiliar task. All were disbanded by 1946, like much of the rest of the American military machine.

The German dream that had begun in Versailles in 1871 with the crowning of the Prussian king as the first kaiser of the newly established German Reich had reached a final and sad ending. All that remained to be done by the victors was to strip Germany of its intellectual scientific capital, and that, in 1946, was a project in progress for

Americans, English, French, and Russians. For Americans, the resolution of the German scientist issue—how to bring them to the United States and how best to use them once there—was first addressed by Project Overcast (although certainly inadequately) and finally resolved by Project Paperclip. With the implementation of Project Paperclip and the prospect of permanent employment for German scientists in the United States, Dr. von Karman's last worry was resolved. He feared that if the German scientists evacuated to the United States knew that permanent employment was not contemplated, they would cease contributing anything of value and return to Germany with new knowledge gained in the United States. Von Karman was concerned that these German scientists would again form "disguised aeronautical associations" and that scientific activities in that field would continue, as it had after World War I.[17] Germany as a security issue was finally off the table. The world was at peace, or so it seemed.

Although the acquisition of the German jets was a memorable experience for both Watson and his Whizzers, in a broader sense the German aircraft had little impact other than that gained through the public air shows and exhibits. The major influence on America's future scientific path was exerted through the information gained from the tons of captured German scientific documentation and drawings of advanced designs, from state-of-the-art test facilities uncovered and brought to the United States, such as the Kochel wind tunnel, to the 138 different types of guided missile designs found during the disarmament and exploitation phase. Most of all, though, it was the German scientists that would make up America's science deficit. It would be these men, Germany's top *Wissenschaftler*, with their unconventional dreams, who would take up the Soviet Sputnik challenge of October 1957 and eventually take America to the moon. These same men would accelerate the move away from conventionally powered straight-winged aircraft to the swept-wing supersonic jets which would soon define America's airpower. Said Watson in a presentation on March 24, 1981, "The equipment, documents, interrogation of scientists, designers, and manufacturers, the German basic and applied research we recovered, the interrogation reports of top-flight fighter aces, all of this, when analyzed and plugged into our U.S. program, moved our research and development program ahead rapidly four and a half to five years."[18] To put it in monetary terms, the Air Documents Division of T-2 noted that "Information extracted from more than 1,000 tons of captured air documents, films, and drawings tends to bear out previous reports that the Germans were considerably ahead of the Allies in certain fields of aeronautical research and development, including rocket propulsion and related phases of aerodynamics. . . . The Germans unintentionally saved the Allies many millions of dollars."[19]

Colonel Don Putt, speaking to members of the Dayton Country Club on May 7, 1946, addressed the same issue of where we stood and where we needed to go and how we could get there. "It must be said that in many fields the Germans were ahead of us," Putt declared cautiously, "in some instances of from two to fifteen years . . . ahead of us in the fields of rockets and guided missiles, jet engines, jet-propelled aircraft, synthetic fuels and supersonics. . . . The developments in these fields are now of first order importance to us because they provide the simplest means of obtaining previously unheard-of speeds in air transportation with the possibility of flight high in the stratosphere and some day, perhaps, interplanetary transportation. So, I might ask, with this information in our possession, should we or the American taxpayer spend additional time and money to supplant facilities and work which has already been accomplished by German science and is now available for our use? . . . If we are not too proud to make use of this German-born information, much benefit can be derived from it and we can advance from where Germany left of. . . . Many of our experimental aircraft which were on the drawing boards on V-E Day were quickly changed when the theories developed by the Germans on the use of the swept back wing were learned."[20]

Putt was right. Engineers and test pilots at Boeing, Bell and North American didn't have to be convinced of the merits of German developments in the field of aeronautics—they had seen with their own eyes the shape of the future, had talked to German test pilots and to German scientists who had tested swept-wing aircraft models in state-of-the-art supersonic wind tunnels. Boeing Aircraft Corporation would emerge four years later with the B-47 bomber, its swept-back wings, six jets, ribbon drag-and-brake chutes, and aerodynamic shape permanently altering military and civil aircraft design concepts. The B-47 aircraft development, like no other aircraft, assured America's readiness for the protracted Cold War, which had yet to be recognized and given a name.

North American Aviation, like Boeing, dropped what it was doing on the XP-86 and incorporated many of the features of the Me-262, as well as advanced concepts tested and validated in German wind tunnels, into its F-86 Sabrejet—including an even greater swept-back wing and automatic leading edge slats. With the F-86, not the struggling P/F-80 design, America was ready to meet the Korean War challenge of the Soviet MiG-15 jet fighter. Bell Aircraft, which built the unexciting YP-59 jet, came up with the Bell X-1, which would take Chuck Yeager through the sound barrier on October 14, 1947. Bell engineers had learned from their German counterparts that this barrier, if approached properly, wasn't really there. The X-1 engineers, and others working on even more advanced test vehicles, readily took advantage of the insights Colonel Putt's *Wissenschaftler* provided. Interviews with German scientists at Wright Field became a frequent occurrence. In time the German scientists became on-site consultants to America's defense industry, and when the immigration issues were resolved, they went to work for these same aircraft companies, universities, research centers, and government laboratories. These men and women of science, as American citizens, continued to influence the future of air and space design for years to come. The German scientists of Project Paperclip became the yeast in a fast-rising postwar transformation of American aviation and space science.

None of these achievements came easily or without opposition. New aircraft shapes and power plants were initially viewed by some in the field as no more than passing fancies, neat little toys with no real practical application. Said Putt in a 1974 interview, "The jet aircraft was pooh-poohed by a lot of people that were authorities in their day. Of course, initially when it came out, those early jet engines burned an awful lot of fuel, so you thought of them as only short-legged aircraft . . . one that takes off, shoots down an airplane almost over the base, and lands. . . . I recall one incident, and this must have been before I went overseas [in January 1945]. . . . General [Franklin] Carroll, who was then Chief of the Engineering Division [at Wright Field], had been trying to get the engine companies to get interested in doing some development work in turbine engines. So he invited Pratt & Whitney, Wright Aeronautical, and the Allison people to Wright Field to talk about this. . . . I did sit in the conference with the Pratt & Whitney people. They were very firm in their conviction that the turbine engine would never be much of a threat. The piston engine was going to be with us forever; it was the way to go. There might be some place for a turboprop, but for a straight jet, forget it. At this point in time we had already, over in the aircraft lab, been doing some design studies in which they had made some allowance for future possible developments in the jet engine itself. They had looked at those hypothetical engines in bombers, and we had shown a possible radius of twelve hundred miles, probably only carrying two thousand pounds of bombs. So I mentioned that, and, you know, complete disbelief. Impossible. Can't be done. So then they went back home. And in a couple or three weeks I got a copy of a report that they did after they had been out to Wright Field proving conclusively that they were right. . . . I'm sure they were sincere in what they were saying and really believed that what they were saying was correct. But it turned out to be wrong. . . . Of course, they quickly became the leaders in the jet engine business when they finally decided that there was a future in it."[21]

It took some convincing and some time to bring change not only to those who built the power plants for military and civil aircraft, but also to the engineers who designed and mated airframes to jet engines. Aircraft designers continued to stick with the old-fashioned straight or only mildly tapered wing, such as Republic's uninspiring F-84G Thunderjet, Northrop's equally plodding F-89 Scorpion, and Lockheed's F-80-based F-94 Starfire interceptor. Even the Bell X-1 which carried Chuck Yeager through the sound barrier in 1947 had straight wings. All subsequent X-series aircraft, though, had varying degrees of wing sweep. In the late fifties and early sixties the Century series of fighters, F-100 through F-106, finally emerged as a successful blend of all that was new in aircraft propulsion and airframe design. By then no one remembered saying that the piston engine was going to be with us forever. The impact of German scientific thought on aerodynamics, on jet propulsion and ballistic missile technology, reshaped America's Air Force. When German scientific concepts were coupled with American developments in radar and the atomic bomb, change became drastic. The Air Force that emerged, with its fleets of jet bombers and fighters, nearly exclusively armed with nuclear weapons, unwittingly gave up a great amount of flexibility to respond effectively to a variety of military threats that would arise in the mid-sixties. By 1965, in the brief span of twenty years, the United States Air Force was almost totally a jet force wrapped around the atomic bomb.

If jets and ballistic missiles were largely overlooked in World War II, what was it that we failed to pay attention to in the 1960s? The answer was quick in coming. As the air war against North Vietnam intensified, we found that our nuclear bombs were of little use at the lower end of the conflict spectrum. There was no utility in dropping megatons on a water buffalo economy. What was suddenly needed, beside lots of dumb bombs, were precision guided weapons—PGMs, in military parlance. Here we were in 1966 flying sophisticated jet aircraft in old-fashioned dive bombing attacks against flak and SAM-protected bridges. It seemed like World War II all over again. Nothing appeared to have changed since KG 76 with its Arado 234 jet bombers attempted to drop the Remagen bridge in March 1945 in the same manner, and with about as much success. The Arados didn't hit the Remagen bridge with their dumb bombs; the F-105s only dropped a span or two of the bridges targeted in North Vietnam after the loss of many brave flyers. Was there something we had overlooked?

Among all the "stuff" brought home to Wright Field in 1945, stored in Building 89 and carefully inventoried by Captain Strobell, were the Hs 293 air-to-surface glide bomb designed by Dr. Herbert A. Wagner and the SD 1400 Fritz X free-falling armor-piercing bomb designed by Dr. Max Kramer. Both of the German World War II designs were radio and wire guided. Wagner and his design team were among the first brought to the United States by the U.S. Navy in May 1945. Navy interest in those weapons waned after the Japanese surrender; Army Air Forces interest apparently never developed. It was an unfortunate and costly oversight. Television guidance for the Hs 293D, for instance, had already been developed and tested at Peenemünde-West as early as 1944, and seventy actual weapon-release tests had been conducted by the Germans against a stationary shipwreck lying in the Baltic Sea.[22] Dr. Vannevar Bush had, of course, heard of TV guidance as early as 1944, but wrote it off as a "Buck Rogers" idea. "There was even one form in which the bomb carried a television transmitter in its nose," he wrote, "but this verged on the warfare of Buck Rogers and Flash Gordon."[23] A scientist should not have the privilege of laughing off any idea but would be better advised to prove or disprove.

In addition to German precision bomb developments there were our own, such as the Azon (azimuth controlled only) glide bomb used effectively, Bush recalled, "in Burma, where an air effort to take out important bridges had been under way for a long time without much success, controlled bombs were introduced and took them out promptly, the records indicating that one controlled bomb was worth one hundred ordinary ones." How could we forget so soon? The Razon (range and azimuth) bomb was under development in 1945, and there was a Navy version as well, known as the Bat. After 1945, change came quickly in many fields and forms, but this was an option nearly totally ignored in the shadow of the atomic bomb. After all, who needed weapons with yields of no more than a ton or two of conventional explosive when we already had the ultimate area weapon? In the crucible of war, priorities shift. By the mid-seventies the deliberate oversight of precision guided weapons began to be remedied. Today we can't even imagine going to war without precisely aimed weaponry. If the past is a guide to the future, what was it we gave scant attention to in the seventies and the eighties? What was it we deemed unimportant for one good reason or another and therefore neglected, to our future detriment? This time the answer was long in coming, but when it came its consequences were grim and obvious to all.

In 1949 Dr. Vannevar Bush wrote quite perceptively that "The principal element of our preparation for possible surprise attack is an intelligence system of high effectiveness, capable of warning us clearly if an attack is being prepared. . . . There is no reason why we should not know reasonably well what is afoot."[24] That statement is, of course, a truism. It was how we won World War II—by having a much better intelligence gathering and interpretation system than either Germany or Japan, by breaking their critical secret codes and being silent listeners to their most closely guarded plans and dialogue. As von Braun and his whiz kids designed and built ever more sophisticated missiles of intercontinental range, we achieved something that Dr. Bush in 1949 presumed to be in the realm of fantasy—putting objects in earth orbit. Bush pooh-poohed "high-trajectory guided missiles . . . spanning thousands of miles and precisely hitting chosen targets" and "missiles fired so fast that they leave the earth and proceed about it indefinitely as satellites, like the moon, for some vaguely specified military purposes."[25]

All those things came to pass soon after the Soviets, with the help of their German scientists, launched the eye-popping Sputnik I, in October 1957. Twenty years later reconnaissance satellites were circling the earth collecting photint, comint, sigint, elint, and any number of other "ints." However, there was one thing satellites couldn't deal with—intentions. The face-to-face dialogue between people, humint in military jargon, the age-old business of one man spying on another, found itself without advocates. Money became scarce as it was put into satellites, which, after all, were so much cleaner to handle than the messy business of human intelligence. On September 11, 2001, we paid a bitter price for our neglect of the most basic of all forms of intelligence gathering—the human spy. The world had changed again on us and we scrambled to rebuild what we had failed to maintain.

The question remains with us in response to the 9/11 catastrophe— what is it this time that we are overlooking or de-emphasizing? What is it that we are relegating to a category of unimportance, such as the jets, missiles, precision guided munitions, and the human spy of years gone by, only to have it emerge at some future date to punish us? The world will continue to change and we have to change with it to survive. There are lessons in our past which can help us to do better, and there is no reason why we can't.

After 1945, change was largely driven by technology that came to the fore during the war years. It was change of a magnitude never before witnessed in human history—for many, difficult to digest, yet totally impossible to ignore. Still, the horse cavalry tried to preserve a niche for itself in a postwar world of jet planes and rockets and bravely laid out its plans for its future participation in world affairs.

By 1947, though, it had run its course, and the horse cavalry joined the fate of the coast artillery. The nature of the technological change that had descended on the postwar world made no allowance for such anachronisms from the past. Nor was there room to reject German scientific achievements for reasons of political ideology. Men like Arnold, Spaatz, Knerr, Putt, and Watson knew that. They looked coldly at the marvels of technology, at the possibilities that presented themselves for the future, and proceeded to add to them. "Wicked, wicked, wicked," muttered General Spaatz to Colonel Watson after reviewing the German jets at Melun, France. "When I first saw an Me-262 I was . . . spell-bound," wrote Watson. General Arnold took a practical tack as early as 1944, being fully aware of the change technology was forcing on his largely antiquated yet victorious air force. "Our prewar research and development," Arnold wrote to Dr. von Karman, "has often been inferior to our enemies. . . . Obsolete equipment, now available in large quantities, may stalemate development and give Congress a false sense of security. . . . More potent explosives, supersonic speed, greater mass offensive efficiency, increased weapon flexibility and control, are requirements. . . . Human-sighted (and perhaps radar or television assisted) weapons have more potential efficiency and flexibility than mechanically assisted weapons. . . . Is it not now possible to determine if another totally different weapon will replace the airplane? Are manless remote-controlled radar or television assisted precision military rockets or multiple purpose seekers a possibility?"[26] General Arnold was far ahead of his time, and of some of the nation's best scientists, in visualizing the variety of courses change could take in the fog-shrouded future. Dr. von Karman's study *Toward New Horizons*, which emerged as a result of Arnold's perceptive questions, remains to this day a classic in open-minded, long-range planning. Yet its findings too were overshadowed by the emergence of the atomic bomb, and only failure in Vietnam forced us to look back and pick up where we had lost our way.

Yet, there is something reassuringly human in the fact that, regardless of the scope of technological change, some things stay the same—we remain straight-line thinkers and have great difficulty imagining that which falls outside our carefully structured paradigms. Once we set our righteous course, those who continue to advocate unconventional ideas are driven out and labeled delusional, with their ideas seen as verging on the warfare of "Buck Rogers or Flash Gordon." It seems that only catastrophe guarantees a brief and precious window of time for new ideas to emerge and be considered. Let us hope that we live in such a time of grace and intellectual tolerance—our future depends on it.

AFTERWORD

What Became of All These Good Men?

Colonel Harold E. Watson (later Major General Watson) continued his pursuit of building a lasting technical intelligence organization for the United States Air Force. Wright Field, renamed Wright-Patterson Air Force Base in 1947, remained Watson's focus for the remainder of his career. Watson headed the Collection Division of Air Technical Service Command's Technical Intelligence Directorate, T-2, in 1945. He then attended the Industrial College of the Armed Forces at Fort McNair, Washington, D.C., served a tour of duty in the Pentagon, and returned in 1949 for three more years as the T-2 director, this time assuming the position previously held by his friend and former boss, General Donald L. Putt.

In May 1951, T-2 became the Air Technical Intelligence Center, ATIC. While T-2 had focused on the exploitation of German technology, ATIC shifted its sights toward the Soviet Union. The most notable project under Watson as ATIC's commander was the evaluation of the Soviet MiG-15 jet fighter. ATIC engineers made estimates of the fighter's performance from pictures and information gained from various sources, but what they really wanted was a MiG—pilot and all.

At first the ATIC engineers had to console themselves with some MiG engine parts recovered by an intrepid ATI team in Korea. The question was, what kind of an engine was the MiG-15 using? It was suspected that the British had sold a copy of their Nene engine to the Soviets before relations soured and that a Soviet version of the Nene powered the MiG. Recalled **Fred McIntosh**, "We had a team in Korea, two men. They went behind the lines to bring out some parts of a crashed MiG. The aircraft had dug itself into soft ground but the engine was accessible. The problem was how to get it out. One of the two had a couple of hand grenades, and he threw them up the tailpipe of the wrecked MiG, breaking loose

[443]

some parts. They brought out a rotor, part of a turbine wheel, the shroud, and some other pieces. I went out to Travis AFB in California in April 1951 in a C-54 and picked up the pieces for analysis. That confirmed the Nene engine theory." The Rolls-Royce Nene engine adapted by the Soviets for use in the MiG-15 used centrifugal rather than axial flow and first flew in 1947.

Fred McIntosh had been released from active duty in 1946, and, like many of his fellow World War II flyers, he was recalled to active duty in March 1951, after North Korea invaded its southern sibling. Watson got hold of McIntosh and put him to work in T-2 setting up a school for technical analysts, turning a group of Air Force reservists, engineers, photographers, and Russian linguists into old-fashioned ATI specialists. In July 1951 a joint British-American operation recovered the better part of a MiG from the mud of the Ch'ongch'on River estuary, using a cherry picker mounted on a barge. The MiG parts included the forward section of the fuselage, both wings, landing gear, the tail assembly, its 23 mm gun, and lots of bits and pieces. "I was running our technical analyst school," McIntosh recalled, "when Colonel Watson got a phone call from Travis that the Navy had recovered a MiG-15. I and another officer grabbed a C-54 and flew from Wright-Patterson to Travis Air Force Base. The MiG was at Travis all right, in bamboo baskets, mostly in bits and pieces. I forget how many baskets there were, but we damn near filled the entire airplane. When we got back to Wright-Patterson we gave all that stuff to the engineers at ATIC to make sense of it. Watson gave the engineers ten days, and it quickly became obvious that they had trouble putting that airplane back together. About this time we were through with our school. We put on a graduation party on the Great Miami River that runs through Dayton. One of our boys was from Louisiana and had a barrel of shrimp and all that stuff brought up from the bayous. We were having a great time and the beer was flowing freely when Watson showed up. 'I got some good news for you, Major,' he said. 'You and your schoolkids have to help us put that airplane back together. I need to know certain things about this airplane. My engineers are stuck. You've been living with these guys for the past couple of months; tell me, do you think they can put the MiG back together again?' "

"I'll give it a try, I told Watson. Do you have a deadline for me? He hemmed and hawed around for a bit, then he said, 'Yeah, I can give you two weeks.' Let me think about it, I told him. 'Think about it while you are sleeping,' Watson said. 'I am asking you to not let this party get to the point where your guys can't work tomorrow. I got everything else ready: photographers, girls to type up the reports. Everything.' That night all fifteen of us were in the hangar developing our plan of how to put that bird back together again. Watson stayed away from us, apparently trying not to interfere. We slept in the hangar, worked twenty-four hours a day. I finally went over to Watson and asked him to please stop by at least once a day.

This MiG-15 was flown in September 1953 to Kimpo airfield by a defecting North Korean pilot. It confirmed the findings of ATIC and vindicated Watson's efforts to build the best foreign technical analysis organization in the country. (RW)

Show them you are interested in their work. We could use a little morale lifter, I told him. It's damn tedious work. When we had put the airplane back together, we found that it had a wing-flutter problem. The Russians had solved it simply by putting a cast-iron slug in the tip of each wing. A single man could hardly carry the weight, it was that heavy. When the engineers had done their preliminary analysis, and the girls had typed up the report, Watson flew to Washington to present his report on the MiG to the Air Force chief of staff. He took the cast-iron counterweight along and put it on General Vandenberg's desk." General Hoyt S. Vandenberg was the second Air Force chief of staff, having succeeded **General Carl A. Spaatz** on April 30, 1948—just in time for the Berlin airlift. "This act of bravado was typical Watson, taking the MiG wing-weight along and putting it on the chief's desk. He had a knack for the dramatic, and it always worked for him. When the guys with the slide rules at ATIC finished their analysis and came up with their final report, their findings were within 5 per cent of the actual perform-ance of the MiG-15. It was the MiG-15 story that put ATIC on the map, and in 1961 led to the creation of the Foreign Technology Division, FTD."

The ATIC engineers eventually got their wish for a flyable MiG-15 when a defecting North Korean, Noh Kum Suk, landed his armed MiG at Kimpo Air Base near Seoul, South Korea, on September 21, 1953, to collect a one-hundred-thousand-dollar reward. The MiG and its pilot were promptly flown to Kadena Air Base on Okinawa, where the plane was test-flown by Captain Tom Collins from the Wright-Patterson AFB Flight Test Division and by Major Charles "Chuck" Yeager from the Air Force Flight Test Center at Edwards AFB. They thoroughly wrung out the MiG in eleven flights, producing what they called "a wealth of quantitative performance data as well as qualitative stability and control data throughout the speed range from below to well above the airplane's placarded limits."[1]

After a tour of duty at Headquarters, Allied Forces Southern Europe, AFSOUTH, in Naples, Italy, Watson returned to Wright-Patterson AFB and again assumed command of ATIC, this time as a freshly minted brigadier general. During the years from 1954 to 1958 the Air Technical Intelligence Center was at the forefront of automation, installing its first computers to analyze missile trajectories, then moving into computer translation of Russian technical and military documentation. Watson reached out and ensured that ATIC maintained close ties to the Air Force laboratories, test centers, industry, and academic institutions to make certain that the organization he had built was in fact able to function as the central analytical center for foreign air and space developments. In 1958 Watson received his second star, and, true to past practice, he sent a telegram to his mother, Louise, in Waterford, Connecticut. "PLEASE GO OUT AND BUY YOURSELF THE BIGGEST STEAK EVER AND SEND THE BILL TO YOUR SON MAJOR REPEAT MAJOR GENERAL HAL WATSON WHO IS PRETTY THRILLED TODAY. LOVE AND KISSES, HAL." Little had changed between the two since Hal had sent his mother that first telegram in 1937 announcing his promotion to second lieutenant in the regular Army. He was still as devoted to his mother as he had ever been. He also sent a telegram to his older brother, Allan, in Plainville, Connecticut: "THOUGHT YOU WOULD BE INTERESTED TO KNOW THAT MAJOR GENERALS WEAR HATS TWO SIZES LARGER. JUST FOUND OUT TODAY. HAL." Allan had served in the Army Air Forces during World War II and understood his brother's pun relating to hat size. Four years later, in 1962, Major General Harold E. Watson retired as Deputy Commander of Air Force Systems Command at Andrews Air Force Base in Maryland. General Bernard A. Schriever, the immigrant from Germany and one-time second lieutenant assigned to the Flying Branch when Watson, also a second lieutenant, was assigned to the Power Plant Laboratory at Wright Field, was the commander of AFSC and led the retirement ceremony.

As for **Fred McIntosh**, he separated from the Air Force in 1961 in the rank of lieutenant colonel and accepted a position as vice president of the National Business Aircraft Association. Fred flew 104 combat missions in the P-47 in Europe. He said that "flying German airplanes for Watson was one of my life's highlights. A time I'll never forget." Watson brought **Bob Strobell** to Wright Field after he recovered from his nearly fatal aircraft accident in Germany and made him the manager of all that "stuff" that had been collected under Operation Lusty and stored in Building 89. Bob decided to leave the Air Force in the late forties. He remained close to airplanes throughout his life, first working as curator at the National Air and Space Museum, in later years doing volunteer work at the College Park Aviation Museum in College Park, Maryland. Bob died in January 2001 at age eighty-two, nine months after I interviewed him for this book.

Lieutenant Colonel Malcolm Seashore, the man who so expertly handled all of Watson's logistics and transportation needs in Europe, became Watson's assistant deputy chief in the T-2 Collection Division at Wright Field in 1945. In August 1946, upon Watson's departure for the Industrial College of the Armed Forces, Colonel Seashore was appointed chief of the collection division. Malcolm Seashore, retired long ago from the Air Force, resides in a retirement community near Fort Belvoir, Virginia. **Bob Anspach**, one of the Whizzer pilots, had more than his share of incidents and accidents flying German aircraft for Watson. Bob got out of the Air Force after all the German airplanes had been flown to Freeman Field, attended college under the generous provisions of the World War II GI bill of rights, and obtained a degree in mechanical engineering. Like McIntosh, Anspach was recalled to active duty and flew the F-86 Sabrejet in the Korean War. Said Bob of that experience, "It was the perfect airplane to fly." After Korea the Air Force sent him to the Air Force Institute of Technology at Wright-Patterson AFB, where he obtained a master's degree in mechanical engineering. Bob then developed the flight simulator for the F-100 Supersabre. In 1969 he retired from the Air Force in the rank of lieutenant colonel and settled in Orlando, Florida.

Roy Brown had enough points to get out of the Army Air Forces when HMS *Reaper* dropped anchor at the Brooklyn Navy Yard in July 1945. He was soon reunited with his young bride, Francis, and went to work as a chemical engineer for Goodyear Tire and Rubber Company in Akron, Ohio. There Roy was in charge of developing de-icing systems for airplane propellers, wing and tail leading edge surfaces, helicopter rotor blades, and engine inlets. Then he transferred to the uranium enrichment plant at Piketon, Ohio, from which he retired in 1983 as manager of the technical division. Roy, an avid jogger, and Fran reside in Chillicothe, Ohio. **Jim Holt** stayed around until 1947 flying Me-262s at various public events, then decided to call it quits. **Fred Hillis** and **Kenneth Dahlstrom** took their discharge, as Roy Brown did, when the *Reaper* docked in New York harbor. And then, of course, there was **Jack Woolams**, the chief test pilot for the Bell Aircraft Company, who spent so much time with Watson and his people flying most of the German aircraft Watson brought back to the United States. Test piloting in the forties and fifties was dangerous business and not for the fainthearted. Jack Woolams died much too young in an aircraft accident on August 30, 1946.

Major General George C. McDonald, who was largely responsible for putting all intelligence operations under one roof at Headquarters USSTAF during World War II, moved with the headquarters in 1945 to Wiesbaden, Germany, where

USSTAF was redesignated United States Air Forces in Europe, USAFE. Upon his return to the United States in 1947, McDonald became the Air Force's first assistant chief of staff intelligence under General Spaatz, his longtime mentor. Many members of his staff from Headquarters USSTAF, such as **Colonel Peebles**, made the move with him, first going from Paris to Wiesbaden, then following their general to the Pentagon. Wartime is a great bonding experience.

General Carl A. "Tooey" Spaatz capped his long and eventful career by becoming the first chief of staff of an independent Air Force in September 1947. It should be no surprise that Spaatz brought George McDonald to Air Force headquarters to serve as his intelligence chief. The two had been together since the early days of the North African campaign. General Spaatz remained in that position until April 1948, retiring from active duty two months later. Spaatz will always be remembered as one of America's truly great airpower leaders and pioneers. He died in 1974 at the age of eighty-three, and was interred at the United States Air Force Academy in Colorado Springs, Colorado, a fitting place.

Lieutenant General Donald L. Putt saw Project Paperclip through to its conclusion. While Watson brought home the hardware, Putt brought home Germany's intellectual capital. The German scientists he had worked so hard to bring to the United States were eventually absorbed into American industry and government, and their contributions led to rapid and visible advancements in aeronautics. Putt remained at Wright Field until August 1948 when he transferred to the Pentagon. He pinned on his first star in February 1947. In June 1953, as a lieutenant general, he assumed command of Air Force Systems Command, the former Air Research and Development Command, then located in Baltimore. General Putt retired from active duty in 1954 and died in 1988 at age eighty-three.

Major General Hugh Johnston Knerr, the hardheaded, no-nonsense USSTAF deputy commander and subsequent commander of the Air Technical Service Command at Wright Field, will be remembered not only for recognizing his country's technological deficiencies, but also for doing everything in his power to change that situation quickly by bringing Germany's scientists to the United States. He and Putt made a great team. In 1946 this U.S. Naval Academy graduate, class of 1908, handed over his command to Lieutenant General Nathan F. Twining and relocated to Washington. He retired a second time on October 31, 1949. Knerr had been recalled to active duty in October 1942 after retiring for the first time in March 1939 in the rank of colonel. General Knerr passed away in October 1971 at the age of eighty-four.

After returning to the ZI in late 1945, **Master Sergeant Eugene E. Freiburger** decided to stay around the Air Corps a bit longer. He was assigned to Freeman Field, then returned to Germany two years later for a tour of occupation duty,

*Sergeant Freiburger, an avid hunter, is shown here near
Lager Lechfeld in May 1945 with carbine in hand. (DF)*

this time accompanied by his wife, Wilma Jeanne. Upon his return to the United
States he attended Officer Candidate School and was commissioned a second
lieutenant. Captain Freiburger retired in 1962 from the Air Force and returned to
his home town of Antigo, Wisconsin. He accepted a position with the Wisconsin
State Division of Corrections and retired in 1982. In October 2002 Eugene
Freiburger died at the age of eighty-two.

Lieutenant Charlie Johnson, the B-17 navigator whose brand-new B-17G aircraft was shot down by a German Me-262 jet fighter over Hamburg, went back to
England after his liberation from Stalag Luft I at Barth. He recalled how difficult it
was for him the day he walked down Bond Street in London and into a tailor shop
to pick up the Eisenhower jacket he had ordered along with Taub and Cooper

before their shoot-down. "It was waiting for me. I could not bring myself to ask about Taub's or Cooper's—I was haunted by their memory. Why did they have to die and I survived? I could not understand why I was the lucky one. In late July I boarded the *Pierre L'Enfant*, a Liberty ship, and after a fourteen-day Atlantic crossing arrived in Boston, Massachusetts." There Charlie processed through Fort Strong, which only a few weeks later would serve as the processing center for German scientists and test pilots entering the United States under Project Overcast. Lieutenant Johnson was discharged at Fort George Mead in Laurel, Maryland, and in less than an hour he was home in Mt. Rainier. Charlie built a successful family business and still resides within a stone's throw of his place of birth.

Karl Baur, the Messerschmitt chief test pilot who provided such invaluable assistance to Hal Watson in the recovery of the Me-262s and Arado 234 jets, immigrated with his family to the United States in the mid-fifties and settled in Arlington, Texas. He died in October 1963. The likeable **Willie Hoffmann**, after recovering from his injuries sustained in bailing out of the 50-mm-gun-equipped Me-262 jet fighter over France, returned to Soviet-occupied Berlin to move his family to the American occupation zone. Hoffmann was promptly arrested and sent along with his family to the Soviet Union, a common fate for many German scientists, technicians, and test pilots. Ten years later he was allowed to return to Germany. Hauptmann **Heinz Braun**, the one-time Junkers 290 pilot, in 1956 joined the new Bundeswehr of the Federal Republic of Germany. He retired in the rank of Oberst (colonel). Heinz Braun is deceased.

As for the hundreds of **German scientists** who came to the United States voluntarily under Projects Overcast and Paperclip, they became American citizens and helped shape their newly adopted country as countless immigrants had done before them, except that their contributions were focused on science and technology rather than on agriculture, mining, manufacturing, the arts, or medicine. The **von Braun** missile team pretty much remained together, first at Fort Bliss, an Army installation near El Paso, Texas, and later at Huntsville, Alabama. Some went to work at NASA. Their research progressed from the V-2 rocket to the Redstone missile to the Apollo II mission, and, on July 20, 1969, Neil Armstrong became the first man to set foot on the moon, saying, "One small step for a man, one giant leap for mankind." The Wright Field scientists were a more diverse group and in time found work in industry, government laboratories, and academe throughout the country. **Dr. Hans von Ohain**, the coinventor of the jet engine, never left Wright Field, choosing instead to remain active in and later directing the research laboratories of his one-time place of confinement. The more than one hundred scientists who worked for the U.S. Navy found employment in various projects throughout the United States, from the Kochel wind tunnel, installed at White Oak, Maryland, to the Naval Test Center at Point Mugu, California.

Dr. Anthony "Tony" Caccioppo, chief scientist of the Foreign Technology Division, speaking to Major General Harold E. Watson at a 1989 dinner given in Watson's honor. Colonel Harold "Tex" Owens, vice commander of FTD, sits to Caccioppo's right. (RW)

Let me end this story with the man you first met as a young boy growing up near Hartford, Connecticut, **Harold E. Watson**. After retirement from the Air Force in 1962 and a few years of consulting, Watson decided to become a blue-water sailor. "It's just like flying an airplane," he told his wife. Ruth and Hal frequently sailed the Caribbean in their boat, *Phantom*. In 1988 General Watson was honored by the Society of Experimental Test Pilots for his contribution to the flight-testing of foreign aircraft; he was made an honorary member. Such an honor is bestowed by the society only on the most deserving airmen, such as Charles Lindbergh, General Jimmy Doolittle, and Harold E. Watson. In 1989 Watson was feted for one last time at the Foreign Technology Division, the former Air Technical Intelligence Center, which for all practical purposes he had founded and given life. It was a memorable reunion for him and those present. It would be his last visit. Watson died on January 5, 1994, in Jupiter, Florida. In 1995 the National Air Intelligence Center, the successor organization to the Foreign Technology Division and the Air Technical Intelligence Center, named its new foreign materiel exploitation building Watson Hall. Watson is remembered for the lasting contributions he made to the Air Force he loved so much. And yes, he lives on in the hearts and minds of those of us who remember the man, the engineer, the pilot, and the Air Force officer he once was.

NOTES

CHAPTER 1: THE WAY THINGS WERE

1. Colonel Harold E. Watson, "The Battle of Know-How in Peace and War," speech given to the Dayton, Ohio, Civitan Club, 19 March 1946, p. 9.
2. Colonel Donald L. Putt, Commanding General, Technical Intelligence, T-2, Air Materiel Command, Wright Field, Dayton, Ohio, "Technical Intelligence," speech given to the Dayton Country Club, 7 May 1946, p. 5.
3. *Air Technical Intelligence, T-2, Air Materiel Command* briefing to visiting dignitaries on the organization and functions of T-2 and the results of Operation Lusty, 10 April 1946, p. 45.
4. Isolde Baur, "With the 'Watson's Whizzers' and 'Operation Paperclip,'" *American Aviation Historical Society* (winter 1995): 296.
5. Major General Harold E. Watson USAF (Ret.), untitled speech given at the United States Air Force Museum, Wright-Patterson Air Force Base, Ohio, 24 March 1981.
6. Sixteen British Meteor jets were delivered to the RAF in 1944 and were employed against slow German V-1 cruise missiles flying fixed course and altitude. The Meteors met with limited success. Most V-1s were destroyed by American proximity fuzed AAA shells.
7. Harold E. Watson, speech, 24 March 1981, p. 42.
8. Putt, speech, p. 3.

CHAPTER 2: THE GERMAN JETS

1. Raymond F. Toliver, *Fighter General: The Life of Adolf Galland*, AmPress Publishing, Zephyr Cove, NV, 1990, p. 153.
2. J. Richard Smith and Eddie J. Creek, *Arado 234 Blitz*, Monogram Aviation Publications, Sturbridge, MA, 1992. This book provides a comprehensive treatment of Arado 234 development and its employment in 1944–1945.

3. Interview with Lieutenant General Donald L. Putt by Dr. James C. Hasdorff, United States Air Force Oral History Program, 1–3 April 1974, p. 30.

4. Albert Speer, *Inside the Third Reich*, The Macmillan Company, New York, 1970, p. 445.

5. Eric Brown, *Wings of the Luftwaffe*, Airlife Publishing Ltd., Shrewsbury, England, 1993, p. 59.

6. Chuck Yeager and Leo Janos, *Yeager*, Bantam Books, New York, 1985, pp. 60–61.

7. Paul B. Cora, *Yellowjackets! The 361st Fighter Group in World War II*, Schiffer Military History, Atglen, PA, 1993, p. 102.

8. Frederick B. McIntosh, interviews by author, 18 December 2001 and 24 January 2003, Leesburg, Virginia.

9. *Status Report of Exploitation Division*, Headquarters, United States Strategic Air Forces in Europe, Office of the Assistant Chief of Staff, A-2, APO 633, July 17, 1945, Tab G, General Summary of Technical Exploitation, p. 63.

10. Ken Chilstrom and Penn Leery, eds., *Test Flying at Old Wright Field*, Westchester House Publishers, Omaha, NE, 1993, pp. 264–67.

11. Ibid., p. 189.

12. Yeager and Janos, pp. 94–95.

13. Phil H. Butler, *War Prizes*, Midland Counties Publications, Leicester, England, 1994, pp. 208, 219.

14. Vannevar Bush, *Modern Arms and Free Men*, Simon and Schuster, New York, 1949, pp. 49–50.

15. Eric Brown, pp. 92, 98. In 1945 Captain Eric M. Brown was a lieutenant commander in the Royal Navy. He was of German heritage and spoke fluent German. He led the Captured Enemy Aircraft Flight at RAE Farnborough—the Wright Field of the Royal Air Force—from 1945 to 1946. Brown was Colonel Watson's counterpart and was responsible for selecting and flying captured German aircraft to the United Kingdom. Brown briefed Watson in London upon his arrival in England in September 1944.

16. Headquarters Air Technical Service Command in Europe, Director of Technical Services, APO 633, report of visit to the Carl Zeiss Factory at Jena, Germany, dated 9 May 1945, submitted by Captain James Harris to the Director of Intelligence, Headquarters USSTAF. Captain Harris interrogated Dr. Herbert F. Kortum, chief bombsight and gunsight engineer who provided information about the German dive-bombing computer type T.S.A.-2A. "It was the best of the dive bomb sights planned for installation in the FW 190, Me-109, Ar 234 and the Me-262." Two high altitude bombsights for horizontal bombing, Loffe 7H, were also obtained and returned to the Technical Intelligence section at USSTAF. The Loffe 7H was the bombsight installed in the Arado 234 for high altitude, level bombing. "Dr. Kortum had in his possession

a translated copy of the U.S. Air Force Report (1942) covering a test on the Norden Bombsight. He did not know where the report came from but presumed it had been taken from a crashed airplane. He also stated that he had his first look at a Norden Bombsight in 1943. The Germans thought their Loffe Bombsight superior to our Norden. To his knowledge no effort had been made by the Germans to duplicate the Norden sight."

17. Smith, pp. 176–82.

CHAPTER 3: JET ENCOUNTERS

1. The 8th Air Force based in England consisted of three air divisions of heavy bombers kept at a combat strength of around two thousand aircraft. The 1st and 3rd Air Divisions flew the B-17; the 2nd Air Division flew the B-24. The 8th Air Force also had several fighter groups. Heinz "Pritzl" Bär, one of Germany's fighter aces, with 221 aerial victories, described the P-38, P-47, and P-51 in a 1955 interview with Colonel Raymond F. Toliver (Raymond F. Toliver and Trevor J. Constable, *Fighter Aces of the Luftwaffe*, Schiffer Publishing Ltd., Atglen, PA, 1996, p. 301): "In general, P-38 Lightnings were not difficult at all. They were easy to outmaneuver and were generally a sure victory. The P-47 Thunderbolt could absorb an astounding amount of lead. . . . The P-51 Mustang was perhaps the most difficult of all Allied fighters to meet in combat."

2. Davis, Coffin, and Woodward, eds., *The 56th Fighter Group in World War II*, Infantry Journal Press, Washington, D.C., 1948, p. 84.

3. Toliver, p. 289.

4. Yeager and Janos, p. 63. Yeager recalled, "Atrocities were committed by both sides. That fall our fighter group received orders from the Eighth Air Force to stage a maximum effort. Our seventy-five Mustangs were assigned an area of fifty miles by fifty miles inside Germany and ordered to strafe anything that moved. . . . It was a miserable, dirty mission, but we all took off on time and did it. . . . I remember sitting next to [Major Donald H.] Bochkay at the briefing and whispering to him: 'If we're gonna do things like this, we sure as hell better make sure we're on the winning side.' "

5. Charles Johnson, "Memoirs of a Navigator WWII," unpublished. Manuscript in possession of the author.

CHAPTER 4: THE DEFIANT FEW

1. Toliver, pp. 280, 282.

2. Cajus Bekker, *The Luftwaffe War Diaries*, Ballantine Books, New York, 1969, p. 535.

3. Raymond F. Toliver and Trevor J. Constable, *Fighter Aces of the Luftwaffe*, Schiffer Publishing Ltd., Atglen, PA, 1996, p. 314.

4. Kit C. Carter and Robert Mueller, *The Army Air Forces in World War II: Combat Chronology, 1941–1945*, Office of Air Force History, Washington, D.C., 1973, p. 620.

5. Cora, pp. 100–101. Drew's gun camera jammed, failing to record his victories. One of his two wingmen was shot down, and the other aborted because of heavy flak and was unable to confirm that Drew downed the two German jets. There were no apparent witnesses and therefore no confirmation. Drew's victories were confirmed years later when a check with German authorities confirmed that two Me-262s were lost that day at Achmer. Major Georg-Peter Eder, in a third Me-262, had aborted his takeoff because of engine problems. Eder witnessed what happened to his two flight mates, and in May 1983, Drew was awarded the Air Force Cross in Washington, D.C., by then Secretary of the Air Force Verne Orr, based on Eder's confirmation of events. Major Eder, who, after Nowotny's death became a member of JG 7, had a total of more than seventy-eight victories. He is credited with at least twelve confirmed victories in the Me-262 and a possible additional twelve, making him one of Germany's highest-scoring jet aces.

6. Toliver, pp. 289–90, 330–40. According to the surrender terms negotiated, the 50th Fighter Group was supposed to escort the Salzburg Me-262s to Giebelstadt airfield. Aircraft at Innsbruck were to be escorted by the 86th Fighter Group to Gross Gerau, near Darmstadt.

7. *WW II History, 526th Fighter-Bomber Squadron, 86th Fighter-Bomber Group, October, 1944–October, 1945*, p. 231. The history is a compilation of official orders, war diary entries, and mission reports provided by Roy Brown, a former member of the 526th FS and a member of Watson's Whizzers. The 86th FG was assigned to the XII TAC, 1st TAF (Provisional). The history is in the author's possession.

8. Gebhard Aders, *History of the German Night Fighter Force, 1917–1945*, Jane's Publishing, New York, 1980, p. 245. Aders provides a comprehensive listing of German night fighter pilot victories and losses. *Fighter Aces of the Luftwaffe* by Toliver and Constable provides a more comprehensive listing of German day and night fighter aces with five or more victories (the definition of an ace), yet it fails to list Feldwebel Karl-Heinz Becker of JG 11, who, in his Me-262, had a total of seven night victories. None of these or other sources claim that their listings are complete.

9. Report of Operations, Oprep 328, 22 February 1945, for the 366th Fighter Group. Eighty-nine P-47 aircraft were tasked to escort bombers under Operations Order 145, Operation Clarion, and to conduct armed reconnaissance in the Düsseldorf, Elberfeld, Honnef, Bonn area.

10. For an authoritative treatment of the capture of the Remagen bridge and German attempts to destroy it, see Ken Hechler, *The Bridge at Remagen*, Pictorial Histories Publishing Co., Missoula, MT, 1999. For a unique German perspective on the capture of the bridge, see Wolfgang W. E. Samuel, *The War of Our Childhood*, University Press of Mississippi, 2002, pp. 112–26.

11. Davis, Coffin, and Woodward, p. 92.

12. Harold E. Watson, speech, 24 March 1981, p. 22.

CHAPTER 5: COLONEL HAROLD E. WATSON

1. Ruth Watson, interview by author, 28 November 2001, Palm Beach Gardens, Florida.

2. "Colonel Philip G. Cochran, War Hero And Model for 2 Cartoon Figures," obituary in the *New York Times*, 27 August 1979.

3. Wesley Frank Craven and James Lea Cate, *The Army Air Forces in World War II*, vol. 6, *Men and Planes*, Office of Air Force History, Washington, D.C., 1983, p. 352.

4. Headquarters USAFE, A-2, APO 633, *History of Directorate of Intelligence United States Strategic Air Forces in Europe, January 1944–May 1945*, 8 September 1945, p. 4.

5. Ibid., p. 42.

6. James Phinney Baxter III, *Scientists Against Time*, M.I.T. Press, Cambridge, MA, 1968, pp. 235–36.

7. Frederick I. Ordway III and Mitchell R. Sharpe, *The Rocket Team*, Thomas Y. Crowell, New York, 1979, pp. 251–53. Sources other than Ordway and Sharpe give slightly differing number sets for V-1/V-2 launches. Dr. Theodore Beneke writes in *History of German Guided Missiles Development*, Verlag E. Appelhans & Co., Brunswick, Germany, 1957, pp. 2–4: "1,115 of the V-2 were launched against England, and 2,050 against Brussels, Antwerp, and Liege. . . . Out of a total of 8,000 V-1 missiles launched against the London area, 2,000 were lost immediately, or shortly after the start, and of the remaining 6,000 missiles, 2,400 went through the concentrated anti-aircraft firing and reached the target." Beneke did some rounding off, but his numbers essentially confirm those provided by Ordway and Sharpe.

8. Harold E. Watson, speech, 24 March 1981, pp. 5–6.

CHAPTER 6: THE 1ST TACTICAL AIR FORCE (PROVISIONAL)

1. Harold E. Watson, speech, 24 March 1981, p. 9.

2. Putt, interview, p. 240.

3. HQ 1st TAF Service Command, APO 374, *History, Headquarters, First Tactical Air Force Service Command (Provisional), 20* October 1944–20 May 1945, pp. 8–10.

4. Ibid., pp. 11–13.

5. Special Order number 105, 21 April 1945, Headquarters, First Tactical Air Force (Provisional), extended the temporary duty assignments of aircraft company technical representatives assigned to combat squadrons of the 1st TAF.

6. The citation accompanying the award of the Bronze Star Medal read, in part: "Harold E. Watson, 0-21537, Colonel, Air Corps, I Tactical Air Force Service Command (Provisional) . . . was responsible for all phases of repair and maintenance that are required in keeping the maximum number of aircraft in an operational status. This task was made exceedingly difficult by the transfer of tactical organizations from the Mediterranean Theater of Operations to the European Theater of Operations. The highly superior manner in which Colonel Watson discharged his many responsibilities is evidenced by the increase from 66% of all aircraft in an operational status during the month of December 1944 to 84% during the month of March 1945."

7. Robert Strobell, interview by author, College Park, MD, 13 April 2000.

CHAPTER 7: ORGANIZING TO DISARM THE LUFTWAFFE

1. *History of Directorate of Intelligence*, p. 24.

2. Headquarters, First TAF (Prov.), APO 374, *Air Plan For Operation Eclipse*, 20 March 1945, pp. 1–4.

3. Letter from SHAEF, APO 757, to All Concerned, Subject: *Security of Operation "Eclipse,"* 19 March 1945, By Direction of the Supreme Commander, signed, T. J. Davis, Brigadier General, USA, Adjutant General.

4. Plan for Operation Eclipse, p. 1.

5. Letter from Colonel H. D. Sheldon to the Director of Intelligence, A-2 HQ USSTAF, APO 633, Subject: *Review of Intelligence Responsibilities of USSTAF— SHAEF Period and Tripartite Period*, 6 October 1944. General Arnold's direction provided for the establishment of the United States Air Forces in Europe, USAFE, upon the cessation of hostilities. The reorganization was put in effect in August 1945 with the establishment of Headquarters, United States Air Forces in Europe in Wiesbaden, Germany. In the interim Arnold's directive made Spaatz de facto commander of all Army Air Forces in the European and Mediterranean theaters of operation.

6. Headquarters IX Air Force Service Command, *History of the Air Disarmament Division, IX Air Force Service Command, October 1944 to March 1946*, Erlangen, Germany, May 1946, p. 7.

7. Letter from HQ USSTAF, APO 633, to the Commanding Officer, Air Disarmament Command, Subject: *Disbandment of Air Disarmament Command*, U.S. Strategic Air Forces in Europe (Provisional), dated 1 February 1945. The letter, in a few terse words, announced the disbandment of the Air Disarmament Command, by command of Lieutenant General Spaatz.

8. Letter from Headquarters USSTAF, APO 633, to Commanding Generals 9th Air Force and 1st TAF (Provisional), Subject: *Duties and Responsibilities of Ninth Air Force and First Tactical Air Force (Prov), with Respect to Disarmament of the German Air Force*, 16 January 1945. The eleven-page, top-secret document provided detailed guidance on how the disarmament function was to be executed and by whom, how it was to be administered, what its intelligence objectives were, and how captured materiel was to be handled and disposed of.

9. *History of the Air Disarmament Division*, pp. 11–16.

CHAPTER 8: OPERATION LUSTY

1. *History of Directorate of Intelligence*, p. 24. In military terminology the word *combined* refers to organizational entities which include other nationalities, such as the Combined Chiefs of Staff in World War II, which included American and British representatives of their ground, naval, and air forces. The word *joint* refers to national organizations or structures including members from more than one military service, such as the Joint Chiefs of Staff. Combined/joint military operations dating back to the Revolutionary War have been a hallmark of American military doctrine.

2. *History of Directorate of Intelligence*, p. 26.

3. Ibid., p. 57.

4. Ibid., p. 33.

5. Ibid., pp. 37–38. The creation of a centralized intelligence operation at headquarters USSTAF would have far-reaching consequences for the future Air Force. It carried forward into the postwar era when USSTAF became USAFE with its headquarters in Wiesbaden, Germany. General McDonald remained behind as the USAFE intelligence chief. He subsequently moved to the Pentagon when General Spaatz became the first Chief of Staff of a newly independent Air Force and appointed McDonald as his Assistant Chief of Staff for Intelligence on the newly created Air Staff with the rank of major general.

6. Memo from Colonel H. G. Bunker, Director of Technical Services, HQ USSTAF, APO 633, to his officers, dated 8 December 1944, and letter from Major General Hugh J. Knerr, Deputy Commanding General, Administration, USSTAF, to Major General Anderson, Deputy Commanding General, Operations, USSTAF,

Subject: Relationship of Functions of Director of Intelligence and Director of Technical Services, 8 December 1944.

7. *History of Directorate of Intelligence*, p. 31.

8. Letter, Director of Technical Services, Air Service Command, USSTAF, APO 633, to Chief, Technical Training Section, Subject: *Personnel Training*, 28 April 1944.

9. By 1944 Germany had deployed a wide variety of search and ground-control intercept (GCI) radars. The Freya search radar came in fixed and mobile versions with a range of up to one hundred twenty kilometers for a target flying at twenty-four thousand feet. The Würzburg and Giant Würzburg operated from a fixed site and in addition to range and bearing of a target was able to determine altitude as well. The Würzburg served primarily as a GCI radar and had a range of up to seventy kilometers for a target flying at nine thousand feet. The longer-range Freya search radar and the Würzburg GCI radar complemented each other in guiding German fighters toward their targets. Benito was a signal generator which emitted a radio beam for navigational purposes. Windjammer was another navigational aid used in conjunction with German GCI stations and provided bearing and slant range to a target. It was less susceptible to jamming than the Würzburg. Coastwatcher was a coast surveillance and fire control radar used to detect approaching ships and provide range and bearing information. Many of the German radars came in various sizes; some were mobile, others fixed. Later radars, such as the Wasserman and Hoarding, were quite large horizontally and vertically; for instance, the fixed Wasserman antenna was sixty-five feet wide and had a height of forty-five feet.

10. *History of Directorate of Technical Services*, Air Technical Service Command Europe, Section III, Air Intelligence Section, February 1944–September 1945, APO 633, U.S. Army.

11. Air Technical Intelligence, briefing, 10 April 1946, pp. 2–3.

12. Memo from Colonel Eric T. Bradley, Chief, Technical Intelligence Division, HQ USSTAF, APO 633, to Brigadier General George C. McDonald. Subject: *Status of Air Technical Intelligence Teams as Compared with C.I.O.S. Activity*, 16 April 1945.

13. Norman M. Naimark, *The Russians in Germany: A History of the Soviet Zone of Occupation, 1945–1949*, The Belknap Press of Harvard University Press, Cambridge, MA, 1995, p. 207.

14. Air Technical Intelligence, briefing, 10 April 1946, p. 3.

15. Harold E. Watson, speech, 19 March 1946, p. 9.

16. Status Report of Exploitation Divison, Tab L, *General Summary of Non-Technical Exploitation*, pp. 102–3.

17. TWX, Spaatz to Third Air Division, USSTAF, APO 633, *Initiation of Project Designated Operation Lusty*, 25 April 1945.

18. Letter from Office of the Commanding General, USSTAF (Main), APO 633, to all USSTAF commanders less Higher Hq, Subject: *Technically Trained Personnel for the Exploitation of Technical Intelligence Objectives.*

CHAPTER 9: SOLVING THE JAPANESE RIDDLE

1. *History of Directorate of Intelligence*, p. 59.

2. *History of Operation Lusty*, Headquarters United States Air Forces in Europe, APO 633, U.S. Army, 8 January 1946, p. 1.

3. Status Report of Exploitation Divison, Tab K, *Oberkommando der Luftwaffe (OKL) Personnel*, pp. 90–96.

4. *History of Operation Lusty*, pp. 1–2.

5. Status Report of Exploitation Divison, Tab L, *General Summary of Non-Technical Exploitation*, p. 102.

6. Ibid., Tab G, *General Summary of Technical Exploitation*, p. 69.

7. Ibid., Tab A, *Japanese Intelligence, Report IN Re: Collaboration Between Germany and Japan*, pp. 2–3.

8. Ibid., Tab A, pp. 19–33.

9. Ibid., Tab A, p. 32.

10. NAVSEA Undersea Warfare Center Division, Newport, Official U.S. Navy Web Site, http://www.npt.nuwc.navy.mil/PAO/Pr/sub_i52.htm, July 9, 2002.

11. Clay Blair, *Hitler's U-Boat War: The Hunted, 1942–1945*, Modern Library, New York, 2000, pp. 690–94. In addition to the disassembled Me-262 jet fighter, U-234 carried an Me-163B Komet rocket plane, as well as a Henschel 293 glide bomb, the latter much sought after by the U.S. Navy, as well as tons of documentation, Jumo 004 engines, and more.

12. Baur, p. 303.

13. Colonel John L. "Larry" Sutton, USAF (Ret.), interview by author, 14 March 2002, San Antonio, TX.

14. Toliver, p. 295.

15. *History of Operation Lusty*, pp. 15–16.

16. Status Report of Exploitation Divison, Tab A, pp. 4–18.

CHAPTER 10: A MOTHER LODE OF AVIATION TECHNOLOGY

1. *History of the Air Disarmament Division*, p. 10.

2. Naimark, pp. 215–16.

3. Memorandum from D/I HQ USSTAF, APO 633, Subject: *Disarmament Division—Directorate of Intelligence Coordination*, 2 May 1945. This document sets forth agreements reached between IX Air Force Service Command and USSTAF Director of Intelligence, including the establishment of three collection points (Merseburg, Nürnberg, and Stuttgart), responsibilities of the Directorate of Intelligence, and responsibilities of IX AF Service Command. See also Status Report of Exploitation Divison, p. 60.

4. Letter from Headquarters, USSTAF, APO 633, Office of the Commanding General, 22 May 1945, Subject: *Exploitation of German Air Force by United States Strategic Air Forces in Europe*. To: Commanding General Army Air Forces, Washington, D.C. Incl #1—Appendix "A" Operating Procedures for A.T.I. of Technical Intelligence Division.

5. Letter USSTAF, Office of the Commanding General, APO 633, U.S. Army, 22 April 1945, Subject: Request for Billeting Arrangements. To: Commanding General, Communications Zone, ETO, APO 887, U.S. Army. "It is requested that arrangements be made to set aside billeting accommodations for approximately fifty specialist personnel, both civilian and military, with actual or assimilated ranks ranging from Lieutenant Colonel through Major General." Attached to the letter was a list of the names of Dr. von Karman's group of scientists visiting the ETO.

6. Theodore von Karman, *Toward New Horizons*, Headquarters, Army Air Forces, Washington, D.C., 15 December 1945, pp. iii–xv.

7. Memorandum from Director of Personnel, Headquarters USSTAF, APO 633, to the Director of Intelligence, 7 April 1945, subject: *Technical Specialists for Exploitation of Objectives in Germany*, states that: "A letter has just been received from General Hodges, Assistant Chief of Air Staff, Intelligence, listing thirty-three civilian technical specialists in categories which directly concern the Technical Intelligence Division. . . . It is urgent that this entire group be transported to this Theater at the earliest possible moment. Many of the listed targets have already been opened up and there is insufficient personnel possessing the necessary technical qualifications to adequately protect Army Air Forces interests."

8. Exploitation of German Air Force, Appendix "B," *Equipment for Specialists Exploiting Targets in ETO*.

9. Chilstrom and Leery, p. 82.

10. J. H. Carter, Chief Fighter Production Branch, Wright Field, Dayton, Ohio, *The American Jet Propelled Plane, P-80*, briefing presented to Lt. General Spaatz and staff at Headquarters, USSTAF, 19 January 1945.

11. Report, Headquarters USSTAF, APO 633, Office of the Director of Intelligence, 18 January 1945, *An Evaluation of German Capabilities in 1945*.

12. Chilstrom and Leery, pp. 92–93.

13. Harriet Buyer and Edna Jensen, *History of AAF participation in Project Paper-clip, May 1945–March 1947 (Exploitation of German Scientists)*, Historical Office, Executive Secretariat, Air Materiel Command, Wright-Patterson AFB, Ohio, August 1948, p. 44.

14. Status Report of Exploitation Divison, Tabs E and G, pp. 60, 64.

15. Ibid., Tab G, pp. 64–65.

16. Ibid., Tab D, p. 59.

17. *History of Operation Lusty*, p. 2. During Operation Lusty the Doblhoff jet-powered helicopter was referred to in USSTAF documentation as the Dh 243. Once it arrived at Freeman Field, Indiana, it became FE-4615 and WNF 342, the latter prominently painted on its rudder. The WNF stood for Wiener Neustadt Flugzeugwerke, where the prototype was being built up prior to its evacuation and subsequent capture near Zell am See.

18. Status Report of Exploitation Divison, Tab G, p. 66.

19. *History of Operation Lusty*, p. 8.

20. As USSTAF was redesignated USAFE, it was not only the name that was changing for the United States Air Forces in Europe but also its commanders. Major General Cannon initially replaced General Spaatz on 3 June 1945, but then Spaatz returned temporarily to command 13–30 June 1945. He was succeeded by Major General Westside T. Larson from 30 June to 4 July 1945, and Larson was replaced by Major General William E. Kepner, who commanded USAFE 3–13 August. The musical chairs routine then came to an end and Cannon again took over. He was replaced by Major General Idwal Edwards on 2 March 1946. On 14 August 1947 Brigadier General John F. McBain assumed temporary command until 20 October 1947, when Major General Curtis E. LeMay took over. Lieutenant General John K. Cannon returned for one final time on 16 October 1948. The Berlin airlift from 1948 to 1949 was flown largely under Cannon's watch (source, Dr. Roger Miller, AF/HO).

21. Letter from Brigadier General George C. McDonald, ACS/A-2, USAFE, APO 633, "German Underground Structures," 29 August 1945, to Commanding General, USAFE.

22. Status Report of Exploitation Divison, Tab G, pp. 72–73. To obtain optimum results with their surface-to-air missile developments required a proximity fuze or a homing device. According to Post Hostilities Investigation, German Air Defenses, Volume I, page 4, of the four methods of fuzing examined by the Germans—photoelectrical, electrical, acoustic, and infrared—at the end of the war none of the projects had gone past the development stage and no fuze had been developed that was small enough for a flak projectile and could withstand

the shock of being fired from a gun. Proximity fuzing coupled to antiaircraft artillery and SAMs was the most cost-effective approach to defeating Allied air superiority, yet only peripheral resources were brought to bear in this important field, an area in which American science excelled.

23. Ibid., Tab G, pp. 68–72.

24. *History of Operation Lusty*, pp. 9–12.

25. Status Report of Exploitation Divison, Tab G, p. 75; Tab H, List of German Scientific Personnel; Tab I, German Scientific Personnel Withdrawn for Further Interrogation from Areas Evacuated by U.S. Troops.

CHAPTER 11: THE SECRETS OF VÖLKENRODE AND KOCHEL

1. Putt, interview, pp. 25–26.

2. Ibid., pp. 1–8.

3. Ibid., pp. 230–38.

4. Ibid., p. 40.

5. Putt, speech, p. 4.

6. Status Report of Exploitation Divison, Tab B, p. 54.

7. Putt, interview, pp. 26–27.

8. Ibid., pp. 53–54.

9. Status Report of Exploitation Divison, Tab B, pp. 53–56.

10. Putt, interview, p. 39.

11. Status Report of Exploitation Divison, Tab B, p. 56.

12. Putt, interview, pp. 36, 107–8.

13. Ibid., p. 110. Colonel Putt recalled that "at almost the same time that Busemann was developing his theories of swept-back wings in Germany—and, of course, this was during wartime; there was no communication—a chap by the name of R. T. Jones at Langley Field in NACA was developing the same thing. But … his work had not been made public here in the United States yet. But he and Busemann were almost together in developing this theory of the swept-back wing. Jones's wing design was of course classified top secret and still had to overcome much skepticism within the scientific community. It was that coincidence of von Karman and Busemann chatting about Busemann's test results with swept-back wing aircraft models, in the presence of George Schairer, the Boeing Chief Aerodynamicist, which changed the world of aviation."

14. Status Report of Exploitation Divison, Tab B, p. 53.

15. Buyer and Jensen, p. 44.

16. Status Report of Exploitation Divison, Tab B, p. 57.

17. Putt, interview, pp. 27–29.

18. Memorandum, Subject: *1st TAF Guard Facilities for USSTAF D/I Exploitation*, 15 May 1945, from Colonel Stone (1st TAF liaison officer at the 12th TAC) to Colonel Sheldon, Director, Exploitation Division, HQ USSTAF, APO 633. The memo defines arrangements made by the 12th TAC to guard intelligence targets in the 7th Army Area, including 120 men at Salzburg, 130 men at Munich-Riem, 130 men at Holzkirchen, and 120 men at Fürstenfeldbruck. The memo then states that "The 12th TAC were given two important targets to start guarding immediately: (a) The Peenemünde Wind Tunnel—located at Kochel, 40 Kilometers East of Innsbruck Y-7202—Headed by Dr. Heyer [should have read Dr. Hermann, a clerical error], German Scientist. (b) The BMW Plant, Baumwall [Baumwolle] Spinnerei at Munich."

19. Status Report of Exploitation Divison, Tab C, p. 58.

20. Fritz Zwicky, report entitled "Introductory Remarks to the Reports on the Peenemünde Supersonic Wind Tunnels at Kochel," 22 June 1945, Naval Technical Mission, Europe, Report No. 162–45.

21. Status Report of Exploitation Divison, Tab A, pp. 4–7.

22. Clarence G. Lasby, *Project Paperclip: German Scientists and the Cold War*, Atheneum, New York, 1971, pp. 3–4.

CHAPTER 12: THE FEUDIN' 54TH

1. *History, 54th Air Disarmament Squadron (Prov)*, 1 December 1944–31 December 1944, APO 639, pp. 1–4.

2. *History, 54th Air Disarmament Squadron (Prov)*, 1 February 1945–28 February 1945, APO 639, pp. 1–2.

3. *History, 54th Air Disarmament Squadron (Prov)*, 1 March 1945–31 March 1945, APO 639, pp. 9–11.

4. Letter, Subject: *Unit History*. 54th Air Disarmament Squadron (P), Office of the Operations Officer, APO 149. To: Commanding Officer, 2nd Air Disarmament Wing, APO 149 U.S. Army, 6 October 1945. Page 1. The Me-262 recovered at Giebelstadt had no engines; it was shipped to Wright Field but never flew.

5. *History, 54th Air Disarmament Squadron (Prov)*, 1 May 1945–31 May 1945, APO 149, p. 1.

6. *Unit History*, p. 2.

7. *Unit History, 20th Air Disarmament Squadron (Prov)*, May–July 1945, APO 149.

8. Letter, Subject: *Squadron History*. From: 21st Air Disarmament Squadron (Prov), Office of the Commanding Officer, APO 149. To: Commanding Officer, 5th Air Disarmament Group (Prov), APO 149, U.S. Army. Histories for the months of April and May and 1–5 June 1945.

9. Letter, Subject: *Historical Record.* 52nd Air Disarmament Squadron (Prov), APO 149, U.S. Army, 5 June 1945. To: Commanding Officer, Hq, 9th Air Disarmament Group (Prov), APO 149, U.S. Army, pp. 1–2.

10. *History of the Air Disarmament Division*, p. 13. The 1st Air Disarmament Wing, which had its headquarters at Fulda and was responsible for the disarmament of the northern portion of American-occupied territory, encountered only small numbers of Luftwaffe personnel. In contrast, the 2nd Air Disarmament Wing captured 55,000 GAF personnel. Of the 55,000, about 40,000 were transferred to ground forces for processing; 11,500 were lost to escape, and the remainder were turned over to USSTAF ATI teams for interrogation and processing.

11. *History, 56th Air Disarmament Squadron (Prov)*, May 1945, pp. 1–2.

12. *History, 55th Air Disarmament Squadron (Prov)*, 1–31 May 1945, pp. 1–2.

13. *Unit History*, p. 2.

14. *History of the Air Disarmament Division*, p. 114.

15. Aders, p. 217.

CHAPTER 13: WATSON PICKS HIS TEAM

1. Memorandum from Colonel McCoy to Colonel Sheldon, Chief, Exploitation Division, Headquarters USSTAF, Subject: *Draft Statement of Plan for Implementation of Operation Lusty*, dated 25 April 1945, pp. 1–4.

2. Headquarters USSTAF message NT-18-CS, JD117-CS, 16 April 1945; Status Report of Exploitation Division, Tab G, p. 59.

3. Baur, p. 295.

4. Headquarters USSTAF, Directorate of Intelligence, Exploitation Division intra Division Memo—"Hire of German Civilians," APO 633, dated 5 June 1945. The memo provides a listing of names, skills (whether pilot or mechanic), number of children, and monthly payment for each of the twenty-seven former Messerschmitt employees engaged by Colonel Watson at Lechfeld.

5. *History, 54th Air Disarmament Squadron (Prov)*, APO 149, June 1945, p. 2.

6. Baur, p. 295.

7. Eugene Freiburger, taped recollections made 21 March 1994 on Operation Lusty and the recovery of Me-262 jet fighters from Lechfeld, Germany. Tape in possession of Dennis Freiburger.

CHAPTER 14: LAGER LECHFIELD

1. Baur, p. 295.

2. *Dennis* is the Me-262 jet on exhibit in the National Air and Space Museum in Washington, D.C. Sergeant Arnold's aircraft had his combat victories painted on the aft fuselage. According to German protocol, aerial victories were usually shown on the vertical stabilizer and the rudder. American practice was to show victories below the pilot's canopy. At this stage of the war, however, there was little time for harried maintenance crews to follow protocol. The victory markings may have even been applied by Sergeant Arnold himself. This wasn't of any particular interest to Sergeant Freiburger, however. What mattered to him was that *Dennis* was the first flyable aircraft he had ready for Colonel Watson.

3. Status Report of Exploitation Divison, Tab G, p. 74.

4. Harold E. Watson, speech, 24 March 1981, p. 42.

5. Ibid., pp. 47–48.

6. Baur, p. 296.

7. Blair, p. 692.

CHAPTER 15: P-47 JUG PILOTS

1. Headquarters First Tactical Air Force Service Command, pp. 14–17.

2. Listing of personnel working on the Me-262 project issued by the Exploitation Division, A-2, USSTAF, undated. The listing includes both American and German names, but only shows the names of fourteen Germans, which indicates that it was issued at Lechfeld prior to the departure of the aircraft to Melun, France. The fourteen Germans were the ones intended to accompany the aircraft movement and included Gerhard Caroli, superintendent; Karl Baur, pilot; Ludwig Hoffmann, pilot; Hermann Kersting, pilot; Georg Fauser, inspector; Hans Ebner, mechanic; Andreas Sebald, mechanic; Reinhold Maruschke, mechanic; Hans Brand, mechanic; Hans Nabholz, mechanic; Wilhelm Wedemann, mechanic; Fritz Hindelang, mechanic; Richard Huber, mechanic; and Karl Schwenk, mechanic. Kersting was fired by Strobell.

3. Robert Anspach, interview by author, 29 October 2001, Orlando, Florida.

4. Roger A. Freeman, *Zemke's Wolf Pack*, Orion Books, New York, 1988, p. 177.

5. Kenneth O. Chilstrom, interview by author, 28 November 2001, Palm Beach Gardens, Florida.

6. *WW II History, 526th Fighter-Bomber Squadron*, pp. 232–33.

7. Roy Brown, interview by author, 14 November 2001, Chillicothe, Ohio.

8. Strobell, interview.

CHAPTER 16: WATSON'S WHIZZERS

1. Harold E. Watson, speech, 24 March 1981, p. 43.

2. Baur, p. 296.

3. Harold E. Watson, speech, 24 March 1981, p. 61.

4. Strobell, interview.

5. Harold E. Watson, speech, 24 March 1981, p. 45.

6. Anspach, interview.

7. A. Scott Berg, *Lindbergh*, Putnam & Sons, New York, 1998, pp. 464–66.

8. For a detailed aircrew perspective of flying the RB-45C using the J-47 engine, see chapter 8 of Wolfgang W. E. Samuel, *I Always Wanted to Fly: America's Cold War Airmen*, University Press of Mississippi, Jackson, 2001.

9. Strobell, interview.

10. Anspach, interview.

11. Roy Brown, interview.

12. Baur, p. 296.

13. Headquarters, European Theater of Operations, United States Army, *Procurement, Administration and Payment of Civilian Labor in Germany*, APO 887, 28 March 1945.

CHAPTER 17: THE MERSEBURG FAN CLUB

1. McIntosh, interviews.

2. In 1948, again serving as commander of the 56th Fighter Group, Schilling led them across the Atlantic in their new P-80 jets. He finally did get to fly jets, if not the Me-262. In 1956 Colonel Schilling, the victor in twenty-three aerial engagements, died in an auto accident in England. The now-closed Schilling AFB, Salina, Kansas, was named after Colonel David Schilling.

3. Speer, pp. 290–91.

4. Peter W. Stahl, *KG 200: The True Story*, Jane's Publishing, New York, 1981, pp. 46–55.

5. Interview with Major H. Clayton Beaman, Jr., by the Assistant Chief of Air Staff, Intelligence, Headquarters Army Air Forces, Washington D.C., 10 June 1943, p. 5.

6. Michael Turner and Frank Mason, *Luftwaffe Aircraft*, Crescent Books, New York, pp. 124–26.

7. Putt, speech, pp. 41–42. Said Putt of George Goddard, "One we should never forget is [Brigadier General] George Goddard, the photographic proponent. He was the leader in aerial photography and mapping as it applied to reconnaissance. He wielded a tremendous force, not only on the development of equipment within the Air Force itself, but within the industry. He played quite a role at Fairchild Camera and Instruments Company."

8. Harold E. Watson, speech, 24 March 1981, p. 38. There remains the issue of the date of Hauptmann Braun's landing at Munich. Watson wrote that it was

May 6. Peter Stahl, writing in *KG 200: The True Story*, stated that Braun "came via Königgrätz to Munich, where he landed on the last day of the war." The last day of the war was May 8, VE Day. The unconditional surrender was signed on May 7, in Reims, France, and German forces were notified that "All hostilities were to cease at 2301 hours, military time, on May 8."

9. USSTAF Directorate of Intelligence, Exploitation Division, *Daily Activity Report—Technical Intelligence—30 May 1945*, Section IV. Miscellaneous, Paragraph 6, "Merseburg requested to move Collection Point, including radio station and equipment and all personnel to Newbiburg [Neubiberg] Airport, R-85, approximately 3 miles south of Munich. This move should be completed as soon as possible and should start on Saturday, 2 June."

10. The airmen of the 56th Fighter Group didn't dismember the old war veteran after all. The Heinkel bomber remained at Boxted and was acquired by the British when the airbase was closed.

11. McIntosh, interviews.

CHAPTER 18: PROJECT SEAHORSE

1. Message from Headquarters USSTAF, UA69291, approved by George C. McDonald, D/I, to War Department. To Arnold, signed Spaatz, 16 May 1945. Subject: *Information On Mike Easy Two Six Two.*

2. Message from War Department, Number 006/19th R R. To: JEUS, To Spaatz for Knerr, Attention Director Technical Services from Hodges, Signed Arnold. 18 May 1945, sent 182241Zulu time.

3. Letter from Major General James P. Hodges, Assistant Chief of Air Staff Intelligence, Washington, D.C., to Brigadier General George C. McDonald, Director of Intelligence, Hq USSTAF, APO 639, New York, N.Y., 29 May 1945. "Dear Mack: In answer to your letter of 14 May 1945 I feel sure that some of the complications which arose in the Hans Fay incident will not be experienced in similar future cases. It was essential that he be made available without delay to technical authorities at Wright Field. I know that this was the paramount consideration back of your action, and, equally so, it was the primary purpose of our efforts. Since the Fay incident we have had a number of conversations and negotiations with CPM Branch, G-2, with a view to emphasizing the necessity of expediting exploitation and interrogation of enemy prisoners of war, or enemy civilians who reach this country, insofar as these may bear on Air Force subjects."

4. Martin E. James, *Historical Highlights: United States Air Forces in Europe, 1945–1979*, Office of History, Headquarters, United States Air Forces in Europe, APO New York 09012, 28 November 1980, pp. 3–4.

5. Memorandum, Headquarters, USSTAF, A-2, Exploitation Division, Operations Section, Colonel Lloyd K. Pepple. To: Operations, Target Section. Subject: *Project 'Seahorse,'* 14 June 1945.

6. Memorandum from Assistant Chief of Staff Intelligence, A-2, USSTAF, Brigadier General George C. McDonald, to Chief of Staff, USSTAF [Lieutenant General Cannon], Subject: *Necessity of Securing Aircraft Carrier for a Priority Shipment of Captured Enemy Material,* 16 June 1945.

7. Message from War Department, 152207Z No 278/15th R R, To: GR 105 [Headquarters USSTAF]. Subject: *Pending Determination of Navy Ability to Furnish Carrier.*

8. Message USSTAF, Cannon, to War, Arnold, UA70981, 18 June 1945.

9. Message from: NAVTECHMISEU, To: Chief of Naval Operations (OP-16-PT), 20 June 1945.

10. Message, 221402, from COMINCH, To: COMNAVEU, 22 June 1945.

11. Message, 231412, from COMNAVEUR, To: Admiralty, 23 June 1945.

12. Message, 281605, from Admiralty, To: COMNAVEUR, 28 June 1945.

13. Message, 031650, from NAVTECMISEU, To: Admiralty, 3 July 1945.

14. Letter from Colonel Harold E. Watson, Headquarters, USSTAF, A-2, Exploitation Division, Operations Section, to Lieutenant Colonel Seashore. Subject: *To Do List,* June 7, 1945, Part II, *Activity at Cherbourg,* page 2.

15. Ibid., Part I, Activities at A-55, p. 1.

CHAPTER 19: MELUN-VILLAROCHE

1. Butler, p. 270.

2. Harold E. Watson, *Flight Test Report, Operation of ME-262,* Headquarters USSTAF, A-2, Exploitation Division, APO 633, 13 June 1945, pp. 1–2, and Appendices A through F.

3. Baur, p. 296.

4. Harold E. Watson, *Flight Test Report,* p. 2.

5. Memorandum, Headquarters USSTAF, A-2, Exploitation Division, Operations Section, AAF Station 379, Colonel Harold E. Watson. To: Colonel Sheldon, 11 June 1945.

6. Watson's Whizzers ME 262 Project, ATI A-2 USSTAF, Operations Order No. 2, 26 June 1945.

7. Strobell, interview.

8. Harold E. Watson, speech, 24 March 1981, pp. 51–52.

9. Chilstrom and Leery, pp. 119–20.

10. News clipping from the personal collection of Harold E. Watson. The clipping appears to have come from the *New London Evening Day.*

CHAPTER 20: ROAST DUCK AT AALBORG

1. Harold E. Watson, speech, 24 March 1981, p. 29.
2. Ibid., pp. 29–30.
3. McIntosh, interviews.
4. HQ USSTAF, A-2, Exploitation Division Notes, *Operation Seahorse*, APO 633, 20 June 1945.
5. Butler, p. 270.
6. Strobell, interview.
7. Eric Brown, pp. 140–41.
8. Ibid., p. 91.
9. McIntosh, interviews.
10. Harold E. Watson, speech, 24 March 1981, pp. 34–35.

CHAPTER 21: THE ARADO 234 CAPER

1. Butler, pp. 189–90.
2. Harold E. Watson, speech, 24 March 1981, p. 15.
3. Eric Brown, p. 92.
4. Harold E. Watson, speech, 24 March 1981, pp. 16–17.
5. Eric Brown, p. 92.
6. Exploitation Division Notes.
7. Eric Brown, pp. 94–98.
8. Harold E. Watson, speech, 24 March 1981, p. 18.
9. Ibid., pp. 18–19.
10. Baur, p. 296.
11. Harold E. Watson, speech, 24 March 1981, p. 20.
12. McIntosh, interviews. There is no convergence of views about what actually happened on that flight from Sola, Norway, to Melun, France. Many years later Watson claimed to have flown three 234s out of Sola, which is impossible, because two were already at Melun in June for General Spaatz's show-and-tell, and a total of only four Arado 234 aircraft were ever collected for transfer to the United States. Records show that the British originally allocated two Arado 234 aircraft to the AAF—the two flown to Melun in June. The other two aircraft Watson absconded with from Sola, Norway, and that made a total of four. As for Watson making an intermediate fuel stop at Grove, Fred McIntosh in his interview claimed it was Schleswig airfield, not Grove. Grove and Schleswig are less than an hour's flying time from Sola and not likely intermediate refueling stops. Le Culot, an hour's flying time from

Sola, would have been the obvious choice, as recorded by Karl Baur in his diary.

13. Harold E. Watson, speech, 24 March 1981, pp. 21–22.

CHAPTER 22: SO FAR, SO GOOD

1. Baur, p. 296.
2. Strobell, interview.
3. Anspach, interview.
4. Strobell, interview.

CHAPTER 23: THE CONQUERING HERO

1. Memorandum, 8 July 1945, Exploitation Division, Directorate of Intelligence, Headquarters USSTAF, APO 633, from Major Anderson through Colonel Pepple to Colonel Sheldon. Subject: *Pilots and Maintenance Personnel for Jet Aircraft.*
2. Message from HQ COMM Z 261606B To: HQ USSTAF MAIN 262325B, 26 June 1945.
3. General Order No. 98, 17 July 1945, Headquarters USSTAF in Europe, Office of the Commanding General. Award of the Distinguished Flying Cross to Harold E. Watson, Colonel, Army Air Forces, United States Army. Awards of the Oak Leaf Cluster to the Air Medal to Captains Kenneth Earl Dahlstrom and Fred L. Hillis and First Lieutenants Roy W. Brown, Jr., Robert J. Anspach, James K. Holt, and Robert Carl Strobell.
4. Harold E. Watson, speech, 24 March 1981, p. 40.
5. Ibid., p. 41.
6. McIntosh, interviews.
7. Baur, pp. 297–98.
8. Harold E. Watson, speech, 24 March 1981, p. 40.
9. Harry S. Truman, *Memoirs*, Doubleday & Company, Garden City, NY, 1955, vol. 1, pp. 332–414.
10. From a newspaper clipping in the Harold E. Watson collection.
11. From a newspaper clipping in the Harold E. Watson collection.
12. AMC Letter No. 21-17, Headquarters Air Materiel Command, Wright Field, 25 June 1946. Subject: *Freeman Field, Seymour, Indiana.* This letter was a restatement of an earlier ATSC policy letter issued on December 4, 1945, by AMC's predecessor organization, the Air Technical Service Command. Organizational realignments and resulting name changes were common occurrences between 1944 and 1947 as the Army Air Forces coped with vast reductions in personnel

and resources and the achievement of its own independence from the Army in September 1947.

13. General Order No. 136, Headquarters USAFE, Office of the Commanding General, 16 October 1945. Award of the Air Medal to Harold E. Watson, 0-21537, Colonel, Army Air Forces, United States Army.

CHAPTER 24: THE FOCKE-WULF 190 TRAGEDY

1. Chilstrom and Leery, p. 239.
2. This was the aircraft surrendered by Hans Fay in Frankfurt on March 31, 1945. It was disassembled and shipped by Liberty ship to the United States. They forgot to put the guns back in when they reassembled the aircraft; that was one reason why Watson didn't want his airplanes disassembled—they might suffer a similar fate. Why Hans Fay, the German test pilot who surrendered the aircraft at Frankfurt and who had been flown to the United States for interrogation, was not used to supervise his aircraft's reassembly and participate in subsequent flight testing has to remain an open question. The same question can be asked of the German Dornier 335 test pilot Hans Padell. Hans was flown to the United States for interrogation, and, like Fay, wasn't used by the Wright Field flight test division. As a result the Dornier 335 was never flown.
3. Chilstrom and Leery, p. 188.
4. Chilstom, interview.
5. Butler, p. 196.
6. Anspach, interview.
7. Newspaper clipping from the Harold E. Watson collection, datelined Freeman Field, Indiana, 30 September 1945. The piece was by Charles A. Densmore, *Dayton Daily News.*
8. Analysis by Roy W. Brown, *A Trim Control Problem of the Focke-Wulf 190,* November 2001, in possession of the author.

CHAPTER 25: AIR SHOWS AND AIR RACES

1. Newspaper clipping from the Harold E. Watson collection, datelined Freeman Field, Seymour, Indiana, 31 August 1945, *The New London Evening Day.* August 31 is an error; the date should be September 30. The three jets referred to in the article didn't arrive at Freeman Field until the first day of the two-day air show, September 29.
2. Baur, p. 301.
3. Newspaper clipping from the Harold E. Watson collection, datelined Freeman Field, Seymour, Indiana, 31 August 1945, *The New London Evening Day.*

4. Chilstrom and Leery, p. 244.

5. Ibid., p. 250.

6. Robin Olds commanded the 8th TFW in 1966 flying out of Ubon, Thailand. He shot down four MiGs while there. In World War II he scored twelve aerial victories.

7. Harold E. Watson, speech, 24 March 1981, pp. 54–55.

CHAPTER 26: THE BIRTH OF PROJECT OVERCAST

1. Franz Hausmann (name changed by request), interview by author, 19 October 2001, Frederick, Maryland.

2. Memorandum to Commanding General, U.S. Strategic Air Forces in Europe, APO 633, 1 June 1945, from Major General Hugh J. Knerr, Deputy Commanding General.

3. Buyer and Jensen, p. 4.

4. Ibid., p. 5.

5. Letter from Colonel D. L. Putt, USSTAF, APO 633, to Major General K.B. Wolfe, HQ ATSC, Wright Field, Dayton, Ohio.

6. Memorandum for Colonel Donald L. Putt, from Major General Hugh J. Knerr, Deputy Commanding General USSTAF, APO 633, 30 May 1945.

7. Buyer and Jensen, p. 24.

8. Memorandum for Assistant Chief of Air Staff, Intelligence, Washington, D.C., Subject: *German Civilian Technicians*, 21 May 1945, by Major L.F. Crawford, Chief, Interrogation Branch, Office of the Assistant Chief of Air Staff, Intelligence.

9. Buyer and Jensen, p. 6.

10. Memorandum from the Joint Chiefs of Staff, Washington, D.C., for Assistant Chief of Staff, G-2, WDGS, and others, Subject: *Code Designation for German Scientists Exploitation Center*, 20 July 1945.

11. Buyer and Jensen, pp. 10–11.

12. Ibid., p. 6.

13. Memorandum, Foreign Technical Seminar Branch, Reference Office, Intelligence, T-2, Air Technical Service Command, Wright Field, Ohio, submitted by Dr. G. Braun, Dr. J. Nöggerath, Dr. R. Edse, and Dr. T. Zobel to Captain H.W. Boesch, Chief Foreign Technical Seminar Branch, T-2, p. 1.

14. Letter from Brigadier General George C. McDonald, Office of the Assistant Chief of Staff, A-2, Headquarters USAFE, APO 633, to Major General Hugh J. Knerr, Commanding General, ATSC, Wright Field, Ohio, 3 November 1945, *Dear Hugh...* , p. 1.

15. Memorandum, Foreign Technical Seminar Branch, pp. 1–4.

16. Buyer and Jensen, p. 105.

17. Ibid., pp. 56–69.

18. Ibid., pp. 105–11.

CHAPTER 27: PROJECT OVERCAST AND ONE MAN'S EXPERIENCE

1. Baur, p. 297.

2. Special Contract For Employment Of German Nationals With The War Department In The United States. War Department, Washington, D.C., p. 1.

3. Buyer and Jensen, p. 105.

4. Baur, pp. 300–7.

CHAPTER 28: FROM OVERCAST TO PAPERCLIP

1. Putt, interview, p. 56.

2. Buyer and Jensen, pp. 94–95.

3. Memorandum from Colonel R. C. Harmon, Acting Judge Advocate, Wright Field, Ohio, to Captain Shurley, *Interpretation of Special Contract for Employment of German Nationals*, 15 October 1945. In the margin of the memorandum was written "Personal for Col D. L. Putt," meaning that a copy of the legal opinion had been forwarded to Colonel Putt, and he was quite aware of how his subordinates had mangled the program.

4. Buyer and Jensen, pp. 95–99.

5. Putt, interview, p. 57.

6. Buyer and Jensen, p. 100.

7. Memorandum from Major Arthur W. Curtis, Headquarters Army Air Forces, Washington, D.C., *Relaxation of Certain Restrictions on 35 German PW to be Selected and Sent to Wright Field for work with German Scientists*, undated, for Chief, Air Information Division. The memorandum was passed to Brigadier General John Weckerling for action.

8. Memorandum for General Banfille from Brigadier General John Weckerling, War Department General Staff, Deputy Assistant Chief of Staff, G-2, Washington, D.C., *Use of Prisoners of War at Wright Field in Connection with OVERCAST*, 13 November 1945.

9. Buyer and Jensen, p. 101.

10. Ibid., p. 102. Although vigorous appeals were initiated to retain at least some German volunteer POWs for the Overcast project at Wright Field, no exceptions were granted. In contrast to the United States, the Soviet Union

did not release the last German POWs until January 1956, the year the Federal Republic of Germany became a NATO member.

11. Buyer and Jensen, pp. 103–4.

12. Ibid., pp. 84–85.

13. *Extract from Report by Colonel McCoy*, to TSRFE/T-2 and TSDIN/T-2, 28 November 1945, from Colonel D. L. Putt, Deputy Commanding General, Intelligence, T-2. Wrote Colonel Putt, "The following are extracts from a report written by Colonel McCoy during his recent trip to Great Britain and Germany and are forwarded as of personal interest to German Scientists now at Wright Field."

14. Memorandum from TSEAL-6G, ATSC, Wright Field, Ohio, to TSEAL-6A, Lieutenant Colonel B. A. Davis, Laboratory Chiefs' Meeting 26 July 1945.

15. Putt, interview, p. 56.

16. Buyer and Jensen, p. 66.

17. Ibid., p. 67

18. Ibid., pp. 67–83.

19. Ibid., p. 125.

20. Letter from Colonel D. L. Putt, Headquarters ATSC, Wright Field, Ohio, to Major General E. R. Quesada, AS/AZ-2, 16 October 1945.

21. Buyer and Jensen, pp. 19–26.

22. War Department, Public Relations Division, Press Section, Washington, D.C., Joint State-Army-Navy Release, *More German and Austrian Scientists to Aid Army-Navy Research Program.*

23. *Newsweek*, 11 November 1946, "Recruiting German Brainpower."

24. War Department, Public Relations Division, Press Section, Washington, D.C., Memorandum to the Press: The story of the presence at various Army installations of German scientists who signed contracts to work in this country will be made available to press, radio and pictorial services. The following installations will be opened to media representatives, on dates noted: Wright Field [Dayton, Ohio] . . . November 18 and 19. Fort Bliss [El Paso, Texas] . . . November 20 and 21.

25. *Dayton Daily News*, 4 December 1946, "Wright Field Reveals 'Operation Paperclip,'" p. D-5.

26. Buyer and Jensen, p. 26.

27. War Department, Washington D.C., Contract for Professional Services [Paperclip Contract], p. 7.

28. Letter, Headquarters Army Air Forces, Washington, D.C., To: Commanding General, Air Materiel Command, Wright Field, Dayton, Ohio, *Approximate Date of Arrival of German Scientists' Families in the United States*, 1 November 1946.

29. *Dayton Daily News*, Thursday, 12 December 1946, "Scientists' Families Here."

30. Buyer and Jensen, p. 125.

31. Ibid., pp. 40–41.

32. *Dayton Daily News*, 24 March 1947, "Ban On German Scientists Asked."

CHAPTER 29: HOW CAPTAIN WENZEL MADE AMERICAN CITIZENS OUT OF ENEMY ALIENS

1. Baur, p. 304.

2. Hans H. Amtmann, *The Vanishing Paperclips: America's Aerospace Secret: A Personal Account*, Monogram Aviation Publications, Boylston, MA, 1988, pp. 11–14.

3. While Colonel Putt and General Knerr struggled to get their German scientists moved to the United States, the Army Service Forces Command in late 1945 quietly assembled the von Braun missile group at Fort Bliss, Texas, by bringing them into the country as part of the routine transfer of American servicemen from Europe to the United States. On Friday, 7 December 1945, the *Cincinnati Times* reported, "Twenty-five German scientists, the second group brought to this country by the Government in recent weeks, for special scientific work here, arrived . . . yesterday among 4,654 American soldiers on the transport *Lejeune* from Le Havre. The voyage of the scientists was a secret and Army officers guarding the men as they disembarked at Pier 51, North River [New York], kept the party herded closely together. On orders from Washington they kept reporters and photographers away and declined to say where the group would go when they left the pier. A similar group arrived on the transport *Argentina* on November 16. The *Lejeune*, a former German liner . . . came from Havre with service men and twenty-five civilians in addition to the Germans."

4. *Dayton Daily News*, 24 March 1947.

5. Special Order 149, Headquarters, Sacramento Air Materiel Area, McClellan Field, California, 29 July 1946, paragraph 1. Reassignment of Captain Lloyd M. N. Wenzel from McClellan Field, California, to Wright Field, Ohio.

6. Special Order 112, Headquarters Air Materiel Command, Wright Field, Dayton, Ohio, 9 June 1947, paragraph 9. Appointment of Captain Lloyd M. N. Wenzel as Class A Agent Finance Officer.

7. Colonel Lloyd Wenzel, USAF (Retired), interview by author, Tequesta, Florida, 9 April 2002.

8. McDonald, pp. 2–3.

9. Buyer and Jensen, pp. 40–41.

10. Special Order 114, Headquarters Wright-Patterson Air Force Base, Dayton, Ohio, 11 June 1948, paragraph 26. Appointment of Captain Lloyd M.N. Wenzel as Responsible Property Officer for German Scientists.

CHAPTER 30: THE WAY THINGS CHANGED

1. Robert S. Drew, interview by author, Hill City, South Dakota, 19 July 2002.
2. Harold E. Watson, speech, 19 March 1946, p. 11.
3. Air Technical Intelligence, briefing, 10 April 1946, p. 30.
4. Letter HQ AAF, Washington, D.C., 14 May 1946. TO: Commanding General, Air Materiel Command, Wright Field, Dayton, Ohio. Subject: AAF Technical Intelligence.
5. Bush, p. 6.
6. Ibid., pp. 98–99.
7. Ibid., p. 100.
8. Ibid., pp. 76–77.
9. Ibid., p. 83.
10. Ibid., p. 99.
11. *Toward New Horizons* was the seminal study initiated by General Arnold in late 1944, and produced by Dr. von Karman and the Scientific Advisory Group.
12. Truman, p. 341.
13. Samuel, *I Always Wanted to Fly*, pp. 181–82.
14. James, pp. 6–14.
15. Harold E. Watson, speech, 24 March 1981, pp. 62–63.
16. *History of Directorate of Intelligence*, pp. 19–20.
17. Letter from Dr. Theodore von Karman, Director, AAF Scientific Advisory Group, to General of the Army, H. H. Arnold, Headquarters, Army Air Forces, Washington, D.C., Subject: *Disposition of German Scientists*, 16 October 1945.
18. Harold E. Watson, speech, 24 March 1981, p. 64.
19. Air Technical Intelligence, briefing, 10 April 1946, p. 1.
20. Putt, speech, pp. 7–8.
21. Putt, interview, pp. 31–34.
22. Theodore Benecke and A. W. Quick, *History of German Guided Missiles Development, First Guided Missiles Seminar, Munich, Germany, April, 1956.* Published for and on behalf of the Advisory Group for Aeronautical Research and Development, North Atlantic Treaty Organization, Verlag E. Appelhans & Co., Brunswick, Germany, 1957, pp. 154–55. The greatest German successes with the

Fritz X and Hs 293 were the sinking of the defecting Italian battleship *Roma* near Sicily on 9 September 1943 and the troop ship *Rohna* off the North African coast on 26 November 1943. Over a thousand American soldiers perished in the *Rohna* disaster.

23. Bush, p. 44.
24. Ibid., p. 135.
25. Ibid., pp. 84–85.
26. Karman, pp. iii–v.

AFTERWORD: WHAT BECAME OF ALL THESE GOOD MEN?

1. Chilstrom and Leery, pp. 178–82.

SOURCES

ARCHIVAL SOURCES

Citations from letters and memoranda between and from various military head-quarters in the United States and Europe and citations from general orders and regulations were obtained from material maintained in and by the Air Force History Support Office, Reference and Analysis Branch, AFHSO/HOR, Bolling Air Force Base, Washington, D.C., 20032, including the following studies, histories, and analyses:

An Evaluation of German Capabilities in 1945. Office of the Director of Intelligence, Headquarters, USSTAF in Europe, APO 633, 19 January 1945.

Duties and Responsibilities of Ninth Air Force and First Tactical Air Force (Prov), with Respect to Disarmament of the German Air Force. Deputy Commander, Operations, F. L. Anderson, Headquarters USSTAF in Europe, APO 633, U.S. Army, 16 January 1945.

German Air Defenses, Post Hostilities Investigation, Volume I. United States Air Forces in Europe, Office of the Assistant Chief of Staff, A-2, APO 633, U.S. Army, undated.

History of AAF Participation in Project Paperclip May 1945–March 1947 (Exploitation of German Scientists). Prepared by the Historical Office, Executive Secretariat, Air Materiel Command, Wright-Patterson Air Force Base, Ohio, by Harriet Buyer and Edna Jensen, Historians, August 1948.

History of the Air Disarmament Division, IX Air Force Service Command, October 1944 To March 1946. Erlangen, Germany, May 1946.

History of Directorate of Intelligence, United States Strategic Air Forces in Europe, January 1944–May 1945. Assistant Chief of Staff, A-2, USAFE, APO 633, 8 September 1945.

History, Headquarters First Tactical Air Force Service Command (Provisional), 20 October 1944–20 May 1945. By authority of Commanding General, I TAF Service Command, 20 May 1945.

History of Operation Lusty, Air Scientific and Technical Intelligence Exploitation in Germany, 6 June 1944–1 February 1946. Scientific and Technical Intelligence Branch, Assistant Chief of Staff for Intelligence, Headquarters USAFE, APO 633, U.S. Army, February 1946.

Operation of ME-262. Headquarters USSTAF, Office of the Assistant Chief of Staff A-2, Air Force Station 379, APO 633, U.S. Army, 13 June 1945. Prepared by Colonel Harold E. Watson, Colonel, Air Corps, Chief A.T.I. Field Teams.

Operations Order No. 2, Watson's Whizzers, Me-262 Project, ATI A-2 USSTAF, prepared by Captain, A.C., Operations Officer, Fred L. Hillis, By order of Colonel Watson, undated.

Plan for Operation ECLIPSE. Headquarters First Tactical Air Force (Prov), APO 374, 20 March 1945.

Status Report of Exploitation Division, Headquarters USSTAF, Office of the Assistant Chief of Staff A-2, Air Force Station 379, APO 633, U.S. Army, 17 July 1945, submitted to the Commanding General, United States Strategic Air Forces in Europe.

INTERVIEWS

Anspach, Robert. Personal background and participation in Operation Lusty. Orlando, FL, October 2001.

Beaman, H. Clayton. Interview with assistant chief of air staff, intelligence, re visit to Tunis and Bizerte, North Africa. Washington D.C., June 1943 (source: AFHSO).

Brown, Roy. Personal background and participation in Operation Lusty. Chillicothe, OH, November 2001.

Chilstrom, Kenneth O. Personal background and participation in test flying of captured German aircraft at Wright Field, Ohio. Palm Beach Gardens, FL, November 2001.

Drew, Robert S. Reflections of a combat infantryman. Hill City, SD, July 2002.

Freiburger, Dennis. Recollections of his father, Eugene Freiburger, and his participation in Operation Lusty; tape recording of Eugene Freiburger on his participation in Operation Lusty made on 21 March 1994. Antigo, WI, January 2003.

Hausmann, Franz. Personal background and piloting experience in Heinkel 177 and Junkers 88 and participation in Project Overcast, Frederick, MD. October 2001.

McIntosh, Frederick. Personal background and participation in Operation Lusty. Leesburg, VA, December 2001, January 2003.

Putt, Donald L. Interview of Lieutenant General Donald L. Putt by Dr. James C. Hasdorff. Atherton, CA, 1–3 April 1974 (source: AFHSO).

Strobell, Robert. Personal background and participation in Operation Lusty. College Park, MD, April 2000.

Sutton, John. Personal background and participation in interrogation of German air staff, 1945, San Antonio, TX, March 2002.

Watson, Ruth. Background on Harold E. Watson. Palm Beach Gardens, FL, November 2001.

Wenzel, Lloyd. Personal background and participation in Project Overcast and Project Paperclip. Tequesta, FL, November 2001.

PRESENTATIONS AND SPEECHES

Bentley, Colonel W. C., Collection Division, T-2, Air Materiel Command, Wright Field, Ohio. "Air Technical Intelligence." Speech given to students of Class 46–47, Air Command and Staff School, Air University, Maxwell Field, Alabama, 26 October 1946 (source: AFHSO).

Putt, Colonel Donald L., Deputy Commanding General, Intelligence, T-2, Air Materiel Command, Wright Field, Ohio. "Air Technical Intelligence." Speech given to members of the Dayton Country Club, 7 May 1946 (source: AFHSO).

Watson, Colonel Harold E., Chief, Collection Division, Air Materiel Command, Wright Field, Ohio. "The Battle of Know-How in Peace and War." Speech given to the Dayton, Ohio, Civitan Club, 19 March 1946 (source: AFHSO).

Watson, Colonel Harold E., Chief, Collection Division, T-2, Air Materiel Command, Wright Field, Ohio. "Engineering Division Tour." Speech given to a group of visiting dignitaries, 10 April 1946 (source: AFHSO).

Watson, Major General Harold E., U.S. Air Force (Retired). Untitled speech (describing Watson's exploits as part of Operation Lusty) given at the United States Air Force Museum, Wright-Patterson Air Force Base, Ohio, 24 March 1981 (source: U.S. Air Force Museum).

BOOKS AND MONOGRAPHS

Aders, Gebhart. *History of the German Night Fighter Force 1917–1945*. London, England: Jane's Publishing Company Limited, 1979.

Amtmann, Hans H. *The Vanishing Paperclips: America's Aerospace Secret: A Personal Account*. Boylston, MA: Monogram Aviation Publications, 1988.

Ashcroft, Bruce. *Major General Harold E. Watson: Intelligence Pioneer, Air Force Warrior*. Wright-Patterson AFB, OH: National Air Intelligence Center, 1994.

Baxter, James P. *Scientists Against Time*. Cambridge, MA: The M.I.T. Press, 1946.

Bekker, Cajus. *The Luftwaffe War Diaries: The German Air Force in World War II*. New York, NY: Da Capo Press, 1994.

Benecke, Theodore, and A. W. Quick. *History of German Guided Missiles Development*. Brunswick, Germany: Verlag E. Appelhans & Company, 1957.

Berg, A. Scott. *Lindbergh*. New York, NY: G. P. Putnam's Sons, 1998.

Blair, Clay. *Hitler's U-Boat War: The Hunted, 1942–1945*. New York: Modern Library, 2000.

Boehme, Manfred. *JG 7*. Atgler, PA: Schiffer Military History, 1992.

Brown, Eric. *Wings of the Luftwaffe*. Shrewsbury, England: Airlife Publishing Ltd, 1993.

Bush, Vannevar. *Modern Arms and Free Men*. New York, NY: Simon and Schuster, 1949.

Butler, Phil. *War Prizes*. Leicester, England: Midland Counties Publications, 1994.

Caldwell, Donald L. *JG 26 Top Guns of the Luftwaffe*. New York, NY: Ivy Books, 1991.

Chilstrom, Ken, and Penn Leery. *Test Flying at Old Wright Field*. Omaha, NE: Westchester House Publishers, 1993.

Cora, Paul B. *Yellowjackets! The 361st Fighter Group in World War II*. Atglen, PA: Schiffer Military History, 2000.

Craven, Wesley F., and James L. Cate. *The Army Air Forces in World War II*. Vol. 6, *Men and Planes*. Washington, DC: Office of Air Force History, 1983.

Cross, Kenneth. *Straight and Level*. London, England: Grub Street, 1993.

Davis, Albert H., Russell J. Coffin, and Robert B. Woodward. *The 56th Fighter Group in World War II*. Washington, DC: Infantry Journal Press, 1948.

Eisenhower, Dwight D. *Crusade in Europe*. Garden City, NY: Doubleday & Company, 1948.

Fighter Group Association, 352nd. *The Bluenosed Bastards of Bodney: A Commemorative History, 352nd Fighter Group*. Dallas, TX: Taylor Publishing Company, 1990.

Freeman, Roger A. *Zemke's Wolf Pack*. New York, NY: Orion Books, 1988.

Green, William, and Gordon Swanborough. *The Complete Book of Fighters*. London, England: Salamander Books Limited, 2001.

James, Martin E. *Historical Highlights United States Air Forces in Europe 1945–1979*. APO New York 09012: Office of History Headquarters United States Air Forces in Europe, 1980.

Karman, Theodore von. *Toward New Horizons*. A report to General of the Army H. H. Arnold, submitted on behalf of the A.A.F. Scientific Advisory Group. Washington, DC: Headquarters, Army Air Forces, 1944.

Kranzhoff, Joerg Armin. *Arado: History of an Aircraft Company*. Atglen, PA: Schiffer Military History, 1997.

Lasby, Clarence G. *Project Paperclip: German Scientists and the Cold War*. New York, NY: Atheneum, 1971.

Mason, Frank, and Michael Turner. *Luftwaffe Aircraft*. New York, NY: Crescent Books, 1986.

Maurer, Maurer, ed. *Air Force Combat Units of World War II*. Maxwell AFB, AL: USAF Historical Division, Air University, Department of the Air Force, 1960.

Miller, Kent D. *Escort: The 356th Fighter Group on Operations over Europe 1943–1945*. Fort Wayne, IN: Academy Publishing Corporation, 1985.

Naimark, Norman M. *The Russians in Germany: A History of the Soviet Zone of Occupation, 1945–1949*. Cambridge, MA: Harvard University Press, 1995.

Ordway, Frederick I., and Mitchell R. Sharpe. *The Rocket Team*. New York, NY: Thomas Y. Crowell, Publishers, 1979.

Samuel, Wolfgang W. E. *I Always Wanted to Fly: America's Cold War Airmen*. Jackson, MS: University Press of Mississippi, 2001.

Smith, J. Richard. *Arado 234 Blitz*. Boylston, MA: Monogram Aviation Publications, 1992.

Spaete, Wolfgang. *Test Pilots*. Bromley, England: Independent Books, 1999.

Speer, Albert. *Inside the Third Reich*. New York, NY: The Macmillan Company, 1970.

Staerk, Hans. *Fassberg, Geschichte des Fliegerhorstes und des gemeindefreien Bezirk's Fassberg in der Lüneburger Heide*. Fassberg, Germany: Selbstverlag des Verfassers, 1971.

Stahl, Peter W. *KG 200: The True Story*. London, England: Jane's Publishing Company Limited, 1981.

Tannehill, Victor C. *First TACAF: First Tactical Air Force in World War II*. Arvada, CO: Boomerang Publishers, 1998.

Toliver, Raymond F. *Fighter General: The Life of Adolf Galland*. Zephyr Cove, NV: AmPress Publishing, 1990.

Toliver, Raymond F., and Trevor J. Constable. *Fighter Aces of the Luftwaffe*. Atglen, PA: Schiffer Publishing Ltd., 1996.

Truman, Harry S. *Memoirs*. Garden City, NY: Doubleday & Company, 1955.

Yeager, Chuck. *Yeager*. New York, NY: Bantam Books, 1985.

MISCELLANEOUS PUBLICATIONS AND SOURCES

Army Air Forces Installations Directory, Foreign Countries and U.S. Possessions. Washington, DC: Headquarters, Army Air Forces, 15 March 1946 (source: AFHSO).

Baur, Isolde. "With the 'Watson's Whizzers' and 'Operation Paperclip.'" *American Aviation Historical Society* (winter 1995): 294–307.

Brown, Roy. "A Trim Control Problem of the Focke-Wulf 190." Unpublished paper, November 2001. In possession of the author.

Die Funkmessgeräte Der Luftwaffe. Berlin, Germany: Generalnachrichtenführer, Ln-Inspection, 6. Abteilung IE, 30 July 1944. In possession of the author.

General Marshall's Victory Report: Biennial Report of the Chief of Staff of the United States Army, 1943 to 1945, to the Secretary of War. Washington, DC: War Department of the United States of America, 1 September 1945.

Johnson, Charles P. "Memoirs of a Navigator, WWII." Unpublished memoir of Johnson's World War II experiences from April 1943 until his discharge from the Army Air Forces in August 1945. In possession of the author.

Jumo 004 B-1 Bedienung. Dessau, Germany: Junkers Flugzeug- und Motoren Werke A.G., September 1944. In possession of the author.

Malayney, Norman. "ATI and Operation Lusty." *American Aviation Historical Society*, part 1 (spring 1995): 16–25; part 2 (summer 1995): 110–25; part 3 (fall 1995): 162–77.

Watson, Ruth. Personal memorabilia of Harold E. Watson, lent to the author for the purpose of this project and including news clippings, photos, telegrams, postal cards, class rosters, graduation certificates, and a variety of other written and pictorial material.

WW II History, 526th Fighter-Bomber Squadron, 86th Fighter-Bomber Group, October, 1944–October, 1945. A compilation of original squadron historical reports, squadron war diary entries, and general orders. In possession of the author.

PHOTOGRAPHS

Photographs came from the personal collections of the following individuals and are identified in the text by abbreviations:

Harold Austin collection (HA)
Roy Brown collection (RB)
Kenneth Chilstrom collection (KC)
Dennis Freiburger collection (DF)
John Hay collection (JH)
Wolfgang Samuel collection (WS)
Ruth Watson collection (RW)

INDEX